THE GUINNESS
DICTIONARY OF
YET MORE

Poisonous

QUOTES

G 19852

COMPILED BY COLIN JARMAN

GUINNESS PUBLISHING

Design: Mandy Sedge

First published in 1993 by Guinness Publishing Ltd
Publishing copyright © Guinness Publishing Ltd 1993
Published in Great Britain by Guinness Publishing Ltd.,
33 London Road, Enfield, Middlesex

Typeset in Plantin Light by
Ace Filmsetting Ltd, Frome, Somerset
Printed and bound in Great Britain by
Cox & Wyman, Reading, Berkshire

'Guinness' is a registered trademark of Guinness Publishing Ltd

A catalogue record for this book is available from the
British Library

ISBN 0–85112–729–0

Dedicated to Fred, Sylvia, Graeme, Maureen, Roger, Catherine,
Annabel and David

CONTENTS

HOW TO USE THIS BOOK

All quotes are alphabetically listed within their individual sections.

The contents pages list the sub-sections within major groups.

Yet More Poisonous Quotes has been compiled to be used as either reading or reference material.

1. Reading

Reading sections as a whole will give an insight into each subject, in both an entertaining and educational way.

2. Reference

By using the extensive index certain subjects or reviewers can be traced through the book.

There are two indexes – one is a general subject index and the other lists all the names of the quoters and quotees.

EDITORIAL NOTES

Sections containing specific reviews are alphabetically listed in two ways – either by subject or (as in 'Dramatic') by reviewer.

Where possible the year of the subject (book, film, play, etc) has been given, as has the year of the actual quote. These dates are given more as a means to place each quote chronologically rather than for historical correctness.

CRITICISM

Our friends the reviewers
Those clippers and hewers
 Are judges of mortar and stone, sir!
But of meet or unmeet
In a fabrick complete
I'll bodily complain they are none, sir!
Robert Burns

Critics kind – never mind!
Critics flatter – no matter!
Critics blame – all the same!
Do your best – damn the rest!
 *Sir Arthur Conan Doyle – 'Through the
 Magic Door'*

Critics never worry unless they are right –
but that does not often occur. *Noël Coward*

The average English critic is a don
manque, hopelessly parochial when not
exaggeratedly teutonophile, over whose
desk must surely hang the motto
(presumably in Gothic lettering) 'Above
all no enthusiasm'.
 Constant Lambert – 'Opera' (1950)

We TV critics are the scum of the earth
and deserve retribution from on high.
 *Victor Lewis-Smith – 'Evening Standard'
 (1992)*

The conscientious Canadian critic is one
who subscribes to the *New York Times* so
that he knows at first hand what his
opinion should be.
 Eric Nicol – 'A Scar Is Born' (1968)

CRITICS

Anon

Thou eunuch of language; thou butcher,
imbruing thy hands in the bowels of
orthography; thou arch-heretic in
pronunciation; thou pitch-pipe of
affected emphasis; thou pimp of gender;
thou scape gallows from the land of
syntax; thou scavenger of mood and
tense; thou pickle-herring in the puppet-
show of nonsense. *Robert Burns (1791)*

Elkan Allan (TV critic of the *Sunday Times*)
'Bumptious' is described by *Webster's Dictionary* as 'presumptuously self-assertive', a phrase which, as your weekly column clearly demonstrates, fits you like a glove. To it, I would add 'smug', 'arrogant', 'odious' and 'puerile'.
 Anon letter

Clive Barnes (drama critic for the *New York Times*)
It seems to me that giving Clive Barnes his CBE for services to the theatre is like giving Goering the DFC for services to the RAF. *Alan Bennett*

Garry Bushell (TV critic of the *Sun*)
Garry 'Gal Gonad' Bushell. *'Private Eye'*

Charles Catchpole (TV critic of the *News of the World*)
Appearing on Ulster TV's 'Kelly' – A miracle cure for insomnia.
 Garry Bushell – the 'Sun' (1992)
[*Unfortunately for Bushell, his 'review' came two weeks before Catchpole appeared on the show, prompting* – Apologies for that Charlie Catchpole review. It must have been a dreadful premonition – like when people have nightmares about air disasters that happen a few days later.]

Bosley Crowther (film critic for the *New York Times*)
A man with a head full of wood shavings.
 Penelope Gilliatt

Gail Greene (food critic of *New York*)
The Judith Krantz of foodies. *Anon*

Gail doesn't write restaurant reviews, she does schtick. Her schtick is simulated masturbatory frenzy, for which there

seems to be an inexhaustible market.
Jay Jacobs – 'Gastronome' (1986)

Eduard Hanslick
I think that the violence of Dr. Hanslick
was as much inspired by the desire to
write a readable article as by any just
indignation.
Philip Hale – 'Boston Journal' (1893)

Harold Hobson (drama critic of the *Sunday Times*)
The characteristic sound of the English
Sunday: Harold Hobson barking up the
wrong tree. *Penelope Gilliatt*

Samuel Johnson (and Thomas Boswell)
The more one learns of Johnson, the
more preposterous assemblage he appears
of strong sense, of the lowest bigotry and
prejudices, of pride, brutality, fretfulness,
and vanity; and Boswell is the ape of most
of his faults, without a pose of his senses.
It is the story of a mountebank and his
zany. *Horace Walpole*

Victor Lewis-Smith (TV critic of the *Evening Standard*)
His humour is constantly short-circuiting
itself and treating ideas like clockwork
toys to be wound up for the pleasure of
seeing where they will fall. *Anon (1990)*

Dwight MacDonald
Don't you realize, Dwight, you have
nothing to say, only to add?
Gore Vidal – 'Two Sisters' (1970)

Richard Meltzer (US music critic)
You have a half-horsepower brain,
pulling a two-ton mouth. *Anon letter*

Sheridan Morley (drama critic for *Punch*)
You rank as a dramatic critic on the same
level as Sheridan Knowles ranked as a
dramatist. *Anon*

Christopher North (a.k.a. John Wilson) – literary critic of *Blackwood's Magazine*
You did late review my lays,

Crusty Christopher;
You did mingle blame and praise.
Rusty Christopher –
When I learnt from who it came,
Musty Christopher;
I forgave you all the blame,
Fusty Christopher –
I could not forgive the praise.
Alfred, Lord Tennyson

Penny Perrick (literary critic of the *Sunday Times*)
Her review [of Kurt Vonnegut's *Hocus
Pocus*] suffered from Hennessey's disease
– named after Val Hennessey [*Daily
Mail*]. This is a mental condition where
the reviewer thinks that his or her own
warm and caring personality is as
interesting as the work under review.
William Startle – 'Sunday Telegraph' (1990)

Brian Sewell (art critic of the *Evening Standard*)
I suppose even his mother wouldn't
admire him. *David Lillington (1992)*

G. B. Shaw
This bright, nimble, fierce and
comprehending being – Jack Frost
dancing bespangled in the sunshine.
Sir Winston Churchill

Mimi Sheraton (food critic for the *New York Times*)
Snuffled around in her feedbag, wearing
blinkers and more or less oblivious of
anything that couldn't be put in her
mouth. *Jay Jacobs – 'Gastronome' (1986)*

John Simon (drama critic of *New York*)
You have obviously spent so much time
with your head wedged between your
buttocks that your vision has been
obscured by the reflection of your own
putrid entrails. *Anon letter*

His warp is worse than his woof.
Bill Cole

Jack Tinker (drama critic for the *Daily Mail*)
On his cabaret act – He sings and he

dances, and his tiny talent should take him as far as the end of the nearest pier – or just beyond.

Nicholas De Jongh – 'Guardian'

Gottfried Weber (German music critic)

Oh, you arch-ass – you double-barrelled ass! *Ludwig van Beethoven*

Alexander Woollcott

As a host at his breakfast parties, although lacking the essential grace and fragility of an eighteenth-century marquise, being as a rule unshaven and clad in insecure, egg-stained pyjamas, he managed in his own harum-scarum way to evoke a certain 'salon' spirit. *Noël Coward*

A butterfly in heat. *Louis Untermeyer*

GOSSIP

In the days of old of barbarism, the people fought with hatchets. Civilised men buried the hatchet, and now fight with gossip.

Edgar W. Howe – 'Country Town Sayings' (1911)

GOSSIP COLUMNISTS

Nigel Dempster

Nigel Pratt-Dumpster – the famous social climber. *'Private Eye'*

SELF-CRITICISM

Anyone is to be pitied who has just sense enough to perceive his own deficiencies.

William Hazlitt – 'Characteristics' (1823)

THE CRITICAL SELF

Reinhold Aman

Each of us is deviant in some way. For instance, I wear glasses, I'm five-foot-seven, 20 pounds overweight, have short

hair and a Kissinger accent. So you could start off calling me a fat, four-eyed, runty, reactionary, sewer-mouthed Kraut.

'Time' (1978)

Mrs Paddy Ashdown

I'm nothing but a loud-mouthed slag.

(1988)

Rick Astley

I'm not your classically handsome devil, and I haven't got animal magnetism. I'm bit of a git, really. *(1991)*

Nancy Astor

Take a close-up photograph of me! You might as well use a picture of a relief map of Ireland!

Francis Bacon

How can I take any interest in my work when I don't like it?

When asked 'What do you do?' by Lord Rothermere – I'm an old poof.

Cilla Black

I'm the most sexless person on TV.

(1992)

Helena Bonham-Carter

I seem to be better when I keep my mouth shut. Maybe I should move into silent films. *(1992)*

George Bush

What's wrong with being a boring kind of guy?

Cyril Connolly

I have always disliked myself at any given moment; the total of such moments is my life.

Noël Coward

I not only muck up some of my plays by writing them but I frequently muck them up by acting in them as well.

On his nickname 'The Master' – Oh, you know 'Jack of all trades, master of none.'

John De Lorean
Would you ever buy a used car from me?
(1984)

Eddie 'The Eagle' Edwards
After having a lengthy brain scan – They
finally found one. *(1989)*

Emerson, Lake and Palmer
Our name sounded like a firm of
chartered accountants. *Carl Palmer (1992)*

Sarah Ferguson
I want to be a good sailor's wife. *(1988)*

Keith Floyd
My producer will tell you that I'm the
most difficult, awkward, obnoxious,
single-minded, arrogant, f★★★ing pig that
ever slid across the earth . . . and I'm not
a dickhead, but everybody thinks I am a
dickhead.

Samantha Fox
I am neither a movie star or a singer and
really these days not much, other than an
inflated swimsuit. *(1992)*

Vitas Gerulaitas
What can you do when you have a name
that sounds like a disease?

Graham Gooch
I know I look like a totally miserable sod
on TV. I wish I didn't, but there you are.
(1990)

Jimmy Greaves
I look in the mirror and this big blob
stares back.

Gilbert Harding
I am full of the milk of human kindness,
damn it. My trouble is that it gets clotted
so easily.

Debbie Harry
My solo album might be called 'Deaf,
Dumb and Bland'. *(1988)*

Mick Jagger
I don't think of the Rolling Stones as an
institution, more a mental home.

John Harvey Jones
Everyone thinks I'm a smart-arse who can
solve any bloody problem. I'm not. I'm
just a very old businessman . . . who
made every mistake in the book. *(1992)*

Vinnie Jones
I'm the worst player in the First Division.

Stubby Kaye
I'm so fat that when I have my shoes
cleaned I have to take the shoeshine boy's
word for it.

Norman Lamont
I'm not an expert on the economy. *(1992)*

Philip Larkin
Gloomy old sod, aren't I?

T. E. Lawrence
On his book 'The Mint' – In some ways it's
a horrible little book. Like over-brewed
tea.

Gary Lineker
I'm not as nice as all that . . . In fact, I
swore only the other week. *(1992)*

Brian London
Cassius Clay can't insult me, I'm too
ignorant.

Zeppo Marx
You ever see me act? You could give me
every good line since Chaucer, and I'd
ruin it.

Robert Maxwell
I have always been an outsider. *(1988)*

Liza Minnelli
I'm so normal, it'd bore you. *(1989)*

Cecil Parkinson
I wish I'd been born short, fat and ugly.
Then at least people would have listened
to my ideas. *(1992)*

Dolly Parton
It takes a lot of money to look this cheap.

I just look like the girl next door – to a fun-fair, that is.

I'm not offended at all, because I know I'm not a dumb blonde. I also know I'm not a blonde.   *(1992)*

General Pinochet
I'm not a dictator. It's just that I have a grumpy face.

Cybill Shepherd
People used to say I had all the star

quality of a dead hamster.

Frank Sinatra
I could go on stage and make pizza and they'd still come to see me.

Elizabeth Taylor
I have the face and body of a woman and the mind of a child.

Terry Wogan
I am, by nature, placid. Boring, even.

INSULTS

GENERAL

A repartee is an insult with its dress suit on.   *Anon*

Take not God's name in vain, select a time when it will have effect.
Ambrose Bierce

The man who first abused his fellows with swearwords instead of bashing their brains out with a club should be counted among those who laid the foundations of civilisation.   *John Cohen*

Iron, when heated in the flames and pounded, becomes a fine sword. Wise men and saints are tested by abuse.
Nichiren Daishonon (c. 1250)

If something you say doesn't offend someone, then you're not saying anything.   *Terence Trent D'Arby (1989)*

Being a star has made it possible for me to get insulted in places where the average Negro could never hope to get insulted.
Sammy Davis Jr.

I'm free of all prejudices. I hate everyone equally.   *W. C. Fields*

Abuse is the weapon of the vulgar.
S. G. Goodrich

No character, however upright, is a match for constantly reiterated attacks, however false.   *Alexander Hamilton*

Fate never wounds more deeply the generous heart,
Than when a blockhead's insult points the dart.   *Samuel Johnson*

Man loves malice, but not against one-eyed men nor the unfortunate, but against the fortunate and proud.
Martial – 'Epigrams' (AD 86)

We live in a climate of insult.
Sir Peter Parker (1983)

It won't take much to get me psyched up to hating anyone.   *Jeff Thomson*

TARGET UNKNOWN

She's as popular as rabies in a guide dogs' home.

If you're not a rogue you should take a libel action against your face.

He was as welcome as a French kiss at a family reunion.

Her heart's in the right place – what a pity the other thirteen stone aren't.

He was about as useless as the Pope's testicles.

There was nothing wrong with her that a vasectomy of the vocal chords wouldn't fix. *Lisa Alther – 'Kinflicks'*

I could never understand what he saw in her until I saw her at the Caprice eating corn-on-the-cob. *Coral Browne*

She has the bear's ethereal grace,
The bland hyena's laugh,
The footsteps of the elephant,
The neck of a giraffe. *Lewis Carroll*

He had a face like what Cardinal Newman's would have been if he had gone into the army instead of the Church, grown an Old Bill moustache, lost most of his teeth, and only shaved on Saturday, before preaching. *Joyce Cary*

She's one of those high-hatting dames. She'd high-hat her own father if she knew who he was. *Noël Coward*

He's so dumb he can't take a shower and sing at the same time. *Chubb Feeny (1965)*

She resembles the Venus de Milo: she is very old, has no teeth and has white spots on her yellow skin. *Heinrich Heine*

You're so ugly, I bet that if I followed you home someone ugly would open the door.
Thomas 'Hollywood' Henderson

Had your father spent more of your mother's immoral earnings on your education you would not even then have been a gentleman. *Seymour Hicks*

He was an Outrageous Stinker, a Jelly-bellied Flagflapper.
Rudyard Kipling – 'Stalky & Co' (1899)

To a tennis spectator – What other problems do you have besides being unemployed, a moron and a dork?
John McEnroe (1992)

When God gave you teeth, he spoiled a bloody good arse. *Bernard Manning*

She spoke with the breathless haste of one to whom repartee comes as rarely as the finding of a gold-handled umbrella. *Saki*

I am debarred from putting her in her place – she hasn't got one. *Edith Sitwell*

She was a blonde – with a brunette past.
Gwyn Thomas

My nose bleed's for you.
Herbert Beerbohm Tree

He had a face like a carving abandoned as altogether too unpromising for completion. *H. G. Wells*

He looked like a halibut which had been asked by another halibut to lend it a quid till next Wednesday. *P. G. Wodehouse*

Her mouth had the coldly forbidding look of the closed door of a subway express when you have just missed the train.
P. G. Wodehouse

A small, shrivelled chap. Looks like a haddock with lung-trouble.
P. G. Wodehouse

Had his brain been constructed of silk, he would have been hard put to find sufficient material to make a canary a pair of cami-knickers. *P. G. Wodehouse – 'Mr Mulliner Speaking' (1929)*

He looked like an owl with a dash of weasel blood in him. *P. G. Wodehouse – 'Mulliner Knights' (1933)*

He looked like a pterodactyl with a secret sorrow. *P. G. Wodehouse – 'Right Ho, Jeeves' (1934)*

If ever there was a pot-bellied little human louse who needed to have the stuffing knocked out of him and have his remains jumped on by strong men in hobnailed boots, it is you.
P. G. Wodehouse – 'Uncle Fred in Springtime' (1939)

He spoke very highly of himself.
P. G. Wodehouse – Ibid (1939)

He was a small man with the face of an untrustworthy monkey, the sort of monkey other monkeys would have shrunk from allowing to come within arm's reach of their nut ration.
P. G. Wodehouse – 'Money in the Bank' (1946)

He had just enough intelligence to open his mouth when he wanted to eat, but certainly no more. *P. G. Wodehouse – 'Full Moon' (1947)*

His IQ was somewhat lower than that of a backward clam – a clam, let us say, which has been dropped on its head when a baby. *P. G. Wodehouse – 'Barmy in Wonderland' (1952)*

She has about as much brain as a retarded billiard ball. *P. G. Wodehouse – 'Galahad at Blandings' (1964)*

He resembled a frog that had been looking on the dark side since it was a slip of a tadpole. *P. G. Wodehouse – 'Aunts Aren't Gentlemen' (1974)*

RETORTS

Otto Abetz (Nazi Ambassador in Paris)
Upon seeing the painting 'Guernica' – Oh, it was you, Mr Picasso, who did that?
Pablo Picasso
No, it was you.

Anon actress
Telegram to G. B. Shaw: Am crazy to play St Joan!
Reply: I quite agree.

Anon Labour MP
Must you fall asleep when I am speaking?
Sir Winston Churchill
No, it is purely voluntary.

Nancy Astor
You are really becoming too grand for words, never leaving the royal stand. You might as well be the court dentist.
Duke of Roxburgh
If I ever do have to pull out the King's teeth, I shall certainly come to you for the gas.

Barbara Castle
Margaret Thatcher is physically very attractive – but she will be still more attractive when she bothers less about whether her hair is in place.
Margaret Thatcher
Barbara is a very talented politician. I only hope I look as good as she does when I get to her age. *(1978)*

Cecil B. De Mille
How can you say good pictures lose money? My pictures are invariably profitable.
Arthur Mayer
But yours are the run of De Mille pictures.

Michael Foot
Don't you ever talk like that to me again. I'll have your head off your shoulders, and the skin off your back.
Roy Hattersley
You couldn't knock the skin off a rice pudding.

Sandra Harris
Have English class barriers broken down?

Barbara Cartland
Of course they have, or I wouldn't be sitting here talking to someone like you.

Journalist
Mr Coward, haven't you anything to say to *The Star*?
Noël Coward
Twinkle!

Gertrude Lawrence
On reading through Noël Coward's script for 'Private Lives' – Nothing wrong that can't be fixed.
Noël Coward
Nothing to be fixed except your performance.

Frederic Leighton
My dear Whistler, you leave your pictures in such a crude sketchy state. Why don't you ever finish them?
J. M. Whistler
My dear Leighton, why do you ever begin yours?

Duchess of Portsmouth
Why, woman, you are fine enough to be a queen.
Nell Gwynne
You are entirely right, madam, and I am whore enough to be a duchess.

Otto Preminger
You're the shortest, fattest man I've ever seen.
Jimmy Rushing
And you're the tallest, baldest man I've ever seen.

Denise Robins
I've just written my 87th book.

Barbara Cartland
I've written 145.
Denise Robins
Oh, I see, one a year.

Wallace Stevens
The trouble with you is you write about things.
Robert Frost
The trouble with you is you write about bric-a-brac.

Harry S. Truman
I wouldn't appoint John Lewis as a dogcatcher.
John L. Lewis
The President could ill afford to have more brains in the dog department than in the Department of State.

Erich von Stroheim –
Defending his endless shots of a character's shoes in 'The Merry Widow' – The character has a foot fetish.
Irving Thalberg
And you have a footage fetish!

Henry Wallace
This country should raise more wheat.
Anon Farmer
What about hay?
Henry Wallace
I am speaking about food for mankind, but I'll get around to your case in a minute.

Alexander Woollcott
What is so rare as a Woollcott first edition?
Franklin P. Adams
A Woollcott second edition.

VISUAL ARTS

PAINTING

Artists are scared by the past and don't believe in the future.
Robert Hughes – 'The Times' (1992)

A living is made by selling something everybody needs at least once a year. And a million is made by producing something that everybody needs every day. You artists produce something nobody needs at any time.
Thornton Wilder – 'The Matchmaker'

MOVEMENTS AND STYLES

Abstract Art
A little more of the abstract art and we'd both have gone potty. What is there to bite on in the abstract? You might as well eat triangles and got to bed with a sewing machine.
Joyce Cary – 'The Horse's Mouth'

Modernism
All you need is a brass neck and a plentiful supply of sucker.
John Naughton (1992)

Post-impressionism
There has been nothing like this outbreak of Philistinism since Whistler's day.
Roger Fry

Post-modernism
Post-modernism is a cartoon-cat version of modernism; that cat keeps running even though he has only air beneath him.
John Updike (1990)

Surrealism
I regard the Surrealists as 100 per cent fools.   *Sigmund Freud*

The Group of Seven
All their pictures look pretty much alike, the net result being more like a gargle or gob of porridge than a work of art.
H. F. Gadsby – 'Toronto Star' (1913)

ARTISTS

Anon modern painting
I couldn't have that hanging in my home. It would be like living with a gas leak.
Dame Edith Evans

Various
Usual modern collection:
Wilson Steer, water in water-colour;
Matthew Smith, victim of the crime of slaughtercolour;
Utrillo, whitewashed wall in mortarcolour;
Matisse, odalisque in scortacolour;
Picasso, spatchcock horse in tortacolour;
Rouault, perishing Saint in thoughtacolour;
Epstein, Leah waiting for Jacob in squawtacolour.
Joyce Cary – 'The Horse's Mouth'

Ferdinand Delacroix
Covering his eyes in front of an anonymous painting – I've no need to know how not to do it.   *William Blake*

Henry Fuseli
Shockingly mad, madder than ever, quite mad.   *Horace Walpole*

Gilbert and George
Penis, Penis, Penis – Surely the word on the street is not *Penis, Penis, Penis,* but 'What a pair of c***s Gilbert and George are.'   *Tony Rushton – 'Private Eye'*

Augustus John
On sitting for his portrait – Who is this chap? He drinks, he's dirty and I know there are women in the background.
Lord Montgomery

Jasper Johns
Recently he has taken to cobbling together fragments from Picasso, Grunewald, ceiling decorations and whatever else. It has become disparate and random. *Tim Hilton – 'Guardian' (1989)*

If Johns is a master, it is one of distraction and disguise.

William Packer – 'Financial Times' (1989)

Jeff Koons

'Jeff in the position of Adam' – The last bit of methane left in the intestine of the dead cow that is post-modernism.

Robert Hughes (1992)

Proved that it is not necessary to be able to paint, sculpt or do anything else in order to become a successful modern artist. *John Naughton – 'Observer' (1992)*

The South Bank Show was doing its usual job of massaging an already inflated ego.

Chris Peachment – 'Sunday Telegraph' (1993)

Henri Matisse and Pablo Picasso

Walter Sickert could paint pictures that make Matisse look like a man of empty tricks and cyphers, and Picasso look a fraud.

Brian Sewell – 'Evening Standard' (1992)

Jackson Pollock

Who among us has not gazed at a painting of Jackson Pollock's and thought: 'What a piece of crap'?

Rob Long – 'Modern Review' (1992)

Henri Toulouse-Lautrec

A tiny Vulcan with pince-nez, a little twin-pouched bag in which he stuck his poor legs. *Jules Renard*

David Tremlett

Tremlett tries our patience with short words culled from longer – a child's alternative to Scrabble – as many as 15 of them all in a row . . . The 15 long words were the names of places visited in the past 15 years, and the short words are of the ilk of AIR from Zaire, ASK from Alaska, SIN from Abyssinia – I observe in passing that he could we have taken EGO from Herzegovina.

Brian Sewell – 'Evening Standard' (1992)

Andy Warhol

He is the most creepy, ghoulish, exploitative pain in the ass you'd ever meet. *Albert Goldman (1989)*

You're a killer of art, you're a killer of beauty and you're even a killer of laughter. I can't bear your work!

Willem de Kooning

OTHER

Art dealers

They are lice on the backs of artists.

Marcel Duchamp

Banff School of Fine Art

Campus in the Clouds.

Donald Cameron (1956)

William Beckford Collection

The only proof of taste Beckford has shown in his collection is getting rid of it.

William Hazlitt

Mona Lisa

She has the smile of a woman who has just dined off her husband.

Lawrence Durrell

Munich Exhibition

On being awarded the Gold Medal, Second Class by a Munich art exhibition – Pray convey my sentiments of tempered and respectable joy to the gentlemen of the Committee, and my complete appreciation of the second-hand compliment paid me. *James M. Whistler*

John Pope-Hennessy (curator of the British Museum)

That a man bereft of human experience, who has never seen a child born or, one assumes, a woman naked (shades of Ruskin), should be considered an authority on those masterpieces of Western art that celebrate the most impassioned and most mysterious of human experiences. *J. G. Ballard*

Royal Academy

All an artist needed to paint to get into the RA was a very bad picture.

Walter Sickert

Royal Academy Summer Show (1956)
Bits of nonsense.   *Sir Alfred Munnings*

The Turner Prize
The razzamatazz of a huge party and announcement is not going to encourage a more sensitive, receptive appreciation of art. It's just showbiz.
Helen Chadwick (1992)

Before the 1992 award – It has deteriorated into a chilling technical exercise which insults the memory.
Daniel Farson – 'Mail on Sunday'

After the 1992 award – The Turner Prize went to a sculptor of giant bottle tops. This must have made Turner spin in his palette. *Daniel Farson – 'Mail on Sunday'*

The Turner Prize never has been about using one's eyes and head, or the intuitions of one's heart. It's about keeping the hearse of the modern movement trundling along, years after life has gone out of the body.
Peter Fuller – 'Sunday Telegraph' (1989)

It represented the narrow and obscure taste of a contemporary art mafia, out of touch with mainstream art and taste, obscure, self-serving and of dubious merit.   *'The Independent' (1992)*

The annual farce of the Turner Prize is now as inevitable in November as is the pantomime at Christmas . . . This prize is a monument to prejudice.
Brian Sewell – 'Evening Standard' (1992)

The Turner Prize draws attention to . . . a sad little band of late labourers in the exhausted pastures of international conceptual art.
Brian Sewell – 'Evening Standard' (1992)

Madame Tussaud's
After the 1980 US presidential election – Madame Tussaud's must have been all set for a Reagan victory. Within minutes of the announcement, an effigy that looked nothing like him was being lifted into position, while the effigy that had looked nothing like Carter was taken away to be given a new haircut and labelled as someone else – Gary Cooper, perhaps.   *Clive James – 'Observer'*

ARCHITECTURE

There are three arts – painting, music and ornamental pastry-making; of which past architecture is a sub-division.
Anon pastry chef

Most artists, or people who think of themselves as such, have to get the public to watch or listen before they can sod it. The famous pile of bricks at the Tate Gallery was powerless against those who never went to see it, and while still on the shelf *Finnegan's Wake* is impotent. Architects are different. They have the unique power of sodding the consumer at a distance, not just if he lives or works in the building concerned, or just when he passes it a couple of times a day, but also when he happens to catch sight of it miles away on the skyline.
Kingsley Amis – 'The Spectator: Sodding the Public' (1985)

The American sign of civic progress is to tear down the familiar and erect the monstrous.   *Shane Leslie – 'American Wonderland' (1936)*

Architecture is a profession which seems to have stopped thinking.   *Jean Nouvel*

Most new buildings in Britain are wrong-headed, if not actively offensive.
Deyan Sudjic – 'Guardian' (1992)

Arson, after all, is an artificial crime . . . A large number of houses deserve to be burnt.   *H.G. Wells – 'The History of Mr. Polly'*

BUILDINGS & CITIES

Acropolis, Athens
Those who tiptoe round the Acropolis

today in their thousands hardly realise that they are looking at something like an empty barn.

Lawrence Durrell – 'Sicilian Carousel' (1977)

Albert Memorial, London

There has often been an affectionate place in human hearts for the supremely bad. Think of the wobbly operatic arias of Florence Foster Jenkins . . . Think of the Albert Memorial. *Arthur Marshall (1971)*

The Ark, London

A giant crouching toad? A beached liner? An old-fashioned bath? . . . This is the strangest building in London for years.

Naomi Stungo – 'Independent on Sunday' (1992)

Astrodome, Houston, Texas

It's like watching a game from the Goodyear blimp.

Anon American football fan (1976)

It shows what you can get if you really look through the Neiman-Marcus catalogue. *Ray Woolston (1965)*

Atlanta, USA

The architecture of Atlanta is rococola.

Anon

Barcelona Cathedral, Spain

One of the most hideous buildings in the world.

George Orwell – 'Homage to Catalonia' (1938)

Belmont Racecourse, USA

I was shocked – I couldn't believe Belmont could have been that bad. They've done the best they could, but my God, that grandstand!

Frank Lloyd Wright (1956)

Berlaymont, Brussels (European Community headquarters)

Berlaymonster. *Anon*

Berlin Wall, Germany

The wall is a masterpiece of the squalid,

the cruel and the hideous. It is quite incredibly ugly.

Goronwy Rees – 'Diary' (1964)

Birmingham, England

A city that once destroyed a beautiful library to build a lousy bus station . . . If they'd had the Parthenon in this city, they would have knocked it down.

Chris Arnot – 'The Independent' (1992)

British Library, London

An academy for secret policemen.

Prince Charles – 'Omnibus' (1988)

Canary Wharf, London

Has the Canary turned into a turkey?

'Evening Standard' (1992)

Channel Tunnel

A tunnel too far. *Anon (1990)*

Chateau de Chantelaup, Amboise, France

It ought to be seen as affording a superb specimen of the wretchedness of French taste.

Henry Matthews – 'Diary of an Invalid' (1820)

Edinburgh, Scotland

Such things as the new St Andrew's House and the St James's Centre, the ruination of Princes Street and Leith Street would be offences even in, say, Birmingham. In Edinburgh, they are crimes against civilisation.

Piloti – 'Private Eye' (1992)

Edinburgh Castle, Scotland

It would make a good prison in England.

Samuel Johnson (1773)

Edmonton Airport, Canada

International meaningless.

Harold Merrilees (1964)

Empire State Building, New York

The Empty State Building. *Anon*

Eurodisney, France

This great fantasy temple to schmalzy

and whimsical American culture.
Peter Tory – 'Daily Express' (1993)

Graceland, Memphis, Tennessee

Graceland looked like the type of property owned by Leicester hosiery factory owners . . . Elvis's shrine is underwhelming – a mish-mash of scrubby rosebushes and round-the-world architecture. It is inside Graceland that the horror begins. Elvis, obviously a stranger to *Interiors* magazine . . . favoured leopard and tiger skin, and he had a particular penchant for lime-green shag pile. He was so fond of it that its use is not confined to the floor, it spreads up the walls and over the ceilings. It is like being entombed in Wembley turf.
Sue Townsend – 'Independent on Sunday' (1992)

Hastings, Sussex

Could not get in at Hastings whose architectural style according to Leo is divided between Early Wedding Cake and Late Water Closet.
James Agate – 'Ego 2' (1934)

Hayward Gallery, London

The Hayward's facade is like that of some enormous nuclear fall-out shelter.
Frank Whitford – 'Sunday Times' (1993)

Hotel du Palais, Biarritz, France

That Gilded Caravansery of all Unrealities.
Rudyard Kipling – 'Letter' (1925)

Humber Bridge, England

The bridge that goes from nowt to nowt. A bridge too far.
Local Humberside saying (1980)

Ladbroke Gardens, London

Coffin Row.   *Local nickname*

A graveyard of buried hopes . . . naked carcasses, crumbling decorations, fractured walls, slimy cement.
'Building News'

Lanesborough Hotel, Hyde Park Corner, London

That great monument to mis-timed opulence.
Craig Brown – 'Sunday Times' (1992)

Lloyds of London Headquarters

Looks like a kid's been let loose with a Lego set . . . festooned with chicken-wire balconies and stainless steel plumbing running round the outside walls.
Brian Hitchen – 'Daily Star' (1992)

Longleat House, Wiltshire

The house disappointed me . . . What makes it look dull is the uniform plate-glass which has been put in every window. It is astonishing how this destroys the beauty of old buildings. It is as though the eyes in a beautiful face had been put out and replaced with spectacles.   *W. S. Blunt – 'Diary' (1896)*

Mincing Lane, London

The biggest and most awful new building in the City is a dung-coloured office development in Mincing Lane, made of marble, stone, glass and plastic . . . It is inspired by both Mad King Ludwig of Bavaria and Walt Disney. The only way to deal with this architectural atrocity is to make it disappear. A controlled explosion is probably the best answer.
Stephen Fry – 'Evening Standard' (1991)

National Theatre, London

Looks like a nuclear power station in the middle of London.
Prince Charles – 'Omnibus' (1988)

Nemausas, Nîmes, France

Commissioned to design public housing for the city of Nîmes, Jean Nouvel produced Nemausas, a block which looks like a ship painstakingly fabricated out of old Citroën vans.
Kenneth Powell – 'Sunday Telegraph' (1992)

Palais des Papes, Avignon, France

The Palais has little or no aesthetic interest . . . An impression unpleasant,

mean and particularly medieval.
Arnold Bennett – 'Journal' (1926)

As desolate as it is dirty.
Henry James (1882)

No. 1 Poultry, London
Like a 1930s wireless set. *Prince Charles*

The Pyramids, Egypt
A practical joke played on history.
Peter Forster – 'Letter' (1946)

They will not last a moment compared to
the daisy. *D. H. Lawrence (1932)*

**Rideau Hall (Government House),
Ottawa**
A miserable little house.
George Brown (1804)

Saltire Court, Edinburgh
The much-vaunted Saltire Court beneath
the castle is just standard international
Post-Modern trash.
Piloti – 'Private Eye' (1992)

**Shakespeare Memorial Theatre,
Stratford-upon-Avon**
There is only one thing that can be said in
favour of the new Memorial Theatre. It is
a tremendous, overwhelming argument
against war. Only a nation that has been
bludgeoned by four years' incessant
warfare into a state of insensitivity –
mental, moral and (one might almost say)
physical – could possibly have allowed
itself to put up a structure of such
unspeakable hideousness: and in such a
spot!
A. Cripps – 'Daily News Chronicle' (1951)

Shepherd's Hotel, Cairo
As a whole the Shepherd's Hotel is more
like a pigsty mixed with a bear garden or
a horribly noisy railway station than
anything I can compare it to.
Edward Lear – 'Letter' (1867)

Sheraton Hotel, Edinburgh
The insultingly mediocre Sheraton.
Piloti – 'Private Eye' (1992)

St. James' Palace, London
The English say that their palaces are like
hospitals and their hospitals like palaces;
and the exteriors of St. James' Palace and
Greenwich Hospital justify the saying.
Robert Southey – 'Letter' (1807)

Suez Canal
A dismal, but profitable ditch.
*Joseph Conrad – 'An Outcast of the Islands'
(1896)*

Sydney Harbour Bridge, Australia
As inspiring as a coat-hanger. *Anon*

Tower of London
An Englishman cares nothing about the
Tower, which to us is a haunted castle in
dream-land.
*Nathaniel Hawthorne – 'Our Old Home'
(1863)*

FASHION

Q. What does a fashion director actually
do?
A. Oh darling – she gets 50% discount at
Harvey Nix. *'Absolutely Fabulous' (1992)*

I never cared for fashion much – amusing
little seams and witty pleated skirts.
David Bailey (1990)

Half-a-dozen well-dressed men would be
indistinguishably alike if you decapitated
them. It is notorious that men are the
slaves of fashion.
*Arnold Bennett – 'The Meaning of Frocks'
(1911)*

Don't ever wear artistic jewellery; it
wrecks a woman's reputation.
Colette – 'Gigi' (1940)

American women mostly have their
clothes arranged for them. And their faces
too, I think. *Noël Coward*

How apt fashionable men are to be fond
of slang diction. *George Daley*

The provocative gyrations of women

earning a crust on the catwalk in frocks that often seem designed for the hooking and bondage classes.

> *Peter Dunn – 'Independent on Sunday'*
> *(1992)*

Inflation is a man-made disaster – like Southern beer and nylon shirts.

> *Roland Long (1990)*

The only thing louder than the voices of children's TV presenters is their clothes.

> *'Mail on Sunday' (1992)*

The fashion industry is largely run by men who wouldn't know a real woman if they found one in their black satin bed-sheets. *Jilly Parkin – 'Daily Express' (1992)*

Women who are not vain about their clothes are often vain about not being vain about their clothes. *Cyril Scott*

When seen in the perspective of half-a-dozen years or more, the best of our fashions strike us as grotesque.

> *Thorstein Veblen – 'The Theory of the*
> *Leisure Class' (1899)*

DESIGNERS

Cecil Beaton

His baroque is worse than his bite.

> *Hank Brennan*

Karl Lagerfeld

His black mini topped by ankle-length chiffon is an idea that should have stayed in his sketch book.

> *Lowri Turner – 'Evening Standard' (1991)*

FASHION VICTIMS

Today Hollywood film stars – even the real lookers like Michelle Pfeiffer and Winona Ryder – are shy, troubled creatures who dress like something Cat Stevens dragged in from the local Saturday night sackcloth-and-ashes hop.

> *Julie Burchill – 'Mail on Sunday' (1993)*

Kathleen Battle

A Carnegie Hall Christmas Concert (1992) – Kathleen Battle sang like an angel, but

her dress suggested she'd squeezed between two scarlet armchairs and brought them with her.

> *Allison Pearson – 'Independent on Sunday'*

Cher

A bona fide fashion fiasco – from nose to toe she's the tacky tattooed terror.

> *Mr Blackwell (1991)*

Bill Clinton

Have you ever seen how he dresses to jog? He wears what looks like a pair of Babe Ruth's old swimming trunks and a P.E.-issue plain grey T-shirt. I mean, I still believe in a place called Hope – unless it's where he shops for jogging clothes.

> *Rick Reilly – 'Sports Illustrated' (1992)*

Cindy Crawford

In the flesh, Cindy Crawford is, inevitably, more plastic than perfect. Like her Hambro namesake, she seems so plastic and perfect I had this insatiable urge to pull down her trousers to see if she had any reproductive organs.

> *Nicola Davidson – 'Modern Review' (1992)*

Jerry Hall

Try interviewing her sometime. It's like talking to a window. *Bryant Gumbel*

Nigel Kennedy

The violinist who plays like an angel and dresses like Vivienne Westwood on a bad day. *Jilly Parkin – 'Daily Express' (1992)*

Benito Mussolini

There is something wrong, even histrionically, with a man who wears white spats with a black shirt.

> *Ernest Hemingway – 'Toronto Daily Star'*
> *(1923)*

Sinead O'Connor

A monastic monstrosity in baggy rags and combat boots – a creepy cross between Joan of Arc and Kojak.

> *Mr Blackwell (1991)*

Rifat Ozbek

Whose personal wardrobe favours a kind of Cardboard City chic.

> *Peter Dunn – 'Independent on Sunday'*
> *(1992)*

Judy Steel [wife of MP David]

Tell me the history of that frock, Judy. It's obviously an old favourite. You were wise to remove the curtain rings.

Dame Edna Everage – 'An Audience with Dame Edna' (1984)

Elizabeth Taylor

Elizabeth Taylor is wearing Orson Welles designer jeans.   *Joan Rivers*

Ivana Trump

A middle-aged laughing stock, a matron desperately in search of a career after being dumped for this year's model.

Julie Burchill – 'Mail on Sunday' (1992)

CLOTHING

Animal furs

It takes up to forty dumb animals to make a fur coat, but only one to wear it.

Bryn Jones

Drab chic

Also known as 'Le Style Dull' or 'Le Breakfast Television Look'. This involves wearing simple, unflashy clothes. The aim is to look like a BBC weather forecaster (think: Michael Fish), or off-duty librarian.

Peter Freedman – 'Glad to be Grey' (1985)

Hats

Is that a hat or a threat you're wearing?

Eddie Condon

For this lady, who had very black hair, had stuck over her right ear the pitiable corpse of a large white bird, which looked exactly as if someone had killed it by stamping on its breast, and then nailed it to the lady's temple, which was presumably of sufficient solidity to bear the operation. *G. B. Shaw – 'Letter' (1905)*

Lingerie

I don't like those chiffon nighties . . . they show your vest.   *Joyce Grenfell*

Sportswear

To his American football players – If you want to wear bell-bottoms, join the navy; if you want long hair, become a hippie; if you want to wear a headband, get a job as an Indian in a movie.   *Norm van Brocklin*

I never could understand tennis players who wore nice dresses but showed dreary garments underneath.   *Teddy Tinling*

Training shoes

The 'trainer' – the ugliest species of footwear ever devised.

'The Weasel' – 'Independent' (1993)

LITERARY

FICTION

Many authors, when one meets them for the first time, are comparatively unimpressive compared to their books.
John Betjeman

There is no rule which says that sex between two people who are in love has to be as dull as watching spermicide dry, but you wouldn't know it from reading modern blockbusters.
Julie Burchill – 'Modern Review' (1992)

Bunyan spent a year in prison, Coleridge was a drug addict, Poe was an alcoholic, Marlowe was killed by a man he was trying to stab, Pope took a large sum of money to keep a woman's name out of a vicious satire and then wrote it so that she could be recognised anyway, Chatterton killed himself, Somerset Maugham was so unhappy in his final thirty years that he longed for death . . . do you still want to be a writer?
Bennett Cerf

Fill an author with a titanic fame and you do not make him titanic; you often merely burst him.
*Frank M. Colby –
'The Margin of Hesitation' (1921)*

Erotic literature is a moral vulture which steals upon our youth, silently striking its terrible talons into their vitals, and forcibly bearing them away on hideous wings to shame and death.
Anthony Comstock

Writing a novel without being asked seems a bit like having a baby when you have nowhere to live.
Lucy Ellman

A book on cheap paper does not convince. It is not prized, it is like a wheezy doctor with pigtail breath who needs a manicure.
Elbert Hubbard

There can hardly be a stranger commodity in the world than books. Printed by people who don't understand them, sold by people who don't understand them; bound, criticized and read by people who don't understand them, and now even written by people who don't understand them.
Georg Lichtenberg – 'Scattered Occasions'

In some modern literature there has appeared a tendency to replace communication by a private maundering to oneself which shall inspire one's audience to maunder privately to themselves – rather as if the author handed round a box of drugged cigarettes.
F. L. Lucas – 'Style'

The multitude of books is a great evil. There is no limit to this fever for writing: everyone must be an author; some out of vanity, to acquire celebrity and raise up a name; others for the sake of mere gain.
Martin Luther – 'Table-talk' (1569)

I would sooner read a timetable or a catalogue than nothing at all. They are much more entertaining than half the novels written.
W. Somerset Maugham

As regards Canadian literary criticism, it is woefully lacking in scholarship, poise and judicial discrimination. All our goslings are swans.
Thomas O'Hagan (1927)

All writers are vain, selfish, and lazy, and at the very bottom their motives are a mystery.
George Orwell

Book reviewing is in danger of becoming a blood-sport.
'Private Eye'

You simply cannot imagine London producing a Saul Bellow or Tom Wolfe. While our writers have never been intellectuals, never have they so collectively given the impression that they have lost their belief in moral, intellectual and spiritual progress. Instead, the more affluent they have become, the less creative.
Nicholas Shakespeare – 'Daily Telegraph'

Authors have a very feeble grip of reality.
G. B. Shaw

Writing is not a profession, but a vocation
of unhappiness. *Georges Simenon*

Literature with a capital L is rubbish.
Georges Simenon

American writers want to be not good but
great; and so are neither.
Gore Vidal – 'Two Sisters' (1970)

One book's very like another – after all
what is it? Something to read and be done
with. It's not a thing that matters like
print dresses or serviettes – where you
either like 'em or don't, and people judge
you by. *H.G. Wells – 'Kipps'*

One should not be too severe on English
novelists, they are the only relaxation of
the intellectually unemployed. *Oscar Wilde*

'American dry goods? What are they, I
wonder?' enquired Lord Henry.
'American novels?'
Oscar Wilde – 'Picture of Dorian Grey'

FICTION WRITERS

Anon
My dear Sir,
I have just read your novel. Oh, my dear
Sir!! Yours sincerely. *John Murray (1803)*

Alice Adams
While I admire the cool surfaces of Alice
Adams's stories, they leave me wanting
more heat.
*Ron Carlson – 'New York Times Book
Review' (1989)*

Glenda Adams
'Games of the Strong' (1989) – What
audience is going to be captivated by a
passive, jinxed, self-despising, female
nerd?
*John Tranter – 'American Book Review'
(1990)*

Kingsley Amis
An over-estimated writer affecting the

high social style of club curmudgeon.
Saul Bellow

Martin Amis
'London Fields' (1990) – Bloated,
tendentious, at the same time fat and
woefully thin . . . A bicycle pump has
been applied to a very average idea.
Martin Cropper – 'Sunday Telegaph'

Jane Austen
If Jane Austen were alive today she'd
probably be writing books called things
like 'Sex and Sensibility' and 'Pride and
Passion'.
Julie Burchill – 'Modern Review' (1992)

Jane Austen's books, too, are absent from
this library. Just that one omission alone
would make a fairly good library out of a
library that hadn't a book in it.
Mark Twain – 'Follow the Equator'

Paul Auster
'Leviathan' (1992) – It may start with a
bang, but *Leviathan* finishes with the
sound of someone simply banging on.
Tom Shone – 'Independent' (1992)

Jean Baudrillard
'Seduction' (1990) – *Seduction* is often little
more than an excuse for some
nauseatingly dated fantasies about
women.
Rosalind Coward – 'New Statesman'

Samuel Beckett
'Molloy; Malone Dies; The Unnameable'
(1959) – The suggestion that something
larger is being said about the human
predicament won't hold water, any more
than Beckett's incontinent heroes can.
'The Spectator'

Max Beerbohm
It always makes me cross when Max is
called 'the incomparable Max.' He is not
incomparable at all . . . He is a shallow,
affected, self-conscious fribble.
Vita Sackville-West – 'Letter' (1959)

Hilaire Belloc
Mr Hilaire Belloc
Is a case for legislation ad hoc.

He seems to think nobody minds
His books being of all different kinds.
E. C. Bentley

C. T. Boyle

'East is East' (1990) – Boyle should do
more with his considerable gifts than
squander them on cynical conceits like
East is East. *Oliver Conant – 'New Leader'*

Charlotte Brontë

'Jane Eyre' – Blatantly such stuff as
daydreams are made on. Reading *Jane
Eyre* is like gobbling a jar full of schoolgirl
stickjaw.
*Brophy, Levey & Osborne – '50 Works of
Literature We Could Do Without' (1967)*

Emily Brontë

'Wuthering Heights' (1847) – Wild,
confused, disjointed and improbable.
'The Examiner'

'Wuthering Heights' (1847) – A
particularly lack-lustre contribution to the
literature not of domestic terror but of the
terror of domesticity.
David Pascoe – 'Literary Review' (1992)

John Bunyan

'Pilgrim's Progress' – It is impossible to
rate his naïve and fevered imagination
any higher than that of the gentlemen
who walk through the West End of
London with sandwich boards imploring
us to flee from the wrath to come.
*Brophy, Levey & Osborne – '50 Works of
Literature We Could Do Without' (1967)*

Julie Burchill

'Ambition' – Just a list of 80s things with
some pornography thrown in.
Stephen Duffy (1989)

'No Exit' – When I was asked to review
No Exit I told myself I would like it . . .
However, as a simple reader, I have to say
that this book stinks . . . The romantic
pulp genre depends on characters with
whom one can identify . . . I defy anyone
to care about the well-being of any one of
the cardboard cut-outs (and badly cut out

at that) who fail to people this text.
Sara Maitland – 'The Spectator' (1993)

Anthony Burgess

He is like someone on a quiz-show who
insists on giving answers in greater detail
than is actually necessary.
*William Leith – 'Sunday Correspondent'
(1989)*

Niven Busch

'The Titan Game' (1989) – Readers are
advised to allow *The Titan Game* to
disappear quickly. Pass this one by.
Elda Pendleton – 'Library Journal'

John Cage

'I-VI: Charles Norton Lectures' (1990) –
Very much like Joyce's *Finnegan's Wake*,
John Cage's *I-VI* is at once unreadable
and rereadable.
Ronald Kostenlanetz – 'Notes'

Albert Camus

'The Fall' (1957) – The style is
unattractive if apt, being the oblique
stilted flow of a man working his way
round to asking for a loan.
Anthony Quinton – 'New Statesman'

Truman Capote

On hearing of his death – Good career
move. *Gore Vidal*

Thomas Carlyle

It is embarrassing how he harps on his
wife's dimensions: brave little heart, noble
little creature, indomitable little soul – he
only just stops short of 'wee cowering
crimson-tippit Beastie.' *Sylvia T. Warner*

Alejo Carpentier

'The Harp and the Shadow' (1990) – A
failed experiment of interest only to
literary historians.
Paul Stuewe – 'Quill Quire'

Barbara Cartland

A tireless purveyor of romance and now a
gleaming telly-figure with a Niagara of
jabber, and the white and creamy look of
an animated meringue.
Arthur Marshall (1971)

Louis F. Céline

'Journey to the End of the Night' (1934) –
Most readers will find this a revolting
book; its vision of human life will seem to
them a hideous nightmare . . . If this is
life, then it is better not to live.

> *J. D. Adams – 'New York Times Book
> Review'*

G. K. Chesterton

Poor G. K. C., his day is past -
Now God will know the truth at last.

> *E. V. Lucas*

Here lies Mr Chesterton,
Who to heaven might have gone,
But didn't when he heard the news,
That the place was run by Jews.

> *Humbert Wolfe*

Agatha Christie

Her stories are puzzles, not novels. The
characters aren't even lifelike enough to
be caricatures. I don't like Agatha Christie
at all.   *Ruth Rendell (1992)*

Tom Clancy

All Clancy's characters sound exactly the
same.   *Paul Gray – 'Time' (1991)*

'The Sum of All Fears' (1991) – A whizz-
bang page-turner, but to be honest not all
the pages get read.   *Morton Kondracke –
'New York Times Book Review'*

Jackie Collins

'Lady Boss' (1990) – The most awful book
I have ever reviewed. The prose is banal
. . . and the many bursts of sexual activity
have the quality of short-time couplings
in a brothel. One weeps for the noble
trees that had to be pulped to enable this
concoction to be published.

> *Anthony Looch – 'Sunday Telegraph'*

Ivy Compton-Burnett

'A God and his Gifts' – Novels by Miss
Compton-Burnett can no more be read

for their narrative impetus or their
development of character than those
problems in which Harry is taller than
Dick, who is shorter than Bill.

> *Brigid Brophy – 'New Statesman' (1963)*

Shirley Conran

'Crimson' (1992) – Brand-name upon
brand-name. Cattleprod psychology.

> *D. J. Taylor – 'Sunday Times'*

'Crimson' – Has more plots than a
municipal cemetery.

> *Val Hennessy – 'Daily Mail'*

Dennis Cooper

'Closer' (1989) – Mr Cooper's offerings
seem to have more in common with run-
of-the-mill pornography, particularly its
grinding obsessiveness and fantastic lack
of material consequences.

> *William Ferguson – 'New York Times Book
> Review'*

Jilly Cooper

Barbara Cartland without the iron
knickers.   *Anon*

Pete Davies

'Dollarville' (1989) – Much of this book
endlessly and tediously reinvents the
wheel . . . and the political statement . . .
is no more than another poster to paste
on the wall.   *Roz Kaveney –
'Times Literary Supplement' (1990)*

Simone de Beauvoir

Mlle de Beauvoir is a plodder par
excellence. Not for her the masterstroke
which cuts a long story short; she opts
every time for the Long March – the long
plod.

> *Brigid Brophy – 'New York Times' (1965)*

Thomas De Quincey

De Quincey had the face of a child, but of
a child that had seen Hell.

> *Thomas Carlyle*

Len Deighton

'Spy Sinker' (1990) – Len Deighton has
exhausted the cold war as a lively topic in
the 28 years and 20 odd books he's
written. *Spy Sinker* suggests the topic has

also exhausted him.   *Morton Kondracke –*
'New York Times Book Review'

Ethell M. Dell

She rode the trash-horse hell-for-leather.
Rose Macaulay

Jane Delynn

'Don Juan in the Village' (1990) – Again
and again, it made me feel like a
bartender with a single customer and a
long night ahead.   *Bertha Harris –*
'New York Times Book Review'

Charles Dickens

'Pickwick Papers' – Mr Dickens writes too
often and too fast. If he persists much
longer in this course, it requires no gift of
prophecy to foretell his fate – he has risen
like a rocket, and he will come down like a
stick.   *Anon (1838)*

'A Tale of Two Cities' – It was a sheer
dead pull from start to finish. It all
seemed so insincere, such a transparent
make-believe, a mere piece of acting.
John Burroughs – 'Century Magazine'
(1897)

A totally disinherited waif.
George Santayana

'Hard Times' – On the whole, the story is
stale, flat, and unprofitable: a mere dull
melodrama, in which character is
caricature, sentimental tinsel, and moral
(if any) unsound.
Richard Simpson – 'The Rambler' (1854)

'Pickwick Papers' – The general theory of
life on which it is based is not only false,
but puerile. Fifty years hence most of his
wit will be harder to understand than the
allusions in the *Dunciad*; and our
grandchildren will wonder what their
ancestors could have meant by putting
Mr Dickens at the head of the novelists of
his day.   *James F. Stephens –*
'Saturday Review' (1858)

John Dos Passos

'The 42nd Parallel' (1930) – He is like a
man who is trying to run in a dozen
directions at once, succeeding thereby
merely in standing still and making a
noise. Sometimes it is amusing noise and
alive; often monotonous.
V. S. Pritchett – 'The Spectator'

Norman Douglas

A mixture of Roman Emperor and
Roman cab-driver.   *Reginald Turner*

Theodore Dreiser

'An American Tragedy' (1925) – His style,
if style it may be called, is offensively
colloquial, commonplace and vulgar.
'Boston Evening Transcript'

An Indiana peasant, snuffling absurdly
over imbecile sentimentalities, giving a
grave ear to quackeries, snorting and eye-
rolling with the best of them . . . He is still
in the transition stage between Christian
Endeavour and civilisation.
H. L. Mencken

Brett Easton Ellis

Ellis is about 15, isn't he?
Martin Amis (1988)

'American Psycho' (1991) – It reads like an
endless brand-name catalogue.
John Heilpern – 'Independent On Sunday'

'American Psycho' – Every bad thing you
have read about this book is an
understatement. It's ineptly written. It's
sophomoric. It is, in the truest sense of
the word, obscene . . . It would take more
space than the task deserves to catalogue
all of Ellis' myriad ineptnesses.
Terry Teachout – 'National Review'

'American Psycho' – The single most
boring book I have ever had to endure.
Imagine a Dantesque circle devoted to the
sin of namedropping.
Naomi Wolf – 'New Statesman'

Henry Fielding

'Tom Jones' – I scarcely know a more corrupt work.   *Samuel Johnson*

Carrie Fisher

'Surrender the Pink' (1990) – Fisher often writes scenes as if she knows her agent is shopping the movie rights.
          Cathleen McGuigan – 'Newsweek'

'Surrender the Pink' – It is utterly unmemorable.   *John Skow – 'Time'*

F. Scott Fitzgerald

'The Great Gatsby' (1925) – A little slack, a little soft, more than a little artificial. *The Great Gatsby* falls into the class of negligible novels.   *'Springfield Republican'*

Ford Madox Ford

What he really is or if he is really, nobody knows now and he least of all . . . He is a system of assumed personas.   *H. G. Wells*

Dick Francis

Off-form, he can be smug, sexist and narky: Surrey with a whinge on top.
          Julie Burchill – 'Sunday Times' (1992)

'Straight' (1989) – This time Francis doesn't make it into the winner's circle.
          Paul Stuewe – 'Quill Quire'

William Gaddis

'The Recognitions' (1955) – The main fault of the novel is a complete lack of discipline . . . Most of the time he just lets his pen run on.   *'Kirkus Reviews'*

John Galsworthy

'The Forsyte Saga' – A thoroughly middle-class substitute for real literature.
          Brophy, Levey & Osborne – '50 Works of Literature We Could Do Without' (1967)

Maggie Gee

'The Burning Book' – If Faber continue to publish this sort of book as a lead-title it will not be long before the portrait of T. S. Eliot should be taken from the boardroom and hung in the servants' lavatory.   *Charles Hawtrey – 'Spectator'*

André Gide

An unattractive man with a pale green complexion.   *Steven Runciman*

What a strange and hollow talent! Gide appears to be completely indifferent to human nature, none of his characters have characters, and he hangs bits of behaviour on them just as one hung different paper hats on flat paper mannequins.   *Sylvia T. Warner*

George Gissing

Gissing's books . . . as grey as a stevedore's vest.
          P. G. Wodehouse – 'Ice in the Bedroom' (1961)

William Golding

After winning the 1983 Nobel Prize for Literature – A little English phenomenon of no special interest.   *Arthur Lundkvist*

Maxim Gorky

You talk about yourself a great deal. That's why there are no distinctive characters in your writing. Your characters are all alike. You probably don't understand women; you've never depicted one successfully.
          Leo Tolstoy (1900)

Alisdair Gray

'Poor Things' – Poor readers is more to the point . . . reading the bloody book is more akin to a mental exercise on *Krypton Factor* than a pleasurable experience.
          Julie Emery – 'Time Out' (1992)

Thomas Hardy

The best prose is usually written by poets – Shakespeare wrote the best seventeenth century, and Shelley the best nineteenth; and I don't think I'm going too far when I say that Mr Hardy has written the worst.
          George Moore

'The Return of the Native' (1878) – We maintain that the primary object of a story is to amuse us, and in the attempt to amuse us Mr Hardy breaks down.
          'Saturday Review'

Joseph Heller
'Catch 22' (1961) – The book is an emotional hodgepodge.
'New York Times Book Review'

Ernest Hemingway
'A Farewell to Arms' – A footnote to the minor art of Gertrude Stein, an appendix to the biography of the great novelist Scott Fitzgerald, and the Ouida of the thirties.
Brophy, Levey & Osborne – '50 Works of Literature We Could Do Without' (1967)

'For Whom the Bell Tolls' (1940) – Mr Hemingway: . . . please leave stories of the Spanish Civil War to Malraux.
'Commonweal'

'The Sun Also Rises' (1926) – His characters are as shallow as the saucers in which they stack their daily emotions.
'The Dial'

He got hold of the red meat of the English language and turned it into hamburger. *Richard Gordon*

Oliver Herford
An embarrassed field-mouse.
Frank Crowninshield

Stewart Home
'Pure Maniac' (1989) – DON'T buy this for your mum, unless she's a pulp-novel junkie with a finely developed sense of the absurd. *Nik Houghton – 'Time Out'*

Aldous Huxley
'Point Counter Point' – He writes in the half clinical, half with-genteel-attention-averted manner of someone obliged to clean the lavatory.
Brophy, Levey & Osborne -'50 Works of Literature We Could Do Without' (1967)

'Antic Hay' – Which is the more despicable – witless smut or witty smut? Which is the more pestiferous – dirty dullness or dirty brilliance? Which is the more poisonous – stupid indecency or intellectual lubricity? Which is the more dangerous – the swinish dullard or the

hog of genius? There is no pardon for the artist who bedaubs his own visions and befouls his own dreams. Mr Aldous Huxley is beyond question a diabolically clever young man and 'Antic Hay' is a witty novel, but its wit compels the reader to hold his nose.
James Douglas – 'Sunday Express' (1923)

'Brave New World' (1932) – A lugubrious and heavy-handed piece of propaganda.
'New York Herald-Tribune'

Henry James
He was like a butler listening at the keyhole to hear what the Duchess and the Duke were saying to each other.
W. Somerset Maugham

He talked as if every sentence had been carefully rehearsed; every semicolon, every comma, was in exactly the right place, and his rounded periods dropped on the floor and bounced about like tiny rubber balls. *Alfred Sutro*

I have just read a long novel by Henry James. Much of it made me think of the priest condemned for a long space to confess nuns. *John B. Yeats*

Tama Janowitz
'The Male Cross-Dresser Support Group' (1992) – It had the same effect on me as watching Terry Wogan; too forced and obvious to do much more than provoke irritation. *Andrea Stuart – 'Literary Review'*

James Joyce
'A Portrait of the Artist as a Young Man' (1917) – As a treatment of Irish politics, society or religion, it is negligible.
'Catholic World'

Bloody awful . . . labouring to be trivial.
Nigel Frith

Probably Joyce thinks that because he prints all the dirty little words he is a great novelist. *George Moore*

I could not write the words Mr Joyce uses: my prudish hands would refuse to form the letters. *G. B. Shaw*

M. M. Kaye

'The Far Pavilions' – One of those big, fat paperbacks intended to wile away a monsoon or two; if thrown with a good overarm action, will bring a water buffalo to its knees.

Nancy Banks-Smith – 'Guardian'

Frank Kermode

A jumped-up book-drunk ponce.

Philip Larkin – 'Letter'

Stephen King

Everyone knows Stephen King's flaws: tone-deaf narration, papier-mâché character, clichés, gratuitous vulgarity, self-indulgent digressions.

Andy Solomon – 'New York Times Book Review'

Rudyard Kipling

Kipling is a jingo imperialist, he is morally insensitive and aesthetically disgusting.

George Orwell

Ivan Klima

'Love and Garbage' (1991) – Some of its loving superfluity could surely have gone in the waste-bin.

James Naughton – 'Times Literary Supplement'

Judith Krantz

'Scruples Two' (1992) – I've never come across a book which was such a slog to finish – and that includes *Gravity's Rainbow* and *Ancient Evenings*. When we are told that *Scruples* is 'the story that millions of readers never wanted to end', I think we can safely take that one with a fair-sized Siberian salt-mine.

Julie Burchill – 'Modern Review' (1992)

Books like *Scruples Two* like to present themselves as daringly taboo-busting, full of 'virile', 'raunchy' women who go after what they want when they want it, but they are as dull as any Mills and Boon barndance.   *Julie Burchill – 'Ibid'*

'Princess Daisy' – As a work of art it has the same status as a long conversation between two not very bright drunks.

Clive James

D. H. Lawrence

Filth. Nothing but obscenities.

Joseph Conrad

'The Plumed Serpent' (1926) – If this writing up of a new faith is intended for a message, then it is only a paltry one, with its feathers, its bowls of human blood and its rhetoric.   *'The Spectator'*

T. E. Lawrence

If he hides in a quarry he puts red flags all around.   *G. B. Shaw*

Warren Leamon

'Unkind Melodies' (1990) – It does not, as the title borrowed from Keats suggests, capture the tunes of pipers forever young. Rather, it sounds the notes of a transient player whistling 'Dixie' out of tune.

Shelby Hearon – 'New York Times Book Review'

John Le Carré

'The Secret Pilgrim' (1991) – Little more than a loose bit of string to tie various good ideas for stories that never made it into his other books.

Ian Buruma – 'New York Review of Books'

Sinclair Lewis and Dorothy Thompson

On their marriage – Red will drink and Dorothy will talk until they both go meshuggah . . .   *H. L. Mencken*

I just had dinner with Dorothy Thompson and her husband, whom I'd never met before. I began by thinking how awful they were, but ended by deciding they were not so bad – though she is ignorant and so silly that one wonders why anybody has ever let her go into print about politics and he is one of those all-too-heavy jolly Viennese lightweights.   *Edmund Wilson*

Susan Lewis
'Dance While You Can' (1989) – A precocious schoolgirl might have penned this by torchlight.
    Anthony Looch – 'Sunday Telegraph'

Ian McEwan
The Booker Prize was a complete waste of time this year. I'm glad McEwan didn't win, he looks squirty and his books sound squirtish – though I've never read any of them.   *Colin Haycraft (1992)*

Norman Mailer
If he has a taste for transcribing banalities, he also has a talent for it.
    'New Republic'

'Harlot's Ghost' (1991) – The last line of this immense book [1310 pages] reads 'To Be Continued'. The thought is enough to send a reader in search of a drink.   *Peter S. Prescott – 'Newsweek'*

'Harlot's Ghost' – The author does come across as a punch-drunk writer trying to outbox all competition, real or imaginary.
    John Simon – 'New York Times Book Review'

W. Somerset Maugham
'Of Human Bondage' (1935) – Largely a record of sordid realism.   *'Athenaeum'*

George Meredith
As a writer he has mastered everything except language: as a novelist he can do everything except tell a story: as an artist he is everything except articulate.
    Oscar Wilde

Henry Miller
'Tropic of Cancer' – . . . is without literary value.
Brigid Brophy – 'London Magazine' (1963)

George Moore
Elegy on Any Lady *by G. M.*
That she adored me as the most adorable of males,
I think I may securely boast . . . Dead women tell no tales.   *Max Beerbohm*

Jan Morris
'Sydney' (1992) – Her anecdotes are as weak as Earl Grey tea with too much milk.
    Kathy Lette – 'Independent on Sunday'

Iris Murdoch
I should much rather be even a minor character in a Jane Austen novel than a major figure in a Iris Murdoch one.
Malcolm Muggeridge – 'Things Past' (1978)

Vladimir Nabokov
'Lolita' (1958) – Very literate pornography.   *'Kirkus Reviews'*

Mr Nabokov is in the habit of introducing any job of this kind which he undertakes by the announcement that he is unique and incomparable and that everybody else who has attempted it is an oaf and ignoramus, usually with the implication that he is also a low-class person and a ridiculous personality.   *Edmund Wilson*

Frank Norris
'McTeague' (1899) – Grossness for the sake of grossness.   *'The Literary World'*

Flannery O'Connor
'Wise Blood' (1952) – Her idea of humour is almost exclusively variations on the pratfall . . . Neither satire nor humour is achieved.   *'Saturday Review of Literature'*

Daniel Odier
'Cannibal Kiss' (1989) – *Cannibal Kiss* took me three hours to read carefully, and I'm a slow reader; unfortunately the book's anaemic prose left me with the impression that the novel hadn't taken much longer to write.
William Mooney – 'American Book Review'

George Orwell
Tall, pale, with his flaccid cheeks, large spatulate fingers and supercilious voice, he was one of those boys who seem born old.   *Cyril Connolly*

Thomas Paine
'Common Sense' (1776) – Shallow, violent and scurrilous. *William E. H. Lecky (1882)*

Edgar Allan Poe

A verbal poet merely; empty of thought, empty of sympathy, empty of love for any real thing . . . he was not human and manly. *John Burroughs – 'The Dial' (1893)*

Anthony Powell

A horse-faced dwarf.

Philip Larkin – 'Letter'

Marcel Proust

A society creep and snivelling hermit.

Andrew Hope (1990)

'Remembrance of Things Past' (1928) – So full of dignitaries, so devoid of dignity.

'Saturday Review of Literature'

Jonathan Raban

'Hunting Mr Heartbreak' (1990) – We need understanding. What we don't need is another queasy sourpuss clearing his sinuses and calling it sociology . . . another man with ants in his pants. *Hunting Mr Heartbreak* reads like a mid-life crisis masquerading as a travel book . . . a waste of time, money and motion, and not to mention talent.

James Wolcott – 'Observer'

Ruth Rendell

'Going Wrong' (1990) – What has happened to Ruth Rendell? . . . *Going Wrong*'s title is an all-too-accurate description of its content. *'Quill Quire'*

Frank Richards [Charles Hamilton]

A charming and courteous robot-writer.

Arthur Marshall (1965)

Marquis de Sade

A French noble keen on inflicting pain, primarily through several execrable novels. *Mike Barfield – 'The Oldie' (1992)*

J. D. Salinger

The greatest mind ever to stay in prep school. *Norman Mailer*

George Sand

She has the habit of speaking and writing concerning chastity in such terms that makes the very word become impure.

Philip Hale

George Santayana

The perfection of rottenness.

William James

William Saroyan

'The Human Condition' (1943) – An excessively simple and very, very sentimental little concoction.

'Times Literary Supplement'

Sir Walter Scott

'Kenilworth' – A wonderful human being and a monumentally boring writer. I would love to have dined with him but I cannot bring myself to read *Kenilworth*.

Richard Huggett – 'The Wit of Publishing'
(1986)

George Bernard Shaw

'The Adventures of a Black Girl in her Search for God' – A profoundly stupid book and a profoundly ignorant book.

Archbishop of York (1934)

Thomas Sheridan

Why, Sir, Sherry is dull, naturally dull; but it must have taken him a great deal of pains to become what we now see him. Such an excess of stupidity, Sir, is not in Nature. *Samuel Johnson (1762)*

Clement Shorter

There is nothing whatever to be said for Clement Shorter, a snuffling, go-getting louse in the locks of literature.

Rupert Hart-Davis

Osbert, Sacheverell and Edith Sitwell

Two wiseacres and a cow. *Noël Coward*

C. P. Snow

Not only not a genius, he is intellectually as undistinguished as it is possible to be.

F. R. Leavis

He doesn't know what he means and doesn't know he doesn't know.

F. R. Leavis

Laurence Sterne

He has that terrible, professional, nonstop pedantry of the Irish. One feels, sometimes, that one has been cornered by some brilliant Irish drunk, one whose mind is incurably suggestive.

V. S. Pritchett

Robert Louis Stevenson

A Presbyterian pirate.   *Doris Dalglish*

Jacqueline Susann

She looks like a truck driver in drag.

Truman Capote

Jonathan Swift

'Gulliver's Travels' (1726) – Evidence of a diseased mind and lacerated heart.

John Dunlop – 'The History of Fiction'
(1814)

Dear Swift, by his lordship's own account, was so intoxicated with the love of flattery, he sought it amongst the lowest of people and the silliest of women; and was never so well pleased with any companions as those that worshipped him, while he insulted them.

Lady Mary W. Montagu

Donna Tartt

'The Secret History' (1992) – . . . naïve and poised by turns . . . like a B-movie written by a schoolgirl.

Kathy O'Shaughnessy – 'Vogue'

'The Secret History' – We've seen it all before – the money, the Hollywood deals, the author profiles. As for this new girl Donna Tartt, even her name sounds like a confection cooked up by marketing.

Harvey Porlock – 'Sunday Times'

D. M. Thomas

'Memories and Hallucinations' – Thomas the Wank Engine.   *'Private Eye'*

J. R. R. Tolkien

On reading a new manuscript – Oh f★★★! Not another elf!   *Hugo Dyson*

His appeal is to readers with a lifelong appetite for juvenile trash.

Edmund Wilson

Leo Tolstoy

'Anna Karenina' (1887) – Sentimental rubbish . . . Show me one page that contains an idea.   *'The Odessa Courier'*

Rose Tremain

'Sacred Country' (1992) – Tremain teaches creative writing at the University of East Anglia and it shows . . . like watching a cricket master demonstrating batsmanship to the under-11s. It's all straight from the textbook. But good textbooks make bad art.

David Robinson – 'Sunday Telegraph'

Anthony Trollope

Trollope! Did anybody bear a name that predicted a style Trollopy?   *George Moore*

Mark Twain

'The Adventures of Huckleberry Finn'
(1884) – The adolescent dream goes on, lulling the reader into an immature climate where goodness somehow triumphs and yet every tribute is paid to the abstract concept of boyishness. It is a vision that can be achieved only by that ruthless dishonesty which is the birthright of every sentimentalist.

Brophy, Levey & Osborne – '50 Works of
Literature We Could Do Without' (1967)

'The Adventures of Huckleberry Finn' – A gross trifling with every fine feeling . . . Mr Clemens has no reliable sense of propriety.   *'Springfield Republican'*

Barry Unsworth

A Daphne du Maurier costume dramatist.

Valentine Cunningham – 'Observer' (1992)

John Updike

'Rabbit Run' (1960) – The author fails to convince us that his puppets are interesting in themselves or that their plight has implications that transcend their narrow world.   *Milton Crane – 'Chicago Tribune'*

'Rabbit at Rest' (1990) – Had Updike done more dramatising and less editorising he

might have created a series that would outlive its period. But the book's bogged down in opinion, and opinion is a poor substitute for appetite.

James Wolcott – 'Observer'

Mary Augusta Ward

That shapeless mass of meaningless flesh – all old and sordid and insignificant.

Lytton Strachey

Evelyn Waugh

He looked, I decided, like a letter delivered to the wrong address.

Malcolm Muggeridge

H. G. Wells

An anti-semitic misogynist obsessed with the creation of a racially pure master race.

Michael Coren (1992)

Edith Wharton

She is always pitying workers; poor things, how they do have to work.

Louise Bogan

Oscar Wilde

'The Picture of Dorian Gray' (1891) – Unmanly, sickening, vicious and tedious.

'Athenaeum'

Ian Wilson

'Black Jenny' (1992) – If you gave Ted Hughes' much mulled-over Shakespearean fantasy to a re-write team of Judith Krantz and Umberto Eco, something like this hybrid monster would result . . . a bucketful of ludicrous tripe concocted by a prankster, marketed by cynics and aimed at (largely male) readers who crave an airport-bookstall fix with a patine of science and no giveaway glitter on the cover.   *Boyd Tonkin – 'Observer'*

Sloan Wilson and Herman Wouk

If the Man in the Grey Flannel Suit married Marjorie Morningstar on my front porch at high noon, I wouldn't bother to go the wedding.

Nelson Algren

Godfrey Winn

'Dreams Fade' and *'Squirrel's Cage'* – An

anthologist would not know where to begin were he to select a paragraph for an 'Oxford Book of English Slop'.

Cyril Connolly – 'New Statesman'

Tom Wolfe

The nonchalant master of the neon-piped sentence.   *Hugh Kenner*

Mary Wollstonecraft

A philosophising serpent . . . that hyena in petticoats.   *Horace Walpole*

Virginia Woolf

V. Woolf's *'A Writer's Diary'* – usually done in 'fifteen minutes before dinner.' What a monster of egotism she was!

Louise Bogan

Biographies of Virginia Woolf will continue to be written until one of them convinces us all that she existed.

Russell Davies – 'Daily Telegraph'

'The Waves' (1931) – This chamber music, this closet fiction, is executed behind too firmly closed windows . . . The book is dull.

H. C. Harwood – 'Saturday Review of Literature'

'To the Lighthouse' (1927) – Her work is poetry; it must be judged as poetry, and all the weaknesses of poetry are inherent in it.   *'New York Evening Post'*

She had been a peculiar kind of snob without really belonging to a social group with whom to be snobbish.

Edmund Wilson

SCIENCE FICTION

Science fiction, like Brazil, is where the nuts come from.

Thomas M. Disch – 'Observer' (1987)

SCIENCE FICTION WRITERS

Isaac Asimov

'Nemisis' (1989) – Reads more like an

outline for an Asimov novel.
Gerald Jonas – 'New York Book Review'

NON-FICTION

Most jazz books possess all the charm and wit of manuals on the construction of gas-cooled nuclear generators.
Clive Davis – 'Literary Review' (1992)

NON-FICTION WRITERS

Anon
'Biography of Leonid Brezhnev' – Here is a book so dull that a whirling dervish could read himself to sleep with it. If you were to recite a single page in the open air, birds would fall out of the sky and dogs drop dead.				*Clive James*

Leo Abse
'Margaret: Daughter of Beatrice' – A Psycho-biography of Margaret Thatcher (1989) – The evidence for this steaming pot-pourri could be assembled on a couple of sheets of A4 . . . This book would have made an amusing pamphlet but at nearly 300 pages it has used up too many trees.
John Turner – 'Times Literary Supplement'

Steve Allen
'On the Bible, Religion and Morality' (1990) – This work is so relentlessly belligerent that one is not surprised to find that he originally planned to publish it posthumously.
Richard S. Watts – 'Library Journal'

Naim Attallah
'Singular Encounters' (1990) – Bland enough to do credit to an in-flight magazine.
Brenda Maddox – 'Sunday Correspondent'

Dr. Christian Barnard (and Curtis Bill Pepper)
'One Life' (1970) – An autobiography written by two persons hardly inspired confidence. Who provided what? Presumably the Professor and his hospital records made with the facts, while Curtis Bill Pepper tidied it all up and fed in the mush.				*Arthur Marshall*

Anthony Bianco
'Rainmaker' (1991) – Mr Bianco recently condensed the essential elements of his [486-page] book into 12 pages for *New York* magazine. The sad part is nothing of significance was lost.
Kurt Eichenwald – 'New York Times Book Review'

Victor Bockris
'Keith Richards' (1992) – Keith Richards comes across as a decent man, but . . . reading about a junkie – even a junkie who played guitar on 'Jumping Jack Flash' – is depressing and dull . . . It is as lopsided as the other partisan biography, *Diana – Her True Story*, with Mick Jagger cast as the Prince of Wales.
Tony Parsons – 'Sunday Telegraph'

Tom Bowers
'Maxwell: The Outsider' – The Maxwell book has chapters in it so tedious that a Roy Harper concert would be more enjoyable. *Steve Grant – 'Time Out' (1992)*

Michael Caine
'What's It All About?' (1992) – He writes like he acts – with yawning monotony.
Simon Garfield – 'Independent on Sunday'

Lady Colin Campbell
'Diana in Private' (1992) – She calls herself a royal confidante but I doubt if she could spot Princess Diana in a police line-up. She is a female Walter Mitty. Her book is fantasy, fabrication and fatuous. It is bile, laced with bitchiness, and layered with vitriol.				*'Daily Mail'*

John Cleese and Robin Skynner
'Life and How to Survive It' (1993) – The first thing to say about this book is that it's unreadable. You could feed it to a bookworm with galloping dysentery and I promise you the creature would have died from acute literary constipation by page ten.		*Andro Linklater – 'The Spectator'*

Charles Darwin

'Origin of the Species' – I started *Origin of the Species* today but it's not as good as the television series.

> *Sue Townsend – 'The Secret Diary of Adrian Mole' (1982)*

Peter Davies

'All Played Out' (1990) – This is petty, vicious, sub-Tom Wolfe, pseudo-Gonzo journalism.

> *Adrianne Bleu – 'New Statesman'*

Andrea Dworkin

Andrea Dworkin looked pretty nutritionally challenged: the coastal shelf of her bosom barely contained in the papoose of a mighty pair of dungarees.

> *Allison Pearson – 'Independent on Sunday' (1992)*

Sigmund Freud

'Moses and Monotheism' (1939) – This book is poorly written, full of repetitions, replete with borrowings from unbelievers, and spoiled by the author's aesthetic bias and his flimsy psycho-analytic fancies.

> *'Catholic World'*

Good Food Guide

The bible-cum-Pseuds'-Corner of modernist cooking. Here one can read about three-dimensional seasoning and self-congratulatory mousses.

> *Kingsley Amis – 'The Spectator' (1988)*

Ann Gray

'Video Playtime' – Check out the vile, meaningless graphics on the jacket. The moral? DO judge a book by its cover.

> *Ruth Picardie – 'Modern Review' (1993)*

Germaine Greer

'The Female Eunuch' – Ego-serving, malignant, posturing and false.

> *Neil Lyndon – 'No More Sex War' (1992)*

'The Female Eunuch' – Her book reads like nothing so much as the wild cries of a woman at bay.

> *Malcolm Muggeridge – 'Things Past' (1978)*

Ronald Hayman

'Proust: A Biography' (1990) – Remembrance of fibs past.

> *Headline – 'Evening Standard'*

'Proust: A Biography' (1990) – A la recherche de l'auteur perdu.

> *Headline – 'Independent on Sunday'*

Denis Healey

'The Time of My Life' (1989) – The book doesn't live up to its title.

> *Fred Inglis – 'Nation' (1990)*

Samuel Johnson

Insolent and loud, vain idol of a scribbling crowd . . . who, cursing flattery, is the tool of every fawning, flattering fool. Features so horrid, were it light, would put the devil himself to flight.

> *Charles Churchill – 'Letter' (1765)*

'Dictionary' (1775) – I can assure the American public that the errors in Johnson's *Dictionary* are ten times as numerous as they suppose; and that the confidence now reposed in its accuracy is the greatest injury to philology that now exists' 　　*Noah Webster – 'Letter' (1807)*

Kitty Kelley

'Nancy Reagan' (1991) – Should this book be taken seriously? Perhaps, but only by people who can shine a flashlight directly through one ear and have light come out the other.

> *Joe Queenan – 'New York Review of Books'*

'His Way' (1986) – I hope the next time she crosses the street four blind guys come along driving cars.　　*Frank Sinatra* [*One of Sinatra's P.R. aide's called Kelley* – Modern mudslinging's minuscule mistress of malice]

Neil Lyndon

Like every one-thesis writer, Neil is a bit of a bore.

> *S.J. Taylor – 'Evening Standard' (1992)*

Madonna

'Sex' (1992) – Mae West made sex funny. It was a joke. Madonna is not intelligent

enough to see that. She herself gets no further than sex as a self-indulgence. Her book is a perversion of the book as a literary object.
Anthony Burgess – 'Start of the Week'

'Sex' (1992) – . . . mechanical soft porn, a listless cross between Henry Miller and Jackie Collins . . . The whole compilation . . . would hardly earn a place on the top shelf of your average Notting Hill newsagent.
Ian Hamilton – 'Sunday Telegraph'

'Sex' (1992) – As for tenderness, the only soft touch she's interested in is those paying £25 for the book.
Jilly Parkin – 'Daily Express'

'Sex' (1992) – The book's erotic text is so dumb (eg. 'My pussy has nine lives') that it makes the dialogue from an X-rated Ginger Lynn movie sound like vintage Anaïs Nin. *Sex* is, forgive the expression, an anti-climax. *'Rolling Stone'*

'Sex' (1992) – Madonna wasn't nominated for any Grammy Awards this year, she put all her efforts into winning the Pulitzer. *Garry Shandling (1993)*

'Sex' (1992) – If you publish photographs of nude bodies they should at least be good bodies. This cannot be said of the wretched Madonna pictures.
Lord Shawcross

'Sex' (1992) – I don't know. What's the next step? Scratch and sniff, I guess?
Damon Wayans

Karl Marx
'Das Kapital' (1867) – A big bad book on Victorian economics written by an old man with a beard in Tufnell Park.
Ian Mackay

Desmond Morris
'Christmas Watching' (1992) – He answers questions which have tormented us for centuries – Why do we eat mince pies at Christmas? Why do we send Christmas cards? . . . One question in *Christmas*

Watching remains unanswered. It is: Why do we give each other crap books at Christmas?
Nicholas Lezard – 'Modern Review' (1992)

Andrew Morton
'Diana: A Private Story' (1992) – Andrew Mortonsofgarbage. *'Private Eye'*

Barry Phelps
'P. G. Wodehouse: Man & Myth' (1992) – It feels a bit like listening to someone who has mugged up for *Mastermind*, and it lacks an alternative perspective. Phelps does not quite capture his subject.
Janet Barrow – 'Literary Review' (1992)

The Spectator
'View of the Thatcher Decade: Britain in the 80s' (1989) – The sound is a little too audible of a barrel being scraped.
Anthony Howard – 'The Spectator'

Geoffrey Wheatcroft
'Absent Friends' (1989) – Separating the wheat from the naff. *'Private Eye'*

A. N. Wilson
'Jesus' (1992) – . . . little more than a warmed-up rehash of Erneste Renan's *Origines de Christianisme* written a century ago; a better title might be 'Let's Upset Christians And Sell A Few More Copies'.
Victor Lewis-Smith – 'Mail on Sunday'

TRAVEL WRITING

A travel writer is a man with a hole in his soul; someone who is by definition looking for something, and not smart enough to settle for religion. *Julie Burchill*

Travel writing is the art of the bum's rush, a soft touch for any cultural dilettante or voyeur who can hold a pen.
Anthony Quinn – 'Independent on Sunday' (1992)

POETRY

Travellers, poets and liars are all of one
significance.
Richard Braithwaite – 'The English
Gentleman' (1631)

Poets have become unamiable,
untamable, innumerable, unnameable.
Louis Dudek (1971)

You certainly wouldn't turn to
contemporary poets for guidance in the
twentieth-century world.
Northrop Frye (1963)

Poetry means nothing to me. It confuses
me. I always want to translate it back into
prose. *Beatrice Webb*

Poets, as a class, are business men.
Shakespeare describes the poet's eye as
rolling in a fine frenzy from heaven to
earth, from earth to heaven, and giving to
airy nothing a local habitation and a
name, but in practice you will find that
one corner of that eye is generally glued
on the royalty returns.
P. G. Wodehouse – 'Uncle Fred in the
Springtime' (1939)

War poetry – passing suffering is not a
theme for poetry. *W. B. Yeats*

POETS

Anon
Though he tortures the English language,
he has never yet succeeded in forcing it to
reveal his meaning. *'Beachcomber'*

What does pain me exceedingly is that
you should write so badly. These verses
are execrable, and I am shocked that you
are unable to perceive it.
Edmund Gosse (1898)

A poem written on a typewriter by a
typewriter. *Randall Jarrell*

W. H. Auden
He wound up as a poor old fag at bay,

Beleaguered in the end as at the start
By dons appalled that he could talk all
day
And not draw breath although pissed as a
fart. *Clive James (1992)*

There is a terrible weightlessness behind
Auden's brilliance from which all his wit
and erudition cannot save him.
Lawrence Norfolk – 'Times Literary
Supplement' (1991)

Alfred Austin
I write poetry to keep the wolf from the
door. *Alfred Austin*

Oh, so you read your poems to the wolf
then!
Frank Harris

Pam Ayres
On her inclusion in the 'Oxford Dictionary
of Modern Quotations' – Who is Pam
Ayres, and why is her dreadful poetry
worth including?
Sandy Whiteley – 'Booklist' (1990)

Edmund Blunden
A little over-written because Mr Blunden
is no more able to resist a quotation than
some people are to refuse a drink.
George Orwell

Rupert Brooke
'1914 Sonnets' – Don't go in for flag-
waving if you're limp-wristed.
Brophy, Levey & Osborne – '50 Works of
Literature We could Do Without' (1967)

Robert Browning
McCay was of a romantic and
sentimental nature. The sort of man who
. . . knew Ella May Wilcox by heart, and
could take Browning without
anaesthetics. *P. G. Wodehouse –*
'The Man Upstairs' (1914)

Lord Byron
'Don Juan' – It is indeed truly pitiable to
think that one of the greatest poets of the
age should have written a poem that no
respectable bookseller could have
published without disgracing himself –
but a work so atrocious must not be

suffered to pass into oblivion without the infliction of that punishment on its guilty author due to such wanton outrage on all most dear to human nature.

'Blackwood's Magazine' (1819)

'Hours of Idleness' (1807) – We counsel him to forthwith abandon poetry . . . He is at best an intruder in the groves of Parnassus.

Henry Brougham – 'The Edinburgh Review'

In his endeavours to corrupt my mind he has sought to make me smile first at Vice, saying, "There is nothing to which a woman may not be reconciled by repetition or familiarity." There is no Vice with which he has not endeavoured in this manner to familiarise me.

Annabella Milbanke [Lady Byron]

Colley Cibber

In merry Old England, it was once the Rule,
The King has his Poet, and also his Fool.
But now we're so frugal, I'd have you to know it,
That Cibber can serve both for Fool and for Poet. *Alexander Pope*

Cibber! write all your verse upon Glasses,
The only way to save 'em from our Arses.
Alexander Pope

John Dryden

Ev'n copious Dryden, wanted, or forgot,
The last and greatest Art, the Art to blot.
Alexander Pope

T. S. Eliot

'The Waste Land' – Unintelligible, the borrowings cheap and the notes useless.
F. L. Lucas – 'New Statesman' (1923)

Ralph Waldo Emerson

Belongs to a class of gentlemen with whom we have no patience whatever – the mystics for mysticism's sake.
Edgar Allan Poe (1842)

Robert Frost

A nice, acrid, savage, pathetic old chap.
I. A. Richards

Allen Ginsberg

That beard in search of a poet.
Caesar Bottom

Gerald Manley Hopkins

'Poems' – The poetry of a mental cripple.
Brophy, Levey & Osborne – '50 Works of Literature We Could Do Without' (1967)

A. E. Housman

'A Shropshire Lad' – As far as writing *A Shropshire Lad*, I shouldn't have thought A. E. Housman capable of reading it.
Anon

Ted Hughes

Ted Hughes
Wasn't much of a hand at clerihews.
His besetting sin
Was that cheerlessness was always breaking in. *Coco – 'The Spectator' (1986)*

Patrick Kavanagh

Mr Kavanagh's mind, when he abandons poetry and fiction, is like a monkey-house at feeding time. *Hubert Butler*

John Keats

That dirty little blackguard Keats . . . Why don't they review and praise 'Solomon's Guide to Health'? It is better sense and as much poetry as Johnny Keats. *Lord Byron*

'Endymion' – The first two books are, even in his own judgement, unfit to appear, and the 'last two' are, it seems, in the same condition – and as that is the whole number of books, we have a clear and, we believe, a very just estimate of the entire work.

John W. Croker – 'The Quarterly' (1818)

Philip Larkin

The celebrated mouldy fig.
Clive Davis – 'Literary Review' (1992)

Who kept his trousers up, a-raging all the while,
We learnt, was Philip Larkin in his letters,
Stumped for a line, so letting out his bile

On women, Lefties, blacks, and all his
betters.   *William Scammell –
'Elegy at Closedown' (1992)*

A miserable, masturbating old drunk who
railed against 'niggers' and 'wogs'.
          The Weasel – 'The Independent' (1992)

Richard Le Gallienne

If you call Le Gallienne a minor poet you
might just as well call a street lamp a
minor planet.   *Edward Marsh*

William McGonagall

There has often been an affectionate
place in human hearts for the supremely
bad. Think of the uninhibited and free-
flowing verse of William McGonagall.
                    Arthur Marshall (1971)

John Milton

'Paradise Lost' (1667) – I could never read
ten lines together without stumbling at
some Pedantry that tipped me at once out
of Paradise, or even Hell, into the
schoolroom, worse than either.
          Edward Fitzgerald – 'Letter' (1876)

'Lycidas' (1638) – The diction is harsh,
the rhymes uncertain, and the numbers
unpleasing . . . Its form is that of a
pastoral – easy, vulgar and therefore
disgusting.   *Samuel Johnson –
Lives of the English Poets' (1779)*

Charles Montagu

Fortunately for himself, and for his
country, he early quitted poetry.
                    Thomas Macaulay

Frederick Nolan

If there's any more verse from Frederick
Nolan
I shall do something dreadful with a semi-
colon.   *Desmond Aarlington*

Wilfred Owen

Owen's tiny corpus is perhaps the most
over-rated poetry in the twentieth
century.   *Craig Raine*

I consider him unworthy of the poets'
corner of a country newspaper.
                    W. B. Yeats

Ambrose Phillips

Namby-Pamby's doubly mild,
Once a man and twice a child . . .
Now he pumps his little wits
All by little tiny bits.   *Henry Carey*

Fiona Pitt-Kethley

'Dogs' (1993) – It is all rather like Pam
Ayres on a wobbly soap-box, except that
Pitt-Kethley has read too much to be an
effective populist and has thought too
little to write stimulating verse.
                    Martin Cropper – 'Daily Telegraph'

Alexander Pope

Translation of Homer's 'Iliad' – A very
pretty poem, Mr Pope, but it's not
Homer.   *Richard Bentley*

'The Dunciad' – Beyond all question full
of coarse abuse.
          Leslie Stephens – 'Life of Pope' (1880)

Ezra Pound

He was a crackpot.   *Nigel Frith*

William Shakespeare

The sonnets beginning CXXVII to his
mistress are worse than a puzzle-peg.
They are abominably harsh, obscure and
worthless. The others are for the most
part better . . . Their chief faults – and
heavy ones they are – are sameness,
tediousness, quaintness, and elaborate
obscurity.   *William Wordsworth*

Percy Bysshe Shelley

Shelley should not be read, but inhaled
through a gas pipe.   *Lionel Trilling*

Edmund Spenser

'The Faerie Queen' – The punishing
length, utter confusion and unremitting
tedium of Spenser's contribution serves
not merely to impress uncreative minds,
but to illustrate generally that English
literature is not an easy option.
          *Brophy, Levey & Osborne – '50 Works of
Literature We Could Do Without' (1967)*

Gertrude Stein
The words employed by Gertrude Stein may be said to resemble poetry because poetry consists of words, and so does her crazy clatter.
'Boston Evening Transcript' (1927)

'Sacred Emily' –
The fault I'm sure is solely mine,
But I cannot root for Gertrude Stein.
For Gertrude Stein I cannot root;
I cannot blow a single toot.   *Ogden Nash*

Wallace Stevens
Not-quite-Milton, a sort of origami Milton, the paper phoenix fluttering in the wizard's hand.   *Hugh Kenner*

Alfred, Lord Tennyson
To think of him dribbling his powerful intellect through the gimlet holes of poetry!   *Thomas Carlyle*

A dirty man with opium-glazed eyes and rat-taily hair.   *Lady Frederick Cavendish*

Alfred Lawn Tennyson.   *James Joyce*

Dylan Thomas
Thomas was an outstandingly unpleasant man, one who cheated and stole from his friends and peed on their carpets.
Kingsley Amis

The insolent little ruffian, that crapulous lout.
When he quitted a sofa, he left a smear.
My wife says he even tried to paw her about.   *Norman Cameron –*
'The Dirty Little Accuser'

He was cartilaginous, out of humanity, the Disembodied Gland, which was my coinage; Ditch, which was Norman Cameron's; the Ugly Suckling, which was Bernard Spencer's, indicating a wilful and at times nasty babyishness.
Geoffrey Grigson

Walt Whitman
'Leaves of Grass' – The title is eclipsed in the pages of this heterogenous mess of bombast, egotism, vulgarity and

nonsense. The author should be kicked from all decent society as below the level of a brute – it seems he must be some escaped lunatic, raving in pitiable delirium.   *'Boston Intelligencer' (1856)*

He is the laureate of the empty deep incomprehensible.
'Cincinnati Commercial' (1860)

'Leaves of Grass' – An auctioneer's inventory of a warehouse . . . a singular blend of Bhagavad Gita and the *New York Tribune*.   *Ralph W. Emerson*

Of all the writers we have perused, Walt Whitman is the most silly, the most blasphemous, and the most disgusting.
'Literary Gazette' (1860)

Whitman laid end to end words never seen in each other's company before outside of a dictionary.   *David Lodge*

'Leaves of Grass' – The chief question raised by 'Leaves of Grass' is whether anybody – even a poet – ought to take off his trousers in the market-place.
'New York Tribune' (1881)

The poetry of barbarism.
George Santayana (1900)

Whitman, like a large shaggy dog, just unchained, scouring the beaches of the world baying at the moon.
Robert L. Stevenson – 'Familiar Studies'
(1882)

As to his originality in the matter of free speaking, it need only be observed that no remarkable mental gift is requisite to qualify man or woman for membership of a sect mentioned by Dr Johnson – the Adamites, who believed in the virtue of public nudity.   *Algernon Swinburne*

William Wordsworth
An old half-witted sheep.   *J. K. Stephen*

W. B. Yeats
Yeats is second-rate, but the rest are fourth-rate.   *Nigel Frith*

'The Wind Among the Reeds' – Neither rhyme nor reason do I find in one single page . . . these books are to me absolutely empty and void.   *John Morley (1900)*

THE BOOK TRADE

Some publishers are honest and never rob their clients of more than 200%.
          Miles Franklin

Publishing is not a very difficult business – most people are so bad at it that it is very easy to look good.
          Colin Haycraft (1992)

Publisher: The patron saint of the mediocre.   *Kin Hubbard –*
          'The Roycroft Dictionary' (1923)

One day we shall strangle the last publisher with the entrails of the last literary agent.   *David Mercer*

I don't believe in publishers who wish to butter their bannocks on both sides while they'll hardly allow an author to smell treacle. I consider they are too grabby altogether and like Methodists they love to keep the Sabbath and everything else they can lay their hands on.
          Anna Ross (1910)

Take an idiot man from a lunatic asylum and marry him to an idiot woman, and the fourth generation of this connection should be a good publisher from the American point of view.   *Mark Twain*

The Booker Prize
'B' stands for Booker. It also stands for Boring.   *Richard Huggett*

André Deutsch
You can trust André Deutsch as far as you can throw George Weidenfeld.
          'The Wit Of Publishing' (1986)

Stephen Fletcher (bookseller)
He was a very proud, confident, ill-natured, impudent, ignorant fellow, peevish and forward towards his wife (whom he used to beat), a great sot, and a whoring prostituted wretch, and of no credit.   *Thomas Hearne*

FICTIONAL CHARACTERS

Billy Bunter (created by Frank Richards)
Obese and, one suspects, impotent . . . seems in person and in character to have more in common with a gin-swilling, petty-cash fiddling, perspiring middle-aged business man endlessly swapping dirty stories with the lads and chatting up Miss Loosely in the snug . . . the deplorable dumpling.
          Arthur Marshall (1965)

Krystle Carrington (created by Aaron Spelling)
The new perfume 'Forever Krystle' is like its namesake [Linda Evans' character in *Dynasty*], a bit too sweet, cloying and only to be applied in very small amounts. In fact, a little squirt among perfumes.
          Sue Peart

Donald Duck (created by Walt Disney)
There is nothing on land or sea, nothing in the air or in the bowels of the earth, that bores me so abysmally as the later pictures of Walt Disney. Which goes for Donald Duck too. I would rather sit at the bottom of a coal-mine, in the dark, alone, and think of nothing, than go to see any of the successors to *Fantasia*. I would rather listen to Bloch's String Quartet played in a goods-yard, with shunting operations in full swing and all the Jews trying to get into or out of Palestine (I never know which) wailing up against the walls – there is no noise known to me, including the road drill and the later compositions of Bela Bartok, that I execrate so deeply as the squawking of that abominable fowl.
          James Agate – 'Ego 9' (1946)

Miss Marple (created by Agatha Christie)
A horrible, old village spinster . . . a tiresome busybody.   *Ruth Rendell (1992)*

DRAMATIC

THEATRE

There is such a phoney respect for the theatre that anyone who enters its hallowed mezzanines automatically becomes as blank as a plank.

Julie Burchill – 'Mail on Sunday' (1992)

I find writing about the Canadian theatre or drama depressingly like discussing the art of dinghy-sailing among bedouins.

Merrill Denison

Drawing-room plays are inimical to our theatre, because they declare that the stage need not be concerned with life, and they are dangerous to our society, because they imply that it is perfect and invincible. *Bernard Levin (1959)*

One of the thousand reasons I quit going to the theatre when I was about twenty was that I resented like hell filing out of the theatre just because some playwright was forever slamming down his silly curtain. *J. D. Salinger*

Musical comedy is the Irish stew of drama. Anything may be put into it, with the certainty that it will improve the general effect.

P. G. Wodehouse – 'The Man with Two Left Feet' (1917)

THEATRELAND

Broadway, New York

At the turn of the century, exiles from Middle America came to Broadway to find their dreams; these days, Broadway – and New York City – is a nightmare you're lucky to escape from.

Julie Burchill – 'Sunday Times' (1992)

The Royal Court, London

Lots of plays at the Royal Court are about people who talk away for hours and still can't communicate with each other and become more and more wretched.

Noël Coward

PLAYWRIGHTS & LYRICISTS

There is no surer sign of mental and moral obliquity than a taste for decadent literature and art – the morbid trash of such authors as Ibsen, Pinero and Maeterlinck. No man who is in good health ever bestows attention upon stuff of that kind. He would just as soon haunt a slaughterhouse to smell the offal.

William Winter – 'New York Tribune' (1900)

Francis Beaumont & John Fletcher

For ten pounds Beaumont and Fletcher will write you any one of a dozen plays – each indistinguishable from the other.

Caryl Brahms and S. J. Simon

Samuel Beckett

Try as I have been since *Waiting for Godot* in the late 50s, I cannot find in Mr Beckett's work anything that remotely qualifies him to be a playwright, let alone a respected one . . . There are times when I suspect that Beckett is a confidence trick perpetrated by a theatre-hating God. He is surely the naked emperor.

Sheridan Morley (1973)

His symbols are seldom more demanding than a nursery version of *Pilgrim's Progress*. If occasionally we get them wrong or do not get them at all, we can safely assume they were not worth deciphering.

Milton Shulman – 'Evening Standard' (1955)

Howard Brenton

Reviewing 'The Romans in Britain' (1980) – It is hard to understand why Howard Brenton occupies the quasi-official position that he does at the National; he has shown no sign of being able to write a play so far and the reiterated limitations of class confusion and socio-sexual immorality are stridently boring.

Bryan Robertson – 'The Spectator'

Rick Fenn and Peter Howarth
'Robin – Prince of Sherwood' (1993) – Fenn and Howarth indulge in 'Carry On up the Sherwood' . . . their lyrics contain more clichés than a speech by John Major.

Jane Edwardes – 'Time Out'

Ben Jonson
'The Alchemist' – So charmlessly pronounced is its lack of personality that it might have been produced by a computer.

Brophy, Levey & Osborne – '50 Works of Literature We Could Do Without' (1967)

Molière
Molière was a smart French plagiarist who hired three guys to do his thinking for him. *D. W. Griffith (1921)*

Harold Pinter
A sort of cockney Ivy Compton-Burnett.

Noël Coward

Harold Pinter, John Osborne, John Arden and Arnold Wesker
The four hoarse men of the new apocalypse. *Tom Stoppard (1977)*

Thomas Shadwell
Some beams of wit on other souls may fall,
Strike through and make lucid interval.
But Shadwell's genuine night admits no ray,
His rising fogs prevail upon the day.

John Dryden

William Shakespeare
I am more easily bored with Shakespeare and have suffered more ghastly evenings with Shakespeare than with any other dramatist I know. *Peter Brook*

There is an upstart crow beautified with feathers. That with his tyger's heart wrapt in a player's hide, supposes he is as well able to bombast out a blank verse as the best of you; and being an absolute

Johannes Factotum, is, in his own conceit, the only Shakescene in a country.

Robert Greene (1590)

G. B. Shaw
I remember coming across him at the Grand Canyon and finding him peevish, refusing to admire it or even look at it properly. He was jealous. *J. B. Priestley*

Bernard Shaw had discovered himself and gave ungrudgingly of his discovery to the world. *Saki [H. H. Munro]*

Concerning no subject would Shaw be deterred by the minor accident of total ignorance from penning a definitive opinion. *Roger Scruton*

It is disappointing to report that George Bernard Shaw appearing as George Bernard Shaw is sadly miscast in the part. Satirists should be heard and not seen.

Robert Sherwood

The way Bernard Shaw believes in himself is very refreshing in these aesthetic days when so many people believe in no God at all. *Israel Zangwill*

Arnold Wesker
What does he show? Lentils boiling in a pot while six men march up and down. Is that entertainment? *Noël Coward*

Oscar Wilde
A fatuous cad. *Henry James*

Wilde and his epigrams are shown up as brilliant bores.
Before the unpretentious penetration of the comment that –
It never rains but it pours.

Ogden Nash – 'I'll Take the Bromide, Please' (1940)

PLAYS & MUSICALS
(listed by reviewer)

Anon
Ivor Novello's 'Fresh Fields' (1933) – The frocks were charming.

'Not to Worry' (1962) – In the 1930s there was a revue that was so bad that on the first night the management did not raise the curtain after the interval. They showed no such leniency last night.

Kenneth Tynan's 'Oh! Calcutta!' (1970) – Smithfield with songs.

Clive Barnes
'The Cupboard' – Bare.

Sandra Barwick
Harold Pinter's 'No Man's Land' (1992) – There is neither plot nor realism, but metaphor, evasion, pretension, bizarre behaviour, hints at deep meaning that may exist and, then again, may not. It occurred to me, halfway through, that a hand-held Nintendo set, sound turned off, would be useful during the longer pauses. 'The Independent'

Robert Benchley
'Abie's Irish Rose' – In its second year, God forbid. 'Life'

Michael Billington
Harold Pinter's 'Betrayal' (1978) – What distresses me is the pitifully thin strip of human experience it explores and its obsession with the tiny ripples on the stagnant pond of bourgeois-affluent life. 'Guardian'

Leslie Bricusse's 'Sherlock Holmes' (1989) – As a librettist, Mr Bricusse succeeds in doing something that no other adaptor has ever accomplished: he makes Holmes look stupid . . . no cliché of musical theatre is left unexcavated . . . It makes this musical seem like a fossil worthy of David Attenborough's investigation. 'Guardian'

Moby Dick' (1992) – Lacking logic, style, coherence or sense, it turns Melville's great Dostoyevskian novel into a campy, vulgar, schoolgirl spoof. 'Guardian'

Alan Brien
Harold Pinter's 'The Birthday Party' (1958) – . . . like a vintage Hitchcock

thriller which has, in the immortal tear-stained words of Orson Welles, been 'edited by a cross-eyed studio janitor with a lawn-mower'. 'The Spectator'

T. S. Eliot's 'The Elder Statesman' (1958) – A zombie play designed for the living dead . . . It is a play in which Mr Eliot mistakes snobbery for ethics, melodrama for tragedy, vulgarity for wit, obscurity for poetry and sermonising for philosophy. 'The Spectator'

Shelagh Delaney's 'A Taste of Honey' (1958) – Twenty, ten, even five years ago, before a senile society began to fawn upon the youth which is about to devour it, such a play would have remained written in green long-hand in a school exercise book on the top of the bedroom wardrobe. 'The Spectator'

John Arden's 'The Workhouse Donkey' (1963) – It is useless to pretend that The Workhouse Donkey is anything except a theatrical folly, an enormous rambling warren of dead ends and blank walls without any architectural merit.
'Sunday Telegraph'

Friedrich Dürrenmatt's 'In the Meteor' (1966) – Mr Dürrenmatt has said that he prefers comedy to tragedy because it is 'the mousetrap in which the public is easily caught'. For this mouse, I'm afraid, the bait needs to be a good deal fresher.
'Sunday Telegraph'

Ivor Brown
William Shakespeare's 'Taming of the Shrew' – A play so loutish in its humour, and so lacking in appeal to the mind, that Hollywood naturally made it first choice when the filming of Shakespeare began.

Julie Burchill
Andrew Lloyd-Webber's 'Sunset Boulevard' (1993) – What was that great line of Gloria Swanson's in the film when William Holden tells her she used to be big? 'I'm still big; it's the pictures that got small.' Now it's the ticket prices which

are still big – and the shows which got small. *'Mail on Sunday'*

Ronald Butt
Kenneth Tynan's 'Oh! Calcutta!' (1970) – Its game is basically the sort of exhibition of sexual voyeurism that used to be available to the frustrated and the mentally warped in the side-turnings of a certain kind of sea-port. If Mr Tynan and his friends wished to satisfy themselves by this sort of thing in strict private, I suppose the rest of us would have no cause for reaction, except pity. But, in fact, they seek to thrust it down the heaving throats of the majority.
'The Times'

F. Osmond Carr
Jerome K. Jerome's 'Biarritz' (1896) – Two minutes of *Biarritz* would reconcile a Trappist to his monastery for life.
'Saturday Review'

Michael Coveney
'The Gift of the Gorgon' (1992) – A score by Judith Weir, who has obviously exchanged her clear-cut 'Night at the Chinese Opera' for a muddled evening at the Greek takeaway. *'Observer'*

English Shakespeare Company's 'The Tempest' (1992) – My worst night of the year . . . The hideous urban concrete setting proves nothing except that this troupe's visual and political aesthetic is now entirely exhausted.
'Independent on Sunday'

Noël Coward
Lionel Bart's 'Blitz' – It was very close to the real thing – but it seemed to last twice as long and be just as noisy!

'Charley's Aunt' – J. R. Crawford directed rehearsals with all the airy deftness of a rheumatic deacon producing 'Macbeth' for a church social.

U.S. production of Chekov's 'The Cherry Orchard' – A month in the wrong country.

'Summer Stars' – Some are not!

'This Was a Man' – The first night in New York was fashionable to a degree. Everybody who was anybody was there – that is they were there till the end of the second act.

Nym Crinkle
G. B. Shaw's 'Mrs Warren's Profession' (1905) – The limit of stage decency was reached last night in one of Mr Shaw's 'unpleasant comedies' . . . If New York's sense of shame is not aroused to hot indignation at this theatrical insult, it is indeed a sad plight. *'New York Herald'*

Nick Curtis
Susan Gott's 'Watching and Waiting' (1992) – Her own one-woman play about fatness . . . makes for a slender show. The play is pointless but all too familiar: coming soon, no doubt, will be 'Prepare To Meet Thy Dome', a searing drama about receding hairlines. *'Time Out'*

Tom Kempinski's 'When the Past is Yet to Come' (1992) – Tom Kempinski has armoured himself against the criticism of writing veiled autobiography (*Duet for One* and *Separation*); here the main character is Tom Kempinski . . . true and painful as this chunk of psychobabble may be, it's certainly no stage play. Kempinski's problems deserve understanding and sympathy – but not a paying audience. *'Time Out'*

Robert Cushman
Peter Nichols' 'The National Health' (1969) – The closing sections of this play are among the ugliest stretches of writing I remember. *'The Spectator'*

'The Mitford Girls' (1981) – . . . bursting with calculated high spirits, not one of which managed to raise mine. *'Observer'*

R.S.C's 'Hamlet' (1981) – At the beginning of *Hamlet* the stage looks like a Build-Your-Own Elsinore set. *'Observer'*

Lillian Hellman's 'The Little Foxes' (1982) – I merely say that the first night is as

grisly as an undertaker's picnic and may
be grislier.   *'Observer'*

Daily Mirror

'The Force of Habit' (1976) – It is said that
the quickest way to empty a theatre is to
yell 'Fire!' Another method slightly
slower, is to put on the current National
Theatre production of *The Force of Habit.*

Daily Telegraph

Henrik Ibsen's 'Ghost' (1891) – The play
performed last night is simple enough in
plan and purpose, but simple only in the
sense of an open drain; of a loathsome
sore unbandaged, of a dirty act done
publicly; or of a lazar-house with all its
doors and windows open.

W. A. Darlington

*Harold Pinter's 'The Birthday Party'
(1958)* – It turned out to be one of those
plays in which an author wallows in
symbols and revels in obscurity. Give me
Russian every time . . . The one sane
character is Meg's husband but sanity
does him no good. He is a deeply
depressed little man, a deckchair
attendant by profession. Oh well, I can
give him one word of cheer. He might
have been a dramatic critic, condemned
to sit through plays like this.
                                   'Daily Telegraph'

*Tom Stoppard's 'Rosencrantz And
Guildenstern Are Dead' (1967)* – It is the
kind of play that one might enjoy more at
a second hearing, if only the first time
through hadn't left such a strong feeling
that once is enough.   *'Daily Telegraph'*

Noel Davis

Sir Peter Hall's 'The Oresteia' (1982) –
This puts the English theatre back 2000
years.

Alan Dent

T. S. Eliot's 'The Cocktail Party' (1950) –
The critic in me is alarmed that a play so
deplorably weak in playcraft should be
hailed as something like a masterpiece.
The critic in me is despondent when
wilful obscurity is greeted as subtlety,

when affected persiflage passes for wit,
when plain flat prose cut into lines of
arbitrary length is loosely given the name
of poetry.   *'News Chronicle'*

Jane Edwardes

'Robin – Prince of Sherwood' (1993) – It's
as authentic as an evening at the local
mock Tudor hotel . . . if *Camelot* was a
symbol for the Kennedy administration
then this could well typify the shambles of
life under Major.   *'Time Out'*

James Fenton

*Howard Brenton's 'The Romans in Britain'
(1980)* – The play is a nauseating load of
rubbish from beginning to end. It is
written in a ludicrous pseudo-poetic yob-
talk; such themes as it possesses are banal
beyond belief; and the intended bravery
of the acting company amounts to no
more than an embarrassing exhibitionism.
If I were Sir Peter Hall and had instigated
such a production, I would take myself
out to dinner and very tactfully but firmly
sack myself over the dessert. Mrs
Whitehouse should stop persecuting the
police. She should force them to sit
through *The Romans in Britain.*
                                    'Sunday Times'

Financial Times

'Which Witch' (1992) – A musical from
hell.

Bamber Gascoigne

*Arnold Wesker's 'Chips with Everything'
(1962)* – I could fill a short book in
describing why Arnold Wesker's *Chips
with Everything* is a bad play.
                                    'The Spectator'

Roger Gellert

David Turner's 'Semi-Detached' (1962) –
David Turner is a talented writer, Tony
Richardson is a talented director, Sir
Laurence Olivier is our greatest actor . . .
I make this profession of faith before
going on to profess my contempt for the
results of their combined efforts.
                                    'New Statesman'

Jeremy Gerard

'The Show Off' (1992) – If someone can figure out what the point of all this was, we'd love to know.   *'Variety'*

Steve Grant

'Travels with My Aunt' (1992) – A fun experiment in Edinburgh, perhaps, but in the West End – do me a favour.
'Time Out'

John Gross

'Other People's Money' (1990) – It is probably just the thing for tired business-men, but I don't think it has much to offer wide-awake ones. *'Sunday Telegraph'*

Anton Chekhov's 'Three Sisters' (1990) – Strident, cacophonous, clamorous, clashing, discordant, grating, harsh, jangling, jarring, loud, rasping, raucous, screeching, shrill, stridulent, stridulous, unmusical. There are times when only a thesaurus will do, and *Three Sisters*, at the Queen's Theatre, is one of them. Not that a single bunch of adjectives can exhaust the horrors of this much heralded Redgrave-dominated production. You would need lots of others to suggest exactly how flashy it is, exactly how crude, exactly how calculated to ruin Chekhov's effects.   *'Sunday Telegraph'*

'Carousel' (1992) – 'You'll Never Walk Alone' – which has always seemed to me an embarrassment, the show's one resounding dud. Or am I alone?
'Sunday Telegraph'

'The Gift of the Gorgons' (1992) – It is the work of one of our leading playwrights, Peter Shaffer. It stars one of our leading actresses, Judi Dench. It is produced by one of our leading directors, Peter Hall. It is quite amazingly awful.
'Sunday Telegraph'

Clive Hirschorn

Harold Pinter's 'Betrayal' (1978) – A very insubstantial so-what piece of work . . . The play is, to say the least, a far from stimulating experience.
'Sunday Telegraph'

Keith Waterhouse's 'Bookends' (1990) – Little more than a pair of bookends, with precious little in between. A very slim volume indeed. And very likely to be remaindered.   *'Sunday Express'*

'Travels with My Aunt' (1992) – Little more than an indulgent exercise for four actors.   *'Sunday Express'*

Harold Hobson's 'Guys and Dolls' (1953) – An interminable, and overwhelming, and in the end, intolerable bore.
'Sunday Times'

Philip Hope-Wallace

Henry Livings' 'Big Soft Nellie' (1961) – The thing – it seems perverse to call it a play – makes a weak wet impact like a sponge full of tepid water dropped into sawdust.   *'Guardian'*

David Turner's 'Semi-Detached' (1962) – The play slowly capsizes. It is poor stuff in a poor school and the presence of great talent only underlines the deficiencies. Tony Richardson's production is unflinching. It was we who flinched.
'Guardian'

Tom Stoppard's 'Rosencrantz and Guildenstern Are Dead' (1967) – I had a sensation that a fairly pithy and witty theatrical trick was being elongated merely to make an evening of it. Tedium, even kept at bay, made itself felt.
'Guardian'

Kenneth Tynan's 'Oh! Calcutta!' (1970) – There were stretches which seemed more like a long, dirty schoolboy joke than 'elegant eroticism'.   *'Guardian'*

Nigel Howard

David Touguri's 'Lust' (1992) [based on Wycherley's 'The Country Wife'] – If only this treatment had the wit, characterisation and subtlety of the original; billed as 'a free adaption' surely it should not be so free as to get lost completely – a bad book interlaced by bad songs.   *'Plays and Players'*

Martin Hoyle
'Valentine's Day' (1992) – A mortifyingly
vapid experience.   *'The Times'*

Kenneth Hurren
Snoo Wilson's 'The Beast' (1974) – 'The
Beast' . . . strikes me as the sort of thing
they should leave to the remoter outposts
of the 'fringe', where tastes are
notoriously as indulgent as they are
bizarre . . . as aimless and trivial as it is
dreary.   *'The Spectator'*

*English Shakespeare Company's 'Macbeth'
(1992)* – Thanes ain't what they used to
be.   *'Mail on Sunday'*

Rick Jones
'Lullaby for Mrs Bentley' (1992) – At 35
minutes, this is half an hour too long, and
even with free tickets, too expensive.
                                      'Time Out'

Nicholas de Jongh
'Stages' (1992) – David Storey reworks his
old familiar themes of breakdown, class
guilt and alienation into what is virtually
an undramatic and obsessive monologue
of reminiscence.   *'Evening Standard'*

'Which Witch' (1992) – It is impossible to
take this musical seriously or any other
way, unless as camp extravaganza . . .
The music, vaguely reminiscent of mid-
70s soft rock and aural wallpaper, rarely
rises above the level of tuneful blandness.
                          'Evening Standard'

Walter Kerr
'Burrito Square' – During the overture
you hoped it would be good. During the
first number you hoped it would be good.
After that you just hoped it would be
over.

'The Red Rainbow' – The *Red*, I believe,
stood for communism. The 'Rainbow'
stood for the light in the heavens on the
day Communism took over. The
audience stood for more than could be
possibly imagined.

'Sing Till Tomorrow' – It had two strikes

against it. One was the fact you couldn't
hear half of it. The other was the half you
could hear.

Francis King
*Howard Brenton's 'The Romans in Britain'
(1980)* – As in the outfitting of the *Titanic*,
no expense has been spared on this
production. Sadly, it meets with a fate not
dissimilar.   *'Sunday Telegraph'*

David Lardner
'Anon' – The plot was designed in a light
vein that somehow went varicose.

Bernard Levin
Franco Zeffirelli's 'Othello' (1961) – For the
eye, too much; for the ear, too little; for
the mind, nothing at all.

Iris Murdoch's 'The Severed Head' (1963) –
The whole thing is written in a kind of
prose that is not so much stilted as
paralysed from the waist down, like some
huge, mad parody of infidelity and its
consequences.   *'Daily Mail'*

Harold Pinter's 'The Homecoming' (1965) –
Long stretches of the second act seem to
be no more than the actions of a tired
man keeping the ball in the air; the
positive motivelessness becomes
negatively aimless and shallow; he seems
to be imitating his own style, asking
himself what Pinter would do now, and
then doing it.   *'Daily Mail'*

*Bertolt Brecht's 'The Days of the Commune'
(1977)* – It has the depth of a cracker-
motto, the drama of a dial-a-recipe
service and the eloquence of a
conversation between a speak-your-
weight machine and a whoopee-cushion.
                                  'Sunday Times'

David Lewin
John Whiting's 'Marching Song' (1954) –
The general dies at dawn in Whiting's
new play – but, oh, the talk that goes on
through the night before death. Talk
about hope, talk about defeat, talk about
love – and just talk.   *'Daily Express'*

Peter Lewis
Kenneth Tynan's 'Oh! Calcutta!' (1970) –
It is five years too late . . . A so-called
erotic revue which is anti-erotic and in
which nearly every sketch is embarrassing
– not because it is rude, but because it
isn't funny with it.   *'Daily Mail'*

Los Angeles Times
'Applause!' – Should be called 'Clap!'

'Macbeth' – Prompter steals the show in
U.C.L.A. *Macbeth.*   *Headline (1919)*

Manchester Guardian
*Harold Pinter's 'The Birthday Party'
(1958)* – What all this means, only Mr
Pinter knows, for, as his characters speak
in *non sequiturs*, half-gibberish and lunatic
ravings, they are unable to explain their
actions, thoughts or feelings.

Frank Marcus
Lindsay Kemp's 'Flowers' (1974) – At it's
worst, *Flowers* descends to 'high Kemp'.
                'Sunday Telegraph'

Charles Marowitz
David Rudkin's 'Afore Night Come' (1962) –
. . . intellectually one-celled and rhythmically
monotonous.   *'Plays and Players'*

*James Saunder's 'Next Time I'll Sing for
You' (1963)* – I squirmed and wriggled
through its agonising longeurs and feel
the need to revenge myself. The play
connects solidly with my most inflexible
prejudices viz literary theatre, discursive
hokum, de-animated action, verbal rather
than spatial imagery . . . my overriding
conviction is that the theatre should not
be used this way . . . it is simply a kind of
diarrhoea of the cerebrum and when one
begins to discern the spiritual overtones,
it positively palls.   *'Plays and Players'*

Ann McFerran
Steam Factory's 'Telephone Belles' (1992) –
Ultimately a tedious waste of time –
chewing gum for a very tired imagination.
                'Time Out'

Sheridan Morley
'Mandrake' – Which disappeared with
deserved speed from the Criterion (as did
this critic at the interval).

'Oh! Calcutta!' (1970) – If you expect an
evening in the theatre to include vestiges
of wit, intelligence, fine acting or subtle
direction you are in for a grave
disappointment . . . The cast conveys the
impression that at best it's amateur
concert party night in a nudist colony.

'Phil the Fluter' (1970) – A curiously
witless, tasteless, pointless entertainment.

'The Dirtiest Show in Town' (1971) – This
theatrical gangbang is as tasteless,
shapeless and aimless as an off-Broadway
jamboree as it has ever been my painful
duty to endure.

'Isabel's a Jezebel' (1971) – A deeply
unattractive musical fable built around no
less than three dozen songs by Gail
MacDermott, all of which left me before I
had even reached for my coat.

'No Sex Please – We're British' (1971) –
One of those inexplicable farces which
capture the hearts of countless London
theatre-goers, despite plots of appalling
banality and dialogue that writers of cat
food commercials might well spurn.

'The Wild Duck' (1971) – A curiously
wooden translation was uncharacteristi-
cally lifeless. As things were, it was rather
like being trapped for far too long with the
Archers' nordic ancestors.

'Jesus Christ Superstar' (1972) – For the
success of a show like this, technically
brilliant and editorially mindless, suggests
that it is possible to put together a musical
with all the soul of a Boeing 747 and
roughly the same sense of style.

Arnold Wesker's 'The Old Ones' (1972) –
Sadly, 'The Old Ones' turned out to be
nothing more than a sort of Jewish
intellectual's version of 'Waggoner's
Walk'.

Alan Bennett's 'Forty Years On' (1973) – Little more than a dramatised reading of seaside postcards.

Anthony Newley's 'The Good Old Bad Old Days' (1973) – It manages momentarily to rise above being 'Oh What A Lovely Bore'.

John Kerr's 'Mistress of Novices' (1973) – The hills are alive with the sound of clichés: *Mistress of Novices* is one of those truly bad plays that if seen in sufficient quantity, drive dramatic critics to drink.

'No No Nanette' (1973) – What the theatre is not all about, mercifully, is *No No Nanette*, a production at Drury Lane of such mind-bending awfulness that only the laws of libel prevent me from dwelling on it at even greater length.

'Beyond the Rainbow' (1978) – Apparently choreographed by a marine gym instructor on a bad morning . . . Italian musicals, on this evidence, have many of the qualities of a school play and not the better ones: very simple, very slow, and very loud.

Howard Brenton's 'The Romans in Britain' (1980) – The scandal here concerns . . . the artistic administration of a state-subsidised company [National Theatre] which could allow this play to get beyond the Xerox machine, let alone into first rehearsal. Not because it is scandalous, or tasteless, or shocking, but because it is an underwritten and overproduced pageant which would look inadequate if performed as a school play. *'Punch'*

Jeffrey Archer's 'Beyond All Reasonable Doubt' (1987) – Mr Archer's play seems to have been not so much written as assembled from spare parts.

RSC's 'Carrie' (1988) – Nothing can hide the gala kitsch of a gimmicky, flashy and ultimately empty show, set somewhere between *Grease* and a nightmare by Norman Rockwell.

Leslie Bricusse's 'Sherlock Holmes' (1989) – It has the curious look of a show that has been locked in a time vault for 20 or 30 years . . . preserved in all its awful tourist-coach-party predictability.

George Jean Nathan
R. C. Sherriff's 'Journey's End' (1942) – There are times in his play when, judging from the comportment of his soldiers in their dugout, one can't be sure whether what is going on outside is a war or a Pinero rehearsal.

New York Herald
G. B. Shaw's 'Mrs Warren's Profession' (1905) – The only way to expurgate *Mrs Warren's Profession* is to cut the whole play out. You cannot have a clean pig stye. The play is an insult to decency . . . And, worst of all, it countenances the most revolting form of degeneracy.

Benedict Nightingale
Snoo Wilson's 'The Beast' (1974) – I left 'The Place' feeling that someone had been endlessly sniffing around the bottom of my trousers; but why, I could not tell.
'New Statesman'

Keith Waterhouse's 'Bookends' (1990) – No kick, no sting, no after-life.   *'The Times'*

'Moby Dick' (1992) – . . . like being sucked into somebody's very silly, very private joke.   *'The Times'*

Philip Norman
Stephen Sondheim's 'Into the Woods' – After Sondheim's *Into the Woods*, I have resolved not to go to another West End musical unless supplied with a written affidavit that it contains at least three hummable tunes. *'The Independent' (1993)*

Brian Friel's 'Dancing at Lughnasa' – That particular kind of sentimental stage Irishness, see-sawing between hyperbole and bathos, almost brings me out in hives.   *'The Independent' (1993)*

Charles Osborne
Ben Travers' 'Thark' (1989) – At the final

curtain, there are so many loose ends that one is in danger of tripping over them as one leaves the theatre.   *'Daily Telegraph'*

Dorothy Parker

Anon – If you don't knit, bring a book.
'Vanity Fair'

Samuel Pepys

William Shakespeare's 'Twelfth Night' (1663) – After dinner to the Duke's house, and there we saw *Twelfth Night* acted well, though it be but a silly play, and not related at all to the name or the day.
Samuel Pepys' 'Diary'

Stewart Permutt

Piers Haggard's 'Which Witch' (1992) – Mr Haggard has presented us with a production of such gross banality the like of which I have never before witnessed on a professional stage. It all looks like a children's Halloween party that has gone hopelessly wrong.   *'Plays and Players'*

John Peter

Larry Shue's 'The Nerd' – The lesson of the evening is that writing comedy is quite a serious business, and Mr Shue is much to small for his boots.
'Sunday Times'

Neil Simon's 'Jake's Women' (1992) – A crushingly vacuous play. The writing is slick and dreary, full of those amiable New York wisecracks that can yawn so wide between theatre and reality.
'Sunday Times'

Norman Phelps

Michael Langham's 'A Midsummer Night's Dream' (1960) – Langham could not make his mind up apparently, whether this was a funny play or an office party.
'Daily Post'

Andrew Porter

Olga Neuwirth's 'Physical Changes' (1992) – Six characters 'searching desperately for someone to listen to them', but nothing they sang was worth listening to.
'Independent on Sunday'

Punch

Oscar Wilde's 'Vera or the Nihilists' (1882) – It must have been vera, vera bad.

Caroline Rees

Albert Camus' 'Caligula' – Two-hours of nihilism run amok.

Frank Rich

Andrew Lloyd-Webber's 'Phantom of the Opera' (1988) – Impoverished of artistic personality and passion. *'New York Times'*

David Hare's 'The Secret Rapture' (1989) – A pallid imitation of life. *'New York Times'*

Anthony Seymour

Harold Pinter's 'The Homecoming' (1965) – Mr Pinter guides us into his strange wasteland of 20th-century loneliness and then deserts us. We are soon lost in the labyrinth of dead ends, unmade roads and confusing signposts. He is more cruel, gruesome and deliberately offensive in this two-act horror than in his previous plays. On its face value, it is callous and empty enough: what lies in its Freudian depths one dreads to think. *'Yorkshire Post'*

Milton Shulman

John Osborne's 'Look Back in Anger' (1956) – It sets up a wailing wall for the post-war generation of under-thirties. It aims at being a despairing cry but achieves only the stature of a self-pitying snivel.
'Evening Standard'

Ian Shuttleworth

Andrew Lloyd-Webber's 'Starlight Express' (1992) – Not even worth a low commotion.   *'City Limits'*

Neil Smith

'Speed the Plow' (1992) – Director Jon Best and his trio of American actors are all at sea in the woolly, quasi-existential verbiage of the inscrutable (and insufferable) mid-section . . . To make matters worse, the cast speak their lines as if reciting the Holy Gospel.
'What's on in London'

Charles Spencer
'Robin – Prince of Sherwood' (1993) –
Awesomely awful new musical . . . The
show seems like the theatrical equivalent
of cheap and tasteless bubblegum.
'Daily Telegraph'

David Storey's 'Stages' (1992) – A half-
baked recipe for unmitigated boredom
. . . Lindsay Anderson's direction is as flat
and uninspired as the beige box set.
'What's on in London'

Hilary Spurling
David Mercer's 'Belcher's Luck' (1966) –
Outlandish, grotesque, gummy. What the
RSC is doing with this kind of
meretricious rubbish I cannot imagine.
'The Spectator'

*Tom Stoppard's 'Rosencrantz and
Guildenstern Are Dead' (1967)* – Nothing if
not bland . . . a single idea is developed
without imagination and in language of
tedious brutality.   *'The Spectator'*

Alan Bennett's 'Forty Years On' (1968) –
The effect of Mr Bennett's text is deeply
dispiriting . . . the quality of this endless
bludgeoning nostalgia, as sapping as a
dose of bromide, which somehow reduces
everything to a deathly sameness . . . a
common insipidity.   *'The Spectator'*

David Storey's 'Life Class' (1974) – . . .
puts in a keen entry for the Most Boring
Play of the Year Award . . . it is an
indolent approach to the dramatist's craft
if ever there was one.   *'The Spectator'*

Barrie Stacey
'The Mousetrap' – Could it be time to
change the brand of cheese?
'Plays and Players' (1992)

Mark Steyn
'Time' – If I honestly thought Cliff
Richard singing 'Tragedy is a Malady'
was the planet's only virtue, I'd press that
ol' nuclear button myself.
'Evening Standard'

Hannen Swaffer
'Lucky Girl' (1928) – . . . contains more

machine-made jokes than any musical
comedy I have seen for years.
'Daily Express'

Jeffrey Taylor
'Kiss of the Spider Woman' (1992) – It will
leave you cold, lost . . . as moved as an
evening snuggled down with the
'Complete Works of Katharine
Mansfield'.   *'Plays and Players'*

Paul Taylor
'Valentine's Day' (1992) – An evening of
virtually non-stop insipidity enlivened
only by the odd spasm of acute
embarrassment. A cloying archness
prevails over the entire evening which
gives you, on occasion, a pretty fair sense
of what it must be like to be suffocated
with a lavender bag.   *'The Independent'*

Time Out
'Barnum' (1992) – Cutely orchestrated big
ensemble numbers are interspersed with
scenes that feel like curled-up Sellotape –
sticky and irritating . . . this is something
of a yawn.

'Carmen Jones' (1992) – It's now looking
decidedly tatty at the edges with a tired
cast on auto-pilot and a small chorus of
children who carry on as if they're still in
rehearsal.

'Cyrano de Bergerac' (1992) – There has to
be something wrong with a production if
this most heart-rending of finales is not
played to a background of audience sobs.
This one isn't.

The Times
*Harold Pinter's 'The Birthday Party'
(1958)* – This sort of drama is all very well
if the writer is able to create theatrical
effects out of his symbolic dialogue. Mr
Harold Pinter's effects are neither comic
nor terrifying: they are never more than
puzzling, and after a while we tend to give
the puzzle up in despair.

Jack Tinker
'Children of Eden' (1992) – There are
shows where the very stench of sudden

death hangs over the billboards announcing their arrival. *Children of Eden* had it been borne along on the music of angels (which it wasn't), gave off a distinctly queasy feel even before we had taken our seats. The posters were as inviting as a Greenpeace barn dance.
'Daily Mail'

'Moby Dick' (1992) – It is undoubtedly mad. It is at times flagrantly bad.
'Daily Mail'

'Private Lives' (1992) – That flat-footed attempt at Noël Coward's sophisticated high comedy . . . had about as much hope of rousing Broadway out of its torpor as I have of turning out with Will Carling's boys at Twickenham.   *'Daily Mail'*

'Some Like It Hot' (1992) – This leaden vehicle rolls ponderously over Billy Wilder's [1959 film] light soufflé, and all we are left with are the eggs. Not that this grotesquely pantomimed production helps to lighten its load . . . Hot? Not even lukewarm.   *'Daily Mail'*

J. C. Trewin
Harold Pinter's 'The Birthday Party' (1958) – I was as baffled by the piece as by the play I saw in London years ago that began, if I remember rightly, in Tibet and ended in Picadilly Circus Tube Station, with nothing much to tell us what had chanced on the way.
'Illustrated London News'

John Osborne's 'West of Suez' (1971) – . . . for once the most fluently dogmatic of dramatists has run out of ideas. What are left are opinions.   *'Birmingham Post'*

Kenneth Tynan
T. S. Eliot's 'The Elder Statesman' (1958) – On the whole, however, the evening offers little more than the mild pleasure of hearing ancient verities tepidly restated.
'The Observer'

Irving Wardle
Peter Barnes' 'The Ruling Class' (1968) –

Mr Barnes will have to try again.
'The Times'

Kenneth Tynan's 'Oh! Calcutta!' (1970) – It is a ghastly show: ill-written, juvenile and attention-seeking.   *'The Times'*

Paula Webb
'The Lament for Arthur Cleary' (1993) – The final result is less genuine lament than prolonged whinge.   *'Time Out'*

Arthur Wimperis
'Anon' starring Earl Carroll – I saw it at a disadvantage – the curtain was up.

P. G. Wodehouse
Chekhov's 'Seagull' – What with the strain of trying to follow the cockeyed goings-on of characters called Zarietchnatya and Medvienko . . . my suffering had been intense.   *'Jeeves in the Offing' (1960)*

Alexander Woollcott
Anon – The audience strummed their catarrhs.

T. C. Worsley
John Arden's 'The Workhouse Donkey' (1963) – Mr Arden has been hawked round by his young admirers as a leading British playwright on the strength of one failure and two rather interesting muck-ups. Now he has added an ambitious piece that is both a downright failure and a muck-up and is far, far from interesting.
'The Financial Times'

Michael Wright
'Frankenstein' (1992) – Rather than breathing new life into Mary Shelley's gothic monster novel, Doug Rollin's attempt at directing, designing and acting in his own adaption of the work has a nasty smell of decomposing flesh.
'Time Out'

B. A. Young
Howard Brenton's 'The Churchill Play' (1974) – Mr Brenton's play amounts to little but a routine disapproval of authority. It lacks any depth of thought or characterisation . . . to quote Dorothy

Parker [!], 'there is less in it than meets the eye'.

'Financial Times'

[*The quote is not one of Parker's but Talullah Bankhead's comment on Maurice Maeterlinck's* 'Algavine and Selysette' – *See* Poisonous Quotes, *1990*]

DANCE

No sober man dances, unless he happens to be mad.   *Cicero*

Dancing is a very crude attempt to get into the rhythm of life.

G. B. Shaw – 'Back to Methuselah' (1921)

BALLET

My own personal reaction is that most ballets would be quite delightful if it were not for the dancing.   *'Evening Standard'*

I feel that classic ballet with its rigis discipline is a very, very narrow medium – it doesn't have a wide or deep range of expressiveness.   *Denise Loverton*

BALLET COMPANIES & DANCERS

Royal Ballet

'The Tales of Beatrix Potter' (1992) – An indigestible surfeit of steps as mice, piglets and squirrels wend their way about the stage . . . this new, unforgivable production. One thing is certain Sir Frederick Ashton would have been appalled.   *Mary Clarke – 'Guardian'*

Christopher Gable

'Swan Lake' (1992) – When is *Swan Lake* not *Swan Lake*? When it is produced by Christopher Gable for the Northern Ballet Theatre. His trite and tawdry travesty of the story amounts to a breach of the Trade Descriptions Act.

Edward Thorpe – 'Evening Standard'

Matthew Madsen

'Swan Lake' (1992) – As Rothbart, seeking to usurp the throne, he stalks through the ballet like a character in search of the

Addams Family.

Edward Thorpe – 'Evening Standard'

Rudolf Nureyev

Farewell Tour (1991) – Flat foot Nureyev leaves them shouting for money back.

Headline – 'Daily Mail'

On being described as 'The Nureyev of American Football' – Who's Nureyev?

Jack Lambert (1976)

Farewell Tour (1991) – Rudolf is ballet awful.   *Headline – 'The Sun'*

Farewell Tour (1991) – Nureyev dances to discord and cries of refund.

Headline – 'The Times'

TANGO

We condemn the dance of foreign origin known as the Tango, which by its lascivious nature offends morality. Christians ought not in conscience to take part in it. Confessors must in the administration of the sacrament of penance enforce these orders.

Archbishop of Paris (1914)

A dance peculiar to the houses of ill-fame in Buenos Aires, and is never cultivated in respectable gatherings.

Argentine Ambassador to Paris

If this Tango-dancing female is the new woman, then God spare us from any further development of the abnormal creature.   *Cardinal O'Connell of Boston*

Dancing with abandon, turning a tango into a fertility rite.   *Marshall Pugh*

MODERN DANCE

I have rarely seen modern dance that seemed to reach the kind of depth and subtlety, and have the range of language, arts, or music.   *Denise Loverton*

MODERN DANCERS

Anon

Their faces are so sad, but their bottoms are so gay.   *Anon French diplomat (1918)*

Dancing with her was like moving a piano.   *Ring W. Lardner*

The Chippendales

The guys with that humble pouch, just big enough for some small change and maybe a buffalo.   *Ruby Wax*

No No Nanette

There is a quality of desperate teeth-gritted gaiety about Anna Neagle's dancing which is more than can be said for the rest of the dancers who perform as if in constant fear of landmines.
Sheridan Morley (1973)

Paul Taylor

'Oz' (1992) – At best Taylor's trawling of his subconscious can produce troubling, disorientating, even traumatic work. But at worst, it can show him as a self-indulgent screwball – nowhere more so than in *Oz* . . . Much of the choreography is threadbare stuff which is designed to look crazy and chirpy, but is actually repetitively banal.
Judith Mackrell – 'Independent'

The Young Generation

A bland Pepsi-generation bunch going through routines that are marginally more exciting than the eternal Palladium-Tiller techniques but in some danger of becoming equally clichéd.
Sheridan Morley (1971)

Everytime Virginia Bottomley advocates 'safe sex', I picture the Young Generation prancing in their Crimplene jumpsuits to 'Love Grows (Where My Rosemary Goes)'.

Mark Steyn – 'Evening Standard' (1991)

CINEMA

Popcorn is the last area of movie business where good taste is still a concern.
Mike Barfield – 'The Oldie' (1992)

Whenever the British Film Institute attaches itself to a project, you know you are in for a gargantuan dose of rural hardship.
Anne Billson – 'Sunday Telegraph' (1992)

Trying to write honestly about pornographic films is like trying to tie one's shoes while walking.
Vincent Canby – 'New York Times' (1973)

The cinema has become more and more like the theatre, it's all mauling and mumbling.
Shelagh Delaney – 'A Taste of Honey'

You get a feeling that if the *Wizard of Oz* were remade today the yellow brick road would be brought to you courtesy of Carpeteria.
Peter Rainier – 'Los Angeles Herald Examiner'

CRITICS

I wouldn't take the advice of a lot of so-called critics on how to shoot a close up of a teapot.   *Sir David Lean*

Judging films should be the same as judging jokes. It's no good saying this is a wonderful joke if no one laughs at it.
Anthony Lejeune – 'Sunday Telegraph' (1992)

Pearson's First Rule of Film Criticism: The further a film deviates from the critical norm – ie. serious drama – the less reliable the criticism of it.
Harry Pearson – 'Films in Review' (1992)

Critics don't represent anyone but themselves. They don't like popular films because they don't want to associate themselves with the great unwashed.

Cinema is about light relief after a hard day, not high art.

> *Michael Winner – 'Sunday Telegraph' (1992)*

[Poor Michael Winner, he shouldn't be so proud of his ignorance. Film is about art.

> *Philip Dodd – 'Sight and Sound' (1992)*]

DIRECTING & PRODUCING

Successful ones seem to become so powerful, through their ability to attract star actors and so on, that they can be self-indulgent, whimsical, mannered and digressive as they please. If a new film comes along and you recognise it's director's name, think twice about going.

> *Kingsley Amis – 'The Spectator' (1985)*

There are maybe one or two good directors. The rest are atmosphere.

> *Robert Blake – 'Esquire' (1976)*

You could spend the rest of your life explaining *The Elephant Man* to Warner Bros.   *Mel Brooks (1989)*

Bad directors are the ones who want to control everything.   *Anthony Hopkins*

DIRECTORS & PRODUCERS

Pedro Almodovar

'Women on the Verge of a Nervous Breakdown' (1988) – The best to be said for it is that Almodovar makes a good interior decorator.

> *Mark Finch – 'Monthly Film Bulletin'*

Robert Aldrich

'Hush Hush Sweet Charlotte' (1964) – Aldrich only just manages to keep this side of being disgusting and that side of being ridiculous.   *'Films and Filming'*

'Hustle' (1975) – Even with such a meandering script as this, one expects more than the paltry fare Aldrich offers.

> *Paul Coleman*

Woody Allen

The only person who takes Woody Allen seriously is Woody Allen . . . His face has the slackness of an old onion; his hair seems to fall in clumps whenever he moves; his voice, squeezed with difficulty through those grimly pursed lips, has the whine of a child screaming for more – more of everything.

> *Peter Ackroyd – 'The Spectator' (1981)*

Robert Altman

'McCabe and Mrs Miller' (1971) – Altman directed *M*A*S*H*, which wandered and was often funny; then *Brewster McCloud*, which wandered and was not funny; now this, which wanders and is repulsive.

> *Stanley Kauffmann*

Michaelangelo Antonioni

'Zabriskie Point' (1969) – He has tried to make a serious movie and hasn't even achieved a beach party level of insight.

> *Roger Ebert*

Anthony Asquith

'Moscow Nights' (1935) – Completely bogus . . . The direction is puerile.

> *Graham Greene – 'The Spectator'*

Sir Richard Attenborough

Sir Dickie puts the sick into sycophantic.

> *Anon (1992)*

John G. Avildsen

'Slow Dancing in the Big City' (1978) – The earnestness and shamelessness of the director are so awesome that if the picture fails as romance, it succeeds as camp.

> *'New Yorker'*

Ingmar Bergman

'Persona' (1966) – A characteristic piece of self-indulgence on Bergman's part – Bergman talking to himself again.

> *David Wilson – 'Monthly Film Bulletin'*

Luc Besson

'The Big Blue' (1988) – The director's future as a significant cinematic navigator

looks, on this evidence, rather less than watertight.

Philip Strick – 'Monthly Film Bulletin'

Peter Bogdanovich

'Daisy Miller' (1974) – Appallingly crass . . . directed with all the subtlety of a sledgehammer. *Michael Billington – 'Illustrated London News'*

'Texasville' (1990) – Making a hash of trying to adapt Larry McMurty's extremely long and dense novel, Bogdanovich has simply thrown away all the flesh and kept the bones.

Tom Milne – 'Monthly Film Bulletin'

John Boorman

'Excalibur' (1981) – Left entirely to his own devices, Boorman seems to run in self-defeating circles.

Richard Combs – 'Monthly Film Bulletin'

Mel Brooks

'Spaceballs' (1987) – At its worst, it displays a colossal ego at work and humour better left to home movies.

'Daily Variety'

'High Anxiety' (1977) – Brooks has no idea of how to build a sequence, how to tell a story, when to leave well enough (or ill enough) alone.

Philip French – 'Observer'

'High Anxiety' (1977) – A child's idea of satire – imitations, with a comic hat and a leer. *'New Yorker'*

Tod Browning

'Outside the Law' (1930) – One of the worst examples of claptrap since sound came in . . . no continuity and the director lets the cast run wild. *'Variety'*

Frank Capra

'Mr Deeds Goes to Town' (1936) – I have an uneasy feeling he's on his way out. He's started making films about themes instead of people. *Alistair Cooke*

Michael Curtiz

'Life with Father' (1947) – The director is totally out of his element in this careful, deadly version. *'New Yorker' (1978)*

Cecil B. De Mille

'Unconquered' (1947) – De Mille bangs the drum as loudly as ever but his sideshow has gone cold on us. *Richard Winnington*

Jonathan Demme

'Last Embrace' (1979) – A case study of late seventies movie-making which does everything in its power to avoid taking risks. *John Pym – 'Monthly Film Bulletin'*

John Derek

'Bolero' (1984) – Only two films in recent history come close to rivalling this junk for stupidity and ineptitude, and both of them just happen to have been by Derek. They were *Tarzan: The Ape-Man* and *A Boy . . . A Girl*. Derek could open his own turkey farm. *'Motion Picture Guide'*

Clint Eastwood

'Sudden Impact' (1983) – Eastwood presumably takes credit for such gems of authorial self-awareness as replacing the orang-utang of the *Which Way* films, with a farting dog.

Paul Taylor – 'Monthly Film Bulletin'

Blake Edwards

'Skin Deep' (1989) – Edwards' undeniable personal obsessions are winding up as bland, uniform, nothing-in-particular films like this.

Kim Newman – 'Monthly Film Bulletin'

Nora Ephron

'This is My Life' (1992) – The directing debut of screenwriter Nora Ephron. On this evidence she should stick to writing because she hasn't a clue about pace and comic timing.

Anne Billson – 'Sunday Telegraph'

'This is My Life' (1992) – On the evidence of her directorial debut, she should not give up her day job.

Nigel Floyd – 'Time Out'

Federico Fellini

'Satyricon' (1969) – Part of the gradual
decomposition of what was once one of
the greatest talents in film history . . . a
gimcrack, shopworn nightmare.

John Simon

Abel Ferrara

'Bad Lieutenant' (1992) – What's truly
offensive is Ferrara's flagrant pretension
to Art. *Tom Charity – 'Time Out'*

John Frankenheimer

'Year of the Gun 2' (1992) – So much of
his direction would make a first-year film
student blush, and the whole thing has
that 'made for TV' – make that 'badly
made-for-TV' – look to it . . . File under
'Frankenheimer's Monsters'.

Peter Keighron – 'Film Review'

Paul Michael Glaser

'The Cutting Edge' (1992) – The whole
frozen farrago is brought to you by
director Paul Michael Glaser of *Starsky
and Hutch* fame. He deserves a kick up
the ice. *Nigel Kendall – 'Time Out'*

'Amazons' (1984) – Another dodgy
direction job by Starsky, or was it Hutch?
'Time Out' (1992)

Menahem Golan

'The Magician of Lublin' (1979) –
California Polish accents grapple with
hamfisted direction and a script of
surpassing banality. *'Sight and Sound'*
[Golan also co-wrote the screenplay]

Menahem Golan and Yoran Globus

'House of the Long Shadows' (1983) –
Golan and Globus seem to have inherited
Lord Grade's habit of assembling
advertising packages with movies
appended as an afterthought.

Kim Newman – 'Monthly Film Bulletin'

Amy Heckerling

'Look Who's Talking Too' (1990) –
Whenever Heckerling runs out of
inspiration, which is every couple of
minutes, she slaps an old rock'n'roll
record on the turntable and transforms
the film into a music-video.

Philip French – 'Observer'

Charlton Heston

'Antony and Cleopatra' (1972) – The
Biggest Asp Disaster In The World.
Anon headline

Anthony Hickox

'Waxwork' (1988) – Film-making by
numbers. *'Monthly Film Bulletin'*

Alfred Hitchcock

'The Secret Agent' (1936) – How
unfortunate it is that Mr Hitchcock, a
clever director, is allowed to produce and
even to write his own films, though as a
producer he has no sense of continuity
and as a writer he has no sense of life.
Graham Greene

'Psycho' (1960) – A reflection of a most
unpleasant mind, a mean, sly, sadistic
little mind. *Dwight MacDonald*

'Mr and Mrs Smith' (1941) – A slight
Hitch. *'Time Out' (1992)*

Brian G. Hutton

'High Road to China' (1983) – As scripted
and abominably directed, the thing is as
flat as a pancake. *'Guardian'*

Jerry Jameson

'Raise the Titanic' (1980) – Laughably
phony trick work and clunky direction
that makes *Voyage of the Damned* seem
inspired by comparison. *'Variety'*

Norman Jewison

'Fiddler on the Roof' (1971) – Jewison
hasn't so much directed a film, as
prepared a product for world
consumption. *Stanley Kauffmann*

Nathan Juran

'East of Sudan' (1964) – Juran could direct
this kind of thing blindfold, and for once
would appear to have done so.
'Monthly Film Bulletin'

Stanley Kramer

The only memorable character in
Kramer's films over the past twenty years
is Hal the computer.
Pauline Kael – 'New Yorker' (1987)

'Judgment at Nuremberg' (1961) – Some believe that by tackling such themes Kramer earns at least partial remission from criticism. How much? 20 per cent for effort? *Stanley Kauffmann*

Stanley Kubrick

'Lolita' (1962) – The director's heart is apparently elsewhere. *Andrew Sarris*

Fritz Lang

'The Secret Behind the Door' (1948) – Lang gets a few wood-silky highlights out of this sow's ear, but it's a hopeless job and a worthless movie. *James Agee*

Frank Launder

'I See a Dark Stranger' (1945) – Essentially this seems to me a supercilious drama, as if it had been made by bright young men who had decided to package and toss a bone to the groundlings. *James Agee*

Rowland Lee

'One Rainy Afternoon' (1935) – Mr Lee has given a useful demonstration of how not to direct this kind of story: his only idea of humour is speed and noise, not speed of thought or situation, but just liberal speed of walking and talking. *Graham Greene – 'The Spectator'*

Spike Lee

'Malcolm X' (1992) – The message is: 'Send a boy to do a man's job.' *Stanley Crouch*

This is a sick little guy, a merchant of shame. *Roy Innis (1992)*

Claude Lelouch

'A Man and a Woman' (1966) – When in doubt, Lelouch's motto seems to be, use a colour filter or insert lyrical shots of dogs and horses; when in real doubt, use both. *Tom Milne – 'Monthly Film Bulletin'*

Brian Levant

'Beethoven' (1992) – It's directed by Levant, helmsman of the anally obsessed abomination *Problem Child 2*, and it's definitely looking like dog shit for supper. *Nigel Floyd – 'Time Out'*

George Lucas

'Star Wars' (1977) – Heartless fireworks ignited by a permanently retarded director with too much clout and cash. *'Time Out' (1984)*

Herman Mankiewicz

To know him was to like him. Not to know him was to love him. *Bert Kalmar*

Joseph L Mankiewicz

'There Was a Crooked Man' (1970) – Directed in the Grand Rapids style of moviemaking. *Pauline Kael – 'New Yorker'*

Christopher Miles

'Priest of Love' (1981) – Miles has assigned himself a missionary role, but he is not up to the task.
Jill Forbes – 'Monthly Film Bulletin'

John Milius

'Red Dawn' (1983) – When is Mr Milius going to put his toy soldiers away and grow up? *'Motion Picture Guide'*

Otto Preminger

'Hurry Sundown' (1967) – Preminger's taste is atrocious. His idea of erotic symbolism is Jane Fonda caressing Michael Caine's saxophone. *'Cue'*

'The Human Factor' (1979) – Unfortunately, Preminger stages it all as if he was just trying to get all the actors through their line readings in under two hours, allowing no breathing room or time for character nuance in a tale which resolutely calls for quiet moments.

'Variety'

David Puttnam

'Memphis Belle' (1990) – Another chapter in Puttnam's peculiar cinema of history lessons without cinematic depth or sound dramatic portfolio.
Richard Combs – 'Monthly Film Bulletin'

Herbert Ross

'The Seven Per Cent Solution' (1976) – A heavyweight spoof in which Sherlock Holmes is placed under hypnosis by Sigmund Freud. The audience is then

placed under hypnosis by director Herbert Ross.

Michael Billington – 'Illustrated London News'

Ken Russell

'Savage Messiah' (1972) – No list of the most awful films of the year would be complete without something by Ken Russell.

Vincent Canby – 'New York Times' (1973)

'Mahler' (1974) – Whether the title of the opus happens to be 'Strauss' or 'Tchaikovsky' or 'Elgar' or 'Brubeck', the real title is always 'Russell'.

Benny Green – 'Punch'

'The Lair of the White Worm' (1988) – He proves incapable of handling straight suspense, horror, or supernatural sequences. *'Monthly Film Bulletin'*

'Crimes of Passion' (1984) – Just when you thought it was safe to go see a Ken Russell movie and that he'd gotten over his excesses, his indulgences and his ego, along comes *Crimes of Passion* to prove you wrong. *'Motion Picture Guide'*

'The Devils' (1970) – Ken Russell doesn't report hysteria, he markets it.

'New Yorker' (1976)

'Lisztomania' (1975) – Russell's first completely unmitigated catastrophe in several years. *Tony Rayns*

'Lisztomania' – This gaudy compendium of camp, second-hand Freud and third-rate pastiche is like a bad song without end. *'Sight and Sound'*

'The Devils' (1970) – . . . the Torquemada School of Film Direction.

Alexander Walker – 'Evening Standard'

Martin Scorsese

'Cape Fear' (1992) – It not only leaves a nasty taste, it is a clumsy, less than effective thriller. Yet it does have

incidental, unintended worth, by betraying how Scorsese and his peers see the world – and what sort of people they think we are. Their world is rotten, teeming with hollow men, and filmgoers are slow-witted, sensation-seekers who must have everything spelled out. In capital letters.

Shaun Usher – 'Daily Mail' (1992)

David O. Selznick

Selznick gave the impression that he stormed through life demanding to see the manager – and that, when the manager appeared, Selznick would hand him a twenty-page memo announcing his instant banishment to Elba. *Lloyd Shearer*

Philippe Setbon

'Mister Frost' (1990) – It would be kindest not to comment on Philippe Setbon's direction.

Christopher Tookey – 'Sunday Telegraph'

Don Siegel

'Black Windmill' (1974) – Direction as blank as the expression on Michael Caine's face throughout.

'Sight and Sound'

Steven Spielberg

He doesn't know anything about actors, that's for sure.

Bruce Dern – 'Films Illustrated' (1978)

'Close Encounters of the Third Kind: Special Edition' (1980) – One is inclined to feel that with all the money [$20m] at his disposal, Spielberg might have got it right the first time. *Derek Malcolm – 'Guardian'*

Sylvester Stallone

'Staying Alive' (1983) – Stallone doesn't bother much with character, scenes or dialogue. He just puts the newly muscle-plated John Travolta in front of the camera, covers him with what looks like oil slick, and goes for whambams.

Pauline Kael – 'New Yorker'

George Stevens

'The Greatest Story Ever Told '(1965) – George Stevens was once described as the

water buffalo of film art. What this film more precisely suggests is a dinosaur.
'Monthly Film Bulletin'

Howard Storm

'Once Bitten' (1985) – Mr Storm might have found his ideas for the tone of this movie written on high school locker walls.
'People'

Rachel Talalay

'Freddy's Dead' (1992) – And if you think the S-FX are poor, the direction is spectacularly muddled and mundane.
James Cameron-Wilson – 'Film Review'

Irving Thalberg

Irving Thalberg was a sweet guy but he could piss ice water.   *Eddie Mannix*

Jean-Claude Tramont

'All Night Long' (1981) – A directorial style no more advanced than the type used to film baby's first tooth.
Merrill Shindler – 'Los Angeles Magazine'

Luchino Visconti

'Death in Venice' (1971) – A prime contender for the title of Most Overrated Film of All-Time.   *'Time Out' (1985)*

Orson Welles

'Touch of Evil' (1958) – Pure Orson Welles and impure balderdash, which may be the same thing.
Gerald Weales – 'Reporter'

Billy Wilder

His critiques of films are subtle and can be very amusing, especially of the ones he hasn't seen.   *David Hockney*

Michael Winner

'Scorpio' (1972) – Relying on moments of violence for effect, Winner directs with typically crass abandon.   *'Time Out' (1984)*

'Scream for Help' (1984) – Winner again comes up a loser.   *'Motion Picture Guide'*

'Bullseye' (1990) – In this film, he aims for the lowest common denominator and

misses. This asinine, loutish piece of work is certainly not the future of British films: it is more like Ealing comedy as re-interpreted by Neanderthal man.
Christopher Tookey – 'Sunday Telegraph'

Darryl F. Zannuck

The only man who can eat an apple through a tennis racquet.   *David Niven*

Franco Zeffirelli

'The Taming of the Shrew' (1967) – With his misty-glow Renaissance decor, he manages to smother Shakespeare in pizza-Sennett.   *Judith Crist*

Robert Zemeckis

'Death Becomes Her' (1992) – Death is Zemeckis' attempt at an adult film (adult in the sense of it being aimed over the heads of 13-year-olds).
Graham Linehan – 'Select'

Mai Zetterling

'Loving Couples' (1964) – That air of packaged neurosis so peculiar to the Swedish cinema.
Tom Milne – 'Monthly Film Bulletin'

SCRIPTWRITING & SCRIPTWRITERS

Movie script-writing is no worse than playing piano in a whorehouse.
S. J. Perelman

Anon

That man is so bad he shouldn't be left alone in a room with a typewriter.
Herman J. Mankiewicz

'Rapid Fire' (1992) – The story is as stale as my aunt's rock cakes.
James Cameron-Wilson – 'Film Review'

'Mambo Kings' (1991) – The plot is as corny as a can of Niblets.
Neil Norman – 'Evening Standard' (1992)

'Far and Away' (1992) – A great deal of effort went into getting the period detail

accurate. It is a pity that such attention was not lavished on the script, which at times is so banal it would have been rejected by *Home and Away*.

Andy Pritchard – 'Film Review'

Jay Presson Allen

'Just Tell Me What You Want' (1980) – Allen has adapted her trashy novel into a trashy picture. *'Variety'*

Edward Anhalt

'The Madwoman of Chaillot' (1969) – The remnants of Jean Giradoux' slight, whimsical play can still be perceived in Anhalt's vile modernisation.

Pauline Kael – 'New Yorker'

George Axelrod

'Paris When It Sizzles' (1963) – The new script embalms the original instead of reviving it.

Stanley Kauffmann – 'New Republic'

Ralph Bakshi

'Cool World' (1992) – Bakshi's animation is almost as incontinent as the plot.

Anne Billson – 'Sunday Telegraph'

Michael Blake

'Dances with Wolves' (1990) – *Dances with Wolves* would be easier to love if screenwriter Blake had resisted the temptation to plug every positive stereotype about Native Americans.

Michael Dorris – 'Premiere'

Leslie Bricusse, Laurence Marks and Maurice Gran

'Bullseye' (1990) – The screenplay seems to have been written by drunken caption writers from *The Sun*.

Christopher Tookey – 'Sunday Telegraph'

Alan Campbell

On their divorce – Oh, don't worry about Alan. He will always land on somebody's feet. *Dorothy Parker*

Jules Furthman

'Jet Pilot' (1957) – One of the most childish, tedious and futile cold war spy dramas yet concocted by a Hollywood screenwriter. *John Gillett*

Graham Greene

'The Comedians' (1967) – So thick and fast do the cliches come that one feels the script can only have been salvaged from some *New Statesman* competition.

Tom Milne

John Hale

'Mary Queen of Scots' (1971) – Without a better script, Hercules couldn't lift this story off the ground.

Pauline Kael – 'New Yorker'

James B. Harris

'Fast-Walking' (1981) – What do people think of when they write a script these days? Don't they have any sense of human values or human decency?

Arthur Knight

Hal Hartley

'Simple Men' (1992) – The plot doesn't so much thicken as curdle.

Kevin Jackson – 'The Independent'

John Hopkins and Richard Maibaum

'Thunderball' (1965) – The screenplay stands on tiptoe at the outermost edge of suggestion and gazes yearningly down into the obscene. *John Simon*

Joseph Howard

'Sister Act' (1992) – The script is completely and utterly unfunny. Even Whoopi Goldberg . . . can't make it funny. It's enough to give feminism a bad name. *Ruth Picardie – 'Modern Review'*

Richard Kaufman

'Freebie and the Bean' (1974) – A tasteless film from a spit-ball script. *'Variety'*

Stephen King

'Pet Sematary' (1989) – Every event can be seen coming before the dud script gets to it. *Alexander Walker – 'Evening Standard'*

David Lynch

'Dune' (1984) – An incomprehensible, ugly, unstructured, pointless excursion into the murkier realms of one of the most confusing screenplays of all time.

Roger Ebert

Tom Mankiewicz

'Mother, Jugs and Speed' (1976) – The writer has found a way to get into the underbelly of a city, to survey the twilight territory where tragedy and comedy trip over each other and make un unsightly mess.   *'Time'*

Gene Markey

'Let's Live Tonight' (1935) – A parrot gets most of the laughs, which tips off the script.   *'Variety'*

Harold Pinter

'The Quiller Memorandum' (1966) – In disposing of most of the original storyline Pinter has virtually thrown out the baby with the bathwater; all that remains is a skeleton plot which barely makes sense and is totally lacking in excitement.
Brenda Davies

'The Handmaid's Tale' (1990) – Nothing can salvage Harold Pinter's screenplay . . . Pinter's approach has the subtlety of a 60s rant by Germaine Greer . . . File under F for Fiasco.
Christopher Tookey – 'Sunday Telegraph'

David O. Selznick

'Since You Went Away' (1944) – Selznick wrote the script himself, intending to be moving and simple, along epic lines; the result is pedestrian in a peculiarly grandiose manner.   *Pauline Kael*

Peter Shaffer

'Equus' (1977) – It sets Peter Shaffer's worst ideas on a pedestal.   *Pauline Kael*

Don Sharp

'Bear Island' (1980) – A script as stiff as the Arctic setting.   *'Variety'*

Stirling Silliphant

'The Poseidon Adventure' (1972) – The script is the only cataclysm in this waterlogged *Grand Hotel.*   *'New Yorker'*

Mayo Simon

'Marooned' (1969) – A computer fed a

dictionary could come up with better dialogue.   *Judith Crist (1973)*

'Marooned' – A space epic with a horse-and-buggy script.   *Pauline Kael*

Neil Simon

'Only When I Laugh' (1981) – One can almost hear the click of the typewriter.
Geoff Brown – 'Monthly Film Bulletin'

Andrew Stone

'Julie' (1956) – Some of the dialogue reaches a fine pitch of banality.
'Monthly Film Bulletin'

Tom Stoppard

'Medicine Man' (1992) – Some of the comedy inserted by our own Tom Stoppard seemed more appropriate for a Hale and Pace sketch.
James Cameron-Wilson – 'Film Review'

Robert Thom

'Death Race 2000' (1975) – The script is hardly Swiftian, and therefore treads a delicate line between mockery and exploitation.
Michael Billington – 'Illustrated London News'

Fernando Trueba

'The Mad Monkey' (1990) – He probably has talent as a director; but his abilities in that direction are more than cancelled out by his near total ineptitude as a scriptwriter.
Christopher Tookey – 'Sunday Telegraph'

Roger Waters

'Pink Floyd: The Wall' (1982) – A vacuous, bombastic and humourless piece of self-indulgence.
Steve Jenkins – 'Monthly Film Bulletin'

Damon Wayans

'Mo' Money' (1992) – Wayans is an actor of considerable talent, but as a screenwriter he needs to read a few more chapters of his how-to-do-it manual.
Iain Johnstone – 'Sunday Times'

Hugh and Margaret Williams
'The Grass is Greener' (1960) – The stars do not glitter or even glow. Instead of being liberated and propelled by the screenplay, they are chained and sunk.
James Powers – 'Hollywood Reporter'

'Flame in the Streets' (1961) – Its methods belong more to the writer's study than to life.   *John Gillett*

Peter Yeldham
'The Long Duel' (1967) – The dialogue seems to have been written by a computer fed a programme of execrable films on the same theme.   *'Monthly Film Bulletin'*

SOUNDTRACKS

John Barry
'Chaplin' (1992) – What is stunningly bad about *Chaplin* is John Barry's music . . . He has done two pricelessly awful scores in recent memory: *Out of Africa* and *Dances with Wolves* . . . In *Chaplin*, if you close your eyes and ask yourself what exactly Barry is trying to communicate the answer turns out to be 'epic' and 'Oscars'.   *Vanessa Letts – 'The Spectator'*

'The Dove' (1974) – Postcard views flick by to the strains of a saccharine score.
David McGillivray

Howard Blake
'Scream for Help' (1984) – Over the moronic characterisation, daft dialogue, inept performances and opportunistic camerawork, music has been poured like a constant stream of cold gravy, making a sound that on occasions resembles, not inappropriately, a growling stomach.
Philip Strick – 'Monthly Film Bulletin'

Donovan
'Brother Sun, Sister Moon' (1973) – The film is scored to a point that makes your teeth hurt with awful songs.
Vincent Canby – 'New York Times'

Bob Dylan
'Pat Garrett and Billy the Kid' (1973) – The music is so oppressive that when it stops we feel giddy with relief, as if a tooth had suddenly stopped aching.
Vincent Canby – 'New York Times'

Ernest Gold
'Ship of Fools' (1965) – The music score unremittingly fills your nostrils with acrid exhalations.   *John Simon*

FILM REVIEWS (listed by reviewer)

Anon
'The Night of the Living Dead' (1968) starring Judith O'Dea – The best film ever made in Pittsburgh.

'Off and Running' (1992) starring Cyndi Lauper – So was I.

Gilbert Adair
'Moment by Moment' (1979) starring John Travolta – Little more than an animated snapshot of its leading man, baring body and soul to various effects . . . truly terrible.   *'Monthly Film Bulletin'*

Renata Adler
'The Graduate' (1967) starring Dustin Hoffman – Seeing *The Graduate* is a bit like having one's brilliant friend to dinner, watching him become more witty and animated with every moment, and then becoming aware what one may be witnessing is the onset of a nervous breakdown.

James Agate
'Show Of Shows' (1929) starring Frank Fay – Colour photography of the crudest, most garish kind, the resulting impression being that a child of seven has been let loose with a shilling box of paints.

'King's Row' (1942) starring Ronald Reagan – Half masterpiece and half junk.

'North Star' (1943) starring Anne Baxter – Putting American villagers into Russian

costumes and calling them by Russian names is never going to deceive this old bird.

'Hanover Square' (1945) from Patrick Hamilton's novel – The worst betrayal of a first class novel that I can remember.

James Agee
On Hollywood musicals – If music be the breakfast food of love, kindly do not disturb until lunch time. *'Age of Film'*

'Cry Havoc' (1943) from Allen Kenward's play 'Proof Through the Night' – A sincere fourth-rate film made from a sincere fifth-rate play.

'The Heat's On' (1943) starring Mae West – A stale-air musical in which good people apathetically support the almost equally apathetic Mae West.

'Here Come the Waves' (1944) starring Bing Crosby – An almost totally negligible musical.

'Mr Skeffington' (1944) starring Bette Davis – An endless woman's page dissertation on 'What To Do When The Beauty Fades'.

'The Miracle of the Bells' (1948) starring Fred MacMurray – I hereby declare myself the founding father of the Society for the Prevention of Cruelty to God.

David Aldridge
'Blue Ice' (1992) starring Michael Caine (as Harry Anders) – An interminably Long Good Friday . . . Also risible is the plot, both hugely implausible and so skilfully mazy that I sought for Hampton Court among the end credits . . . All great fun for Caine, no doubt, but I wasn't wild about his Harry. *'Film Review'*

'Carry On Columbus' (1992) starring Jim Dale – By and by, this is more wet than wit . . . Half-a-dozen good lines. But

1,492 less hale and me-hearties ones. *'Film Review'*

'Daydream Believer' (1992) starring Martin Kemp – No foaling, but this horse's arse of a movie is nothing to ride home about. *'Film Review'*

'For the Boys' (1992) starring Bette Midler – As corny as Kansas in August, and as hammy as the meat counter at Sainsbury's. *'Film Review'*

'Meet the Feebles' (1992) directed by Peter Jackson – Jim Henson must be high-speed spinning in his grave. *'Film Review'*

'My Girl' (1992) starring Macaulay Culkin – I wouldn't worry about leaving *Home Alone* without it. American excess? *My Girl* will overdo nicely. *'Film Review'*

'Problem Child 2' (1992) starring John Ritter – I branded the first *Problem Child* as 'brash trash' . . . Ditto for *Problem Child 2* – but with bells on! . . . Protracted barf-and-fart sequences add new meaning to the term 'box-office gross'. *'Film Review'*

'Shining Through' (1992) starring Melanie Griffith – *Shining Through* stands unshiningly exposed as just a mediocre and silly *Girl's Own Paper* romp. *'Film Review'*

'Stepkids' (1992) starring Griffin Dunne – You watch it. You mentally compile your shopping list. You stop watching it. And you don't give it a second thought. Unless, that is, you have to write a review of it. *'Film Review'*

'Straight Talk' (1992) starring Dolly Parton – The film is so corny that it makes Kansas in August seem positively cropless by comparison. *'Film Review'*

'Strictly Ballroom' (1992) starring Paul Mercurio – As camp as a Boy Scout

jamboree, and as corny as a chiropodists' convention. *'Film Review'*

'Till There Was You' (1992) starring Mark Harmon – Like God, movie distributors move in mysterious ways . . . It's a tame tale, tepidly told. And the cast couldn't put bums on seats if they all changed jobs and became ushers and usherettes. *'Film Review'*

'Wuthering Heights' (1992) starring Juliette Binoche – This is a Wuthering that fails to scale the Heights. *'Film Review'*

Geoff Andrews
'Batman Returns' (1992) starring Michael Keaton – If you're satisfied with stars in funny costumes playing shallow characters involved in a murkily obscure battle to the death, fine; but if huge sets, special effects and a blaring score are not enough, you may find it a long haul. *'Time Out'*

Ed Barrett
'Singles' (1993) starring Matt Dillon – I suspect it is destined to follow in the footsteps of the stewardess's friend *Splash*, gently sending future generations of students and OAPs to sleep on coaches up and down the nation's motorways. *'Modern Review'*

Michael Billington
'The Possession of Joe Delaney' (1971) starring Shirley MacLaine – Some see this film as a political allegory; I see it as a piece of political tosh. *'Illustrated London News'*

'Huckleberry Finn' (1974) starring Jeff East – It transforms a great work of fiction into something bland, boring and tasteless. *'Illustrated London News'*

'Network' (1976) starring Peter Finch – Too much of this film has the hectoring stridency of tabloid headlines. *'Illustrated London News'*

'A Star is Born' (1976) starring Barbra Streisand – A clear case for the monopolies commission. *'Illustrated London News'*

Anne Billson
'Chaplin' (1992) – starring Robert Downey Jr. – This is the *Readers' Digest* run-down of Chaplin's life . . . it washes over you like a TV mini-series . . . It's not even a film that one can hate – it simply wears you down with its relentlessly middlebrow lack of approach. *'Sunday Telegraph'*

'Home Alone 2: Lost in New York' (1992) starring Macaulay Culkin – Never mind – there's always the prospect of the next sequel. With any luck, this one will be called 'Home Alone 3: Christmas in the Workhouse'. *'Sunday Telegraph'*

'Traces of Red' (1992) starring Jim Belushi – There are so many twists in this plot it should have been called 'Traces of Red Herring'. *'Sunday Telegraph'*

Boxoffice
'Meteor' (1979) starring Sean Connery – There are moments that make *Godzilla* look like a masterpiece.

Patrick Boyle
'Sneakers' (1992) starring Robert Redford and Sidney Poitier – *Sneakers* is a bore. It's like a superior episode of *The A- Team* or *Mission Impossible*. *'Modern Review'*

Marie Brenner
'A Star is Born' (1976) starring Barbra Streisand – Hollywood's biggest joke. *'New Times'*

Anwar Brett
'Split Second' (1992) starring Rutger Hauer – As enjoyable as a trip to the dentist, but nothing like as useful, *Split Second*'s only virtue is its length – 90 minutes. But it's time which could be more usefully spent figuring out what the title has to do with the story. *'Film Review'*

Geoff Brown

'Mame' (1974) starring Lucille Ball – It makes one realise afresh the parlous state of the Hollywood musical, fighting to survive against misplaced superstars and elephantine budgets matched with minuscule imagination.

'Madame Sousatzka' (1988) starring Shirley MacLaine – No amount of technical finesse, or polite musical trappings, can make the film seem other than an unswallowable, old-fashioned, overlong slab of confectionery.
'Monthly Film Bulletin'

'Basic Instinct' (1992) starring Sharon Stone – See this film, and a little more of your humanity gets chipped away.
'The Times'

Luis Buñuel

'Metropolis' (1927) directed by Fritz Lang – Two movies glued together by their bellies.

Julie Burchill

'Night and the City' (1993) starring Robert de Niro – This is Noir Lite; you'd drink it at home quite happily, but you wouldn't go out for it.
'The Tatler'

James Cameron-Wilson

'Afraid of the Dark' (1992) starring James Fox – In short, *Afraid of the Dark* is very unpleasant, poorly realised and a damned cheek. I felt I was led up the garden path – and then tripped over.
'Film Review'

'Barton Fink' (1992) starring John Turturro – In the end, *Barton Fink* is nothing more than an extremely well-made but overlong film in search of a better plot.
'Film Review'

'Bill and Ted's Bogus Journey' (1992) starring Keanu Reeves – It boasts some of the dumbest minutes since 'Attack of the Killer Tomatoes'.
'Film Review'

'The Favour, the Watch and the Very Big Fish' (1992) starring Bob Hoskins – Forget the Fish. It's a red herring.
'Film Review'

'Freddy's Dead: The Final Nightmare' (1992) starring Robert Englund – Freddy's always been dead, but he's never been this dead boring.
'Film Review'

Vincent Canby

'Mackenna's Gold' (1969) starring Gregory Peck – A western of truly stunning absurdity.

'The Grissom Gang' (1971) directed by Robert Aldrich – Offensive, immoral, and perhaps even lascivious.

'Mary Queen of Scots' (1972) starring Vanessa Redgrave – It's a Christmas card sale in January.
'New York Times'

'Portnoy's Complaint' (1972) from the Philip Roth novel – It proves once again that there are some things that simply can't be filmed – *The Yellow Pages, The Bible, Search of Things Past*, most film reviews, and *Portnoy's Complaint*.
'New York Times'

'Young Winston' (1972) directed by Richard Attenborough – It had all the charm and grace of a report by the keeper of the exchequer.
'New York Times'

'. . . and Hope to Die' (1973) starring Robert Ryan – Just remember the title, and if you have to, break your leg to avoid seeing it.
'New York Times'

'Class Of '44' (1973) – Winner of 1973 'Old Songs, Old Cars, Old Haircuts, Don't Make A Movie Award'.
'New York Times'

'The Exorcist' (1973) directed by William Friedkin – The film cost $10m. The money could have been better spent subsidizing a couple of beds at the Paine-Whitney Clinic . . . It is also an early but leading candidate for 'The Most Expensive Clap-Trap of the Decade Award'.
'New York Times'

'Lost Horizon' (1973) directed by Charles Jarrott – A big, stale marshmallow . . . for the film, in addition to packing all of the dramatic punch of a Moral Re-Armament pamphlet, is surprisingly tacky in appearance . . . A better film might have resulted by equipping the original *Lost Horizon* with muzak.   *'New York Times'* [*Neither was Canby impressed with the set –* The Dalai Lama's Palace looks like Pickfair remodelled as a motel.]

'The Way We Were' (1973) starring Barbra Streisand – Adapted by Arthur Laurents from his novel, it looks like a 747 built around an elephant. It seems to have been constructed of prefabricated parts that were then bolted together as best they could considering the nature of the beast.   *'New York Times'*

Brian Case
'Chaplin' (1992) directed by Richard Attenborough – A bit of a beached whale.   *'Time Out'*

'Patriot Games' (1992) starring Harrison Ford – So duff that you wonder why they didn't ask Roger Moore to star.   *'Time Out'*

'Shadows and Fog' (1992) directed by Woody Allen – An inconclusive charade for celebrity guests.   *'Time Out'*

Charles Champlin
'A Place for Lovers' (1969) directed by Vittorio de Sica – The worst movie I have seen all year and possibly since 1926.   *'Los Angeles Times'*

'End of the Game' (1976) written and directed by Maximilian Schell – A more addled, overreaching, misjudged, ill-made, wasteful, polarising, uninteresting, and tedious little epic has not toddled into town in years.   *'Los Angeles Times'*

Tom Charity
'Rollerball' (1975) starring James Caan – There's not an ounce of sincerity in this film . . . As for the game itself, wouldn't you rather go to the movies?   *'Time Out' (1993)*

'Rocky IV' (1985) starring Sylvester Stallone – This is film with the depth of music promo – and the aesthetics to match.   *'Time Out' (1993)*

'Lethal Weapon' (1987) starring Mel Gibson – An integrationist buddy movie with paper-thin characters and a stunningly banal script. *'Time Out' (1993)*

Jay Cocks
'Jonathan Livingstone Seagull' (1973) – If one must spend two hours following the adventures of a bird, far better that the hero be Donald Duck.   *'Time'*

Richard Combs
'Head' (1968) starring The Monkees – Random particles tossed around in some demented jester's wind machine.   *'Monthly Film Bulletin' (1978)*

'Shampoo' (1975) starring Warren Beatty – It has the bursting-with-talent but fuzziness-of-effect aspect of a movie made by a group of friends for their own amusement.

'Nasty Habits' (1976) starring Glenda Jackson – The sort of material just about fit for a half-hour TV sketch.   *'Monthly Film Bulletin'*

'High Anxiety' (1977) written and directed by Mel Brooks – It basically shambles along, in search of the next big set-piece to send up.   *'Monthly Film Bulletin'*

Pam Cook
'Cookie' (1989) starring Peter Falk – *Cookie* has all the feel of a worn-out vehicle grinding to a halt. *'Monthly Film Bulletin'*

Judith Crist
'The Second Time Around' (1961) starring Debbie Reynolds – Keep a lemon handy for sucking to ward off an attack of the terminal cutesies.

'A Global Affair' (1963) starring Bob Hope – Squaresville incarnate, with a side trip into leersville.

'My Six Loves' (1965) starring Debbie Reynolds – Enough to make you settle for cyclamates – or cyanide.

'The Sound of Music' (1965) starring Julie Andrews – Square and solid sugar. Calorie-counters, diabetics and grown ups from eight to eighty had best beware.

'Dracula: Prince of Darkness' (1966) starring Christopher Lee – Run-of-the-coffin stuff.

'The Night of the Generals' (1967) starring Peter O'Toole – The 'who' is obvious from the first and the 'dunnit' interminable.

'Dracula Has Risen from the Grave' (1968) starring Christopher Lee – A bloody bore.

'The Only Game in Town' (1969) starring Elizabeth Taylor – It epitomizes the disaster the studio and star systems foist on films . . . the only two-character tale around to cost $11 million.

'El Condor' (1970) starring Jim Brown – The kind of film you can find at your local neighbourhood abattoir.

'How Do I Love Thee?' (1970) starring Jackie Gleason – Nauseated embarrassment for participants and onlookers.

'I Love My Wife' (1970) starring Elliot Gould – A leer-laden, anti-feminist tract disguised as comedy.

'The Landlord' (1970) starring Beau Bridges – Bad taste from start to finish . . . not an avenue of offensiveness to any race is left unexplored.

'Night of the Lepus' (1972) starring Stuart Whitman – For insomniacs with lax standards.

'Murder on the Orient Express' (1974) starring Albert Finney – Audiences appear so hungry for this type of entertainment that maybe it hardly matters that it isn't very good.

Martin Cropper
'Carry On Columbus' (1992) starring Jim Dale – This is not so much a movie as a gesture of cultural piety, an illuminated obituary notice. Where you might have expected to see trousers at half-mast there are only limp flags.   *'Modern Review'*

Bosley Crowther
'Four Jills in a Jeep' (1944) directed by William A. Seiter – It gives the painful impression of having been tossed together in a couple of hours.

'Pin Up Girl' (1944) starring Betty Grable – A spiritless blob of a musical, and a desecration of a most inviting theme.

Daily Express
'No Orchids for Miss Blandish' (1948) starring Jack La Rue – The morals are about level with those of a scavenger dog.

Daily Mail
'Breathless' (1983) starring Richard Gere – Not much more than an ego trip for a bankable star.

Mike Davies
'As You Like It' (1992) starring Griff Rhys-Jones – Ultimately, since it's hard to see this appealing to a non-Shakespeare audience, it all boils down to how you prefer your Bard. A case of like it or leave it.   *'Film Review'*

Jan Dawson
'Portnoy's Complaint' (1972) from Philip Roth's novel – The spectator is forced into the doubly uncomfortable position of a voyeur who can't actually see anything.

'Slaughter' (1972) starring Jim Brown – The cast perform their trigger-happy tasks with all the passionate conviction of a team of well-oiled robots.

Jeff Dawson
'Jersey Girl' (1992) starring Jami Gertz – In transatlantic terms, an Essex girl joke stretched beyond breaking-point. *'Empire'*

Peter John Dyer
'Pocketful of Miracles' (1961) starring Bette Davis – The effect is less one of whimsy than of being bludgeoned to death with a toffee-apple.

Roger Ebert
'A Place for Lovers' (1969) directed by Vittorio de Sica – The most God-awful piece of pseudo-romantic slop I've ever seen.   *'Chicago Sun-Times'*

'The Texas Chainsaw Massacre' (1974) directed by Tobe Hooper – It's without any apparent purpose, unless the creation of disgust and fright is a purpose.

'Shogun Assassin' (1980) starring Tomisaburo Wakayama – No one bleeds like this unless they have garden hoses for veins.

'Death Wish II' (1981) starring Charles Bronson – It doesn't contain an ounce of life. It slinks onto the screen and squirms for a while, and is over.

'History of the World Part One' (1981) starring Mel Brooks – Most of the time it's just expensive sets sitting around waiting for Brooks to do something funny in front of them.

'Pennies from Heaven' (1981) starring Steve Martin – All flash and style and no heart.

'Educating Rita' (1983) starring Michael Caine – If only I'd been able to believe they were actually reading the books, everything else would have fallen into place.

Otis Ferguson
'The Cowboy and the Lady' (1938) starring Gary Cooper – Just a load of old chestnuts pulled out of other people's dead fires.

'Only Angels Have Wings' (1939) starring Cary Grant – All these people did the best they could with what they were given – but look at it.

Nigel Floyd
'Toxic Avenger II' (1988) starring Ron Fazio – Puerile garbage with a memory half-life of about ten seconds.   *'Time Out'*

'Memoirs of an Invisible Man' (1991) starring Chevy Chase – An inflated lightweight comedy whose shortcomings are all too visible.   *'Time Out'*

'Traces of Red' (1992) starring James Belushi and Lorraine Bracco – Why would anyone bother to make an erotic thriller which has neither thrills nor frills? Belushi's nose for stiffs (*K-9* and *Filofax*) explains his presence, one assumes Bracco fancied a few weeks holiday in Florida.   *'Time Out'*

S. Frank
'Logan's Run' (1976) starring Michael York – A science fiction film made by people who don't understand science fiction for the amusement of people who don't care one way or the other.
                    'Los Angeles Panorama'

Philip French
'The Music Teacher' (1988) starring José Van Dam – Culture of this kind makes gun-reaching Goerings of us all.
                                    'Observer'

'Silent Scream' (1989) starring Iain Glenn – I felt as if someone had handed me a bag of jumbled jigsaw pieces and told me to make up my own picture.   *'Observer'*

'The Big Man' (1990) starring Liam Neeson – Rarely plausible, frequently risible, occasionally embarrassing, this morally confused melodrama falls with a dull thud between social realism and mythical fable.
                                    'Observer'

'Bullseye' (1990) starring Roger Moore and Michael Caine – The performances are atrocious, the movie looks like a Pearl and Dean advertisement.   *'Observer'*

'The Krays' (1990) starring Gary and Martin Kemp – The movie comes over like a collaboration between Joan

Littlewood's Theatre Workshop, an ungifted follower of Sigmund Freud and the postcard artist Donald McGill.

'Observer'

Sean French

'Madhouse' (1990) starring Kirstie Alley – Some comedies seem to have been constructed by a computer without a sense of humour.   *'Observer'*

Brendan Gill

'The Greatest Story Ever Told' (1965) starring Max Von Sydow – If the subject matter weren't sacred, we would be responding to the picture in the most charitable way by laughing at it from start to finish.   *'New Yorker'*

Steve Grant

'Columbus – The Discovery' (1992) starring George Corraface – It's hard to fathom the minds of people who could make this kind of tripe. It's boring enough crossing the Atlantic on British Airways, never mind months in a wooden hulk surrounded by exiles from the RSC and the National. Solid gold shit.   *'Time Out'*

Marianne Gray

'Death Becomes Her' (1992) starring Meryl Streep – Well, death doesn't become her here because instead of being a light-as-air comedy brushed together with a feather, it has been sledge-hammered into place bashing all the party pieces like lust, envy, murder most foul into a grimy paste . . . After this, I hope I die before I get old.   *'Film Review'*

Benny Green

'The Outlaw Josey Wales' (1976) starring Clint Eastwood – If only the actors hadn't got in the way of the scenery, it would have been a very beautiful film.   *'Punch'*

'Islands in the Stream' (1977) starring George C. Scott – It's all too awful for words.   *'Punch'*

Graham Greene

'Go West Young Man' (1936) starring Mae West – Quite incredibly tedious, as slow

and wobbling in its pace as Miss West's famous walk. The wisecracks lack the old impudence, and seldom have so many feet of film been expended on a mere dirty look.

'Ourselves Alone' (1936) starring Antoinette Cellier – One of the silliest pictures which even an English studio has yet managed to turn out.   *'The Spectator'*

'The Frog' (1937) starring Noah Beery – Badly directed, badly acted, it is like one of those plays produced in country towns by stranded actors.

Roger Greenspun

'Lady Caroline Lamb' (1973) starring Sara Miles – *Lady Caroline Lamb* is to cinema what the coffee-table book is to literature: a heavy but insubstantial irrelevance.

'New York Times'

Guardian

'The Awakening' (1980) starring Charlton Heston – It is difficult to imagine a film more likely to put you to sleep.

'The Ninth Configuration' (1980) starring Stacy Keach – The pretensions are enough to raise the *Titanic* – and sink it again.

'For Your Eyes Only' (1982) starring Roger Moore – Pretty boring . . . as if the director [John Glen] isn't interested in actors, and Cubby Broccoli forgot to commission a screenplay.

'Enigma' (1982) starring Martin Sheen – The mystery is why they bothered.

'Indiana Jones and the Temple of Doom' (1984) starring Harrison Ford – A two-hour series of none too carefully linked chase sequences. Sitting on the edge of your seat gives you a sore bum but also a numb brain.

Molly Haskel

'Mikey and Nicky' (1976) starring Peter Falk and John Cassavetes – A pretext for Falk and Cassavetes to indulge in one of

those long, lugubrious Actors' Studio exercises that wore out its welcome with the last frame of *Husbands* and the first frame of *The Killing of a Chinese Bookie*.
'Village Voice'

Margaret Hinxman
'The Postman Always Rings Twice' (1981) starring Jack Nicholson – Too cheerless to be erotic, too charmless to be titillating.
'Daily Mail'

'Porky's' (1982) written and directed by Bob Clark – One of those movies that makes you weep for the state of the contemporary commercial cinema – and, even more, for the gullibility of the public that pays to see it. *'Daily Mail'*

Christopher Hudson
'Love Story' (1970) starring Ryan O'Neal and Ali MacGraw – Happiness is a warm bed pan.

Tom Hutchinson
'Boomerang' (1992) starring Eddie Murphy – Taking a cue from its title, this film rebounds to no one's advantage.
'Mail on Sunday'

'Death Becomes Her' (1992) starring Meryl Streep and Goldie Hawn – It is an atrocity exhibition with Streep and Hawn as prize exhibits. *'Mail on Sunday'*

'Muppet Christmas Carol' (1992) starring Michael Caine – Charles Dickens would find it hard to warm to this Nightmare on Sesame Street. *'Daily Mail'*

'The News Boys' (1992) directed by Kenny Ortega – This Disney musical is as leaden-footed as it is heavy-hearted.
'Mail on Sunday'

Independent
'The Reflecting Skin' (1990) directed by Philip Ridley – The film strains for poetic resonance: a puffed-up frog trying to pass as a prince.

Kevin Jackson
'Meet the Feebles' (1992) – The Muppet

Show as seen by a bunch of New Zealand hippies who suffered from inadequate potty training. *'Independent'*

Sheila Johnston
'California Man' (1992) starring Paul Shore – From the film school of Bill and Ted and Wayne and Garth, but inferior in all regards, illustrating the Theory of Reverse Evolution. *'Independent'*

Marshall Julius
'Boomerang' (1992) starring Eddie Murphy – For devoted Murphy fans only. For the rest of the world, this is one boomerang to throw away and hope it doesn't come back. *'What's on in London'*

'Lifeless' (1992) written and directed by Nora Ephron – This is a flat, lifeless movie. *'What's on in London'*

Pauline Kael
'Goodbye Mr Chips' (1938) starring Robert Donat – The movie clogs the nose more than necessary.

'Green Dolphin Street' (1947) starring Lana Turner and Donna Reed – The actors in this stupefyingly flimsy epic seem to be in competition for booby prizes.

'A Connecticut Yankee in King Arthur's Court' (1948) – The tacky pageantry is more suited to the opening of a West Coast supermarket than to an English court in the 6th century.

'So Fine' (1981) starring Ryan O'Neal – A visual insult. *'New Yorker'*

'Return of the Jedi' (1983) starring Harrison Ford – An impersonal and rather junky piece of moviemaking. *'New Yorker'*

'Top Gun' (1986) starring Tom Cruise – A recruiting poster film that isn't concerned with recruiting but with being a poster.
'New Yorker'

'Bright Lights, Big City' (1988) starring Michael J. Fox – The banality comes down on you like drizzle. *'New Yorker'*

Stanley Kauffmann
'The Sound and the Fury' (1959) starring
Yul Brynner – A fourth carbon copy of
Chekhov in Dixie.

'The Hired Hand' (1971) starring and
directed by *Peter Fonda* – When a film
begins with a 'lyrical' shot, your heart has
a right to sink.

'Scarecrow' (1973) starring *Gene Hackman
and Al Pacino* – Here's a picture that
manages to abuse two American myths at
once – the Road and the Male Pair.

Peter Keighron
'By the Sword' (1992) starring *Eric Roberts*
– I'd like to say that *By the Sword* is at the
cutting edge of cinema, or that it has a
rapier-like wit. But curses, foiled again! It
isn't and it doesn't . . . If this is really
more than just a story of some rather silly
men playing with their long pointy things,
then I think we should have been told.
'Film Review'

'Scorchers' (1992) starring *Faye Dunaway* –
The whole thing is based on a play, and
doesn't it show. It's a five-course meal of
words, words, words, words, and more
words. In a word, it's wordy. And it's not
helped by the fact that the entire cast
seem to be under the impression that
someone's forgotten to invent the
microphone. *'Film Review'*

'Year of the Gun' (1992) starring *Sharon
Stone* – We never actually find out why it
was the 'year of the gun'. It just was, like
next year could be the 'year of the bottle-
opener'. *'Film Review'*

Nigel Kendall
'The Cutting Edge' (1992) directed by *Paul
Michael Glaser* – Only a lobotomised ice-
skating obsessive could find anything
praiseworthy in all this predictable,
romantic, ham-fisted tosh, since many of
the skating sequences are choreographed
by former Olympic gold medallist Robin
Cousins. Unsurprisingly, glimpses of the
actors' faces and feet in the same shot are
few and far between. *'Time Out'*

Howard Kissell
'Nickelodeon' (1976) starring *Ryan O'Neal*
– Another collection of scenes from other
people's films. *'Women's Wear Daily'*

Gavin Lambert
'Key Largo' (1948) starring *Humphrey
Bogart* – A completely empty, synthetic
work.

Anthony Lane
'A League of Their Own' (1992) starring
Geena Davis – Should have been ground
into bone-meal and fed to chickens.
'Independent on Sunday'

C. A. Lejeune
'Suddenly Last Summer' (1959) starring
Katharine Hepburn – I loathe this film, I
say so candidly. To my mind it is a
decadent piece of work, sensational,
barbarous and ridiculous. *'Observer'*

Vanessa Letts
'Chaplin' (1992) directed by *Richard
Attenborough* – By the end of the film we
feel as if Attenborough is splashing about
in a bath and can't bring himself to get
out. *'The Spectator'*

'Shadows and Fog' (1993) directed by
Woody Allen – For all its philosophical
pretensions, *Shadows and Fog* gets no
more existential than a series of question
marks. *'The Spectator'*

Ian Lyness
'Unlawful Entry' (1992) starring *Ray Liotta*
– This is really just a superior TV movie
with big-screen pretensions.
'Daily Express'

Dwight MacDonald
'The Sound of Music' (1965) starring *Julie
Andrews* – Pure unadulterated kitsch, not
a false note, not a whiff of reality. *'Esquire'*

Mail on Sunday
'King Solomon's Mines' (1985) starring
Richard Chamberlain – The cinema's
equivalent to junk-food.

Derek Malcolm
'Bird on a Wire' (1990) starring *Mel Gibson*

and Goldie Hawn – One of those star vehicles from deepest Hollywood for which there seems no adequate reason other than to pay someone's mortgage.
'Guardian'

Richard Mallett

'Prince of Foxes' (1949) starring Orson Welles – This pretentious chapter of pseudo-history never rises above the merely spectacular, hovers mostly around the conventionally banal, and descends once to the unpardonably crude. *'Punch'*

'The Lady with a Lamp' (1951) starring Anna Neagle – It may please fans of Anna Neagle but not fans of Florence Nightingale. *'Punch'*

John Marriott

'Necessary Roughness' (1992) starring Scott Bakula – Aimed squarely at teenage Neanderthals in the Mid-West, anyone of them could take his girl to see this at a drive-in, involve himself in noisy conversation, in-depth snogging or the pursuit of popcorn and not miss a thing on screen. *'Daily Mail'*

Adam Mars-Jones

'Patriot Games' (1992) starring Harrison Ford – There is as much political realism in the film as there is in *Naked Gun 2½*, except that in *Patriot Games* it matters.
'Independent'

Colette Maude

'Electric Moon' (1992) starring Rashan Seth – A gentle comedy which is more aimless than amiable. *'Time Out'*

'Folks' (1992) starring Tom Selleck – If your idea of fun is watching a grown man have his toenails twisted off, then this moronic comedy is for you; those in search of humour will find more laughs in an edition of *Panorama*. *'Time Out'*

'A League of Their Own' (1992) starring Geena Davis – Major players, perhaps, but minor league. *'Time Out'*

'Mo' Money' (1992) written and produced by Damon Wayans – Wayans has likened his new film to a cinematic smorgasbord, but this comedy-romance has the substance of a midnight snack. *'Time Out'*

'Stay Tuned' (1993) starring John Ritter – It boasts the emotional depth of a 30-second soup commercial . . . a dismal affair that goes down the tube. *'Time Out'*

Howard Maxford

'Beethoven' (1992) starring Charles Grodin – A more apt title might have been 'Problem Pup'. *'Film Review'*

'Just Like a Woman' (1992) starring Adrian Pasdar – If this film is a hit I'll eat my black lace panties . . . er, hat. *'Film Review'*

'Knight Moves' (1992) starring Christopher Lambert – This is the sort of stuff that makes *Murder, She Wrote* look brilliant . . . Run of the mill; the actors must have done it for the cheque, mate. *'Film Review'*

Tom Milne

'Soldier Blue' (1970) starring Candice Bergen – One is more likely to be sickened by the film itself than by the wrongs it tries to right.

'Huckleberry Finn' (1974) starring Jeff East – It expires in a morass of treacle.

'The Killer Elite' (1975) starring James Caan – Merely a commercial chore.

'Outland' (1981) starring Sean Connery – Acres of footage are expended on the same old dreary electronic gadgetry and the same old hollowy echoing metalwork sets. *'Monthly Film Bulletin'*

Monthly Film Bulletin

'Home at Seven' (1952) directed by and starring Ralph Richardson – A film with a notable absence of imagination in conception, direction and acting is not vindicated because it was made very cheaply in fifteen days . . . it seems ominous that the technique closely resembles that of television.

'Dr. Zhivago' (1965) directed by David Lean – A long haul along the road of synthetic lyricism.

'Not With My Wife You Don't' (1966) starring Tony Curtis – About as frothy as a tin of dehydrated milk.

'Hurry Sundown' (1967) starring Michael Caine – A pantomime version of Greek tragedy.

'The Penthouse' (1967) from J. Scott Forbes' play – Pornography in Pinter's clothing.

'Deadfall' (1968) starring Michael Caine and Eric Porter – The principal protagonists move like many somnambulists through the turgid labyrinth. *Deadfall* merely falls flat on its somewhat ludicrous face.

'A Lovely Way to Die' (1968) starring Kirk Douglas – The net result is rather as though Philip Marlowe had met Doris Day on his not very inspiring way to the forum.

'Snowball Express' (1972) starring Dean Jones – As wholesome and bland as that old American favourite the peanut butter and jelly sandwich.

'Days of Thunder' (1990) starring Tom Cruise – Simply a flashy, noisy star-vehicle for Tom Cruise, one which – like the stock cars he drives – goes around in circles getting nowhere.

Sheridan Morley
'Twin Peaks: Fire Walk With Me' (1992) directed by David Lynch – Truly breathtaking; not for its writing or directing or acting, but for the arrogance of its maker, David Lynch. Lynch assumes that having suffered through the incomprehensibility of the TV series, we are about to sit through another load of old log-cabin cobblers.   *'Sunday Express'*

Leonard Mosley
'Manon' (1949) starring Michel Auclair –

Though I have been going to the pictures since I wore rompers, I do not recall a more horrible film.

Motion Picture Guide
'The Hitchhiker' (1972) starring Misty Rowe – Don't pick this one up.

'The Happy Hooker' (1975) starring Lynn Redgrave – Not sexy, not funny, not good.

'Better Late Than Never' (1983) starring David Niven – As predictable as a rumbling stomach after a bowl of chilli.

'Best Defense' (1984) starring Dudley Moore – The Best Defense a viewer can take against total boredom is to avoid this sad attempt at comedy.

'Cannonball Run II' (1984) co-starring Dean Martin and Dom Deluise – Starring Burt Reynolds and a cast of washed up has-beens, from Screen Actors Guild Hell, who would probably have been more comfortable on TV's *Love Boat*.

'Falling in Love' (1984) starring Robert de Niro and Meryl Streep – The basic flaw in *Falling in Love* is the fact that no one in the film – including the lovers – seem to be in love.

'Friday 13th: The Final Chapter' (1984) directed by Joseph Zito – The open-ending prepared blood-lusting viewer craving for another sequel 'A New Beginning', which is a rather laughable title considering the previous four films came out of a Xerox machine.

'Scream for Help' (1984) produced and directed by Michael Winner – Scream For Help is what the audience will probably do after viewing this film, not out of abject horror, but out of sheer misery of having sat through eighty-eight minutes of this inane attempt at blending intrigue and terror.

Kim Newman
'The Hidden' (1988) starring Kyle MacLachlan – The film appears to

suggest that the universe is entirely peopled with strange creatures who nevertheless conform to American stereotypes.   *'Monthly Film Bulletin'*

'Traces of Red' (1992) starring James Belushi – An absurd double-whammy ending that requires you to swallow contrivances so blatant even Alfred Hitchcock wouldn't let them into a movie.
'Empire'

New Yorker

'Yolanda and the Thief' (1945) starring Fred Astaire – Needs to be seen by anyone who wants to know what killed the MGM musical.

'Che!' (1969) starring Omar Sharif – It goes at the pace of a drugged ox.

'Something for Everyone' (1971) starring Angela Lansbury – Nothing much for anyone, actually.

'The Other Side of Midnight' (1977) from Sidney Sheldon's novel – A fatuous, money-spinning film from the fatuous, money-spinning book.

'Danton' (1982) starring Gerard Depardieu – By any reasonable standard, terrible.

New York Times

'Solomon and Sheba' (1959) starring Yul Brynner – Watch out it doesn't put you to sleep.

Frank S. Nugent

'Housewife' (1934) starring Bette Davis – The dramatic punches are not merely telegraphed, but radioed.

Observer

'No Orchids for Miss Blandish' (1948) starring Jack La Rue – It has all the morals of an alley cat and the sweetness of a sewer.

'The Ninth Configuration' (1980) starring Stacy Keach – Quite astonishingly garbled, trailing yards of portentous religious allegory.

'Raiders of the Lost Ark' (1981) starring Harrison Ford – Children may well enjoy its simple-mindedness, untroubled by the fact that it looks so shoddy and so uninventive.

'The Best Little Whorehouse in Texas' (1982) starring Dolly Parton – Rancid, self-destructive, hypocritical stuff.

'The Pirates of Penzance' (1982) directed by Wilford Leach – Anyone who thinks Gilbert and Sullivan indestructible should see this.

John O'Hara

'The Great Dictator' (1940) starring Charlie Chaplin – No time for Chaplin to preach as he does in those last six minutes, no matter how deeply he may feel what he wrote and says. He is not a good preacher. Indeed, he is frighteningly bad.

Elaine Paterson

'Salsa: The Movie' (1988) directed by Boaz Davidson – It's up to salsa to save the movie, but there's nothing hot and spicy served up here. The finale has the feel of a junior *Come Dancing*.   *'Time Out'*

William S. Pechter

'A Touch of Class' (1973) starring Glenda Jackson - Machine-tooled junk.

People

'Gung Ho' (1986) starring Michael Keaton – A film that's not much of anything except two hours long.

'Tai-Pan' (1986) starring Bryan Brown – With some movies, you're forever checking your watch. With *Tai-Pan* you'll be checking your calendar.

Playboy

'Pocketful of Miracles' (1961) starring Bette Davis – The story has enough cracks in it for the syrup to leak through.

Dilys Powell

'The Virgin Spring' (1959) directed by Ingmar Bergman – When I first saw the

film I thought it was nauseous. At a second view I find it generally tedious, occasionally absurd, and always retrograde.

'Murder by Death' (1976) starring Peter Falk – If you haven't watched the real *Thin Man* and the real Bogie in the real *Maltese Falcon* you won't see the joke; and if you have watched them, the joke is not good enough. *'New York Times'*

'Who Framed Roger Rabbit?' (1988) starring Bob Hoskins – A deplorable development in the possibilities of animation.

Ray Pride
'Passenger 57' (1992) starring Wesley Snipes – It's not *Die Hard*. It's Die, Already. *'New City'*

Tim Pulleine
'The Hills Have Eyes' (1977) written and directed by Wes Craven – Simultaneously risible and nauseating.
'Monthly Film Bulletin'

Tony Rayns
'The Deadly Trackers' (1973) starring Rod Taylor – It is no more than the outline of a shadow.

Rex Reed
'The Chase' (1966) starring Marlon Brando – The worst thing that has happened to movies since Lassie played a war veteran with amnesia.

'The Cheyenne Social Club' (1970) co-starring Henry Fonda – Co-starring Shirley Jones and Rigor Mortis, who enters early and stays through the very last scene.

'A Star is Born' (1976) starring Barbra Streisand – Stupid, cacophonous and unnecessary rock and roll remake of the old potboiler that drowns in a lot of noise and body odour . . . Her clothes looked designed by Lawrence of Poland, her hair looked like fried possum fat, the music was execrable, the dialogue sounded like

it had been rejected by *The Gong Show*. A total disaster – the worst movie of 1976 – about as contemporary as a 1965 student riot.

Frank Rich
'Bugsy Malone' (1976) directed by Alan Parker – All the pizzazz in the world couldn't lift it above the level of empty camp. *'New York Times'*

'Harry and Walter Go to New York' (1976) starring James Caan – This film fails to work as light comedy, as a period piece, as a jigsaw puzzle . . . mainly, it just sits there and dies. *'New York Post'*

'Mikey and Nicky' (1976) starring Peter Falk and John Cassavetes – An impenetrable, ugly and almost unendurable mess. *'New York Post'*

Nick Roddick
'The Bounty' (1984) starring Mel Gibson – A long voyage to nowhere.
'Monthly Film Bulletin'

Jonathan Romney
'Just Like a Woman' (1992) starring Adrian Pasdar and Julie Walters – This is undemanding stuff which could have been made expressly to elicit thought-provoking, mildly racy human-interest articles in the women's monthlies.
'Time Out'

Jonathan Rosenbaum
'The White Buffalo' (1977) starring Charles Bronson – The dried husk of a *Moby Dick* allegory seems to be rattling around here amidst all the other dead wood.
'Monthly Film Bulletin'

William Russell
'Far and Away' (1992) starring Tom Cruise – Far and away the silliest romantic adventure movie ever made – the cinema's equivalent of a Jeffrey Archer novel. *'The Oldie'*

Richard Schickel
'Catch 22' (1970) adapted from Joseph Heller's novel – As hot and heavy as the original was cool and light.

'Midnight Express' (1978) directed by Alan Parker – One of the ugliest sado-masochistic trips that our thoroughly nasty movie age has yet produced. *'Time'*

Arthur Schlesinger Jr.
'2001: A Space Odyssey' (1968) directed by Stanley Kubrick – Morally pretentious, intellectually obscure and inordinately long . . . A film out of control, an infuriating combination of exactitude on small points and incoherence on large ones.

Sight and Sound
'The Russians are Coming, The Russians are Coming' (1966) – Rather amiable, though the film, like its title, seems to repeat most things twice.

'For Pete's Sake' (1974) starring Barbra Streisand – Revives memories of how much more inventive they used to do it thirty years ago.

'Mame' (1974) starring Lucille Ball – The cast seem to have been handpicked for their tone-deafness.

'Orca – Killer Whale' (1974) starring Richard Harris – There are more thrills to be had in the average dolphinarium.
'Tales of Ordinary Madness' (1981) starring Ben Gazzara – By turns, repellant, naïve and risible.

'Terms of Endearment' (1983) starring Shirley MacLaine – An outsize sitcom and a crassly constructed slice of anti-feminism that contrives to rub liberal amounts of soap in the viewer's eyes.

John Simon
'The Cardinal' (1963) directed by Otto Preminger – Very possibly the last word in glossy dishonesty posturing as serious art.

'I Could Go on Singing' (1963) starring Judy Garland – Merely standard fare in an age without standards.

'Ulysses' (1967) based on James Joyce's novel – No amount of pious invoking of Joyce's name can disguise the fact that a cheaply produced film is being sold at exorbitant prices so that someone can make his boodle off 'culture'.

'Charge of the Light Brigade' (1968) directed by Tony Richardson – It is almost as inexcusably muddled as the British commanders at Balaclava.

'Petulia' (1968) directed by Richard Lester – A soulless, arbitrary, attitudinising piece of claptrap.

'The Damned' (1969) starring Dirk Bogarde – The ludicrous flailings of puny puppets in inscrutable wooden frenzies.

'The Madwoman of Chaillot' (1969) starring Katharine Hepburn – Drawn out to gigantic proportions of humourless vacuity, and peopled with a barrelful of non-acting stars.

'Performance' (1970) directed by Nicolas Roeg – You don't have to be a drug addict, pederast, sado-masochist or nit-wit to enjoy it, but being one or more of these things would help.

'Casanova' (1976) directed by Federico Fellini – The most ponderous specimen of imaginative vacuity ever devised.
'New York'

Alan Stanbrook
'The Birds' (1963) directed by Alfred Hitchcock – It amounts to little more than a shaggy-bird story. *'Sunday Telegraph'*

'Arthur 2: On the Rocks' (1988) starring Dudley Moore – It's about as funny as a hangover. *'Sunday Telegraph'*

'Strapless' (1988) starring Blair Brown – Strapless? It's a pretentious metaphor for having no visible means of support.
'Sunday Telegraph'

'Turner & Hooch' (1988) starring Tom Hanks – In truth this movie is a bit of a dog . . . *Witness* meets *Police Academy* in the tackiest buddy-buddy movie yet.
'Sunday Telegraph'

The Star Tribune
Wayne's World (1991) featuring the
negative suffix 'Not!' – Wayne's World is a
surefire Oscar-winner and is destined to
become a Hollywood classic . . . Not!

Jaci Stephens
'Andrew and Fergie: Behind the Palace
Doors' (1992) made for US TV – The
Queen in *Andrew and Fergie* would not
look out of place on the back of a tin of
Mr Dog; Andrew looks like something
you'd buy in a Moscow Spud-U-Like,
and his wife's hair like a Moscow Spud-
U-Like after Diana has eaten it.
'Sunday Times' (1993)

Philip Strick
'Superfly' (1972) starring Ron O'Neal – It
suggests that New York is now nothing
more than a concrete junkieyard.

'Bolero' (1984) starring Bo Derek – The
only ecstatic moment a filmgoer might
derive will be at the discovery that it's
over.   *'Monthly Film Bulletin'*

'The Hit' (1984) starring John Hurt –
Sensitive editing and seductive
camerawork can't disguise that the
exercise is heading nowhere, a road movie
without fuel.   *'Monthly Film Bulletin'*

'Burning Secret' (1988) starring Faye
Dunaway – Producing many exquisite
coils of smoke, but nothing resembling a
fire.   *'Monthly Film Bulletin'*

Sunday Times
'A Change of Seasons' (1980) starring
Shirley MacLaine – The situation soon
melts into a gooey mess, like a Mars bar
left too long in a trouser pocket.

'The Hunter' (1980) starring Steve
McQueen – The final impression is of an
extended TV pilot for yet another police-
boosting serial with more action than
sense.

'Conan the Barbarian' (1981) starring
Arnold Schwarzenegger – A rag-bag of

half-witted kitsch, where even locations
resemble a set, actors look like extras,
violence like a stunt and life a bad dream.

'Merry Christmas, Mr Lawrence' (1982)
starring David Bowie – It always seems
like a cocktail of saleable ingredients
rather than genuine cinema.

'Psycho 2' (1983) starring Anthony Perkins
– It's all very well having your tongue in
your cheek, but it also helps to have a
brain in your head.

'Friday The 13th: The Final Chapter'
(1984) – The censor says you have to be
eighteen to see it. I would suggest you
merely have to be daft.

Kevin Thomas
'Fighting Mad' (1976) directed by Jonathan
Demme – Little more than a blatantly
obvious play to the yahoo mentality.
'Los Angeles Times'

'Harry and Walter Go to New York' (1976)
starring James Caan – Strictly for those
who'll laugh at anything.
'Los Angeles Times'

Time
'Christopher Columbus' (1949) starring
Frederic March – Even ten-year-olds will
find it about as thrilling as an afternoon
spent looking at Christmas cards.

'The Man from Colorado' (1949) starring
Glenn Ford – No more humour than a
lawyer's shingle.

'Circus World' (1964) starring John Wayne
– To sit through this film is something
like holding an elephant on your lap for
two hours and fifteen minutes.

'Mahogany' (1975) starring Diana Ross –
Movies as frantically bad as *Mahogany*
can be enjoyed on at least one level; the
spectacle of a lot of people making fools
of themselves.

Annie (1982) directed by John Huston – Funeral services may be held starting this week at a cinema near you.

Time Out

'Wing and a Prayer' (1944) starring Don Ameche – It doesn't quite take off. *(1992)*

'Up Periscope' (1959) starring James Garner – Sunk without trace. *(1992)*

'Journey Back to Oz' (1974) starring Liza Minnelli – No heart, no brain but whatta noive. *(1992)*

'Shampoo' (1975) directed by Hal Ashby – Ashby makes it gel, but the overall effect is somewhat bouffant.

'Kramer v Kramer' (1975) starring Dustin Hoffman – One of the most undeserved successes of the year: wall-to-wall sentiment.

'Escape to Victory' (1981) starring Michael Caine – The obviously choreographed soccer action bears more resemblance to a first-year ballet class. *(1992)*

'Embassy' (1985) starring Eli Wallach – One that should have been left in the diplomatic bag.

'A Nightmare on Elm Street Part Two: Freddy's Revenge' (1985) - Much as one loves watching unpleasant American teenagers ripped to death, the slasher formula has worn thin of late.

'Poltergeist II' (1986) on the TV screening – Its subtitle is 'The Other Side', which you'd be better off watching. *(1992)*

'Benji the Hunted' (1987) starring Red Steagall – The third in the series about the plucky li'l fella (ie scrawny jumped-up canine) . . . We eagerly await 'Benji the Skinned', 'Benji the Gutted' and 'Benji the Rather Elegant Genuine Fur Handbag'.

'Mac and Me' (1988) co-starring Ronald McDonald – Junk food, junk film.

Christopher Tookey

'Robocop' (1987) starring Peter Weller – Half John Wayne, half biscuit tin.
'Sunday Telegraph'

'Bert Rigsby, You're a Fool' (1989) starring Robert Lindsay – At times, the film is so amateurish that I had to avert my eyes from Robert Lindsay being crushed by his own star vehicle. *'Sunday Telegraph'*

'Return of Swamp Thing' (1989) starring Heather Locklear – The film doesn't work; even as a shaggy bog story.
'Sunday Telegraph'

'Tank Malling' (1989) starring Ray Winstone – Other movies this year have been almost as incompetently scripted, crudely directed and badly acted; but in view of the way *Tank Malling* combines these qualities with grotesque sexism, gratuitous violence and subnormal intelligence, this marks a new low.
'Sunday Telegraph'

'Cadillac Man' (1990) starring Robin Williams – A wreck of a star vehicle . . . slow to start and never fires on all cylinders, it's the kind of all too familiar mass-produced American runabout which confuses noise with entertainment value and chaos with pace.
'Sunday Telegraph'

'Silent Scream' (1990) directed by David Hayman – It looks like hopelessly confused, poorly executed television *Play for Today*. *'Sunday Telegraph'*

'Wings of the Apache' (1990) starring Nicholas Cage – Where *Top Gun* is gung-ho about aeroplanes, *Wings of the Apache* is merely ho-hum about helicopters. The storyline takes unoriginality to frightening extremes, and the worst aspect of all, is that it's too loud to be slept through.
'Sunday Telegraph'

'Young Guns II' (1990) starring Emilio Estevez – The most vacuous Western since *Young Guns* . . . The Wild West has never looked more like a Club 18-30 holiday. *'Sunday Telegraph'*

DRAMATIC

Shaun Usher

*'New York Stories: Life Without Zoe'
(1989) directed by Francis Ford Coppola* –
Finger-down-the-throat cuteness.   *'Daily
Mail'*

*'Once Upon a Crime' (1992) starring John
Candy and James Belushi* – Usher's Law
warns that any comedy in which voices
are raised for more than three consecutive
sentences, is in trouble . . . Whole chunks
of this travelogue with jokes are shouted,
so draw your own conclusions.
                                    'Daily Mail'

'Variety'

*'Little Accident' (1930) starring Douglas
Fairbanks Jr.* – If anybody thinks 82
minutes is the proper time for this film,
they should be made to sit through it
twice.

*'God's Gift to Women' (1931) starring
Frank Fay* – No gift to audiences.

*'The Goldwyn Follies' (1938) starring
Kenny Baker* – An advance glimpse at
next Saturday's amusement section from
any metropolitan newspaper.

'Free and Easy' (1941) starring Nigel Bruce
– This one must have slipped through the
Metro wringer while the brains
department was out to lunch.

*'Goodbye Mr Chips' (1968) starring Peter
O'Toole* – The sum total is considerably
less than the parts.

*'Fist of Fear Touch of Death' (1980)
starring Fred Williamson* – Bruce Lee,
where are you?

*'The Gong Show Movie' (1980) directed
and starring Chuck Barris* – Bong-g-g-g-
g-g!

*'The Hollywood Knights' (1980) directed by
Floyd Mutrux* – Experiencing the 90
minute paean to jerkdom is akin to sitting
in a car while someone else is
continuously punching up different
stations on the AM band.

*'In God We Trust' (1980) written by and
starring Marty Feldman* – A rare
achievement – a comedy without any
laughs.

'Rough Cut' (1980) starring Burt Reynolds
– Could use some polishing.

*'The Shining' (1980) starring Jack
Nicholson* – . . . but not bright.

*'Used Cars' (1980) directed by Robert
Zemeckis* – Also used jokes.

*'Wholly Moses!' (1980) starring Dudley
Moore* – Wholly Cow!

'Birdy' (1984) directed by Alan Parker –
Will fall short of taking full flight at the
box office.

*'City Heat' (1984) starring Clint Eastwood
and Burt Reynolds* – It evaporates from
the mind instantly upon conclusion.

*'Falling in Love' (1984) starring Robert de
Niro and Meryl Streep* – The effect of this
talented pair acting in such a lightweight
vehicle is akin to having Horowitz and
Rubinstein improvise a duet on the theme
of 'Chopsticks'.

*'La Cage Aux Folles III' (1985) starring
Ugo Tognazzi* – Lots of cooks but not
much broth.

'Cat's Eye' (1985) starring Drew Barrymore
– It creeps in on foggy feet.

'Eleni' (1985) starring John Malkovich – As
lofty in ambition as it is deficient in
accomplishment.

'Out of Africa' (1985) starring Meryl Streep
– It's a long way to go for a downbeat
ending.

*'The Money Pit' (1986) starring Tom
Hanks* – It begins unpromisingly and
slides irrevocably downhill from there.

*'Ishtar' (1987) starring Dustin Hoffman and
Warren Beatty* – One can't help but

wonder whether the camel was the only blind creature who had anything to do with this picture.

'Bonfire of the Vanities' (1990) starring Tom Hanks – A misfire of inanities.

'Kickboxer 2: The Road Back' (1990) starring Peter Boyle – Has all the faults of many Stateside chop-suey carbons: slow pacing, fortune-cookie philosophy and fight sequences shot from all the wrong angles.

'The Night of the Living Dead' (1990) starring Tony Wood – A crass bit of cinematic grave-robbing.

'Problem Child' (1990) starring John Ritter – Universal took a step in the right direction by whittling it down to just 81 minutes but didn't go far enough. The studio should have excised another 75 minutes and released this unbelievable mess as a short.

'Total Recall' (1990) starring Arnold Schwarzenegger – While the temptation is to just shrug off *Total Recall* as an excessive but exciting 'no-brainer', enough intelligence and artistry lie behind the numbing spectacle to also make one regret its heedless contribution to the accelerating brutality of its time.

Robert Vas
'On the Beach' (1959) starring Gregory Peck – The characters remain little more than spokesmen for timid ideas and Salvation Army slogans, their emotions hired from a Hollywood prop room; which is all pretty disturbing in a film about nothing less than the end of the world.

Alexander Walker
'Beyond the Valley of the Dolls' (1970) directed by Russ Meyer – The kind of movie that a maladroit Mack Sennet might have made if he had worked in a sex shop not a fun factory.
'Evening Standard'

'Shaft's Big Score' (1972) starring Richard Roundtree – Most of it is so slowly paced you could not only pour yourself a drink between the lines of dialogue, but add ice too. *'Evening Standard'*

'Posse' (1975) starring Kirk Douglas – The kind of film that raises more questions than it answers, like 'Why was it made at all? *'Evening Standard'*

'Rollerball" (1975) starring James Caan – Rollerball looks like a film that film-makers have made in their own, mindless, narcissistic image. *'Evening Standard'*

'Heathers' (1989) starring Winona Ryder – A foiled rag-day skit. *'Evening Standard'*

'The Lord of the Flies' (1990) starring Balthazar Getty – A Technicolour travel brochure in which a pack of already uncivilised kids act rough and talk dirty like children temporarily freed from the vigilance of their parents.
'Evening Standard'

'Grand Canyon' (1991) starring Steve Martin – Should more properly have been entitled 'San Andreas Fault'.
'Evening Standard'

'Basic Instinct' (1992) starring Sharon Stone – *Basic Instinct* is addressed to the basest instincts. To call it a mystery thriller is to dignify it with a human interest it doesn't remotely possess.
'Evening Standard'

'Twin Peaks: Fire Walk with Me' (1992) directed by David Lynch – It is such a mess that even intrepid Peakies who followed the TV serial may give up and walk out, fire notwithstanding. *'Evening Standard'*

Natasha Walter
'Wuthering Heights' (1992) starring Ralph Fiennes – *Wuthering Heights* is a botch job. It's a pick'n'mix of Gothic motifs, Gainsborough fashions, clashing accents and limp lines. *'Independent on Sunday'*

Bruce Williamson
*'What's the Matter with Helen?' (1971)
starring Debbie Reynolds* – A cast of
seasoned troupers cannot quite alter the
impression that they are all working to
revive a stiff.

David Wilson
*'Hello Dolly' (1969) starring Barbra
Streisand* – The film leaves an oddly
negative impression; a good deal of
synthetic effervescence . . . but very little
vitality.

Richard Winnington
'North Star' (1943) starring Anne Baxter –
Its failure is the case history of every
Hollywood film that stepped outside of its
scope.

*'Golden Earrings' (1947) starring Ray
Milland and Marlene Dietrich* – A good
deal of torso work goes on which I can't
help feeling they're a bit old for.

*'The Sundowners' (1960) starring Robert
Mitchum* – The overall impression
remains one of sheer length and repetition
and synthetic naturalism.

Paul D. Zimmerman
*'Jesus Christ Superstar' (1973) starring Ted
Neeley* – One of the true fiascos of
modern cinema.

William K. Zissner
*'The Iron Petticoat' (1956) starring Bob
Hope* – They seem amazed to find
themselves in a comedy that has no
humour, and they go through the motions
grimly, like children at dancing school,
hoping it will all be over soon.

STAR CRITICISM

*'Bitter Sweet' (1940) original play by Noël
Coward* – After Metro-Goldwyn-Mayer's
dreadful film I can never revive *Bitter
Sweet*. A pity. I was saving it up as an
investment for my old age.   *Noël Coward*

*'Raise the Titanic' (1980) produced by Sir
Lew Grade* – It would have been cheaper
to lower the Atlantic.
                              Sir Lew Grade (1987)

'Star Wars' (1977) starring Mark Hamill –
Acting in this movie I felt like a raisin in a
giant fruit salad. And I didn't even know
who the coconuts or canteloupes were.
                              Mark Hamill

*'Seven Thieves' (1960) directed by Henry
Hathaway* – Christ, it was supposed to be
a fun film, and Rod Steiger is far, far
from having a sense of humour.
                              Henry Hathaway

*'Champagne' (1928) directed by Alfred
Hitchcock* – Horrible.   *Alfred Hitchcock*

*'Waltzes from Vienna' (1933) directed by
Alfred Hitchcock* – I hate this sort of thing.
Melodrama is the only thing I can do.
                              Alfred Hitchcock

*'A Kiss for Corliss' (1949) starring David
Niven* – A disastrous teenage potboiler.
                              David Niven

*'The Long Ships' (1963) starring Sidney
Poitier* – To say it was disastrous is a
compliment.   *Sidney Poitier*

'St Joan' (1957) starring Jean Seberg – I
have two memories of *St Joan*. The first
is being burned at the stake in the picture.
The second was being burned at the stake
by the critics. The latter hurt more.
                              Jean Seberg

'The Prodigal' (1955) starring Lana Turner
– A costume stinker! It should have
played Disneyland.   *Lana Turner*

MOVIE INSULTS

Your idea of fidelity is not having more
than one man in bed at the same time . . .
you're a whore, baby, that's all.
                    Dirk Bogarde – *'Darling' (1965)*

If Florence Nightingale had ever nursed
you, she would have married Jack the

Ripper instead of founding the Red Cross.
Bette Davis – 'The Man Who Came to Dinner' (1941)

You have the brain of a four-year-old child, and I'll bet he was glad to get rid of it. *Groucho Marx – 'Horse Feathers' (1932)*

You know you haven't stopped talking since I came here? You must have been vaccinated with a phonograph needle.
Groucho Marx – 'Duck Soup' (1933)

I'll bet your father spent the first year of your life throwing rocks at the stork.
Groucho Marx – 'At the Circus' (1939)

CANNES FILM FESTIVAL

A film festival in the way that Christmas is a religious festival. *Penelope Houston*

HOLLYWOOD

Hollywood maybe thickly populated but

to me it's a bewilderness.
Sir Cedric Hardwicke

Hollywood is the only community in the world where the entire population is suffering from rumortism. *Bert Lahr*

I've had offers, but I couldn't go to Hollywood – they're all such wankers.
Lynda LaPlante (1992)

Hollywood always had a streak of totalitarianism in just about everything it did. *Shirley MacLaine*

Hollywood is where the stars twinkle, then wrinkle. *Victor Mature*

Hollywood is a sunny place for shady people. *Ferenc Molnar*

Where you find a combination of hot heads and cold shoulders. *Gregory Peck*

Hollywood is a piquant mixture of the Main Line, the Mermaid Tavern and any lesser French penal colony. *S. J. Perelman*

CELEBRITIES

Fame is the stepmother of death.
Pietro Arentino (1537)

Fame is rot, daughters are the thing.
J. M. Barrie – 'Dear Brutus'

A sign of celebrity is often that his name is worth more than his services.
Daniel J. Boorstin – 'The Image' (1962)

In show-business most of what you do is fakery and who wants to spend their whole life with a bunch of fakes?
Marcel Orphuls (1990)

ACTING

Actors and actresses are so stupid, ignorant and eaten up with themselves that one can easily forget how lazy they are. Many cannot face the effort of articulating clearly enough to be understood . . . Anything like that is too much trouble, beside the point, in fact, if all you care about is receiving attention and looking good.
Kingsley Amis – 'The Spectator' (1988)

In London, no young actress can be brought to the footlights unless she is pretty. The public does not want to see plain actresses, however great maybe their talent. *Max Beerbohm*

When actors begin to think, it's time for a change. They are not fitted for it.
Stephen Leacock – 'The Decline of Drama' (1921)

Acting is largely a matter of farting about in disguises. *Peter O'Toole*

Actors in Canada are a little too much of the fly-by-night order to hold a high social status. *Horton Rhys (1861)*

I've written for the theatre for many years, and I'd never vote for an actor to represent me for anything. *Irwin Shaw*

ACTORS

Anon
If she was cast as Lady Godiva the horse would steal the show. *Anon*

The fellow is such a ham I bet he wears a clove in his buttonhole. *Irving Lazar*

Benedicte Adrian
'Which Witch' (1992) – Her top register must be responsible for freezing every fjord in Norway . . . she has the stage presence and emotional impact of a bit of leftover smorgasbord.
Stewart Permutt – 'Plays and Players'

Woody Allen
On his affair with Soon-Yi Previn – You couldn't print what I think. As a father I don't have a colourful enough vocabulary. *André Previn (1992)*

Judith Anderson
'The Seagull' (1960) – At no single point is she on the same stage as the rest of the company. Nor for that matter is she in Chekhov's play. *Mervyn James*

Harry Andrews
'Othello' (1956) – He looks and sounds like an outstanding member of the British

General Staff, sunburned after a tour of the Middle East. *'Financial Times'*

Julie Andrews
There's a kind of flowering dullness about her, a boredom in rowdy bloom.
Joyce Haber

Peggy Ashcroft
'The Duchess of Malfi' (1945) – Something more than plaintiveness, however touching, is wanted if 'I am Duchess of Malfi' is not to sound like 'I am still little Miss Muffett'. *James Agate*

Dan Aykroyd
'Sneakers' (1992) – Dan needs a few more workouts, although he's been having trouble in the weight department for a good few movies now.
Patrick Boyle – 'Modern Review' (1992)

Lauren Bacall
'Applause' (1973) – It doesn't actually matter that she is not notably expert at singing or dancing . . . What does matter about Miss Bacall is that she's no great shakes at acting either, so there is a curious vacuum where the middle of the show ought to be. *Sheridan Morley*

Lucille Ball
'Mame' (1974) – So terrible it isn't boring; you can get fixated staring at it and wondering what Lucille Ball thought she was doing. *'New Yorker' (1977)*

Ronnie Barker
'The Cherry Orchard' (1951) – The most monumental bit of mis-casting . . . Never has anyone been so much at sea since Columbus. He cried when he should have laughed, clowned when he should have been serious, and generally had every-thing back to front. *'Oxford Times'*

Diana Barrymore
Diana is a horse's arse, quite a pretty one, but still a horse's arse. *John Barrymore*

Kim Basinger
'Cool World' (1992) – Casting Kim as a two-dimensional doxy – one could almost

say a 'little tramp' – was a stroke of genius. *Anne Billson – 'Sunday Telegraph'*

'Cool World' (1992) – After a career of steam-heated movies Kim Basinger ends up as only a sexy cartoon . . . But it's too late. We've discovered the cartoon acts better than she does.

Tom Hutchinson – 'Mail on Sunday'

Stephanie Beacham

'The Rover' (1987) – Stephanie Beacham comes on dressed like an especially exotic wedding cake to do an eccentric impersonation of a period Zsa Zsa Gabor.

Sheridan Morley

James Belushi

'Traces of Red' (1992) – The decidedly tubby Belushi hardly qualifying as the epitome of a smouldering sex god.

Kim Newman – 'Empire'

Dirk Benedict

'Blue Tornado' (1991) – Benedict has at least had a decent haircut since *Battlestar Galactica* – but still acts like a square-jawed sequoia.   *'Empire' (1992)*

Jill Bennett

'The Eagle Has Two Heads' (1979) – Jill Bennett in the leading role is acted off the stage by her costume.

Nicholas de Jongh – 'Guardian'

Ingrid Bergman

Turning down the role of Rick in 'Casablanca' (1942) – Who's ever heard of Casablanca? I don't want to star opposite an unknown Swedish broad.   *George Raft*

Brian Bosworth

'Stone Cold' (1991) – Bosworth has hair like a blow-dried skunk and a neck twice the size of his head. The 'Boz' has all the superstar charisma of the average fork-lift truck and could take acting lessons from Flipper.   *'Empire' (1992)*

Lorraine Bracco

'Medicine Man' (1992) – Ms. Bracco squeaks like a sugar bat.

Maureen Paton – 'Daily Express'

Kenneth Branagh

If you smeared Germolene over those lips, his mouth would heal over.   *Anon*

'Hamlet' (1992) – At the Barbican that clown prince of British Thespianism Kenneth Branagh is presently proving that every comedian wants to play Hamlet.

Christopher Bray – 'Modern Review'

'Hamlet' (1992) – Branagh underwhelms as the prince charming of Elsinore plc . . . Branagh leaves me, unlike some of my swooning colleagues, lukewarm and underwhelmed.

Nicholas de Jongh – 'Evening Standard'

'Henry V' (1989) – The film's visual tedium, vulgarity and musical mediocrity would be more bearable if Branagh himself were a more persuasive lead actor.   *'Monthly Film Bulletin'*

'Look Back in Anger' (1989) – I can't understand how anyone can compare him to Laurence Olivier . . . I never thought *Look Back in Anger* could be so bland until I saw Branagh's rendering. The angry young men have been replaced by the Ambitious Young Wimps. 'Look Back in Blandness'.

A. N. Wilson – 'Sunday Telegraph'

Marlon Brando

Brando his heart it bleeds for the masses, But the people he works with, he kicks in the asses.   *Anon*

'Columbus: The Discovery' (1992) – Brando, whose voluminous cloak could have concealed the trolley it looks like he was wheeled about on.

David Aldridge – 'Film Review'

'The Freshman' (1990) – Brando has clearly forgotten that comedy should be played at a pace above that expected in a funeral parlour . . . Whenever Brando's whale-like presence fills the screen, the film grinds to a halt and smacks not of freshness, but of stale, starry, self-satisfaction.

Christopher Tookey – 'Sunday Telegraph'

Tony Britton

'A Woman of No Importance' (1968) – His habit of curling his lip villainously and so relentlessly gives one the impression that he has had it permanently waved.

'Plays and Players'

Blair Brown

'The Secret Rapture' (1989) – A matter of lofty smiles and holier-than-thou posturings. *Frank Rich – 'New York Times'*

Michael Caine

When you watch Caine act, even in his best stuff . . . do you ever think: 'Hey, I bet there's a really fascinating man under there with hundreds of secrets'? Of course not. You think: 'Holy shit, this guy is dull as labradors.'

Simon Garfield – 'Independent on Sunday' (1992)

A mediocrity with halitosis. *Peter Langan*

Michael Caine and Roger Moore

'Bullseye' (1990) – Few leading actors as feeble, lazy and self-indulgent as Caine and Moore are in this film could reasonably expect to work again.

Christopher Tookey – 'Sunday Telegraph'

Simon Callow

Shakespeare's 'Sonnets' (1980) – Simon Callow was wildly applauded at the end – but not by me. If he had spent his time with a ferret down his trousers or stuffing his face with hard-boiled eggs, I might have been more impressed.   *Anon*

'Travels with My Aunt' (1992) – Augusta Bertram played by Simon Callow in an accent as variable and as unreliable as our British weather.

Clive Hirschorn – 'Sunday Express'

'Amadeus' (1979) – Mozart, played by Callow as a goonish cross between a chimp and a donkey. *Benedict Nightingale*

Mrs Patrick Campbell

'Ghosts' (1928) – She was like the Lord Mayor's coach with nothing in it.

James Agate

This was an actress who, for twenty years, had the world at her feet. She kicked it away, and the ball rolled out of her reach.   *James Agate (1942)*

She was a sinking ship firing at her rescuers.   *Alexander Woollcott*

Capucine

During filming of 'Walk on the Wild Side' (1962) – If you were more of a woman, I would be more of a man. Kissing you is like kissing the side of a beer bottle.

Laurence Harvey

Adolfo Celi

'The Borgias' (1981) – Pope Rodrigo Borgia is played by Adolfo Celi, looking like Lord Weidenfeld dressed as Father Christmas.   *Clive James – 'Observer'*

Charlie Chaplin

Chaplin became a millionaire by fooling many people much of the time.

Gerald Kaufman

I positively dislike the irritating, cane-twirling, moustache-twitching character he foisted on the public for decades . . . The shameless way he forced pathos down the throats of the audience leaves a nasty taste in the mouth.

Victor Lewis-Smith – 'Independent on Sunday' (1992)

The funniest man who ever lived (we don't think).   *'Time Out'*

Cher

If she has another facelift, she'll be wearing a beard.

'Absolutely Fabulous' – BBC TV (1992)

Maurice Chevalier

A great artiste but a small human being.

Josephine Baker

Diane Cilento
'Naked' (1963) – Diane Cilento, an attractive but unreal blend of Nefertiti and Sheila Hancock, wages a losing battle to convince us that we ought to care.
Roger Gellert – 'New Statesman'

Montgomery Clift
He acts like he's got a Mixmaster up his ass and doesn't want anyone to know it.
Marlon Brando

Joan Collins
At the Cannes Film Festival – She looked like a bag-lady. *Lenny Henry (1989)*

Nancy Reagan has had a face lift. Joan Collins, on the other hand, uses a fork lift.
Joan Rivers

Jason Connery
'Trelawney of the Wells' (1992) – Connery wears an apprehensive look before each utterance, as if thinking, 'Oh Gawd, I have to speak again!'
John Peter – 'Sunday Times'

Sean Connery
'From Russia with Love' (1963) – The sadistic, suave agent is again played by Connery and although he is not very good at it, it seems to be where he belongs.
Stanley Kauffman – 'The New Republic'

Kevin Costner
'Dances with Wolves' (1990) – Costner has feathers in his hair and feathers in his head. *Pauline Kael*

'The Bodyguard' (1992) – Sporting the type of Haircut from Hell Harrison Ford had in *Presumed Innocent,* and swigging orange juice in an attempt at depth.
Mark Salisbury – 'Empire'

Tom Courtenay
'Charley's Aunt' (1971) – Tom Courtenay, as Charley's Aunt, reminded me of Whistler's Mother. *Frank Marcus*

Annette Crosbie
'Twelfth Night' – Annette Crosbie played Viola like a Shetland Pony. *Anon*

Macaulay Culkin
'Home Alone 2' (1992) – He is performing less like a natural-born son of celluloid and more like a hardened professional. You can almost see him calculating his fee as he delivers his smug one-liners and nauseating dollops of folksy wisdom.
Anne Billson – 'Sunday Telegraph'

Jim Dale
'Carry On Columbus' (1992) – It's not so much that his face has lapsed into the semblance of a condemned sofa but that he's given up moving anything save his eyes, which persist in registering embarrassment by jerkily following a notional autocue somewhere over the camera's shoulder . . . Set him in concrete as the big chief and he's just a totem pole.
Martin Cropper – 'Modern Review' (1992)

Marion Davies
On visiting William R. Hearst's 'San Simeon' mansion -
Upon my honour,
I saw Madonna
Hanging within a niche
Above the door
Of the private whore
Of the world's worst son of a bitch.
Dorothy Parker

Bette Davis
Bette and I are very good friends. There's nothing I wouldn't say to her face – both of them. *Tallulah Bankhead (1950)*

'Of Human Bondage' (1934) – A totally obtuse concoction, serving only to demonstrate how untalented an actress Bette Davis was before she perfected those camp mannerisms.
John Simon (1967)

Robert de Niro
'Night and the City' (1993) – A performance by de Niro that distinguishes nothing but his own ego. He has

turned stereotype into cliché . . . Shyster Harry Fabian is a role so threadbare with use that de Niro could play it with one hand tied behind his back. Certainly he could not have given a more artificial performance if he had done it that way.

Tom Hutchinson – 'Mail on Sunday'

Robert de Niro is about as street as George Bush.   *Michael Medved*

'Night and the City' (1993) – For someone who can usually be more expressive with the back of his neck than other actors can with a dramatic monologue, it's a horribly hammy performance – a grotesque parody of all his Scorsese roles. It's Method without reason – he seems to be thinking if he acts hard enough, everything will suddenly make sense.

Chris Savage King – 'Modern Review'

'Midnight Run' (1988) – de Niro proving surprisingly inept at milking laughs from the script. As a comedian he relies too much on mugging and pulling faces.

Alan Stanbrook – 'Sunday Telegraph'

Bo Derek

'Bolero' (1984) – The curvaceous Bo Derek comes off as erotically as a Dresden doll.   *'Motion Picture Guide'*

Kirk Douglas

'Spartacus' (1960) – In his most famous role, as the gladiator, Spartacus, he had such spindly legs that he couldn't happily have carried the whole script for the epic by himself, let alone take on the whole of Rome. *Peter Tory – 'Daily Express' (1992)*

Sonia Dresdel

'Doctor Jo' (1956) – This is a character-study worthy of Joan Crawford; an antiseptic, overdressed, malarial virgin who acquired, in one of my more frivolous nightmares, the nickname of Boofy Schweitzer.

Kenneth Tynan – 'Observer'

Faye Dunaway

Directing her in 'Chinatown' (1974) – She was a gigantic pain in the ass. She demonstrated certifiable proof of insanity.

Roman Polanksi

Sheena Easton

As Aldonza in 'Kiss of the Spider Woman' (1991) – There's too little dirt in this Aldonza, her burnished hair carefully combed and her well-scrubbed face suggesting not a trollop dwelling in the lower depths but a bratty kid doing her best to imitate an alley-cat.

Anon Broadway critic

Clint Eastwood

'Heartbreak Ridge' (1986) – Now looking increasingly like an Easter Island statue, he has a voice pickled in Bourbon, a tongue like a razor wire and a body so full of shrapnel he can't walk through airport metal detectors.   *'Time Out'*

Robert Eddison

'Twelfth Night' (1950) – He plays a conventional Sir Andrew Aguecheek, looking like a dripping toffee-apple.

'Bandwagon'

Nelson Eddy and Jeanette MacDonald

The singing capon and the iron butterfly.

Anon

Linda Evans

She has all the emotion of a goalpost.

Anon

Rupert Everett

I suspect that at least ten per cent of my time in the auditorium was spent with one hand across my eye – although this was often at the sight of Meryl Streep or Rupert Everett, rather than any more ostensible horror.

Peter Ackroyd – 'The Spectator' (1987)

Albert Finney

'Night Must Fall' (1964) – Finney constantly recalls a ventriloquist's dummy.   *'Monthly Film Bulletin'*

'*Tamburlaine the Great*' *(1976)* – With his full mane of curly hair and dressed in a gold-encrusted tightly fitting mini-skirted costume, he struck me as more of an overweight elf than the savage conqueror of Asia.　　　　　*Arthur Thirkell*

Henry Fonda

Durn if I don't like that boy.

Otis Ferguson

Edward Fox

He introduced the *Olivier Awards* as if he were selling a car-cleaning kit.

Jack Hughes – '*Independent on Sunday*' *(1992)*

Clark Gable

On his nickname '*The King of Hollywood*' – If Clark had an inch less he'd be called 'The Queen of Hollywood'.

Carole Lombard

Zsa Zsa Gabor

She has proved beyond doubt that diamonds are the hardest thing in the world – to get back.　　　*Anon former lover*

I have stopped swearing. I now just say 'Zsa Zsa Gabor!'　　　　*Noël Coward*

Judy Garland

A character ruled by petulance.

Anita Loos

John Gilbert

During the filming of '*La Bohéme*' *(1926)* – Oh no! I've got to go through another day kissing John Gilbert.　　　*Lillian Gish*

Julian Glover

'*Antony and Cleopatra*' *(1973)* – Glover's Antony, who enters red, sweaty and with his bow-tie askew, like some raddled, over-used debs' delight.　　　*Anon*

Dorothy Green

On her large nose in '*Antony and Cleopatra*' – Miss Green, like a battleship, commands from the bridge.　　　*James Agate*

Alec Guinness

'*Incident at Vichy*' *(1966)* – Guinness plays it like a garrulous middle-aged Galahad presenting the Grail on Prize Day at Camelot.　　　　'*New Statesmen*'

'*Hitler: The Last Ten Days*' *(1973)* – There are times when Guinness's Hitler reminded me most of Jack Benny.

Alexander Walker – '*Evening Standard*'

Susan Hampshire

'*Married Love*' *(1988)* – Susan Hampshire as Marie Stopes drifts through the action looking like Isadora Duncan with stomach cramps.　　*Sheridan Morley*

Goldie Hawn

'*Death Becomes Her*' *(1992)* – Hawn emotes like a Barbie doll on coke.

Alexander Walker – '*Evening Standard*'

'*Bird on a Wire*' *(1990)* – The 46-year-old Goldie Hawn – supposedly playing a high-powered, successful lawyer – screams and gibbers like a 12-year-old Bonnie Langford with a spider down her back.

Christopher Tookey – '*Sunday Telegraph*'

Tony Haygarth

'*Macbeth*' *(1992)* – Haygarth makes the blood-thirsty king unimaginative, unambitious and utterly unsoldierly. Even at his most furious he has no more passion than a child with a broken toy. The memory of him sitting in an easy chair for a terrifying soliloquy, like Ronnie Corbett settling down to tell a joke, will stay with me for life. He is the teddy-bear Macbeth.

Tom Morris – '*The Independent*'

Robert Helpmann

'*The Fairy Queen*' *(1946)* – He speaks a good deal of verse in his thin, ascetic voice, glowering all the time with his aghast little hatchet face; and he occupies his silences by trying to intimidate the audience with his favourite facial expression: that appalled look out of the corner of his eye, as if to say 'My God, there's an owl on my shoulder!'

Kenneth Tynan

91

Katharine Hepburn

On her memoirs 'Me: Stories of My Life' –
The rampant egotism implied by the title
is all too painfully prominent throughout
this 'long awaited memoir'. Less
embarrassing than having to watch her
tremulous 'nodding dog' television
interviews.   *'Time Out' (1992)*

Katharine Hepburn and Spencer Tracy

'The Desk Set' (1957) – They lope through
this trifling charade like a couple of old-
timers who enjoy reminiscing with simple
routines.

   Bosley Crowther – 'New York Times'

Charlton Heston

Playing the role of a doctor – It makes me
want to call out, 'Is there an apple in the
house?'   *C. A. Lejeune*

'Earthquake' (1974) – Any movie in which
Charlton Heston drowns in a sewer is all
right by me.   *'Time Out' (1992)*

Sophie Heyden

'The Show Off' (1992) – Her emotional
palette seems limited to wide-eyed
girlishness and brow-furrowing conster-
nation.   *Jeremy Gerard – 'Variety'*

Dustin Hoffman

'Hook' (1992) – Rathbone and Fairbanks
used to fence as a natural flourish of
freedom; Dustin Hoffman looks as if he
learnt fencing from a correspondence
course. What we get is Terry-Thomas
posing for Van Dyck.

   Anthony Lane – 'Independent on Sunday'

Ian Holm

Gloucester in 'Richard III' (1963) – He
exhausts his lung-power in the later
scenes, but finishes up on Bosworth
Field, loaded with an armoury of
medieval weapons, crooning to himself
like a baby inside his visor.   *'The Times'*

Mike Holoway

'Robin – Prince of Sherwood' (1993) – Mike
Holoway's bland Robin Hood, who
occasionally looks as though he has been
taking evening classes in acting when he's
not mindlessly celebrating 'the hero who
lives in us all'.

   Jane Edwardes – 'Time Out'

Anthony Hopkins

'Cariolanus' (1971) – Dressed like a cross
between a fisherman and an SS man,
evoking doggedly a Welsh rugby captain
at odds with his supporters' club.   *Anon*

'Magic' (1978) – The gloomily withdrawn
Hopkins has no vulgarity in his soul –
nothing that suggests any connection with
the world of entertainment – and the
picture grinds along.   *'New Yorker'*

Miriam Hopkins

The least desirable companion on a
desert island.   *'Harvard Lampoon' (1940)*

Michael Hordern

'Jumpers' – Michael Hordern looks like a
cross between a tired bloodhound, a
worried owl and the late Sir Alan Herbert.

   J. C. Trewin – 'Birmingham Post'

Bob Hoskins

'The Inner Circle' (1992) – Hoskins
cameos as a leery Beria. He needn't have
bothered. He contributes nothing to the
movie save a 'star' name.

   David Aldridge – 'Film Review'

Gayle Hunnicut

'Peter Pan' (1979) – As this year's Peter,
she supplies an advertising industry view
of the role . . . This Peter is clearly not
going to spend his future camping out in
an obscure tree house.

   Irving Wardle – 'The Times'

John Hurt

'1984' (1984) – As usual he looked just
like Joan of Arc – after she's burnt at the
stake.   *Anon*

William Hurt

'The Doctor' (1992) – An ironically
anaemic performance from William Hurt,
who's fast becoming the big screen's
blandest man.

   David Aldridge – 'Film Review'

Wilfred Hyde White
'Not in the Book' (1958) – Precise, half-desiccated and very wary, Wilfred Hyde White prowls around the stage in search of laughs with all the blank single-mindedness of a tortoise on a lettuce hunt.   *Anon*

Eric Idle
'Missing Pieces' (1992) – Eric Idle just calls to mind a pre-school show-off on amphetamines.
                James Cameron-Wilson – 'Film Review'

Sir Henry Irving
As Romeo he reminds me of a pig who has been taught to play the fiddle. He does it cleverly but he would be better employed in squealing.   *Anon*

He achieved the feat of performing *Hamlet* with the part omitted and all the other parts as well, substituting for it and for them the figure of Henry Irving.
                                        G. B. Shaw

Glenda Jackson
An actress of some talent, whose entire persona, however, is made up of contempt and even hatred for the audience. In almost every play or film she inflicts her naked body on us, which, considering its quality, is the supreme insult flung at the spectators. *John Simon*

'The Music Lovers' (1970) – I watched *The Music Lovers*. One can't really blame Tchaikovsky for preferring boys. Anyone might become a homosexual who had once seen Glenda Jackson naked.
        Auberon Waugh – 'Private Eye' (1981)

LaToya Jackson
'Moulin Rouge' – An inexpressive face and a pinched little voice drained of emotion.
            Agnes Dalbrad – 'Le Parisien' (1992)

Mick Jagger
'Freejack' (1992) – Resembling a skinny ballerina in a role more suited to Arnie, Sly or Clint, he ignores acting by spraying the audience with lots of cod-cockney

'allos' and 'awrights' instead. Looking like he has swallowed the A-Z of acting before appearing on camera, he probably had each monosyllabic grunt engraved on his cuff links.   *John Marriott – 'Daily Mail'*

'Freejack' (1992) – A strangely accented Mick Jagger makes it plain his acting career ended with *Performance* in 1970.
                George Perry – 'Sunday Times'

Barbara Jefford
'Much Ado About Nothing' (1956) – Miss Barbara Jefford's Beatrice delivers herself of her vaunted raillery with brisk competence and dispatch, rather in the manner of a stalwart school captain bossing the hockey team to victory.
            Derek Granger – 'Financial Times'

Celia Johnson
'St Joan' (1947) – Celia Johnson, in the title role, might I feel have played Jim Hawkins in *Treasure Island*.
                            'Daily Graphic'

Sam Jones
'Flash Gordon' (1980) – Jones in the title role has even less thespic range than Buster Crabbe showed in the old Saturday matinee cliff-hangers.   *'Variety'*

Penelope Keith
'The Apple Cart' (1977) – Miss Keith plays Orinthia as though she has lost the last race at Goodwood.   *Anon*

Martin Kemp
'Daydream Believer' (1992) – Kemp inexplicably opts to do a Roger Daltrey impersonation and falls at the first fence.
                David Aldridge – 'Film Review'

Don Knotts
'The Love God?' (1969) – Strictly for the admirers of Don Knotts. Can there really be many?   *'Monthly Film Bulletin'*

Kris Kristofferson
'A Star is Born' (1976) – Kristofferson looked like the Werewolf of London stoned on cocaine and sounded lie a dying buffalo.   *Rex Reed*

Danny La Rue

'At the Palace' (1970) – . . . is, if you'll forgive the expression, tat for tit; a load of incredibly old material . . . jokes and songs that would have shamed the end of a singularly under-privileged pier twenty years ago. The result is a lavishly costumed but scenically and artistically seedy show – the last resting place for some rather elderly smut . . . Perhaps it might have been more acceptable under water or on ice; at the Palace, it is merely proof that all that glitters is not even bronze! *Sheridan Morley – 'The Tatler'*

'At the Palace' (1970) – Mr La Rue has solved the problem of dressing up like the most gorgeous bird in the world; what he has not discovered is quite what to do then. *Sheridan Morley – Ibid*

Jessica Lange

She says she wants 'mother' not 'actress' on her tombstone – and I for one hope she gets it, the sooner the better. In recent years, she has developed into one of the cinema's most overrated actresses with little but a non-specific luminosity to recommend her.

Julie Burchill – 'The Tatler' (1993)

Bonnie Langford

After a horse had defecated on stage – If they'd stuffed the child's head up the horse's arse, they would have solved two problems at once. *Noël Coward*

Charles Laughton

He is a disappointed narcissist.

Simon Callow

'King Lear' (1959) – As Lear, it was one of the oddest we have seen . . . Laughton, makes no attempt to capture grandeur or majesty. His snow-white hair and beard form an almost complete circle round a pudgy face of the utmost benignity, giving him the air of an innocent Father Christmas. *Eric Keown – 'Punch'*

'A Midsummer Night's Dream' (1959) – A ginger-wigged, ginger-bearded Bottom. I confess I do not know what Mr Laughton is up to, but I am sure I would hate to share a stage with it . . . He behaves throughout in a manner that has nothing to do with acting, although it perfectly hits off the demeanour of a rapscallion uncle dressed up to entertain the children at a Christmas party. *Kenneth Tynan*

Eugenie Leontovich

'Antony and Cleopatra' (1936) – The part of Cleopatra was written in English and in verse, Madame Leontovich has neither.

Anon

Sophia Loren

Working with her is like being bombarded by water-melons. *Alan Ladd*

Montagu Love

Mr Love's idea of playing a he-man was to extend his chest three inches and then follow it slowly across the stage.

Heywood Broun

Ralph Lynn

'Wild Horses' (1957) – Mr Lynn is an extraordinary actor. His performance in this Ben Travers' farce, for example, seems to be entirely independent of the part he is called on to play.

Harold Hobson – 'Sunday Times'

Alec McCowen

'Luther' (1965) – An inspired piece of miscasting . . . a frail schizoid pixie in a robust cycloid role . . . it helped if you shut your eyes. *Maurice Richardson*

Sir Ian McKellen

'Hamlet' (1971) – The best thing about Ian McKellen's Hamlet is his curtain-call. *Harold Hobson*

As an actor he has always been vastly overrated. As for his tombstone, I don't give a damn what it says on it. I just think it damnable that he will go to his grave as a knight.

John Junor – 'Mail on Sunday' (1992)

Virginia McKenna

'As You Like It' (1954) – In an attempt to be boyish she raises her voice so loudly

that at times I had the impression she was a desperate auctioneer trying to sell her lines. *Milton Shulman – 'Evening Standard'*

Madonna

'Body of Evidence' (1993) – Watching her act is like seeing an animal in heat. It's celluloid garbage. It's a bomb. It's a really bad film. It gives a new meaning to 'Amateur Night'. *Chuck Henry*

'Body of Evidence' (1993) – Madonna has a long way, and many acting lessons, to go. *'New York Post'*

'Body of Evidence' (1993) – Madonna is guilty as hell. Her crime is that she just can't act, not one stitch – or stitchless. *'USA Today'*

John Malkovich

'Of Mice and Men' (1992) – . . . harder still to believe is Malkovich's shamble and gape, a simian variant of Hoffman's Rainman. *Brian Case – 'Time Out'*

'Of Mice and Men' (1992) – There's a love affair at the centre of this new adaptation of the novel. But it's between John Malkovich and his own acting technique . . . somewhere along the line the story of two friends on the road becomes the Malkovich acting workshop roadshow . . . There's one scene where Malkovich actually seems to react to the other actors, when Sherilyn Fenn makes her entrance in a pretty pink dress. Malkovich starts rubbing his crotch . . . it's also the movie in a nutshell: even when playing opposite someone, Malkovich still plays with himself.

Tom Shone – 'Mail on Sunday' (1992)

Frederic March

March comes in like a lion and goes out like a ham.
Frank S. Nugent – 'New York Times'

Steve Martin

'My Blue Heaven' (1990) – He gives a crude performance which is about as funny as a hernia.
Christopher Tookey – 'Sunday Telegraph'

Anna Massey

'The Elder Statesman' (1958) – Miss Massie, with her puffed cheeks and popping eyes, is torn between ham and hamster – for the more technique she pours into this tiny role the more it overflows into melodrama.
Alan Brien – 'The Spectator'

Keith Michell

'Dear Love' (1973) – Portraying Robert Browning he jockeys on the balls of his feet as if about to dissolve in a waltz and, at the character's more exalted movements, takes flight like a Davis Cup finalist standing in as Peter Pan.
'Catholic Herald'

Bernard Miles

'John Gabriel Borkman' (1961) – Bernard Miles plays the lead like an effigy of Charles Dickens attacked by a fit of the mange. *Alan Brien – 'Sunday Telegraph'*

Sylvia Miles

She would go to the opening of an envelope. *Anon*

Liza Minnelli

That turnipy nose overhanging a forward gaping mouth and a hastily retreating chin. That bulbous cranium with eyes as big and as inexpressive as saucers – those are the appurtenances of a clown.
John Simon

Robert Mitchum

'Winds of War' – Nowadays, Mitchum doesn't so much as act as point his suit at people. *Russell Davies*

Roger Moore

'For Your Eyes Only' (1981) – Roger Moore fronts for a succession of stunt men with all the relaxed, lifelike charm of a foyer poster of himself. *'Sunday Times'*

Eddie Murphy

The word smug could have been invented for him. *Tom Hutchinson – 'Mail on Sunday' (1992)*

Anna Neagle

'Nurse Edith Cavell' (1939) – Miss Neagle

looked nice as Queen Victoria, she looks just as nice as Nurse Cavell: she moves rigidly on to the set, as if wheels were concealed under the stately skirt: she says her piece with flat dignity and trolleys out again – rather like a mechanical marvel for the World's Fair.

Graham Greene – 'The Spectator'

John Neville

'Henry V' (1953) – Here at last, I felt, was the authentic *Richard II*: a lithe, sneering fellow, who curdled the milk of human kindness even as he dispensed it . . . My excitement was marred, however, by the fact that the play presented was *Henry V.*

Kenneth Tynan – 'Evening Standard'

Anthony Newley

Wrinkling his head and pouting in mock self-adoration, he unfalteringly kept up the hilarious pretence that his songs were immortal and that he has a divine mission to sing them.

Clive James – 'Observer' (1980)

'Once Upon a Song' – He has devised an evening of such mind-numbing self-indulgence one wonders why he did not pay us to attend this unabashed audition of his life . . . Mr. Newley's fabled vibrato is so tremulous it is as if he were shaking hands with his own larynx. His appearance has taken on a hunched, even grotesque, gnomic quality.

Jack Tinker – 'Daily Mail' (1992)

Jack Nicholson

There's a total f***ing w***er! There's a smug, loathsome bastard!

Chris Roberts – 'Melody Maker' (1989)

Chuck Norris

An actor whose lack of expression is so profound that it could be mistaken for icily controlled technique.

Nicholas Lezard – 'Sunday Times' (1992)

Michael Oliver

'Problem Child 2' (1992) – No kidding, micro-monster Michael Oliver, who stars, and who in the first film ran the gamut of emotions from A to just after it, here

doesn't even move from A. The brat has one tone of voice – a hideous half-holler. And just two expressions – cod-diabolical and cod-non-diabolical.

David Aldridge – 'Film Review'

Sir Laurence Olivier

Mr Olivier does not speak poetry badly, he does not speak it at all.   *James Agate*

'Othello' (1964) – There is a kind of bad acting of which only a great actor is capable. I find Sir Laurence Olivier's Othello the most prodigious and perverse example of this in a decade.

Alan Brien – 'Sunday Telegraph'

Olivier brandished his technique like a kind of stylistic alibi. In catching the eye, he frequently disengaged the brain.

Russell Davies – 'J'accuse' (1992)

Peter O'Toole

'Macbeth' (1980) – His performance suggests that he is taking some kind of personal revenge on the play.

Robert Cushman – 'Observer'

'Macbeth' (1980) – He delivers every line with a monotonous tenor bark as if addressing an audience of Eskimos who have never heard of Shakespeare.

'Guardian'

'Our Song' (1992) – The spectacular mis-casting of O'Toole as a sexual obsessive given over to a brunette half his age, when the only thing this actor seems to give himself over to is the sound of his own voice.   *Matt Wolf – 'Variety'*

Gregory Peck

'The Sea Wolves' (1980) – Peck's a Britisher in this one, but the affected accent won't fool anyone. *'Variety' (1980)*

Michael Pennington

'Measure for Measure' (1974) – He seems less a self-deceiving Puritan than a soiled Prince Charming from the Actor's Studio.   *Michael Billington*

Natasha Perry

'Hamlet' (1990) – Natasha Perry is a

gravely beautiful and dignified Gertrude, but she seems to be holding everything in reserve for a rainy day or another production. *Michael Coveney – 'Observer'*

Mary Pickford

She was the girl every man wanted to have – as a sister. *Alistair Cooke*

Donald Pleasence

'Henry VIII and His Six Wives' (1973) – Donald Pleasence overdoes his meaching rodent act as Thomas Cromwell; the twanging Northern accent that issues from his pleated lips seem more appropriate to Dickens or even Pinter.
Nora Sayre – 'New York Times'

'The Merchant of Venice' (1953) – I cannot imagine what Donald Pleasence was trying to make of Launcelot Gobbo, who is not, I suggest, an organ-grinder's monkey. *Kenneth Tynan*

Su Pollard

I have no understanding of how she can be a popular British celebrity.
John Lydon (1989)

Denis Quilley

'High Spirit' (1965) – Denis Quilley plays his role with all the charm and animation of the leg of a billiard table. *Bernard Levin*

Charlotte Rampling

A poor actress who mistakes creepiness for sensuality. *John Simon*

'Orca: Killer Whale' (1977) – Miss Rampling is caught on the icefloes, leaping from one to t'other and clad in thigh boots, homespun poncho and a turban, as if she expected David Bailey to surface and photograph her for *Vogue*'s Arctic number.
Alexander Walker – 'Evening Standard'

Robert Redford

His hair is coordinated with his teeth.
Pauline Kael

Oliver Reed

His face looks like mouldy melon with a half-eaten carrot for a nose and topped by a used Brillo pad. *'Variety' (1980)*

Burt Reynolds

'Evening Shade' – This show's sickly sweet, and Burt Reynolds lives up to his character's name: Wood Newton.
Charles Catchpole – 'News of the World' (1992)

Sir Ralph Richardson

His voice is something between bland and grandiose: blandiose perhaps.
Kenneth Tynan

Chita Rivera

'Kiss of the Spider Woman' (1992) – Her numbers are clearly intended to be showstoppers of the 1950s Hollywood vintage. But Miss Rivera doesn't stop the show, she merely slows it down.
Jeffrey Taylor – 'Plays and Players'

Richard Roundtree

'Shaft in Africa' (1973) – As an African tribesman, he looks about as indigenous as, say, during the 1930s heyday of filmed colonialism, Ralph Richardson might have looked if gotten up in blackface to infiltrate the Fuzzy Wuzzies.
Roger Greenspun – 'New York Times'

Antonia de Sancha

A gruesome old slapper.
Richard Littlejohn

A tour is rumoured of *A Woman of No Importance* . . . Has Antonia de Sancha applied for an audition?
Barrie Stacey – 'Plays and Players' (1992)

Carmen du Sautoy

'Hay Fever' (1992) – Her vamp, whose mugging faces and strange postures suggests that she needs sedation.
Jane Edwardes – 'Time Out'

'Hay Fever' (1992) – All nasal drawl and self-conscious twenties modernity, she goes to such great lengths to be a true type of the era that she forgets to be funny.
Jane Langdon – 'What's on in London'

Paul Scofield

'Othello' (1980) – His idea of a black man's movements consisted of a kind of Fairbankian prancing which, in moments of deep anguish, came to resemble an orang-utan choreographed by Sir Frederick Ashton.

Peter Jenkins – 'Spectator'

Serena Scott Thomas

As Princess Diana in 'Diana: Her True Story' (1993) – Serena Scott Thomas looks so unlike Di they might as well have got Dame Edna.   *'Scanners' – 'Time Out'*

Steven Seagal

And if you can make a star out of Steven Seagal, you can make a star out of anyone.

Mike Bygrave – 'Sunday Telegraph' (1992)

'Under Siege' (1993) – Bring back Bruce [Willis] – at least he's funny.

Colette Maude – 'Time Out'

Tom Selleck

'Carry On Columbus' (1992) – A miscast Tom Selleck, as a petulant King Ferdinand, complete with Prince Valiant wig, is a Magnum farce.

David Aldridge – 'Film Review'

Anthony Sher

'Twelfth Night' (1987) – He plays Malvolio like Groucho Marx dressed as a Greek none-too-orthodox priest.

Sheridan Morley

Michael Siberay

Alsemore in 'The Changeling' (1992) – His voice alone could bore the pants back on even the gamest gal.

Jack Tinker – 'Daily Mail'

Simone Signoret

'Macbeth' (1966) – Simone Signoret's Lady Macbeth was in need of both subtitles and microphones.

Thomas Curtiss – 'New York Times'

Jay Silverheels

As the Chief in 'The Man Who Loved Cat Dancing' (1973) – Even the Indians looked fake, including good old Jay Silverheels, who is real.

Roger Greenspun – 'New York Times'

Alistair Sim

'The Tempest' (1962) – Rather than play the part of Prospero, Alastair Sim chooses to reconnoitre it, you might think him a tentative pantomime dame standing in for Tommy Cooper, the music-hall magician whose tricks never work.

Kenneth Tynan – 'Observer'

Christian Slater

'Heathers' (1989) – I wish it wasn't quite so obvious that his acting hero is Jack Nicholson.

Christopher Tookey – 'Sunday Telegraph'

'Mobsters' (1992) – The ultra-modern Slater struggles to play the Prohibition-era gangster 'Lucky' Luciano but ends up as just another victim of criminal miscasting.

Christopher Tookey – 'Sunday Telegraph'

William Squire

'The Elder Statesman' (1958) – William Squire prances and cavorts like a refugee from a horror film in which Peter Lorre was filling in for Boris Karloff.

Alan Brien – 'The Spectator'

Sylvester Stallone

'Escape to Victory' (1981) – A soccer film set in a POW camp, it features actors who can't play football [Michael Caine], footballers who can't act [Pele] and Americans who can do neither [Stallone].

Nick Hornby – 'Sunday Times' (1992)

Tommy Steele

'Some Like It Hot' (1992) – A man whose ego is never at rest long enough to listen. He was out of place in *Singin' in the Rain* and is even more so here. Tommyrot, this oh so tepid show we all liked hot.

Jack Tinker – 'Daily Mail'

'Some Like It Hot' (1992) – Cavorting around the tacky glitter at the Prince Edward with all the innate diffidence of

King Kong, he takes the musical theatre back to the pantomime.
Jack Tinker – 'Daily Mail'

Marti Stevens
'Blithe Spirit' (1964) – You managed to play the first act of my little comedy tonight with all the Chinese flair and light-hearted brilliance of Lady Macbeth.
Noël Coward

Geoffrey Steyne
Mr Steyne's performance was the worst to be seen in the contemporary theatre.
Heywood Broun (1917)
[*Steyne sued Broun for libel, prompting the critic to review sub-judice the plaintiff's next stage appearance* – Mr Steyne's performance is not up to his usual standard.]

Meryl Streep
Despite her almost Nordic looks, she comes across like a bleached Jewish mother with a tongue to match.
Bob Flynn – 'City Limits' (1992)

'Death Becomes Her' (1992) – Streep, having shown how small a talent she had for broad farce in *She-Devil*, goes all out to prove it again . . . Here she's asked to behave as if auditioning for a *Spitting Image* gargoyle.
Alexander Walker – 'Evening Standard'

Barbra Streisand
'The Way We Were' (1973) – She's not really an actress, not even much of a comedienne. She's an impersonator . . . When she goes one way and the movie goes another, it's no contest. The movie is turned to junk.
Vincent Canby – 'New York Times'

'What's up, Doc?' (1972) – She does her own schtick . . . but she doesn't do anything she hasn't already done. She's playing herself – and it's awfully soon for that.   *Pauline Kael – 'New Yorker'*

'A Star is Born' (1976) – Streisand looked and sounded ridiculous trying to be Grace Slick.   *Rex Reed*

'All Night Long' (1981) – Streisand makes no pretence of acting at all. I thought I'd never seen a worse portrayal of an allegedly living, breathing human being than Streisand gave in *The Main Event*, but the lustful little turnip she plays in *All Night Long* puts some of the creatures in *Freaks* to shame.
Merrill Shindler – 'Los Angeles Magazine'

'A Star is Born' (1976) – Gifted with a face that shuttles between those of a tremulous young borzoi and a fatigued Talmudic scholar . . . O, for the gift of Rostand's 'Cyrano' to evoke the vastness of that nose as it cleaves the giant screen from east to west, bisects it from north to south. It zigzags across our horizon like a bolt of fleshy lightning; it towers like a ziggurat made of meat. The hair is now something like the wig of a fop in Restoration comedy; the speaking voice continues to sound like Rice Krispies if they could talk. And Streisand's notion of acting is to bulldoze her way from one end of a line to the other without regard for anyone or anything; you can literally feel her impatience for the other performer to stop talking so she can take over again. This hypertrophic ego and bloated countenance.
John Simon – 'New York'

Janet Suzman
'Antony and Cleopatra' (1972) – Where Shakespeare had written the word 'O', she favoured us with an extended imitation of a hurrying ambulance. *Anon*

Elizabeth Taylor
Since from her appearance, looking like a brunette version of Lady Penelope in *Thunderbirds*, the old girl has obviously had everything sucked out that could be sucked out, and everything lifted that could be lifted. Indeed, from her tight-skinned, 60-year-old face and taut, little body, they must have had to take away the surplus in truckloads.
Lynda Lee-Potter – 'Daily Mail' (1992)

Elizabeth Taylor's so fat, she puts mayonnaise on an aspirin.   *Joan Rivers*

Colin Teague

'Frankenstein' (1992) – As Victor, he seems to have graduated from the *Prisoner Cell Block H* school of acting.
Caroline Rees – 'What's on in London'

Emma Thompson

Why do I keep seeing all those wonderful pictures of Emma Thompson looking so lovely and so talented? I think she might have to go to hospital soon. I think I might have to put her there.
Dawn French (1988)

On learning Kenneth Branagh was to direct 'Frankenstein' – No doubt he's looking for the right person to be the monster, someone whose acting ability won't be affected by a bolt through the neck. E.T. phone home. Your husband has a job for you. *Jilly Parkin – 'Daily Express' (1992)*

David Threlfall

As Prince Charles in 'Diana: Her True Story' (1993) – David Threlfall at least looks like Prince Charles, even if his performance is more parody than portrayal. He speaks through clamped jaws, his mouth stretched permanently to one side , as if trying to capture something to eat at the base of his skull.
Jaci Stephens – 'Sunday Times'

Rip Torn

'Desire Under the Elms' (1963) – Torn, playing Eben like a refugee from a Texas lunatic asylum, giggles when he is in despair, stares blankly when he is unhappy, and spits when he is undecided.
Robert Brustein

Spencer Tracy

'Dr Jekyll and Mr Hyde' (1941) – Which part is he playing now?
W. Somerset Maugham

Lana Turner

She is not even an actress only a trollop.
Gloria Swanson

Jean-Claude van Damme

He has about three moves he uses over and over in every single one of his films. He does that jump-back spin-kick, and that's pretty much all he does.
Brandon Lee – 'For Him Magazine' (1992)

The Village People

'Can't Stop the Music' (1980) – They've a long way to go in the acting stakes. Some scenes one could pulp and thereby solve the world paper shortage, they're so wooden. *'Variety' (1980)*

Harriet Walter

As Viola in 'Twelfth Night' (1987) – Looks as though she would far rather be leading a troupe of Girl Guides in an archaeological dig around the island.
Sheridan Morley

David Warner

'Hamlet' (1965) – I would as lief the town-crier spoke Shakespeare's lines as hear David Warner. He delivers the soliloquies as though he were dictating to the literary pirates jotting down the first-quarto version of the play. He butchers the rhythms, stresses unimportant words, affects new and strange ways of speaking the English language. On his delivery of the part alone, he must stand condemned.
Julian Holland – 'Daily Mail'

'Hamlet' (1965) – His Hamlet would make better sense if he had no cue to passion and were simply wrestling with the Danish equivalent of the Tory magic circle . . . Essentially what Mr Warner presents is yet another variant on his Henry VI – a sweet-natured child entrusted with a task beyond his powers.
'The Times'

Timothy West

'The Merchant of Venice' (1980) – The Jew, played by Timothy West, is that familiar Rialto, the bad-tempered Hungarian economic advisor.
James Fenton

Simon Williams

'The Last of Mrs Cheyney' (1980) – What Mr Williams could use as a performer is a voice that did not always sound

strangulated by black ties.
Ned Challiet – 'The Times'

COMEDY

If British clowns were funny, I would book them. They aren't, so I won't.
Gerry Cottle (1992)

I don't really find any silent comedians funny . . . I don't really identify with it. I've never had to wallpaper a room while delivering a piano upstairs.
Angus Deayton – 'Independent on Sunday' (1992)

COMEDIANS

Alternative Comedians
'Carry On Columbus' (1992) – Here are the bold young Turks: Sayle, Mayall, Planer, Slattery, Richardson, Keith Allen . . . the best joke of the whole enterprise is the notion that the Comic Strip honchos could have hoped to revitalize the vieux jeu conventions. Well they haven't, they're just playing panto. Ian Botham could have played any of their roles.
Martin Cropper – 'Modern Review' (1992)

Alternative comedians have as much chance of raising a laugh as beating Barry Manilow in a photo finish.
Bernard Manning (1992)

They're just a Carry On team for the 80s.
Jerry Sadowitz (1989)

Comic Relief
To me, the idea of 'Comic Relief' is Lenny Henry having a shit.
Jerry Sadowitz (1989)

You don't wear a red nose if you're starving, there's something sick about that.   *Jerry Sadowitz (1989)*

Rowan Atkinson
'One-man Show' (1990) – It's not inconceivable that this comic's biggest fans at home are products of an

upbringing that encourages boys to tame their nasty bowel habits at an early age, with the consequence that their obsession with alimentary products persists right through to Oxford and Cambridge.
Frank Rich – 'New York Times'

David Baddiel
If I were put in charge for one day, my priority would be to arrest the really cocky one from *The Mary Whitehouse Experience* – the one with the supercilious sneer and the silly glasses. I'd lock him in a prison cell and make him listen to every episode of *Round the Horne* and *Hancock's First Half-Hour*, in the hope, probably forlorn, that a tiny particle of talent might rub off. Then I'd throw away the key.
Matthew Norman – 'Mail on Sunday' (1992)

Sandra Bernhard
She is as much fun as barbed wire.
Tom Hutchinson – 'Mail on Sunday' (1992)

Jasper Carrott
Mr Carrott has yet to learn that brevity is often the soul of wit, but he has little to learn about the vast vocabulary of body language.   *'The Times' (1981)*

Julian Clary
'Terry and Julian' – The one-dimensional Clary, a hopeless actor, minced his way through a series of sub-Sir Les Patterson single entendres . . . Isn't it incredible that Clary landed a part in the new *Carry On* film? That some reviewers had the cheek to compare his sorely limited delivery to a talent like Kenneth Williams? Anyone taking a stethoscope to the late great one's grave would be sure to detect the distinct sound of spinning six feet under.
Garry Bushell – 'Modern Review' (1992)

Clary is a tottering marvel of unwatchability.
Martin Cropper – 'Modern Review' (1992)

'Sticky Moments' (1990) – It is not just that he has no idea how to time a gag, or

that he fluffs so many of his lines which makes watching Julian so painful . . . but there is something ditheringly apologetic about his manner, as though he is embarrassed to be making quite such a fool of himself.

A. N. Wilson – 'Sunday Telegraph'

Andrew Dice Clay

If you said irony to Clay, he'd look down at his shirt and think it needed pressing.

Denis Leary

Jim Davidson

'Jim's Blue Christmas Show' (1991) – The programme celebrates 'his machine gun style' that continues 'to endear him to audiences everywhere.' Personally, I would have preferred a firing squad . . . Davidson is a comedian for those without hearts, minds or souls.

Michael Arditti – 'Evening Standard'

Ben Elton

Alexei Sayle opened up stand-up comedy in this country, Ben Elton closed it.

Jerry Sadowitz (1989)

A hypocrite because he's a capitalist making money out of left-wing jokes. I just wish he'd own up and say 'I want to be rich and famous.'

Jerry Sadowitz (1989)

Craig Ferguson

'Mental' (1989) – The album (in what must be a direct contravention of the Trade Descriptions Act) is far from mental.

Matthew Collin – 'New Musical Express'

Stephen Fry

'Clive Anderson Talks Back' – Fry appeared in his habitual role of a 60-year-old don, as convincing as a first-year undergraduate who takes up pipe-smoking in the belief that he will acquire gravitas and not merely catarrh. He mentioned that he had become Rector of Dundee University and discussed his rectal duties and titular functions, using that curious vocabulary of moist, fluffy

and gooey words that he often mistakes for humour.

Victor Lewis-Smith – 'Evening Standard' (1992)

Keith Harris and Orville

They make a remarkable ventriloquist act. Together they amount to a prat with a perm holding a green duck with a squeaky voice dressed in a nappy. The only intriguing thing about their act is trying to figure which one is which.

Stafford Hildred – 'Daily Star' (1992)

Billy Hicks

'Relentless' (1992) – Hicks doesn't tell gags, he is an 'attitude comic'. Trouble is his attitude is so '60s he ought to be wearing a kaftan and cowbells.

Garry Bushell – 'The Sun'

Benny Hill

Benny Hill has been compared to Buster Keaton, but seventy years on Keaton comes up fresh while Hill's forty-year-old peepshow looks hopelessly outdated in a groin-and-bear it age.

Allison Pearson – 'Independent on Sunday' (1992)

Hill's biggest defect was surely not his sexism, but the fact that he repeated himself ad nauseam.

Christopher Tookey – 'Sunday Telegraph' (1992)

Bob Hope

He's an applause junkie. Instead of growing old gracefully and doing something with his money, all he does is have an anniversary with the president looking on. He's a pathetic guy.

Marlon Brando

Barry Humphries (aka Dame Edna Everage)

He uses the disguise of a woman to humiliate other women in a way he couldn't as a man. *Anne Karpf (1993)*

Jerry Lewis

'Ladies' Man' (1961) – Regression into infantilism cannot be carried much further than this. *'Monthly Film Bulletin'*

Apparently some people find him hilariously funny.   *'Time Out' (1992)*

Harold Lloyd
'Feet First' (1930) – That Lloyd was a bit pressed for laughs may be guessed from the fact that he is again dangling from the front of a skyscraper.   *'Variety'*

Marx Brothers
Working for the Marx Brothers was not unlike being chained to a galley car and lashed at ten-minute intervals.
S. J. Perelman

Groucho Marx
The man was a major comedian, which is to say that he had the compassion of an icicle, the effrontery of a carnival shill, and the generosity of a pawnbroker.
S. J. Perelman

Ruby Wax
'The Full Wax' – Talent is not a word you instinctively identify with this brash New York motormouth. As a stand-up comedian, she's wooden and unoriginal. As an interviewer, she's more interested in what she has to say than anything her guest may proffer. Indeed, she doesn't really seem to be good at anything – she's just there, sneering, yelling, wheedling, humiliating and, of course, finding herself funnier than even she might have thought possible. She's not a performer, she's an ego, and *The Full Wax* is nothing if not a

celebration of that ego.
Marcus Berkmann – 'Daily Mail' (1992)

A trappy Yank bow-wow.
Garry Bushell – 'The Sun' (1992)

Ms Wax talks like a cement mixer from Brooklyn . . . freeze-dried, she would have made a perfectly acceptable hat-stand in a Second Empire Turkish Bath.
David Naughton – 'Observer'

Buddy Young
Not only self-destructive but also a thoroughly unpleasant person.
'Los Angeles Times'

OTHER

British Comedy Awards
To create a meritocracy of humour is about as much sense as a group of anarchists drawing up a rule book.
Victor Lewis-Smith – 'Mail on Sunday' (1992)

An endless crocodile of egos in cheap nylon polyamide dinner jackets; Americans appearing 'live via satellite' because they couldn't be bothered to come to London to pick up some tacky bit of tin that even Gerald Ratner would reject . . . The grotesque tinny gold jester wears motley; appropriate dress for a motley event that stars a motley bunch.
Victor Lewis-Smith – Ibid

MUSIC

CLASSICAL MUSIC

All festivals are bunk. They are for the purpose of attracting trade to the town. What that has to do with music, I don't know.
Sir Thomas Beecham

Why are the frequenters of serious concerts so alarmingly ugly? And why do their features usually denote harsh intellectuality and repudiation? Why have they the air of mummies who have crept out of the Pyramids in order to accomplish a rite? Why have they not the air of having come into a public-house to get a pint of beer?

Arnold Bennett – 'Things That Have Interested Me'

I recently reported that a computer had been programmed to enjoy modern concert music (as very few people seemed to want to). *Miles Kington – 'The Times'*

If one plays good music, people don't listen, and if one plays bad music, people don't talk.

Oscar Wilde – 'The Importance of Being Earnest'

COMPOSERS

John Adams

Mr Adams has done for the arpeggio what McDonalds did for the hamburger.
'New York Times'

Béla Bartók

'First Piano Sonata' – He has made big music sound small . . . He has converted the grand orchestra into a mere mandolin . . . He has gone after beauty with hammers and sticks.

'Christian Science Monitor' (1928)

'Concerto for Pianoforte and Orchestra' – He is in music's no man's land, and ingress and egress have been deliberately protected by heavily charged barbed wire. From the vantage point of his own planning he hurls gas bombs in the direction of friend and foe indiscriminately. If you emerge from the conflict without suffering from shell shock, you may consider that you have been a favourite of the gods.

'Cincinnati Enquirer' (1928)

'Violin Sonata' – The bulk of the sonata seemed to me the last word (for the present) in ugliness and incoherence. It was as if two people were improvising against each other.

Ernest Newman – 'Sunday Times' (1922)

'Piano Concerto' – This work from first to last was one of the most dreadful deluges

of piffle, bombast and nonsense ever perpetrated on an audience in these environs.

H. Noble – 'Musical America' (1928)

Ludwig van Beethoven

'Ninth Symphony' – The general impression it left on me is that of a concert made up of Indian war-whoops and angry wildcats. *Anon U.S. critic*

'Quartet No. 13' – Beethoven's imagination in the finale of this quartet suggests a poor swallow flitting incessantly in a hermetically sealed compartment to the annoyance of our eyes and our ears.
H. Blanchard – 'Revue et Gazette Musicale' (1849)

'Ninth Symphony' – The pages of stupid and hopelessly vulgar music. Unspeakable cheapness of the chief tune, 'Freude, Freude'! Do you believe way down in the bottom of your heart that if this music had been written by Mr. John L. Tarbox, now living in Sandown, N.H., any conductor here or in Europe could be persuaded to put it in rehearsal?
Phillip Hale – 'Musical Record' (1899)

'Second Symphony' – A crass monster, a hideously writhing wounded dragon that refuses to expire, and though bleeding in the Finale, furiously beats about with its tail erect.
'Zeitung für die Elegente Welt' (1804)

Alban Berg

Berg is just a bluff. But even if he isn't, it is impossible to deny that his music is a soporific, by the side of which the telephone book is a strong cup of coffee.
Samuel Chotzinoff – 'New York Post' (1935)

Splitting the convulsively inflated larynx of the Muse, Berg utters tortured mistuned cackling, a pandemonium of chopped-up orchestral sounds, mishandled men's throats, bestial outcries, bellowing, rattling, and all other evil noises. Berg is the poisoner of the well of German music. *'Germania' (1925)*

'Wozzeck' – In Berg's opera *Wozzeck* nothing sings and nothing dances. Everything screams hysterically, weeps drunken tears, jitters, spasmodically wriggles, and writhes in epileptic convulsions . . . All is calculated to stun the human ear and to insult the aesthetic sense of any normal and healthy human being. *V. Gorodinsky – 'Music of Spiritual Poverty' (1950)*

'Lulu' – As absolute music, *Lulu* has no value whatever. It is just laboured and ugly, apparently aimless, and surely futile. It meanders and puffs and groans and grunts. It touches no responsive chord in the listener's heart, for it is seemingly without heart.
W. J. Henderson – 'New York Sun' (1935)

Nietzsche said once that there must have been chaos where a star was to be born. Alban Berg has luckily managed to re-establish chaos with the expenditure of great cunning, and waste a considerable quantity of brain fat.
Karl Krebs – 'Tag' (1925)

In Berg's music there is not a trace of melody. There are only scraps, shreds, spasms, and burps . . . I regard Alban Berg as a musical swindler and a musician dangerous to the community. We deal here, in the realm of music, with a capital offence.
Paul Zschorlich – 'Deutsche Zeitung' (1925)

Hector Berlioz
'Fantastic Symphony' – The final movement is a dreary, cacophonous mess, an interminable galimatias.
'Boston Home Journal' (1890)

What Monsieur Berlioz writes does not belong to the art which I customarily regard as music, and I have the complete certainty that he lacks the prerequisites of this art. *F. J. Fetis (1837)*

'Fantastic Symphony' – A nightmare or the delirium tremens set to music.
'Musical Record' (1880)

'King Lear' – Overture to *King Lear* by Berlioz, mere rubbish and rot. Shakespearean overtures by galvanised anthropoid Parisians are becoming a nuisance. *George T. Strong – 'Diary' (1864)*

'Le Carneval Romain' – I can compare *Le Carneval Romain* by Berlioz to nothing but the caperings and gibberings of a big baboon, over-excited by a dose of alcoholic stimulus.
George T. Strong – 'Diary' (1866)

Berlioz writes like a tipsy chimpanzee.
George T. Strong – Ibid

Georges Bizet
'Carmen' – Bizet aimed at originality, and he undoubtedly obtained it, but he obtained monotony at the same time.
'Boston Gazette' (1879)

'Carmen' – *Carmen* is neither scenic nor dramatic. Nourished by the succulent harmonies of the expression of the music of the future, Bizet opened his soul to this doctrine that kills the heart.
Oscar Commettant – 'Le Siècle' (1875)

'Carmen' – I think we must face the fact that *Carmen* by Bizet is no more Spanish than the Champs Elysées. *Noël Coward*

'Carmen' – If it were possible to imagine his Satanic Majesty writing an opera, *Carmen* would be the sort of work he might be expected to turn out.
'Music Trade Review' (1878)

'Carmen' – It is little more than a collocation of couplets and chansons . . . musically, it is really not much above the works of Offenbach. As a work of art, it is naught. *'New York Times' (1878)*

Ernest Bloch
Nearly all of Bloch's music is hot in the mouth with curry, ginger and cayenne, even where one has a right to expect vanilla and whipped cream.
'New York Evening Post' (1917)

The music of Ernest Bloch seems to be a parody of Richard Strauss. It is simply noise for the sake of noise.

Arthur Pougin – 'Le Menestral' (1910)

Johannes Brahms

'Second Symphony' – Whatever he writes, he seems to have to force music out of his brain as if by hydraulic pressure.

W. F. Apthorp – 'Boston Courier' (1879)

'Symphony in C Minor' – Mathematical music evolved with difficulty from an unimaginative brain.

'Boston Gazette' (1878)

'Second Symphony' – It gave the impression that the composer was either endeavouring all the while to get as near as possible to harmonic sounds without reaching them; or that he was unable to find any whatever. *'Boston Traveler' (1882)*

'Symphony in C Minor' – I do not like and I cannot like the C minor *Symphony* of Brahms . . . I am willing to admit without argument that the *Symphony* is grand and impressive and all that. So is a channel fog. This C minor *Symphony* seems to me the apotheosis of arrogance.

Philip Hale – 'Boston Journal' (1893)

'Violin Concerto' – That disappointing work, Brahms' *Violin Concerto*, promises me clear skies at the opening, and only when the violin has squealed up in the air for page after page is the promise falsified.

E. M. Forster – 'The Listener' (1939)

Art is long and life is short: here is evidently the explanation of a Brahms symphony.

Edward Lorne – 'Fanfare' (1922)

'Fourth Symphony' – The orchestration is, like most of Brahms, of a certain sameness, rather thick and of India-rubber-like stiffness.

'Musical Courier' (1887)

'Symphony in C Minor' – Three slow movements following each other become extremely tedious, and the last movement is so much like the finale of Beethoven's *Ninth Symphony* that it should be put in quotation marks. *'New York Post' (1880)*

'Fourth Symphony' – It is charaterised by Brahms' besetting sin – a profuse lack of ideas. *'New York Post' (1886)*

'Symphony in E Minor' – Owing to the misfortune of being a musician, I cannot appreciate Brahms, and least of all Brahms in E minor . . . There is no more intolerably dull symphony in the world than the E minor.

J. F. Runciman – 'Saturday Review' (1897)

Strip off the euphemism from his symphonies and you will find a string of incomplete dance and ballad tunes following one another with no more organic coherence than the succession of passing images reflected in a shop window in Picadilly during any twenty minutes in the day.

G. B. Shaw – 'The World' (1890)

'Symphony in E Minor' – Let Brahms be content that in his E minor Symphony he has found a language which gives the most persuasive expression of his mute despair: the language of the most intensive musical impotence.

Hugo Wolf – 'Salonblatt' (1886)

Anton Bruckner

Bruckner is the greatest living musical peril, a tonal Antichrist . . . his music may radiate the fragrancy of heavenly roses, and yet be poisoned with the sulphur of Hell. *Anon*

We recoil in horror before this rotting odour which rushes into our nostrils from the disharmonies of this putrefactive counterpoint. His imagination is so incurably sick and warped, he composes like a drunkard.

Gustav Dompke – 'Wiener Allgemeine Zeitung' (1886)

'Third Symphony' – The scoring is throughout puerile in the extreme, and the absence of intelligent construction or inventive ability completes the sum total of Herr Bruckner's musical imbecility.
'Keynote' (1885)

Frederic Chopin
He was essentially a drawing-room composer. *'The Times' (1855)*

A composer for the right hand.
Richard Wagner

Aaron Copland
'Piano Concerto' – No dance-hall would tolerate jazz of such badness. *Anon (1927)*

'Piano Concerto' – There is nothing in it that resembles music except as it contains noise . . . It is of all sounds the most illogical, the most anti-human. The piano part of the composition is not played but merely happened upon at random, as it might be if the performer struck the keyboard with his elbows instead of his fingers. *'Boston Evening Transcript' (1927)*

'Piano Concerto' – A shocking lack of taste, of proportion. After thunderous, blaring measures in which one brass instrument vies with another in arrogant announcement, there are gentle purposeless measures for the piano, which is struck by fingers apparently at random, as a child amuses itself by making noises when it is restless in the room. Let us not forget that the leading English reviewers characterised Schumann's Symphony in B flat when they first heard it as belonging to the 'Broken Crockery School.' Our objection to Mr. Copland's broken crockery is that it is not of the first quality.
Philip Hale – 'Boston Herald' (1927)

'Short Symphony' – I cannot describe it more exactly than inane and rainy . . . A quite bewildering piece of creative impotence.
Lazare Saminsky – 'Living Music of the Americas' (1949)

He is a flagrant example of composer by propaganda. *Lazare Saminsky – Ibid*

'Piano Concerto' – There are gargantuan dance measures, as of a herd of elephants engaged in jungle rivalry of the Charleston and dances further south.
Pitts Sanborn – 'New York Telegram' (1927)

Claude Debussy
The music of M. Debussy which professes to dismiss all elements of melody, appears strangely futile, vacuous and non-existent. It splashes little vague notes whose lulling vibration ends by giving a sensation of sea-sickness. This amorphous art, so little virile, seems to be made specially for tired senses, which evokes somehow the idea of falseness and fraud . . . It reduces itself to musical dust, a mosaic of chords . . . a lilliputian art for dwarfish humanity.
Raphael Cor – 'Le Cas Debussy' (1910)

'Afternoon of the Faun' – A strong example of modern ugliness.
Louis Elson – 'Boston Daily Advertiser' (1904)

'Afternoon of the Faun' – It is musical absinthe; there are moments when the suffering *Faun* seems to need a veterinary surgeon.
Louis Elson – 'Boston Daily Advertiser' (1905)

'The Sea' – When we read the title of the first of the sea sketches by Debussy – *From Dawn Till Noon* – we feared that we were to have a movement seven hours long. It was not so long, but it was terrible while it lasted.
Louis Elson – 'Boston Daily Advertiser' (1907)

'The Sea' – We believe that Shakespeare means Debussy's ocean when he speaks of taking up arms against a sea of troubles.
Louis Elson – 'Boston Daily Advertiser' (1907)

I was struck by the unique ugliness of the man. His face is flat, the top of his head is flat . . . he looked more like a Bohemian, a Croat, a Hun than a Gaul. His high, prominent cheekbones lend a Mongolian aspect to his face. The head is brachycephalic, the hair black – the man is a wraith from the East; his music was heard long ago in the hill temples of Borneo; was made as a symphony to welcome the head-hunters with their ghastly spoils of war. *James G. Huneker – 'New York Sun' (1903)*

The music of Debussy has the attractiveness of a pretty tubercular maiden, with her languorous glances, anaemic gestures, whose perversity has the charm of one marked for death. A symphony, a piece of music, are organisms. A Debussyan organism reminds us of the jellyfish whose translucid substance lights up brilliantly at the touch of sunlit wave, but which will never be anything but a protozoan. All this lacks fibre and blood. I have the sensation of originality covering up a kind of impotence.

Alfred Mortier – 'Rubriques Nouvelles' (1909)

'The Sea' – The three parts of which it is composed are entitled 'From Dawn till Noon', 'Play of the Waves', and 'Dialogue of the Wind and Sea', but as far as any pictorial suggestiveness is concerned, they might as well have been entitled 'On the Flatiron Building', 'Slumming in the Bowery', and 'A Glimpse of Chinatown During a Raid.' *'New York Post' (1907)*

Debussy's music is the dreariest kind of rubbish. Does anybody for a moment doubt that Debussy would write such chaotic, meaningless, cacophonous, ungrammatical stuff, if he could invent a melody? *'New York Post' (1907)*

'The Sea' – Dialogue of the Wind and Sea would have sounded as sweet if played backwards or upside-down.

'New York Sun' (1907)

'The Sea' – Persistently ugly . . . It is prosaic in its reiteration of inert formulas . . . Debussy fails to give any impression of the sea . . . There is more of barnyard cackle in it than anything else.

'New York Times' (1907)

'La Demoiselle Elue' – Not a shadow of rhythm; vacillating and fluid harmonies; not even any nuances. All in this music is indeterminate, vague, fleeting, indecisive, deliberately indefinite, formless music without muscle or backbone; grey music forming a sort of sonorous mist which one would like to pierce to see whether there is anything behind it, but whose somnolent opacity makes it impenetrable.

Arthur Pougin – 'Le Menestrel' (1910)

'Afternoon of the Faun' – A vacuum has been described as nothing shut up in a box, and the prelude to *L'Aprés-midi d'un faun* may aptly be described as nothing, expressed in musical terms.

'Referee' (1904)

'Pelleas and Melisande' – The score resembles a curiosity shop of tangled harmonies, a gallery of harmonised abortions.

Hugo Schlemuller – 'Signale' (1907)

'Pelleas and Melisande' – As to the nature of this composition, no one here has an inkling that it is quite feasible to play music of the fourth act to the text of the first, and vice versa, or even turn the score upside down or put it in front of a mirror and perform it in this manner without an essential change in its effect.

F. Spiro – 'Signale' (1909)

César Franck

M. Franck's melodies are born to vanish at once. Oh, arid and grey music, devoid of grace, charm and smile!

Camille Bellaigue – 'Revue des Deux Mondes' (1888)

The Franck Symphony is not a hilarious work . . . charcoal would make a white mark upon the Cimmerian darkness of its first movement. One hears the creaking of the machinery, one watched the development with no greater emotion than would be evoked by a mathematical demonstrator at the blackboard.

*Louis Elson – 'Boston Daily Advertiser'
(1899)*

'Symphony in D Minor' – The symphony drags slowly, painfully . . . It is morose and pompously generates tedium.

'La Menestrel' (1893)

Charles Gounod

'The Queen of Sheba' – The libretto is certainly of deplorably low quality; but the inadequacy of the libretto is no excuse for a musician.

*P. Scudo – 'La Revue des Deux Mondes'
(1862)*

Edvard Grieg

A pink sweet stuffed with snow.

Claude Debussy

Roy Harris

'Symphony No. 3' – How blessed are they who are born deaf, and are spared the agony of listening to the hideous sounds of *Symphony No. 3* by Roy Harris . . . who should have stuck to truck driving instead of insulting music-lovers with his senseless noise.

Letter to 'Radio Times' (1942)

'Gayety and Sadness of the American Scene' – The Overture proved to be not only monumental but colossal – a colossal failure. To face the notes of such a music-less composition without becoming eligible for life membership in the booby hatch is a surprise to me.

'The Hollywood Citizen-News' (1932)

'Cumberland Concerto' – There was one deadly number, a clamorous and incoherent piece entitled *Cumberland Concerto* by Roy Harris. Harris had the gall to come out afterwards and take a bow. *'New York Daily News' (1951)*

'American Creed' – One is tempted to put the whole thing down as insincere and a bad joke. *Virgil Thomson –
'New York Herald-Tribune' (1940)*

Dave Heath

Libel laws prevent discussion of Dave Heath's music. *'The Times' (1984)*

Vincent d'Indy

'Second Symphony' – It shows the work of a musical scientist who takes daring liberties in progressions, juggles chromatics, ascending and descending, in a way to grieve the ear of the average concert attendant. *'Boston Globe' (1905)*

'Second Symphony' – It is one long stretch of ugliness, a single piece of weird tonalities, hideous progressions, barren wastes of mechanism.

'Boston Journal' (1905)

'The Stranger' – The Entr'acte from *The Stranger* was one of the modern 'puzzle' pieces. We might suggest changing the title from the comparative to the superlative.

*Louis Elson – 'Boston Daily Advertiser'
(1904)*

'Second Symphony' – People who do not like harmonies suggestive of rampant lemons and inebriated persimmons will not enjoy this *Symphony*.

W. J. Henderson – 'New York Sun' (1905)

Vincent d'Indy, stepfather of dissonance, fears a theme as something pernicious and vulgar. And the lengths! The stretches of barren, mincing tonal speech!

'Town Topics' (1905)

Ernst Krenek

'Jonny Spielt Auf' – In *Jonny Spielt Auf*, Krenek cynically eliminates every living, warm human emotion. Here love is perverted into an animal, cattle-like concupiscence; there is nothing in it but filth, dirt, cold cruelty and sticky frog-like sexuality, combined with the dry rationalism of a biped calculating machine.

*V. Gorodinsky – 'Music of Spiritual
Poverty' (1950)*

'Fourth Symphony' – It is a pseudo-masterpiece, with about as much savour

to it as a pasteboard turkey.

*Virgil Thomson – 'New York Herald-
Tribune' (1947)*

Franz Liszt

'Faust' – It seems too much like a sheer nothing, on the grandest scale. It may be the Music of the Future, but it sounds remarkably like the Cacophony of the Present.

W. F. Apthorp – 'Musical Review' (1880)

Liszt's orchestral music is an insult to art. It is gaudy musical harlotry, savage and incoherent bellowing.

'Boston Gazette' (1872)

'Divina Commedia' – It appears that Liszt wasted much valuable time in committing this work to paper, as he could have saved his labour by instructing the orchestra to play for fifteen minutes anything that occurred to them at the moment, provided that they never relaxed from making the noisiest and most inharmonious charivari possible.

'Boston Gazette' (1880)

'Dante Symphony' – Music will have fallen irrevocably into a condition of dry rot before such a composition as Liszt's *Dante Symphony* can be received at any higher value than that of a solemn travesty. It is vulgar sensationalism run mad . . . The cacophony of the work is intolerable. It seems as though the composer had attempted to depict in music every moan and howl of pain ever heard by the human kind, from that caused by an agonising colic to that produced by the woes of gout, interspersed now and then by a choice selection of the various shades of expression of which the voice of the nocturnal cat is capable.

'Boston Gazette' (1886)

'Mephisto Waltz' – A hideous, incomprehensible jargon of noise, cacophony and eccentricity, musically valueless, and only interesting to ears that prefer confusion to meaning . . . It had about as much propriety on the programme after Schumann and Handel as a wild boar would have in a drawing-room.

'Boston Gazette' (1887)

'Mephisto Waltz' – The worst of all, and positively devilish. Such music is simply diabolical, and shuts out every ray of light or heaven from whence music sprang.

'Dwight's Journal of Music' (1870)

It is the peculiarity of Liszt to place his passages in those positions of the particular instruments where the most disagreeable sounds can be got. For example, *Hungaria*, the violinists are always capering and scraping nearly up to the bridge, where the tone is apt to resemble the forlorn wail of an amorous cat upon the tiles at midnight. If he has a passage for the bassoon, it is where the tone reminds one most naturally of the sight of a prize pig at a cattle show.

'Era' (1882)

'Inferno' – The clank of steam hammers, the rattle of express trains, the howling of a hurricane, the roar of the ocean, the cries of wild beasts, are tame compared to the terrible uproar to be found in the score of Liszt. *'Era' (1882)*

Liszt's bombast is bad; it is very bad; in fact there is only one thing worse in his music and that is his affected and false simplicity. *Philip Hale*

'Sonata in B Minor' – It is impossible to convey through words an idea of this musical monstrosity . . . At first I felt bewildered, then shocked, and finally overcome with irrestible hilarity. Here all criticism, all discussion must cease. Who has heard that, and finds it beautiful, is beyond help. *Eduard Hanslick (1881)*

'Hell' – The horrible chaos and noise can be compared to nothing but the upsetting of twenty thousand coal-scuttles.

Henry Labouchere – 'Truth' (1885)

'Faust' – Liszt has too often mistaken arrogant self-assertion for the prompting

of genius, confused obscurity for metaphysical profundity, and an insolent contempt of all classical precedents of musical composition for an innate originality that we have hitherto failed to find in his works, otherwise than in an disagreeable and repugnant sense.
'London Daily News' (1880)

'Faust' – Not even the weird fancy of Middle Ages painters has conjured up anything equivalent in repulsiveness to the noises of Liszt. The instruments seem to have gone mad with one consent. If this *Faust* symphony is music at all, it is music degraded.   *'Musical World' (1880)*

His music is all but unplayable by anyone but himself; it represents improvisations without order and without ideas, as pretentious as they are bizarre.
P. Scudo – 'Critique' (1852)

'Piano Concerto in A major' – A more chaotic effect could hardly have been produced had the notes been drawn, haphazard, out of the toy known as the musical kaleidoscope.
'Sporting News' (1874)

'Faust' – Rubbish that gave one a sensation like that produced by eating sour apples or chokeberries.
George T. Strong – 'Diary' (1867)

'Lamento E Trionfo' – The *Lamento* was expressed by dreary phrases of the cellos and double-basses that seemed suggestive of a cow in a strange land seeking an abducted calf and seeking it in vain. The *Trionfo*, by crashing brass chords, illustrated by fantasias on the triangle, apparently descriptive of the triumphant hero with his hands in his pockets, juggling his pennies and his bunch of keys.   *George T. Strong – Ibid*

Gustav Mahler

'Symphony of a Thousand [No. 8]' – If you are perverse enough to endure over an hour of masochistic aural flagellation, here's your chance! This grandiose *Symphony* with all its elephantine forces,

fatuous mysticism and screaming hysteria, adds up to a sublimely ridiculous minus-zero.
R. D. Darrell – 'Down Beat' (1952)

'Fourth Symphony' – The drooling and emasculated simplicity of Gustav Mahler! There is nothing to impress the musician except its grotesquerie . . . The writer of the present review frankly admits that to him it was one hour or more of the most painful musical torture to which he has been compelled to submit.
'Musical Courier' (1904)

'Fifth Symphony' – Mahler hadn't much to say in his *Fifth Symphony* and occupied a wondrous time in saying it. His manner is ponderous, his matter imponderable.
'New York Sun' (1913)

If there is any music that is eminently a routine, reflective, dusty sort of musical art, it is certainly Mahler's five latter symphonies. The musical 'Desert of Sahara' is surely to be found in these unhappy compositions. They are monsters of ennui. and by their very pretentiousness, their gargantuan dimensions, throw into relief Mahler's essential sterility. They seek to be colossal, and achieve vacuity.
Paul Rosenfeld – 'Musical Portraits' (1920)

Alas for the music of Mahler! What a fuss about nothing! What a to-do about a few commonplace musical thoughts, hardly worthy of being called ideas.
L. A. Sloper – 'Christian Science Monitor' (1924)

Jules Massenet
The vulgar and impassioned writings of Massenet.   *Gabriel Fauré (1909)*

Darius Milhaud
'Creation du Monde' – If we must have foreigners as guests, then at least they should be of a different sort than this totally impotent Darius Milhaud, whose arch-amateurish handwork leaves behind a sense of shame . . . This self-torturing impotence is here raised to such a degree

that any layman can diagnose it as hopeless. A more brutal self-accusation of sinning against the spirit of true art is difficult to find. In our times of prevention of cruelty to animals, this sort of thing should really be prevented.
Max Chop – 'Signale' (1929)

'Maximilian' – The composer knows the grammar, the spelling and the language; but he can speak only Esperanto and Volapuk. It is a work of a Communist travelling salesman.
P. B. Gheusi – 'Le Figaro' (1932)

Modest Mussorgsky
'A Night on the Bald Mountain' – As hideous a thing as we have ever heard . . . an orgy of ugliness and an abomination. May we never hear it again!
'Musical Times' (1898)

'Boris Godunov' – Cacophony in Five Acts and Seven Scenes.
Nicolas Soloviev (1874)

'Boris Godunov' – I consign it from the bottom of my heart to the devil; it is the most insipid and base parody on music.
Pyotr Tchaikovsky – 'Letter' (1874)

Mussorgsky is a limited individual devoid of any desire of educating himself. His is a low nature, rough, crude and coarse . . . He flaunts his illiteracy and is proud of his ignorance. So he dashes off whatever comes, hit or miss. A sad spectacle!
Pyotr Tchaikovsky – 'Letter' (1878)

Wolfgang Amadeus Mozart
'Cosi Fan Tutti' – I liked it. The costumes were heavenly! But couldn't they have got some other music for it?   *Anon*

Piddling on flannel.   *Noël Coward*

'The Marriage of Figaro' – Far too noisy, my dear Mozart. Far too many notes.
Archduke Ferdinand

Sergei Prokofiev
'The Love for Three Oranges' – The orchestra is a noble instrument, but it has

seldom been put to so ignoble use as it is in *The Love for Three Oranges*.
Richard Aldrich – 'New York Times' (1922)

'Classical Symphony' – The repellently vulgar performance of Prokofiev's *Classical Symphony* was given heavyweight treatment, with every point so grossly underlined that every scrap of wit vanished.   *'Guardian'*

'Scythian Suite' – A splendid tribute was paid to his *Scythian Suite* in Petrograd by Alexandre Glazunov. The poor tortured classicist walked out of the hall during the first performance of the work. No one walked out of the Aeolian Hall, New York, but several respectable pianists ran out.   *'Musical America' (1918)*

As far back as the days of Hans von Bulow, the Russians were noted for their addiction to dissonantal din in music. The thing gradually came to be a sort of sport – as sportsmen have brought about the evolution of the ugliest possible bulldog, bestowing prizes on those that were most so. There is fierce competition among the composers for this award. The latest comer is always acclaimed as the worst ever. One of these worst evers was exhibited in the Aeolian Hall yesterday afternoon. His name is Sergei Prokofiev.
'New York World' (1918)

'Suggestion Diabolique' – The present writer has heard much more cruel things than Prokofiev's compositions. Seldom, however, has he heard compositions so devoid of all musical interest . . . The recipe for this sort of composition is as simple as that for boiling an egg. Write anything that comes into your head no matter how commonplace. Then change all the accidentals, putting flats in the place of sharps, and vice-versa, and the thing's done.   *'New York World' (1918)*

Giacomo Puccini
'La Tosca' – At first hearing much, perhaps most, of 'Tosca' sounds exceedingly, even ingeniously, ugly.

Every now and then, one comes across the most ear-flaying of chords.

> *W. F. Apthorp – 'Boston Evening Transcipt' (1901)*

'La Bohéme' – Silly and inconsequential incidents and dialogues are daubed over with splotches of instrumental colour without reason and without effect, except the creation of a sense of boisterous excitement and confusion . . . Here the expression is superficial and depends upon strident phrases pounded out by hitting each note a blow on the head as it escapes from the mouths of singers or the accompanying instruments.

> *H. E. Kreihbel – 'New York Triubune' (1900)*

Sergei Rachmaninov

'Symphony in E Minor' – One could hardly escape the idea that the whole affair was some great mechanical contrivance for hypnotising the audience with a complicated scheme of mechanical motion driven by some tremendous engine whose squeakings, and wheezings, and crashings were synchronously adjusted thereto. Rachmaninov – no more for me! *Letter to 'New York Sun' (1914)*

'Piano Concerto No. 2' – It is a little too much like a mournful banqueting on jam and honey.

> *Paul Rosenfeld – 'New Republic' (1919)*

'Rhapsody on a Theme of Paganini' – Sounds like a plague of insects in the Amazon valley, sometimes like a miniature of the Day of Judgment . . . and for a change goes lachrymose.

> *Pitts Sanborn – 'New York World-Telegram' (1936)*

Maurice Ravel

'Equisses Enfantines' – Who can unravel Ravel? If these *Equisses Enfantines* received their proper title, they would be labelled 'Scenes from a Second Childhood'. *Louis Elson – 'Boston Daily Advertiser' (1913)*

To hear a whole programme of Ravel's works is like watching some midget or pygmy doing clever, but very small things, within a limited scope.

> *'The Times' (1924)*

'String Quartet' – Ravel is content with one theme which has the musical potency of one of those tunes which the curious may hear in a Chinese theatre, shrieked out by an ear-splitting clarinet. This theme serves him for four movements during which there is about as much emotional nuance as warms a problem in algebra. It is a drastic dose of wormwood and assafoetida.

> *'New York Tribune' (1906)*

'Bolero' – Although Ravel's biography does not mention it, I feel sure that at the age of three he swallowed a musical snuff-box, and at nine he must have been frightened by a bear. To both phenomena he offers repeated testimony: he is constantly tinkling high on the harps and celesta, or is growling low in the bassoons and double-basses. *Edward Robinson – 'The Naïve Ravel' (1932)*

Max Reger

'Piano Concerto' – A most inflated, pretentious bag of wind, with a very heavily scored and somewhat brutally effective piano part. The orchestration is swollen, thick and prevailingly in bad taste. Little bits of ideas are pretentiously and noisily bunched together, and they get nowhere. What incredibly bad taste, and poor invention!

> *Olin Downes – 'New York Times' (1950)*

'Quartet Opus 109' – Looks like music, it sounds like music, it might even taste like music; yet it remains, stubbornly, not music.

> *Irving Kolodin – 'New York Sun' (1934)*

'Trio' – This pretentious rubbish will probably not be heard again in this enlightened town. *'New York Sun' (1908)*

This Reger is a sarcastic, churlish fellow, bitter and pedantic and rude. He is a sort of musical Cyclops, a strong, ugly creature bulging with knotty and unshapely muscles, an ogre of composition . . . a swollen myopic beetle with thick lips and sullen expression. His works are stereotyped, stale terribly quickly. They are mathematical problems and solutions, sheer brain-spun and unlyrical works.

Paul Rosenfeld – 'Musical Portraits' (1920)

Wallingford Riegger

'Dichotomy' – It sounded as though a pack of rats were being slowly tortured to death, while, from time to time, a dying cow moaned.

Walter Abendroth – 'Allgemeine Musikzeitung' (1932)

Nikolai Rimsky-Korsakov

'Scheherazade' – If the fair Scheherazade related her stories as confusedly and unmeaningly, not to say cacophonously, as the composer has related them musically, the sultan would have ordered her to be bowstrung or have her head lopped off after the second or third night. That he would have permitted her to gabble away, Korsakov-wise, for two years, eight months and odd days, is wholly improbable. The music suggested a parvenu making an ostentatious display of his newly-acquired wealth by surrounding himself with gorgeously inharmonious furniture and wearing an excess of diamonds, in the belief that they will obliterate all indications of his innate vulgarity. *'Boston Herald' (1897)*

'Scheherazade' – It was performed to the amazement of every concert-goer who had been brought up in the paths of Bach and righteousness yet no one dare say that the mountain brought forth a mouse; it was rather a white elephant that emerged.

Louis Elson – 'Boston Daily Advertiser' (1897)

'Sadko' – Programme music in its most unashamed form, a product of barbarism mated with utter cynicism. Such poverty of musical thought, and such impudence of orchestration, we have seldom heard.

Eduard Hanslick (1872)

Edmund Rubbra

'Lauda Sion' – Lauda Sion is dismally stodgy. *'The Observer'*

Carl Ruggles

'Sun-Treader' – Should surely have been renamed 'Latrine-Treader.' This title comes nearer to the character of the music. I for one had only the impression of bowel constrictions in an atonal Tristanesque ecstasy.

Paul Schwers – 'Allgemeine Musikzeitung' (1932)

Camille Saint-Saëns

'Danse Macabre' – Saint-Saëns has succeeded in producing effects of the most horrible, hideous and disgusting sort. Manufacture would be the more proper term; and in some cases, very clumsy manufacture.

'London Daily News' (1879)

'Samson and Delilah' – The most kindly reception has been one of resignation to the inevitable – as one accepts, influenza, fog in November, or a tainted egg in the ration. *'London Musical Opinion' (1953)*

'Deluge' – Bears utter vapidity, spiritual and intellectual poverty, and hopeless emptiness stamped upon its forehead. Every possible noise, whistling, howling, sighing, rustling, roaring, clashing, banging, that can be drawn from a combination of instruments is made for the benefit of the dumbfounded listeners.

'New York Tribune' (1879)

It is one's duty to hate with all possible fervour the empty and ugly in art; and I hate Saint-Saëns the composer with a hate that is perfect.

J. F. Runciman – 'Saturday Review' (1896)

He has, I suppose, written as much music as any composer ever did; he has certainly written more rubbish than any one I can think of. It is the worst, most rubbishy kind of rubbish.

J. F. Runciman – 'Saturday Review' (1898)

Erik Satie

A couple of instruments short of the full orchestra, old Erik.

Martin James – 'Sunday Times' (1992)

Arnold Schoenberg

'Chamber Symphony' – I can only compare the harmonic structure of the work to a field of weeds and turnips mixed together. *Anon Berlin critic (1913)*

'Pierrot Lunaire' – Arnold Schoenberg may be either crazy as a loon, or he may be a very clever trickster who is apparently determined to cause a sensation at any cost. His *Pierrot Lunaire* is the last word in cacophony and musical anarchy . . . A musical, or rather, unmusical ensemble discoursed the most ear-splitting combinations of tones that ever desecrated the walls of a Berlin music hall.

Arthur M. Abell – 'Musical Courier' (1912)

'Pierrot Lunaire' – The impression upon the unattached music lover is simply null, or more or less wearisomely repugnant.
Richard Aldrich – 'New York Times' (1923)

Behind the works of Schoenberg I see only an inhuman lunar landscape; and I cannot warm to it.

Sir Arthur Bliss – 'Music and Letters' (1951)

'Five Orchestral Pieces' – If there is anything more utterly monstrous, more hideous and more artistically squalid than Schoenberg's *Five Orchestral Pieces*, it can only be some other composition by their creator or by one of his disciples. A cat walking down the keyboard of a piano could evolve a melody more lovely than any which came from the Viennese composer's consciousness.

Felix Borowski – 'Chicago Record-Herald' (1913)

'Five Orchestral Pieces' – The normal, that is the usual, ear however, might decide that Schoenberg's emotions are fit subjects for a vacuum cleaner . . . Each of the *Five Orchestral Pieces* ends with every

man choosing his note as by lottery. This is economical music, for what is the need of rehearsal? *'Boston Globe' (1914)*

'Five Orchestral Pieces' – The heroic steed of Wagnerism cavorting amidst a Covent Garden conflagration has been grotesquely diminished to a gaunt and fleshless sea-horse, poking furtively among atonal weeds. *Harriet Cohen – 'Music's Handmaid' (1936)*

'Prometheus' – The product of a once fine composer suffering from mental derangement, and Schoenberg's lucubrations are simply nothing at all. You cannot expect either a journalist or his public to see any difference between a lunatic and an idiot.

Frederick Corder – 'Musical Quarterly' (1915)

If this is 'music of the future', one can only say that Schoenberg is about a thousand years ahead of his time, for the ear, as well as the brain, cannot readily discern the significance, if there is any, of such music. *'Daily Mail' (1912)*

'Five Orchestral Pieces' – To one critic, it suggested 'feeding time at the zoo or a farmyard in great activity while pigs are being ringed and geese strangled.' On another the identical section of the work produced the impression of 'a village fair with possibly a blind clarinettist playing at random'. The same listener heard sounds as of 'sawing steel' and the 'distant noise of an approaching train alternately with the musical sobs of a dynamo.'

'Daily Telegraph' (1914)

'Five Orchestral Pieces' – It sounds like a pandemonium of cross-eyed devils playing a big score without transposing instruments and with careful regard of each and every devil.

Eric De Lamarter – 'Inter-Ocean' (1913)

'Chamber Symphony' – Self-torture of a flagellant who whips himself with a cat-o'-nine-tails, while cursing himself! When a conglomeration of horns pushes

upwards through the strings, it sounds like the words, 'You monster!' A hideous modern song of the scourge! A sort of cat music, whining, wailing, desperate.
Ernst Decsey – 'Signale' (1914)

'Five Orchestral Pieces' – At best, it appears as the music of raw and tortured nerves. *Olin Downes – 'Boston Post' (1914)*

'Variations for Orchestra Op. 31' – Tortuous, meagre-hued music, anaemic music. It is geometrical music, important only on paper; hideous, without vitality, and signifying nothing that matters.
Olin Downes – 'New York Times' (1929)

'Suite for String Orchestra' – A pale monument of lifeless theory, an empty and unbeautiful exhibition. A fatigued person might thus make a show of gymnastics. One! Two! Three! Four! Up go the arms and down go the legs, up go the legs and down go the arms. It is hollow; it is ersatz. Ersatz music, music on and of paper.
Olin Downes – 'New York Times' (1935)

A composer who operates on the theory that if you know how to put a bunch of notes on a piece of score paper you are, presto, a composer.
Rudolph Elie – 'Boston Herald'

'Chamber Symphony' – It never touches any emotion save curiosity, never arouses any mood save speculation on how the conductor can conduct it and how the musicians can count the bars.
Rudolph Elie – 'Boston Herald' (1950)

'Five Orchestral Pieces' – It has been said that it is difficult to score a noise well. In his *Five Orchestral Pieces*, Schoenberg has certainly succeeded in doing this. There were passages that suggested a bomb in a poultry-yard; cackles, shrieks, caterwauls, and, then – crash! *Louis Elson – 'Boston Daily Advertiser' (1914)*

In Schoenberg's later works, all the laws of construction, observed by the masters, from Bach to Wagner, are ignored, insulted, trampled on. The statue of Venus, the Goddess of Beauty, is knocked from its pedestal and replaced by the stone image of the Goddess of Ugliness, with the hideous features of a Hottentot hag.
Henry T. Finck – 'Musical Progress' (1923)

'Quartet in D Major' – The first work on last night's programme was the 'Quartet' allegedly 'in D major'. Of course, it was in no key . . . It was like the babbling of a deranged man. *Glenn D. Gunn – 'Washington Times-Herald' (1952)*

It is the decomposition of the art, I thought, as I held myself close in my seat . . . What did I hear? At first, the sound of delicate china shivering into a thousand luminous fragments. In the welter of tonalities that bruised each other as they passed and repassed, in the preliminary grip of enharmonies that almost made the ears bleed, the eyes water, the scalp freeze, I could not get a control on myself. Schoenberg is the cruellest of all composers for he mingles with his music sharp daggers at white heat, with which he pares away tiny slices of his victim's flesh. *James G. Huneker – 'New York Times' (1913)*

Every composer has his aura; the aura of Arnold Schoenberg is, for me, the aura of original depravity, of subtle ugliness, of basest egoism, of hatred and contempt, of cruelty, and of the mystic grandiose . . . If such music-making is ever to become accepted, then I long for Death the Releaser. *James G. Huneker – Ibid*

'Pelleas and Melisande' – Schoenberg's symphonic poem is not just filled with wrong notes: it is a fifty-minute long protracted wrong note. This is to be taken literally. What else may hide behind these cacophonies is quite impossible to find out. *Ludwig Karpath – 'Signale' (1905)*

Schoenberg sounds like a musical dead-end when compared to Debussy.
Michael Kennedy – 'Sunday Telegraph' (1992)

'Three Piano Pieces Op. 11' – Whether the pianist played the pieces well or badly, I cannot judge, because in this music the listener cannot distinguish between right and wrong.

Hugo Leichtentritt – 'Signale' (1911)

'Five Orchestral Pieces' – I must reject completely the five orchestral pieces of 1909. These sounds conjure up hideous visions; monstrous apparitions threaten – there is no joy and light, nothing that makes life worth living! How miserable would our descendants be, if this joyless gloomy Schoenberg would ever become the mode of expression of their time. Is this destined to become the art of the future? *Hugo Leichtentritt – 'Signale' (1912)*

Imagine the scene of bleating sheep in *Don Quixote*, the sacrificial procession in *Elektra*, and the scene of the opponents in *Heldenleben* all played together, and you will have Schoenberg's idea of orchestral colour . . . We must be content with the composer's own assertion that he has depicted his own experiences, for which he has our heartfelt sympathy.

'London Daily News' (1912)

'Five Orchestral Pieces' – The music resembled the wailings of a tortured soul, and suggested nothing so much as the disordered fancies of delirium or the fearsome, imaginary terrors of a highly nervous infant.   *'London Globe' (1912)*

Schoenberg, in short, is to Strauss at his wildest what Strauss is to Mozart. He does not even end his pieces with recognisable chords.

'Manchester Guardian' (1912)

Schoenberg states: 'I write what I feel in my heart.' If this is really so, we can only assume that from 1908 or so, Schoenberg has been suffering from some unclassifiable and peculiarly virulent form of cardiac disease.

'Musical Opinion' (1949)

'Pierrot Lunaire' – To some of us its 612 bars of etiolated and emasculated shreds

of sound represent the nadir of decadence.   *'Musical Opinion' (1949)*

'Quartet Op. 37' – Mathematics are not music, and to non-dodecaphonists the effect of Schoenberg's works on the ear is one of unintelligible ugliness . . . The multitudinous freak effects and frenetic caperings defeat their own ends by becoming monotonous and afford little beyond a quasi-masochistic pleasure to the uninitiated.   *'Musical Opinion' (1952)*

The name of Schoenberg is, as far as the British public is concerned, mud.

'Musical Times' (1930)

Arnold Schoenberg is the musical Von Tirpitz of Germany. Having failed to capture a hostile world by his early campaign carried on in accordance with the international laws of music, he began to torpedo the eardrums of his enemies, as well as neutrals, with deadly dissonances.

'New York Evening Post' (1915)

'Pelleas and Melisande' – In *Pelleas* he boxes the ears of his hearers with some extremely rude and loud dissonances. He also introduces some bleating noise, which sounded as if a sheep or calf were hidden under the stage.

'New York Evening Post' (1915)

'Piano Pieces Op. 11' – There was a time when the keys of church organs were so wide and so hard to work that fists and elbows were used to press them down. Schoenberg's *Piano Pieces* sounded just as if they were played that way. For a minute of two that sort of thing is quite funny.   *'New York Post' (1915)*

Some of his pages resemble a kitchen fly-paper during the rush-hour on a hot August afternoon.

C. W. Orr – 'The Music Review' (1948)

'Violin Concerto' – A piece that combines the best sound effects of a hen yard at feeding time, a brisk morning in Chinatown and practice hour at a busy

music conservatory. The effect on the vast majority of hearers is that of a lecture on the fourth dimension delivered in Chinese.   *Edwin H. Schloss –*
'Philadelphia Record' (1940)

'Three Piano Pieces Op. 11' – Schoenberg kills tonal perception; his sounds are no longer derived from one another. Debussy only threatens; Schoenberg carries out the threat. His musical progressions represent an anarchistic wandering in colours. They are the result of error followed through with ingenious consistency.   *'Signale' (1910)*

He writes the music of the future millenia, when the sun will hang in the skies only as a glowing red night lamp, and our great-grandchildren will skate on the equator, and will dance in a Greenland dance hall to waltz music in quarter-tones.   *'Signale' (1912)*

'Chamber Symphony' – Fifteen brave musicians presented to us Schoenberg's *Chamber Symphony*. 'Chamber of Horrors Symphony' would be a more fitting title.
August Spanuth – 'Signale' (1913)

'Pierrot Lunaire' – If this is the music of the future, then I pray my Creator not to let me live to hear it again.
Otto Taubamann – 'Borsen-Courier'

'Five Orchestral Pieces' – It was like a poem in Tibetan, not one single soul could possibly have understood it . . . At the conclusion, half the audience hissed.
'The Times' (1912)

Robert Schumann
Schumann is essentially as trivial in idea and as poor in resource as the most intolerable of the Philistines.
'The Athenaeum' (1856)

His general style betrays the patchiness and want of fluency of a tyro; while the forced and unnatural terms of cadence and progression declare neither more nor

less than the convulsive efforts of one who has never properly studied his art, to hide the deficiencies of early education under a mist of pompous swagger.
H. F. Chorley – 'Musical World' (1853)

'Carnival Music' – We can find nothing of the carnival in these fourteen little pieces; which are as insignificant in scale as in a child's lesson, yet without the prettiness and the character which alone make such trifles pass.
H. F. Chorley – 'The Athenaeum' (1856)

Schumann went for his melody to a dried-up well. Schumann's faculty of invention was next door to null; and Schumann, though laboriously studied, was at the best, a half-formed musician.
'Musical World' (1864)

Aleksandr Scriabin
'Second Symphony' – I think there was an error in the programme: instead of 'Symphony' they should have printed 'Cacophony'.
Anton Arensky – 'Letter' (1902)

'Poem of Ecstasy' – Some of this ecstasy was extremely bitter, while some of it reminded me of the ecstasy of the too convivial gentleman who thought that the air was filled with green monkeys with crimson eyes and sparkling tails, a kind of ecstasy that is sold in Russia at two roubles a bottle.
Louis Elson – 'Boston Daily Advertiser'
(1910)

As a kind of drug, no doubt Scriabin's music has a certain significance, but it is wholly superfluous . . . Why must we degrade an art into a spiritual narcotic? Why is it more artistic to use eight horns and five trumpets than to use eight brandies and five double whiskeys?
Cecil Gray – 'Contemporary Music' (1924)

'Poem of Ecstasy' – Most of the time, the violins were whimpering and wailing like lost souls, while strange undulating and formless melodies roved about in the

woodwind. A solo violin spoke occasionally, growing more and more plaintive, and finally being swallowed in a chaos of acid harmonies with violins screaming in agony overhead . . . It all seemed far more like several other things than ecstasy.

W. J. Henderson – 'New York Sun' (1908)

'*Divine Poem*' – The work of a neurotic, a Fourth of July celebration in which every member of the orchestra has signed a Declaration of Independence and makes just as much noise as he possible can.

'Musical America' (1907)

'*Prometheus*' – All the elaborate sanity of technique will not hide the fact that we are in the atmosphere of the revivalist meeting, where zealots speak with tongues and utter strange words divorced from their plain meaning.

'The Times' (1919)

Dimitri Shostakovich

'*Ninth Symphony*' – A farrago of circus tunes, gallop rhythms, and dated harmonic quirks whose smart cleverness resembles the tea-table talk of an ultra-precocious child.

E. Chapman – 'Tempo' (1946)

'*May Day Symphony*' – In impregnating his *Symphony* with political and economic doctrine, the composer unfortunately neglected to transmit to it any musical ideas . . . If this brainless and trivial music with its unrelieved indigence, its blatant banality, its naïve portentousness, is the result of impregnating music with Marxist ideology, all one can say is that aesthetic birth control in Russia is a lamentable failure.

Lawrence Gilman – 'New York Herald Tribune' (1933)

'*Lady Macbeth of Mzensk*' – Shostakovich is without doubt the foremost composer of pornographic music in the history of the art . . . The whole is little better than a glorification of the sort of stuff that filthy

pencils write on lavatory walls.

W. J. Henderson – 'New York Sun' (1935)

'*Fourth Symphony*' – The subject of the fugue is absolutely meaningless and aimless. Its wanderings can continue interminably. The appearance of the second voice does not contribute any new quality to the fugue. Meaninglessness is multiplied by meaninglessness, and instead of one unpleasantness the listener experiences two unpleasantnesses.

Marian Koval – 'Sovietskaya Musica' (1948)

'*Lady Macbeth of Mzensk*' – The music quacks, grunts, growls, strangles itself in order to represent the amatory scenes as naturalistically as possible. 'Love' is smeared all over the opera in the most vulgar manner.

'Pravda' (1936)

Jean Sibelius

'*Fourth Symphony*' – A tangle of the most dismal dissonances. It eclipses the saddest and sourest moments of Debussy.

'Boston Journal' (1913)

'*Fourth Symphony*' – The *Symphony* is neither fish, flesh nor fowl – nor good red herring . . . The third movement is even more incoherent than the first – it would take a Philadelphia lawyer to find any sense of form in it. It sounds like the improvisation of an unskilled organist.

W. H. Humiston – 'Musical America' (1913)

'*Second Symphony*' – Vulgar, self-indulgent and provincial beyond all description.

Virgil Thomson – 'New York Herald Tribune' (1940)

Dame Edith Smyth

It's bad if they don't perform your operas – but when they do, it's far worse.

Camille Saint-Saëns

Richard Strauss

'*Elektra*' – Words fail me and I'm going

home at once to play the chord of C major twenty times over to satisfy myself that it still exists. *Anon British composer*

'Ein Heldenleben' – In no other work has Strauss so deliberately affronted the ear with long-continued din and discord or has so consciously used ugliness in music to represent conceptions of ugliness.
Richard Aldrich – 'New York Times' (1905)

'Also Sprach Zarathustra' – The work is unhealthy; it suffers severely from basstubaculosis; and its utterances are too often basstubathetic. The score is at its worst in 'The Dance Song', a species of symbolic waltz, ushered in with unheard-of caterwauling and with a gruesomeness of execrably ugly dissonances . . . a realistic tone-picture of a sufferer from the worst pangs of sea-sickness.
'Boston Herald' (1897)

'Elektra' – The music reproduces sounds of smashing glass and china, the bursting of bottles, the clashing of shovels and tongs, the groaning and creaking of rusty hinges and stubborn doors, avalanches in the mountains, the crying of babies, the squealing of rats, the grunting of pigs, the bellowing of cattle, the howling of cats and the roaring of wild beasts.
'Boston Herald' (1910)

'Till Eulenspiegel' – Musical obscenity of the most unique and remarkable description; in form a crazy-quilt, in orchestral colour much the same . . . It is a most inexplicable hodge-podge. *Eulenspiegel*'s daily beverage was doubtless beer, and the music is unmistakably beerish.
O. L. Capen – 'Boston Journal' (1896)

Strauss may be characterised in four words: little talent, much impudence.
Cesar Cui – 'Letter' (1904)

'Also Sprach Zarathustra' – The chaos is entitled 'Thus Spake Zarathustra', but Zarathustra shouted and whispered,

mumbled and roared, did everything but speak.
Louis Elson – 'Boston Daily Advertiser' (1897)

'Ein Heldenleben' – We cannot rid ourselves of the idea that the attempt to play in two different keys at the same time is as disastrous as the attempt of two railroad trains to pass each other on the same track. After the Strauss work, the orchestra rinsed our ears with Beethoven's *Second Symphony.*
Louis Elson – 'Boston Daily Advertiser' (1901)

'Elektra' – Strauss lets loose an orchestral riot that suggests a murder scene in a Chinese theatre . . . If the reader who has not heard *Elektra* desires to witness something that looks as its orchestral score sounds, let him, next summer, poke a stick into an ant hill and watch the black insects darting, angry and bewildered, biting and clawing, in a thousand directions at once. It's amusing for ten minutes, but not for two hours.
H. T. Finck – 'New York Post' (1910)

'Ein Heldenleben' – The climax of everything that is ugly, cacophonous, blatant and erratic, the most perverse music I ever heard in all my life, is reached in the chapter 'The Hero's Battlefield'. The man who wrote this outrageously hideous noise, no longer deserving of the word music, is either a lunatic, or he is rapidly approaching idiocy.
Otto Floersheim – 'Musical Courier' (1899)

'Der Rosenkavalier' – A worn-out, dissipated demi-mondaine, with powdered face, rouged lips, false hair, and a hideous leer.
Cecil Gray – 'Contemporary Music' (1924)

Strauss uses music as the vehicle of expressing everything but music; for he has little invention, and his musical thoughts are of little worth.
Philip Hale – 'Boston Post' (1891)

'*Salome*' – If that is art, will somebody set to music that department of Armour's packing house in which they make the sausage? *William R. Hearst –*
'*New York Evening Journal*' *(1907)*

The compositions of Richard Strauss do not even leave a clean taste in one's mouth . . . Strauss is a musical Maeterlinck, a tonal Ibsen.
W. J. Henderson – 'New York Times' (1897)

'*Till Eulenspiegel*' – You may have heard *Till Eulenspiegel*. No gentleman would have written that thing. It is positively scurrilous. There are places for such music, but surely not before miscellaneous assemblages of ladies and gentlemen.
W. J. Henderson – 'Musical Record' (1900)

His music often suggests a man who comes to a social reception unkempt, with hands unwashed, cigar in mouth, hat on, and who sits down and puts his feet on the table. No boor ever violated all the laws of etiquette as Strauss violates all the laws of musical composition.
W. J. Henderson – 'New York Sun' (1907)

'*Salome*' – If this be art, then let the music of the future find her mission in sewer, pest-house and brothel.
W. J. Henderson – 'New York Sun' (1907)

'*Salome*' – Music that offends the ear and rasps the nerves like fiddlestrings played on by a coarse file . . . There is not a whiff of fresh and healthy air blowing through *Salome* except that which exhales from the cistern.
H. E. Krehbiel – 'New York Times' (1907)

'*Salome*' – The deplorable 'Dance of the Seven Veils' with its evocation of a second-rate vamp of the silent film days.
Constant Lambert – 'The Listener' (1938)

Strauss is impotent to create anything new, but as you cannot abuse people in music, he abuses the divine art itself.
'*New York Evening Post*' *(1897)*

Mr Strauss' counterpoint may be compared generally to a motor car charging through the traffic in Cheapside at noon. '*Referee*' *(1905)*

Strauss' music is singularly flat and hollow and dun, joyless and soggy . . . He is indeed the false dawn of modern music.
Paul Rosenfeld – 'The Dial' (1920)

'*Till Eulenspiegel*' – Dreary though most musical humour is, Strauss' is the dreariest that has ever bored me. I contemptuously dismiss *Till Eulenspiegel* as a pretentious piece of smart shoddy.
J. F. Runciman – 'Saturday Review' (1896)

'*Also Sprach Zarathustra*' – A hopeless failure from the musical point of view.
'*The Times*' *(1897)*

Igor Stravinsky

'*Le Sacre du Printemps*' –
Who wrote this fiendish Rite of Spring,
What right had he to write the thing,
Against our helpless ears to fling
Its crash, clash, cling, clang, bing, bang, bing?
He who would write the 'Rite of Spring',
If I be right, by right should swing.
'*Boston Herald*' *(1924)*

'*Le Sacre du Printemps*' – A tone picture of spring-fever in a zoo.
'*Boston Herald*' *(1924)*

The only real form in his work is that kind of primitive repetition which birds and babies also do very well.
Rutland Boughton – 'Musical Times' (1929)

'*Fireworks*' – Stravinsky hurls a whole orchestra at the head of the public, and calls it music . . . What some of the brass dissonances meant, we could not imagine, unless the man who lit the pieces had burned his fingers and made a few resultant remarks.
Louis Elson – 'Boston Daily Advertiser' (1914)

'*History of a Soldier*' – The nearest that any composer of consequence has ever come to achieving complete infantilism in a score that is presumably intended to be taken with some degree of seriousness.
Lawrence Gilman – 'New York Herald Tribune' (1928)

'*Petrushka*' – It is but a disjointed series of funny sounds, squeaks and squawks, imitations of wheezy hand organ and hurdy-gurdy, grunting snatches of tune from a bassoon, clatterings of a xylophone and whirring noises. If we must have music of this kind in the concert-room let us by all means also have moving pictures to explain it.
H. E. Krehbiel – 'New York Tribune' (1923)

Practically the whole of Stravinsky's works are already on the shelf, and they will remain there until a few jaded neurotics once more feel a desire to eat ashes and fill their belly with the east wind.   *'Musical Times' (1923)*

'*Symphony for Wind Instruments*' *written in memory of Debussy* – I had no idea Stravinsky disliked Debussy so much as this. If my own memories of a friend were as painful as Stravinsky's of Debussy seem to be, I would try to forget him.
Ernest Newman – 'Musical Times' (1921)

'*Le Sacre du Printemps*' – Without description or programme, the work might have suggested a New Year's Eve rally of moonshine addicts and the simple pastimes of early youth and maidens, circumspectly attired in a fig leaf apiece.
'North American' (1922)

'*Cantata for Mezzo-Soprano, Tenor, Choir and Five Instruments*' – A mercilessly dull, wholly unleavened essay in boredom . . . The most invigorating sound I heard was a restive neighbour winding his watch.
Philadelphia Evening News

'*Le Sacre du Printemps*' – Listening to the 'Rite of Spring' might be regarded as

more of an affliction than a privilege.
'Philadelphia Evening News' (1922)

'*Concertino*' – Stravinsky music is a drab, rasping, tired, shuffle and breakdown. It is like a locomotive which has fallen off the track, making its wheels revolve in air. Rhythms prolong themselves out of sheer inertia: pound on, wearily.
Paul Rosenfeld – 'The Dial' (1921)

He has reduced melody to the primitive, inarticulate refrain of a Zulu, and has converted the orchestra into a gigantic rattle, the toy and mouthpiece of the new savage.
Lazare Saminsky – 'Music of Our Day' (1939)

'*Le Sacre du Printemps*' – Stravinsky is mechanism become music . . . Of course, it sounds like cacophony because I'm not used to it, and it probably sounds all alike for the same reason that Chinamen all look alike to me: I'm not that well acquainted.
Deems Taylor – 'The Dial' (1920)

Pyotr Tchaikovsky
'*Slavic March*' – One feels that the composer must have made a bet, for all that his professional reputation was worth, that he would write the most absolutely hideous thing that had ever been put on paper, and won it, too.
'Boston Evening Transcript' (1883)

'*Fifth Symphony*' – The furious peroration sounds like nothing so much as a horde of demons struggling in a torrent of brandy, the music growing drunker and drunker. Pandemonium, delirium tremens, raving, and above all, noise worse confounded!
'Boston Evening Transcript' (1892)

'*Eugene Onegin*' – As an opera, it is still-born and absolutely incompetent.
Cesar Cui – 'Nedelya' (1884)

'*1812 Overture*' – A sweet little slumber song, on second hearing, or rather second

deafening, was as loud as the explosion of a powder-mill. The fight between the Marseillaise and the Russian hymn came to an end in one round, the former being knocked out completely. One can best sum up this remarkable earthquake by saying that it is sound and fury signifying – nothing!
Louis Elson –
'Boston Daily Advertiser' (1896)

'Violin Concerto' – The violin is no longer played; it is pulled, torn, drubbed . . . Friedrich Vischer once observed, speaking of obscene pictures, that they stink to the eye. Tchaikovsky's *Violin Concerto* gives us for the first time the hideous notion that there can be music that stinks to the ear.
Eduard Hanslick – 'Neue Freie Presse'
(1881)

'Violin Concerto' – An accumulation of discords, confused climaxes and dressed-up trivialities, covered by the national flag of the most barbarous sort of Russian nihilism. *Theodore Helm – 'Signale' (1881)*

We know that butter comes from cream but how long must we watch the churning arm?
Charles Ives

'Fourth Symphony' – Tittle-tattle in motley orchestration . . . The composer's twaddle perturbed my mood. The confusion in brass and the abuse of the kettledrums drove me away.
'Kleines Journal'

'Fifth Symphony' – In the last movement, the composer's Calmuck blood got the better of him, and slaughter, dire and bloody, swept across the storm-driven score.
'Musical Courier' (1889)

'Francesca da Rimini' – A musical monster . . . ear-flaying horror.
'Musical Review' (1880)

'Fourth Symphony' – If Tchaikovsky had called his Symphony 'A Sleigh Ride Through Siberia' no one would have found this title inappropriate.
'New York Post' (1890)

'Piano Concerto' – In at least a dozen instances the entry of the piano is an impertinent intrusion permitted by the composer because the pianist had to be given something to do.
J. F. Runciman – 'Saturday Review' (1899)

Edgard Varèse

'Ionization' – After hearing Varèse's *Ionization*, I am anxious that you should examine my composition scored for two stoves and a kitchen sink. I've named it 'Concussion Symphony', descriptive of the disintegration of an Irish potato under the influence of a powerful atomiser.
Iona L. Bunk – Letter (1933)

'Hyperprism' – Reminded us of election night, a menagerie or two and a catastrophe in a boiler factory.
Olin Downes – 'New York Times' (1924)

It remained for Varèse to shatter the calm of a Sabbath night, to arouse angry emotions and tempt men to retire to the back of the theatre and perform tympanal concertos on each others' faces.
W. J. Henderson – 'New York Herald'
(1923)

'Octandre' – It shrieked, it grunted, it chortled, it mewed, it barked – and it turned all the eight instruments into contortions. It was just a ribald outbreak of noise.
W. J. Henderson – 'New York Herald'
(1924)

The lover of art can only declare his faith that the time will come when all his decompositions will be swept violently down a steep place into the sea.
W. J. Henderson – 'New York Sun' (1924)

'Hyperprism' – I should say what was at the back of Mr Varèse's mind was an alarm of fire at the Zoo – the lion roaring, the hyena howling, the monkeys chattering, the parrots squealing, with the curses of the distracted attendants cutting through them all.
Ernest Newman – 'New York Evening Post'
(1924)

'Integrales' – It sounded a good deal like a combination of early morning in the Mott Haven freight yards, feeding time at the zoo and a Sixth Avenue trolley rounding a curve, with an intoxicated woodpecker thrown in for good measure.

Ernest Newman – *'New York Evening Sun'* (1925)

Giuseppe Verdi

Verdi was intended by nature for a composer, but I am afraid the genius given him – like girls kissing – is a decided waste of the raw material.

'Dwight's Journal of Music' (1855)

There has not yet appeared an Italian composer more incapable than Verdi of producing what is commonly known as melody. *'Gazette Musicale de Paris'* (1847)

'Macbeth' – His airs are such as a man born deaf would compose by calculation of the distances between notes and the intervals between them.

George T. Strong – *'Diary'* (1853)

Richard Wagner

'Ring' – The most colossal musical swindle that even Germany has ever produced.

Anon – *Letter, 'Musical World'* (1876)

'Ring' – I should like to see all the plot cut out, and the four operas run into one and got through in two hours and three-quarters. *James Agate*

'Tannhäuser' – The score resembles a book written without periods or commas; one doesn't know when to take breath. The listener suffocates. *D. F. A. Auber*

'Lohengrin' – After hearing it, I had a splitting headache, and all through the night I dreamt of a goose.

Mily Balakirev – *'Letter'* (1868)

If we are permitted to express a plain opinion about Wagner, it is music with a stomach ache. It has knots and cramps and spasms, increasing in violence suddenly and subsiding as quickly , but never quite coming to a state of internal rest. The contortions are simply awful and exhibit all the symptoms of musical colic verging on cholera morbus. There are gnashings of teeth, groanings that cannot be uttered, bellowings as of the bulls of Bashan.

'Cincinnati Commercial' (1880)

'Flying Dutchman' – The overture is a musical horror, a mixture concocted of bad taste and brutality in equal doses.

'Deutsche Musikzeitung' (1861)

'Tristan and Isolde' – This is advanced cat music. It can be produced by a poor piano player who hits black keys instead of white, or vice versa.

Heinrich Dorn (1870)

Wagner takes himself for a Dalai Lama and his excrement for the emanation of his godlike spirit. *Heinrich Dorn* (1870)

'Die Meistersinger' – A more horrendous Katzenjammer than Wagner achieves in his *Meistersinger* could not be accomplished even if all the organs grinders of Berlin would have been locked up in Renz's circus, each playing a different waltz. *Heinrich Dorn* (1870)

It is the music of a demented eunuch.
'Figaro' (1876)

'Flying Dutchman' – If the composer wished to depict a storm, he at least produced its most painful effect, for it made me seasick.

P. A. Fiorentino – *'Constitutionnel'* (1860)

'Tannhäuser' – It produces the same effect upon you, and gives you the same pain, as if a hundred needles should enter your ear at once. *P. A. Fiorentino*

'Die Meistersinger' – With scrupulous avoidance of all closing cadences, this boneless tonal mollusk, self-restoring, swims ever on into the immeasurable.

Eduard Hanslick (1870)

'Die Walküre' – The second act is an abyss of boredom . . . This utterly

tuneless, plodding narrative, in a slow tempo, engulfs us like an inconsolable broad sea from which only the meagre crumbs of a few leitmotives come floating towards us out of the orchestra. Scenes like this recall the medieval torture of waking a prisoner by stabbing him with a needle at every nod.

Eduard Hanslick (1876)

He was a crook, a hypocrite, a poseur, and a spiteful, hysterical bastard.

Anthony Hecht

Listening to Wagner's music, every musically healthy person gets a terrible 'Lamnetum Katzarum', that is *Katzenjammer*. *Isaak M. Hersch*

'Die Meistersinger' – The debauchery of *Meistersinger* is the saddest assault ever made upon art, taste, music and poetry.

Ferdinand Hiller (1870)

Wagner, thank the fates, is no hypocrite. He says what he means, and he usually means something nasty. *James Huneker*

Wagner is the Antichrist incarnate of art.

Max Kalbeck (1880)

The wild Wagnerian corybantic orgy, this din of brasses, tin pans and kettles, this Chinese or Caribbean clatter with wood sticks and ear-splitting scalping knives . . . Heartless sterility, obliteration of all melody, all tonal charm, all music . . . This revelling in the destruction of all tonal essence, raging satanic fury in the orchestra, this diabolic, lewd caterwauling, scandal-mongering, gun-toting music, with an orchestral accompaniment slapping you in the face.

J. L. Klein (1871)

The diabolical din of the pig-headed man, stuffed with brass and sawdust, inflated, in an insanely destructive self-aggrandisement, by Mephistopheles' mephitic and most venomous hellish miasma, into Beelzebub's Court Composer and General Director of Hell's Music – Wagner! *J. L. Klein (1871)*

Q. Have you heard Wagner's music?
A. I think so, once.
Q. When?
A. When the lightning struck a sheet iron dealer's store. *'Musical Herald' (1884)*

'Lohengrin' – It has no more real pretension to be called music than the jangling and clashings of gongs and other uneuphonious instruments with which the Chinamen, on the brow of a hill, fondly thought to scare away our English blue-jackets. *'Musical World' (1855)*

'Tannhäuser' – It is not merely polyphonous, but polycacophonous.

'Musical World' (1855)

Everything he touches falls ill: he has made music sick. *Friedrich Nietzsche*

The music of Wagner imposes mental torture that only algebra has a right to inflict.

Paul de Saint-Victor – 'La Presse' (1861)

'Siegfried' – It would kill a cat and would turn rocks into scrambled eggs from fear of these hideous discords. The whole crap could be reduced to one hundred measures, for it is always the same thing, and always equally tedious.

Richard Strauss – 'Letter' (1879)

Wagner writes like an intoxified pig.
George T. Strong – 'Diary' (1866)

'Lohengrin' – It seems uncommon nonsense, with an occasional gleam of smartness, like the talk of a clever man who is just losing his wits.

George T. Strong – 'Diary' (1868)

'Siegfried' – Any half-hour of it, from first to last, would make you blush, if you had a face on you as hard as a bronze statue, and a moral nature as tough as a section of New York pie-crust.

'Sunday Herald' (1882)

This so-called music of the future, with its effects of frying pans and broken china. *Albert Wolff – 'Figaro' (1869)*

Anton von Webern

'Symphony for Chamber Orchestra' – 'The Ultimate Significance of Nothing' – this would be the proper title of this piece. Webern's orchestra suggested nothing so much as a cat, that, arching its back, glared and bristled its fur, and moaned or growled or spat.

> *Olin Downes – 'New York Times' (1929)*

'Quartet' – Webern's *Quartet* is Dead Sea fruit, and Dead End music.

> *Olin Downes – 'New York Times' (1941)*

'Five Pieces' – As clearly significant and symphonic as a toothache.

> *Lawrence Gilman – 'New York Herald Tribune' (1926)*

If modernism depended for progress upon the Weberns, it would get nowhere.

> *'Musical Courier' (1929)*

'Symphony for Chamber Orchestra' – The work had Webern's cardinal merit of brevity. *Oscar Thompson –*
> *'New York Evening Post' (1929)*

CONDUCTORS

Why do we have to have all these third-rate foreign conductors around – when we have so many second-rate ones of our own? *Sir Thomas Beecham*

So many of them are just junked up on the idea of controlling 80 people.

> *Nigel Kennedy – 'Sunday Times' (1992)*

Good conductors put musicians on their feet, but bad ones give them feet of clay.

> *Garry O'Connor – 'The Pursuit of Perfection'*

Sir John Barbirolli

The dancing dervish. *Sir Thomas Beecham*

Sir Thomas Beecham

Opera in the provinces is dying of T. B.
> *Sir Harry Hamilton*

Leonard Bernstein

He looks like a haggard twentieth-century

Prometheus with some sort of vulture tearing at his liver. *Anon*

Sir Adrian Boult

He reeks of Horlicks. *Sir Thomas Beecham*

Colin Davis

Mozart's 'Prague Symphony' – Mr Davis, who is a patchy conductor, ran aground on a bad patch early in the concert and was not, alas, afloat by the end of it.
> *'Daily Telegraph'*

Verdi's 'Requiem' – Is it possible for Verdi's *Requiem* to be a bore? I wouldn't have thought so, but Colin Davis has a damn good try . . . If the Day of Judgement is to be like this, it will be something of an anticlimax.
> *Michael Tanner – 'Classic CD' (1993)*

Mozart's 'Prague Symphony' – His account of Mozart's E flat Symphony No 39 K439 could hardly have been duller.
> *'The Times'*

Herbert von Karajan

Beethoven's 'Fourth Symphony' (1975) – He ruined Beethoven's *Fourth* by offering a mannered, brutal reading that sounded as if it had been designed to get through to Beethoven a year after he went deaf.
> *Stephanie von Buchan – 'Musical America'*

Bach 'Concerts' at Carnegie Hall (1967) – Mr von Karajan's duties seemed to be to wave a hand occasionally at the group, to pluck out the continuo at the second harpsichord, and to turn pages for Miss Bilgram. Otherwise he was a mere ornament, though, to be sure, Mr von Karajan is unquestionably ornamental.
> *Winthrop Sargeant*

Sergei Koussevitzky

That Russian boor. *Arturo Toscanini*

James Levine

Vienna Philharmonic at the Festival Hall (1992) – It was a horrid concert. When not vulgar, Levine was heavy and stodgy; the great orchestra played as if on a

commercial date.
Andrew Porter – 'Independent on Sunday'

Lorin Maazel

Mussorgsky's 'Pictures at an Exhibition' –
With natty, elegant gestures that were cut
and tailored to every bar, Mr Maazel
made at least one of the movements
scamper itself out of breath and almost
into nonsense. Elsewhere he whipped and
forced his brass until they brayed
inexcusably.   *'Daily Mail'*

Zdenek Macal

Mahler's 'Sixth Symphony' – Zdenek
Macal proved a woeful replacement [for
Klaus Tennstedt], the New York
Philharmonic orchestra looked bored
rigid.   *Michael Henderson – 'Guardian'*

Ion Marin

'Ave Maria' (1992) – Some of Marin's
tempi are distinctly sluggish, as though
they were being conducted after a too
heavy Christmas dinner.
Charles Osborne – 'BBC Music Magazine'

Zubin Mehta

*Bruckner's 'Symphony No. 8 in C Minor'
(1992)* – It sounds more like a
demonstration than a performance.
Terry Williams – 'Classic CD'

Paul Paray

Saint-Saën's 'Organ Symphony' (1992) –
When the music gets going it seems to
implode. Either that or the players have
been forced to sit five to a chair. Paray's
performance is a strait-jacketed affair.
Charles Munch can rest easy in his grave.
Terry Williams – Ibid

Johannes Schaff

Mozart's 'Idomeneo' (1989) – A terribly
embittered human being . . . who hates
music and despises the very notion of
love, particularly young love.
Max Loppert – 'Financial Times'

Giuseppe Sinopoli

Wagner's 'Die Walkure' (1992) –
Sinopoli's conducting was so pedantically
accurate he could easily have been

replaced by a digital metronome.
Brian Hick – 'Musical Opinion'

Sir George Solti

The least graceful conductor since
Dimitri Mitropolous . . . His motions are
jittery; his whole body is in motion; his
shoulders as well as hands are responding
to the rhythm; his beat is a series of jabs,
and he looks as though he is shadow
boxing.
*Harold C. Schonberg – 'New York Times'
(1976)*

Verdi's 'Aida' – I have never heard a
worse triumphal march from *Aida*.
Confronted by so many brass instruments
Solti engages in a wild orgy of
fragmentary blasts – rather like the traffic
in Rome (where this was recorded).
Simon Trezise – 'Classic CD' (1992)

Wagner's 'Ring' – After a 'Ride of the
Valkyries' that would be better employed
at frightening birds off the runway at
Gatwick, we have a heartless rendition of
Wotan's farewell in which the vocal line is
played by a trombone!
Simon Trezise – Ibid

Fritz Stiedry

Gluck's 'Orfeo et Euridice' – The
criminally bad conducting of Fritz
Stiedry, both lumpy and unfeelingly
rapid.
Michael Tanner – 'Classic CD' (1992)

Arturo Toscanini

You're no maestro – you're a bully!
Anon violinist (1918)

Verdi's 'La Traviata' (1946) – This
performance is strait-jacketed but it is the
person imposing that garment who seems
mad. *Michael Tanner – 'Classic CD' (1992)*

MUSICIANS

The trouble with women in an orchestra
is that if they are attractive it will upset
my players, and if they are not it will
upset me.   *Sir Thomas Beecham*

Consort not with a female musician lest
thou be taken in by her snares.
Ben Sira – 'Book of Wisdom' (190 BC)

Anon

Clarinettists – The classic cry-babies of
the orchestra . . . who look down their
noses at any kind of vibrato, making it
difficult for them to play in tune (which
they don't). *Harry Ellis Dickson*

Drummer – Young man, you're not a
drummer – you're an anarchist.
Sir Thomas Beecham

Pianist – Oh well, if you have to. You
play Bach your way. I'll play him his.
Wanda Landowska

Trombone player – Are you producing as
much sound as possible from that quaint
and antique drainage system which you
are applying to your face?
Sir Thomas Beecham

Your tone sounds like roast beef gravy
running through a sewer. *Hans von Bulow*

Trumpet player – God tells one how music
should sound but you stand in the way!
Arturo Toscanini

Valery Afanassiev (piano)

Brahm's 'Opus 117' – . . . guaranteed to
induce sleep after only four bars.
Misha Donat – 'BBC Music' (1993)

John Anderson (oboe) and Simon Wynberg (guitar)

'Summertime' (1992) – Pleasant enough
background for your barbecue, I suppose,
but little else. *Terry Blain – 'Classic CD'*

Baltimore Symphony Orchestra

Stravinsky's 'Firebird Suite' (1992) – As far
as the interpretation of Stravinsky is
concerned, it's air from another planet.
Simon Trezise – 'Classic CD'

Béla Bartók (piano)

He will probably feel no more aggrieved
at my denying him 'touch' than would be
the village blacksmith if I refused it to him

in description of his musical performance
with his two-stone hammer upon his red-
hot horseshoe.
Percy A. Scholes – 'Observer' (1923)

Bournemouth Symphony Orchestra (conducted by Sir Vivian Dunn)

'British Concert' (1992) – If I thought this
was the best of British, I'd emigrate.
Jeremy Beadle – 'Classic CD'

Jane Coop (piano)

'Romantic Piano' (1990) – A rag-bag of
schmalzed-up, slow-moving, ivory
ticklers, short movements snippeted from
major composers and strung together in a
shapeless wallow of coffee-table
smoochiness. Yugh!
Terry Blain – 'Classic CD'

Alexander Dreyschock (piano)

Debut concert in Paris – He makes a hell of
a racket. One does not seem to hear one
pianist but three score of them. Since on
the evening of his concert, the wind was
blowing south by west, perhaps you heard
the tremendous sounds in Augsburg? At
such a distance their effect must be
agreeable. Here, however, in this
Department of the Seine, one may easily
burst an ear-drum when the piano-
pounder thumps away. *Heinrich Heine*

Ofra Harnoy (cello)

On the 1990 RCA Poster Campaign –
Simply couldn't persuade anyone that the
quality of her playing justified the picture
of her reclining in a chaise-longue in a
state of unnatural luxury. The lesson
there seems to be that it is no good
turning a second-rate musician into a
second-rate pin-up.
Rupert Christiansen – 'Observer'

Peter Hill (piano)

*Messiaen's 'Vingt Regards sur l'enfant
Jesus' (1992)* – Hill, for all his insights,
sounds as if he is thinking it out as he
goes along. *Ian Macdonald – 'Classic CD'*

Nigel Kennedy (violin)

The Liberace of the 90s.
John Drummond (1992)

The violinist who plays like an angel and dresses like Vivienne Westwood on a bad day.   *Jilly Parkin – 'Daily Express' (1992)*

Trying to come on like a bohemian designed by the *Beano* comic . . . Kennedy looking like a stylist's Armageddon . . . seems to be taking his fashion cues from the hippie travellers. And Dopey of the Seven Dwarfs.
    Robert Sandall – 'Sunday Times' (1992)

Laureate (string ensemble)
'Ain't Misbehavin'' (1992) – This disc is for those who like their sincerity *Dynasty*-style, and who like their music not to penetrate beyond the make-up. Good background music at someone else's party.   *Roderick Swanson – 'Classic CD'*

Signor Lietti (violin)
'The Barber of Seville' (1848) – The orchestra had a leader, Signor Lietti, who did not apparently consider it necessary to indicate the movement by beating the time. On the contrary, he was occupied in playing the first violin part, fully unconscious of the other instruments. In order to guide them, he was possessed with the monomania of playing more loudly and vigorously upon his fiddle than any of subordinates. He trampled on the floor as though he had been determined to work a path through the deal planking, and made a series of the most grotesque faces with his nose, mouth and eyes.   *Max Maretzek*

London Philharmonic Trombones
Ear-splitting Bartlemy-Fair bulls of Bashan.   *'Musical World' (1852)*

London Symphony Orchestra
Prokoviev's 'Ivan the Terrible' (1993) – 'Terrible'? No, 'Ivan the slightly Disappointing' would be nearer the mark.
    Stephen Johnson – 'The Times'

Mannheim Orchestra
Auber's 'La Muette de Portici' (1829) – The crowing, shouting, bawling, and the furious crashing of the orchestra was

enough to split our ears: it was absolutely frightful.   *Vincent Novello – 'Diary'*

Simon Morris (cello) and Leo Debono (piano)
'Romantic and Virtuoso Pieces for Cello and Piano' (1992) – It's hard to take this disc seriously . . . When all is said and done, it could go straight to the tombola in the local summer fête without you really missing anything.
    Roderick Swanson – 'Classic CD'

The Moyzes Quartet
They sound like a bunch of wallflowers at a downbeat party where the beer (and a string or too) has gone flat.
    Samuel Fischer – 'Classic CD' (1992)

New York Philharmonic
Mahler's 'Sixth Symphony' (1992) – A notoriously uneven orchestra were to play Mahler's *Sixth Symphony* . . . and, true to form, the audience wriggled, spluttered and acted for 80 awful minutes.
    Michael Henderson – 'Guardian'

Vladimir De Pachmann (piano)
'Chopinzee'   *James Huneker*

Pantomimic performances with accompaniments by Chopin. *G. B. Shaw*

Sergei Prokofiev (piano)
'First Piano Concerto' (1918) – The composer handled the keyboard – handled is the right word – and the duel that ensued between his ten flail-like fingers was to the death; the death of euphony. The human ear soon accommodates to such monstrous aberrations. Prokofiev wouldn't grant an encore. The Russian heart may be a dark place, but its capacity for mercy is infinite.
    James G. Huneker – 'New York Times'

Erno Sebesteyn (violin) and Josef Myslivecek (cello)
'Violin and Cello Concertos' (1992) – Good for supermarkets, lifts and restaurants.
    Jeremy Nicholas – 'Classic CD'

St Paul Chamber Orchestra (conducted by Hugh Wolff)
Copland's 'Appalachian Spring' (1992) –
As a certain lager advert would have it; good, but not that good.
Paul Riley – 'Classic CD'

OPERA & ORATORIO

Opera can be very staid and boring. It's not liberated enough.
Dame Kiri te Kanawa

Opera is a loosely connected series of songs designed to make a full evening's entertainment out of an overture.
Miles Kington

Richard Strauss' *Capriccio*
Performed at Glyndebourne (1991) –
Is it ever going to end?   *Nicola Bailey*

Handel's *Alcina*
Performed at the Royal Opera House –
You might call it the nouvelle cuisine school of Handel . . . You might call it nouvelle to the point of no cuisine at all.
Michael White – 'Independent on Sunday'

Monteverdi's *The Return of Ulysses*
Performed by the English National Opera (1989) – Even if this is music of a sort, most of it simply isn't very good or very interesting. And what a long evening it makes.
Geoffrey Wheatcroft – 'Evening Standard'

Rossini's *Barber of Seville* (1992)
A down-market job to pull in the audiences over the Christmas period . . . anything that helps fills the coffers is to be welcomed from one point of view. That would be the only justification for this abomination. The whole cast deserves sympathy for being involved in this self-indulgent tripe. A ghastly evening.
Michael Kennedy – 'Sunday Telegraph'

A performance so dismally second rate it cast a sheen of boredom over the whole

auditorium within minutes. Peter Knapp's new script is as flat as a pancake and the comic actors who purveyed it drilled their inadequacies through the audience's skull with a determination that was agonising.
Alexander Waugh – 'Mail on Sunday'

OPERA SINGERS

A tenor is not a man but a disease.
Hans von Bülow

If the expenses are too big, let us cut out the stars. We do not need them. We are stars ourselves. People do not come to hear singers – they come to hear the orchestra.   *Hans Richter*

The hollow, cowlike megaphone tones of the average bass are the most objectionable.   *Sir Henry Wood*

Anon tenor
'Lohengrin' – You are not a knight of the swan but of the swine.   *Hans von Bülow*

Raffaele Arie
Rossini's 'Stabat Mater' (1992) – Arie needs a gentle hint that passion is not always an adequate substitution for accuracy.   *Gwen Hughes – 'Classic CD'*

Ian Bostridge
It is useless to pretend that the voice of tenor Ian Bostridge is big, or even specially well-placed.
Meredith Oakes – 'The Independent' (1992)

Enrico Caruso
'Madame Butterfly' (1907) – Caruso's celebrated singing does not appeal very much more than the barking of a dog in a faraway wood.   *Jihei Hashigushi*

Placido Domingo
Placebo Domino.   *Anon (1990)*

'Mozart Arias' (1992) – A collection of contextless tenor scenes and arias, sung with undoubted passion but

comparatively little grace, is simply too monotonous to make for an edifying – or even satisfying – recital.

Ian Brunskill – 'Classic CD'

'*Barber of Seville*' *(1992)* – This is one of the most humourless characterisations of the Barber on record and Domingo sounds like an Otello who took the wrong turning at the heel of the Italian Peninsula.

Hugh Canning – 'BBC Music Magazine'

'*Barber of Seville*' *(1992)* – A Figaro who sounds like an Otello in need of a new navigator; too light, obviously tenorial in tone, lugubrious in lines which require verbal agility, utterly devoid of wit.

Hugh Canning – 'Sunday Times'

'*Entre dos Mundos*' *(1992)* – About as embarrassing as such things manage to be – which is considerable . . . if you love the Eurovision Song Contest or Barcelona Airport's muzak, you'll love this.

Michael S. Rohan – 'Classic CD'

His name sounds like a resort in Baja California.   *Taki – 'The Spectator' (1992)*

Frau Heink
My dear Schuck, I insist you make the orchestra play louder – I can still hear the voice of Frau Heink!   *Richard Strauss*

Florence Foster Jenkins
There has often been an affectionate place in human hearts for the supremely bad. Think of the wobbly operatic arias of Florence Foster Jenkins.

Arthur Marshall (1971)

Dame Gwyneth Jones
'*Various*' *(1992)* – Gwyneth screams Wagner.   *Michael Tanner – 'Classic CD'*

Dame Kiri te Kanawa
'*Festival of Song*' *(1989)* – Kiri remains frustratingly immature, her technique unadventurous, her grasp of poetic meaning superficial, her range off colour narrow, her delivery of foreign texts

slightly imperfect, her attack bland . . . In opera the sheer dullness of her musical imagination is far less evident than in a recital like this.   *Tom Sutcliffe – 'Guardian'*

Giovanni Martinelli
Giordano's 'Madame Sans-Gene' (1915) – You! You sing like a police dog!

Arturo Toscanini

Jessye Norman
'*Lucky to Be Me*' *(songs by Bernstein, Gershwin, Lerner) (1992)* – If you like this sort of thing, this is the sort of thing you like – I dread the appearance of 'Jessye Sings Kylie'.

Jeremy Beadle – 'Classic CD'

Luciano Pavarotti
'*Don Carlos*' *(1992)* – This evening Verdi is crying.   *Anon heckler*

Alexei Stebilianko
'*Medee*' *(1989)* – As Jason, the Russian tenor, Stebilianko must have had some throat ailment, otherwise, one cannot understand how he came to be selected for the part.

Michael Kennedy – 'Sunday Telegraph'

Dame Joan Sutherland
The ultimate purgatory would be to go to the Opera House and hear Joan Sutherland sing.   *Kerry Packer (1977)*

BALLET MUSIC

Julian Grant
'*Swan Lake*' *(1992)* – Grant's reduction of Tchaikovsky's score is not so much a scissors-and-paste as a hatchet job.

Edward Thorpe – 'Evening Standard'

NATIONAL ANTHEMS

British
The national anthem belongs to the eighteenth century. In it you find us ordering God about to do our political work.   *G. B. Shaw*

MUSICAL INSTRUMENTS

Clarinet
An instrument of torture operated by a person with cotton wool in his ear.
Ambrose Bierce

Drums
So many drummers, so little time.
Arlette Budwig

The sound of the drum drowns out thought.　*Joseph Joubert – 'Pensées'*

The merry chatter of electronic drum-kits, as authentic as dehydrated paella.
Michael S. Rohan – 'Classic CD' (1992)

Oboe
The bass oboe is a strain upon the nervous system of the conductor . . . confounded by the frequent audition of noises that resembled nothing so much as the painful endeavour of an anguished mother-duck to effect the speedy evacuation of an abnormally large egg.
Sir Thomas Beecham

Piano
Little more than a harp in a box.
Leigh Hunt

Theremin
In the theremin we have a machine which in the baritone register suggests a cow in dyspeptic distress.　*'The Times' (1950)*

Violin
What can be more strange than that the rubbing of a little Hair and Cat-gut together make such a mighty altercation in a man that sits at a distance?
Jeremy Collier – 'An Essay on Musick'

POPULAR MUSIC

Music-hall songs provide the dull with wit, just as proverbs provide them with wisdom.

W. Somerset Maugham – 'A Writer's Notebook' (1949)

Music is spiritual. The music business is not.　*Van Morrison*

COMPOSERS

George Gershwin
'An American in Paris' – It is nauseous claptrap, so dull, patchy, thin, vulgar, long-winded and inane, that the average movie audience would be bored by it. This cheap and silly affair seemed pitifully futile and inept.
Herbert F. Peyser – 'New York Telegram' (1928)

Andrew Lloyd Webber
'Evita' – The composer has been particularly applauded for the eclecticism of his idiom, as if drawing on six varieties of rubbish was more praiseworthy, or for that matter, more difficult, than employing one.
Bernard Levin – 'Sunday Times' (1978)

Lloyd Webber is a bleedin' cowboy – he's terrible, absolutely terrible. I don't know how he's ever got anything published, let alone on stage . . . People like that shouldn't be allowed out.
Kirsty MacColl (1989)

Andrew Lloyds-Bank.　*'Private Eye'*

Lloyd Webber's music is everywhere, but so is AIDS.　*Malcolm Williamson (1992)*

PERFORMERS

Charles Aznavour
He's so worn by experience he's got bags under his head.
Clive James – 'Observer' (1974)

Richard Clayderman
He is to piano playing as David Soul is to acting; he makes Jacques Loussier sound like Bach; he reminds us how cheap potent music can be.　*Richard Williams*

Neil Diamond
'The Jazz Singer' (1980) – What is jazz to Neil Diamond and what is Neil Diamond to jazz? Old title has nothing to do with music on display here and would seem

meaningless to modern audiences.

'Variety'

Tom Jones

'A Man and a Half' (1972) – The singer himself appeared looking curiously like Eamonn Andrews . . . he proceeded to work his way through twenty or so numbers, shaking himself the while like an actor auditioning for St Vitus. Baring his teeth like an indignant race-horse, and managing at his best to conjure up memories of John Hanson, Mr Jones mumbled, grunted and sang his way through one of the least inspiring star turns it has ever been my duty to witness.

Sheridan Morley

Peggy Lee

The poodle of pomp.

Ross Fortune – 'Time Out' (1992)

Liberace

Let's get one thing straight . . . Liberace is a skilled artist – but his art is comedy, not music. *Anon (1955)*

The biggest sentimental vomit of all time.

'Daily Mirror' (1956)

[Liberace sued the paper and was awarded £8,000 damages]

Liberace is pure art student gone camping.

Peter Freedman – 'Glad to be Grey' (1985)

Barry Manilow

Barry is bringing out a new range of nose-clippers – to the rest of us, they'll be more recognisable as shears. *Angus Deayton – 'BAFTA Advertising Awards' (1992)*

Ethel Merman

A chorus of taxi-horns. *Anon*

Des O'Connor

During the Strangeways prison rooftop riots – If they don't come down by midnight we are going to play Des O'Connor records. *Anon prison officer (1990)*

Gilbert O'Sullivan

The man with a voice like a cartoon duck.

Ross Fortune – 'Time Out' (1992)

William Shatner

'The Transformed Man' – His 'Lucy in the Sky with Diamonds' is piss-yourself hilarious . . . Instead of singing he disclaims the lyrics as though they were the work of Shakespeare . . . Most of the other tracks are Shakespearean speeches . . . His 'Hamlet''s not bad, but his 'Romeo' sounds like a child molester and should be given a very wide berth.

David Cavannagh – 'Select' (1992)

'The Transformed Man' – . . . like Laurence Olivier on acid. *Creation Records*

'The Transformed Man' – The track-listings suggest Shatner might be short of a dilithium crystal or two.

'Time Out' (1992)

Barbra Streisand

'Mother' – An unqualified bummer . . . in which she belts out the primal scream. A mechanised shriek that has all the humanity of a police siren, it makes an embarrassing mockery of a great song.

Stephen Holden – 'Rolling Stone'

Her work is pretentiously arty, overinvolved and overprojected, and made further intolerable by a vocal tone best described by the Irish word 'keening'. *John Indcox*

'And Other Musical Instruments' – It is overproduced, over-orchestrated and overbearing to the point of aesthetic nausea.

John O'Connor – 'New York Times' (1973)

BRASS

Canadian Brass

'Made in the USA' – Imagine listening to the most saccharine light radio while under the influence of a mild but disagreeable hallucinogenic and you come close to appreciating the crassness of this disc. *Stuart Nickless – 'Classic CD' (1992)*

COUNTRY & WESTERN

Asked if he was allergic to anything –
Country and Western music. *Buddy Rich*

PERFORMERS

Garth Brooks

'We Shall Be Free' – More American lies
and bollocks from the billion-selling man
with the hat who always looks like he's
just farted.

Ross Fortune – 'Time Out' (1992)

Billy Ray Cyrus

'These Boots Were Made for Walking'
(1992) – Well I know for a fact that it isn't
my mum who keeps buying all the Billy
Ray Cyrus records.

Nick Coleman – 'Time Out'

FOLK

A folksinger is a comedian with a guitar
slung from his neck. *Miles Kington*

The whole trouble with folk songs is that
once you have played it through, then
there is nothing much you can do except
play it over again, and play it rather
louder.

Constant Lambert – 'Music Ho!' (1934)

JAZZ

Live jazz – two words which find my
hands instinctively shooting up to protect
my ears.

Craig Brown – 'Sunday Times' (1992)

The 'jazz mania' has taken on the
character of a lingering illness and must
be cured by means of forceful public
intervention.

Boris Gibalin – 'Izvestia' (1958)

American nigger-kike music.
Josef Goebbels

Anon big band – An idiotic little hammer
knocks drily: one, two, three, ten, twenty

knocks. Then, like a clod of mud thrown
into crystal-clear water, there is a wild
screaming, hissing, rattling, wailing,
moaning, cackling. Bestial cries are heard:
neighing horses, the squeal of a brass pig,
crying jackasses, amorous quacks of a
monstrous toad. This excruciating
medley of brutal sounds is subordinated
to a barely perceptible rhythm. Listening
to this screaming music for a minute or
two, one conjures up an orchestra of
madmen, sexual maniacs, led by a man-
stallion beating time with an enormous
phallus. *Maxim Gorky*

Jazz has a bad name because some of it is
crap, and it's boring.
Jools Holland – 'Jazz Express' (1992)

The jazz players were forced upon me; I
regarded them with a fascinated horror. It
was the first time, I suddenly realized,
that I had ever clearly seen a jazz band.
The spectacle was positively terrifying.
Aldous Huxley – 'Do What You Will'
(1929)

Jazz used mainly as an adjective
descriptive of a band. The groups that
play for dancing, when coloured, seem
infected with a virus that they try to instil
as a stimulus to others. They shake and
jump and writhe in ways to suggest a
return to the medieval jumping mania.
Walter Kingsley – 'New York Sun' (1917)

The most irritating quality about the
voodoo, poo poop-a-doop school of jazz
song is its hysterical emphasis on the fact
that the singer is a jazz baby going crazy
about jazz rhythms.
Constant Lambert – 'Music Ho!' (1948)

The musician who invented 'Swing'
ought to. *'New York Times'*

Jazz is either a thrilling communication
with the primitive soul, or an ear-splitting
bore. *Winthrop Sargent*

After the dissemination of jazz, which was
definitely put through by the Dark

Forces, a very marked decline in sexual morals became noticeable. *Cyril Scott*

Jazz will endure just as long as people hear it through their feet instead of their brains. *John P. Sousa*

Jazz has nothing to do with composed music and when it seeks to be influenced by contemporary music it isn't jazz and it isn't good. *Igor Stravinsky*

The White races just now are submerged in a spate of negroid sentiment: Hot Jazz, Fox Trots and Black Bottoms occupy the young folk; Negro Spirituals send the adults into tears; the Crooner wails his erotic inanities every night over the Radio. We have reached the stage of a spineless acceptance of all these phenomena . . . the observant onlooker cannot fail to see that in the not too far distant future the Catholic Church will be standing as the one barrier in the path of this pagan advance.
Sir Richard R. Terry – 'Voodooism in Music'

PERFORMERS

Anon

Kid, you've got a perfect ear. No hole in it. *Jimmy Dorsey*

Don't just do something, stand there!
Jim Hall

Art Blakey

On his stick-twirling showmanship – Son, the music is on the drums, not in the air.
Chick Webb

ECM label

A massive musical mush-making machine, run by one Manfred Eicher, whose avowed purpose it appears to be to turn us all into blancmange. *Anon (1981)*

The ECM sound is as bland as a Ford Pinto full of cream of wheat. *Anon*

Eddy Duchin

Anon: Don't you adore Eddy Duchin, Mr Condon? He really makes the piano talk.

Eddie Condon: He certainly does. And what the piano says is, 'Please take your clumsy hands off of me!'

George Melly

You're a repulsive sweaty faced lout singing love songs. Why, you're past it. Hang your gun up now. And all your dirty jokes leave them to the real comedians. You have a mouth like a duck's ass. You dirty minded oaf. You're a load of rubbish. *Anon letter*

Glenn Miller

Glenn should have lived, and the music should have died. *Al Klink*

Mother Earth

'Hope You're Feeling Better' (1992) – A disgusting, morally indefensible abuse of the Hammond organ.
Nick Coleman – 'Time Out' (1992)

Red Nichols

Red thought he played like Bix Beiderbecke, but the similarity stopped the minute he opened his horn case.
Eddie Condon

Courtney Pine

'Traditions Beckoning' (1988) – Not so much informed by a sense of history as asphyxiated by it . . . Right down to the man's name, which exudes a deep brown dignity, this record is a Reproduction Antique. *Ian Gittins – 'Melody Maker'*

Why does Courtney Pine always looks like a startled dildo?
Bob Mapplethorpe (1988)

'Redemption Song' (1992) – A Bob Marley cover so bland most supermarket/hotel lifts would be ashamed to play it. This record reeks of cocktail bars in Croydon, plastic palm trees and ceiling fans on freezing days. *Mark Morris – 'Select'*

Windham Hill label

All that Windham Hill stuff – it's just music for the hot-tub.
Anon listener – WYNC Radio (1984)

ROCK

Rock is very squalid, impersonal and degrading; an egocentric circus full of people who aren't really human beings.
Adam Ant (1980)

Rock music has one appeal only, a barbaric appeal to sexual desire – not love, not eros, but sexual desire undeveloped and untutored.
Allan Bloom (1992)

I think that some rock'n'rollers are giving it a black eye. They are way off base with their stage contortions. I don't think anything excuses the suggestive gyrations that some go in for. Why do musicians find it necessary to get down on the floor, or quiver like a slab of aspic?
Pat Boone (1957)

Rock'n'roll is our modern version of rituals that have existed in other societies as far back as the time when primitive man shuffled and stomped around a drummer pounding on a hollow log until he fell in a state of mystic frenzy.
Charles Broeckman

Once upon a time, rock music was sung by the young to disgust the old. Now, it seems, it is sung by the old to embarrass the young.
Craig Brown – 'Sunday Times' (1993)

I won't record rock'n'roll. Where's the story value in those songs? Those sax players, for instance, they don't tune up from year to year, let alone day to day, and the singers just have no respect for the basic do-re-mi.
Rosemary Clooney (1955)

The drone which dominates indie music is symbolic of a collective inability to decide which way to progress.
Andy Gill – 'Independent' (1992)

Why is heavy metal so popular? I can't stand the haircuts; they're like shag poodles.
Kim Gordon [Sonic Youth] (1992)

In a year or two rock'n'roll will be as passé as Clara Bow. *Benny Green (1956)*

Rock is a little boy's playground and little boys don't talk about anything that women are interested in or concerned about. Apart from how big their willies are. *Jo [Fuzzbox] (1989)*

Rock'n'roll should be made by truck drivers from Tupelo, Mississippi, not studio musicians with an album commitment to fulfil.
Southside Johnny (1977)

I don't believe in guitar heroes. If I walk out to the front of the stage it's because I wanna reach the audience. I don't want them to suck my guitar off.
Mick Jones [The Clash] (1977)

This is the first time in the history of our business that records have capitalised on illiteracy and bad recording.
Mitch Miller (1957)

Rock'n'roll is musical baby food: it is the worship of mediocrity, brought about by a passion for conformity.
Mitch Miller (1958)

The only thing worse than an average stadium rock group is a pretentious one with too many expensive toys to play with. *Jim Shelley – 'Guardian' (1992)*

Please, please, don't call it rock'n'roll. I don't like rock'n'roll. I do not sing rock'n'roll. *Mel Torme (1963)*

PERFORMERS

The Alarm
'Sold Me Down the River' (1989) – This is not very good. Strange really because The Alarm have never been any good and you'd think, just by the virtue of trial and error, that they'd be good by now. It's such a long time to be completely crap.
The Stud Brothers – 'Melody Maker'

Ashes and Diamond
'Hands of Love' (1992) – In search of some

new rock, ended up with this. Terrible, but Dave Lee Travis will play it.
Will Woodward – 'Time Out'

The Auteurs
'Showgirl' (1992) – With so little muscle, it's amazing they can even hold their guitars. *Laura Lee Davies – 'Time Out'*

Aztec Camera
'Deep and Wide and Tall' – Would like to be wild honey. Is more like lemon curd.
Steve Reynolds

Don Baird
'Love Songs' – Baird comes over as a poor man's Rod Stewart. *Stephen Leigh – 'What's on in London' (1992)*

The Beatles
Bad-mannered little shits. *Noël Coward*

Musically, this reviewer cannot understand the fervour of the Beatles' admirers . . . except for their visual uniqueness, the Beatles are a run of the mill rock'n'roll attraction.
Nat Hentoff (1964)

Chuck Berry
I love his work but I couldn't warm to him even if I was cremated next to him.
Keith Richards

Black Crowes
What they do, they do well but you could say the same thing about Morris Dancers.
'Melody Maker' (1992)

Jon Bon Jovi
He sounds like he's got a brick dangling from his willy, and a foodmixer making puree of his tonsils.
Paul Lester – 'Melody Maker'

Bon Jovi
'Bed of Roses' (1993) – A power ballad so leaden it doubles up as a pencil.
Paul Lester – 'Melody Maker'

'Living in Sin' (1989) – A slushy mumbling piece of shit.
Mick Mercer – 'Melody Maker'

Bon Jovi nanced about the Wembley stage with all the charisma of car park attendants who've watched all the Mick and Rod videos and practised hard in front of their mirrors and still got it wrong. *Steve Sutherland – 'Melody Maker' (1988)*

Bono
If you are one of Bono's brain cells, you'll be lonely. *Tom [Mekons] (1989)*

David Bowie
On his marriage – I hope Iman took a good book on honeymoon.
'Melody Maker' (1992)

How do we hate thee, David? Let us count the ways. *'Melody Maker'*

He's just doing what Phil May of The Pretty Things used to do. He's just wearing different clothes.
Van Morrison (1973)

Carnival Art
'Sucker Punch' (1992) – CRUNGE rock, as in CRap and grUNGE. Like Steppenwolf played through a concrete wall. *Jennifer Nine – 'Melody Maker'*

Carter USM
'The Impossible Dream' (1992) – All that's missing from the full Pink Floydian horror is a ghastly guitar solo. For small mercies we must be thankful.
Mark Morris – 'Select'

'1992: The Love Album' – Their contrived indie bombast saw them take America less by storm and more by chance . . . I guess there'll always be a place for clumsy, right-on comedy sloganeering in music's squalid scheme of things but grubby pantomime pop from smug gutter gobshites we can all do without.
Ross Fortune – 'Time Out'

Tracy Chapman
Tracy Chapman don't mean shit to black people. If the shit don't hit you here and here, then the shit don't mean shit.
Chuck D (1988)

You only notice a Tracy Chapman record when it ends, like a faint humming in your ear that has suddenly stopped.
'Melody Maker' (1992)

Albert Hall concert (1989) – A glum, tedious singalong. The suspicion that this is a high-class form of busking music was emphasised by a tube-tunnel ranter on the journey home.
David Toop – 'The Times'

Alice Cooper
'Bed of Nails' (1989) – Not really as good as 'Poison' which wasn't the least bit good . . . This is a bit like mugging a dosser, it's always unpleasant.
The Stud Brothers – 'Melody Maker'

Kevin Coyne
It's said that he's very big in Germany, which is like saying cricket is popular in Albania.
Angus Deayton – 'Guardian' advert (1993)

Crowded House
They are big in Canada, which sums them up really.
David Stubbs – 'Melody Maker'

The Cult
'Heart of Soul' (1992) – Does Ian Astbury imagine that by clumsily juxtaposing the words 'heart' and 'soul' in this manner, he'll come across as doubly sincere?
'Melody Maker'

Dave Clark Five
Clark leads an ordinary rock'n'roll group with no particular musical direction.
Nat Hentoff (1964)

Def Leppard
'Adrenalize' (1992) – There's never even the slightest suggestion that things might even get a little out of hand, that something unexpected or shocking might occur, which is a sad comment on a supposedly wilde genre.
Andy Gill – 'Independent'

They're the George Bush of rock. They're just pieces of animation, they're

faceless, a blur nobody can define.
Jim Steinman (1989)

Deicide
'Legion' (1992) – They say that the Devil has all the best tunes, which logically would make Cole Porter Satan, and Deicide sitting up there with St Francis of Assisi.
'Melody Maker'

The Dick Nixons
'Paint the White House Black' (1992) – We may deserve the government we get, but do we deserve this?
Jeremy Clarke – 'Select'

Dire Staits
The dullards of rock.
'Time Out' (1992)

Dr. Robert [The Blow Monkeys]
When he has died, I'd like to go and shit on his grave.
Miles Hunt (1989)

Duran Duran
'Girls on Film: The Video' (1981) –
Repulsive piece of gang-bang voyeurism.
Dave Hill (1986)

'Big Thing' (1989) – Would I dig this if I was 13? Or would the pervasive image of Simon le Bon's trouser-minnow be too scary?
Dave Jennings

Bob Dylan
Zimmerman? Zimmerframe more like, you useless, cactus-faced crock of cack.
'Melody Maker' (1992)

How is it possible to play the harmonica, professionally, for 30 years and still show no sign of improvement?
David Sinclair – 'The Times' (1993)

Eggstone
'In San Diego' (1992) – They've got an identity crisis that makes Michael Jackson seem stable. They try to sound like George Michael, The Housemartins, XTC and the theme from *Barbarella*, and can't quite get any of them right.
Mark Morris – 'Select'

Emerson, Lake and Palmer
Live at the Albert Hall (1992) – If it was

Ralph Waldo Emerson, Veronica Lake and Arnold Palmer, the rest of the world would have to sit up and take notice, but it's Keith, Greg and Carl, on the run from the taste police in their leather trousers and horrendous embroidered shirts, ready to perpetrate more aesthetic crimes in the name of pomp-rock.

Ben Thompson – 'Independent on Sunday'

The Farm
'Love See No Colour' – This time they don't even manage football terrace singalongs, just cheap, empty tunes whose only spiritual home is down the pub on Karaoke nite.

Stephen Leigh – 'What's on in London'
(1992)

Fish
'Songs from the Mirror' (1993) – His lack of talent is legend, his delusions of grandeur Napoleonic, yet men and women depend upon him for their livelihoods . . . Casual workers in the rag trade will likely enjoy longer tenure than Fish's minions when *Songs from the Mirror* flings itself suicidally upon the market. Jesus. It's no wonder where in a recession. *David Bennun – 'Melody Maker'*

'State of Mind' (1989) – Fish sounds like he's pushing a wheelbarrow of wet cement up a 1 in 3 slope in a duffle coat, whining as he goes.

Ian Gittins – 'Melody Maker'

Foreigner
I've seen Bauhaus, so I've seen bad, and I've seen Foreigner, so I've seen worse.
Steve Sutherland – 'Melody Maker'

Bob Geldof
'Room 19 (Sha La La La Lee)' (1992) – Bob can't have a shred of dignity left.
'Melody Maker'

Genesis
Earl's Court concert – Games master Phil Collins and his anonymous chums gave full value for money as they paraded their treacly, interminable songs in and out of the fancy hardware. Unfortunately,

atmosphere was not in the air tonight . . . The aural Valium disguised as karmic snooze-surround was apparent . . . Fair's fair. The virtual reality graphics were super. Shame about the actual boredom.
Max Bell – 'Evening Standard' (1992)

'The Way We Walk: Vol 1' (1992) – The continued existence of Genesis provides incontestable proof that there is no God. Featuring, as always, Beelzebub on drums and vocals. *Adam Higginbotham – 'Select'*

Gary Glitter
That bouffant looks ridiculous, it looks more like a mushroom, for God's sake! But then, this is Gary Glitter, after all, a man unacquainted with taste.
Nick Duerden – 'Select' (1992)

The Ugly Sister of rock'n'roll.
Robert Sandall – 'Sunday Times'

The Go-Gos
'Vacation' – Uncool Jerkoffs! *Anon (1982)*

Guns N'Roses
Concert, Slane Castle, Ireland (1992) – It went downhill from the entrance.
'Melody Maker'

Bill Haley and his Comets
They nauseated a whole elder generation although the chubby bunch possessed a similar shock factor to that of Don Estelle. *'Melody Maker'*

Debbie Harry [Blondie]
The face that launched a thousand whores. *Stud Brothers – 'Melody Maker'*

Buddy Holly
He has always struck me as the type more likely to be found serving in a hamburger bar or delivering the soft drinks.
Paul Anka

Hue And Cry
'Ordinary Angel' (1988) – They have been away, haven't they? Well, they're back . . . Perhaps, they could go away again.
Mick Mercer – 'Melody Maker'

Inspiral Carpets

'Dragging Me Down' (1992) – Like
watching a penguin with a broken wing
pathetically trying to get up and waddle
but falling over, over and over again.
'Melody Maker'

Inxs

'Heaven Sent' (1992) – An appalling,
blaring, incoherent, neon nightmare,
rather like staring at a searchlight.
'Melody Maker'

Iron Maiden

They can't have any idea what they
sound like, otherwise they'd sound like
something else.
Ian McCann – 'New Musical Express'

Mick Jagger

How could I possibly have a sexual
relationship with a 50-year-old fossil? I
have a beautiful boyfriend of 28 . . . why
should I swap that for a dinosaur?
Carla Bruni (1992)

He is about as sexy as a pissing toad.
Truman Capote

'Wandering Spirit' (1993) – Wandering
spirit indeed. Prevaricating ponce more
like.   *Nick Coleman – 'Time Out'*

'Sweet Thing' (1993) – A stab at 'modern'
rock-funk but the beat-and-bassline
creaks, I swear, like an arthritic hip . . .
he's trying to come over like a randy
teenager, when he should be into
gardening or something. Leave it out
grandad.

Simon Reynolds – 'Melody Maker'

Jagger sounds like his mouth is full of
putty.   *Chris Roberts*

'Sweet Thing' (1993) – About as exciting
as a weekend in Malaga airport.
Will Woodward – 'Time Out'

Wendy James [Transvision Vamp]

'The Nameless One' (1993) – The
'Talentless One' more like.
Jim Arundel – 'Melody Maker'

She can't sing, she can't rock, and she
can't smoulder . . . James's singing
alternates between her usual breathily
brazen little-girl-lost voice, and the odd
attempt to come on like Marianne
Faithful, while actually sounding more
like Hazel O'Connor trying to shrug off a
cold.   *Ross Fortune – 'Time Out' (1993)*

Wait till I sell my story that I lived with a
pig. Called Wendy.
Nick Sayer [Transvision Vamp] (1989)

Jane's Addiction

'Nothing's Smokin' (1988) – If Jane was
addicted to this, hers must have been a
pretty hollow existence.
Mat Smith – 'Melody Maker'

Jesus and Mary Chain

Miserable f***ers, they are. It hurts. You
wanna just slap 'em. Wake up!
John Lydon (1989)

Elton John

If you mention the Queen to most Aussie
kids, they think you mean Elton John.
Kathy Lette – 'Independent on Sunday'

Kingmaker

'Killroy Was Here' (1992) – Sure it 'works
up a sweat' but a horse can do that.
'Melody Maker'

Kiss

'Crazy Crazy Nights' (1988) – Slade for
the humourless.   *David Quantick*

Mark Knopfler [Dire Straits]

'Money for Nothing' – The singer sounded
like he was having a crap as the vocal was
being recorded.   *Andrew Smith*

Lemonheads

'Confetti' (1993) – Seems rather a spare
wotsit at a wedding.
Will Woodward – 'Time Out'

John Lennon

John could be a manoeuvring swine,
which no one ever realized.
Paul McCartney

John Lennon and Yoko Ono
Some people exist who like to see their
names in print. John Lennon and Yoko
Ono are print junkies.
Germaine Greer – 'Listener' (1973)

Julian Lennon
'Get a Life' (1992) – How apt!
'Melody Maker'

Level 42
Barracuda Club concert – It would have
been better to turn your back and use the
music as a soundtrack.   *Anon (1982)*

Living Colour
The Au-Pairs of Black Rock.
Simon Reynolds

Living in a Box
'Room in Your Heart' (1989) – A ballad as
drippy as frozen chocolate gateau thawing
in the midday sun.
David Stubbs – 'Melody Maker'

Paul McCartney
'Mull of Kintyre' – McCartney should
have been prosecuted for his 'Mull of
Kintyre', which was about as mysterious
as the local gas board.
Peter McKay – 'Evening Standard' (1992)

He has become the oldest living cute boy
in the world.   *Anna Quindlen*

If I hear Paul McCartney going 'Bom
Bom Bom Ayeya' one more time, I'm
going to open fire. It's true. Mark
Chapman did get the wrong guy.
Jon Ronson – 'Time Out' (1992)

Malcolm McLaren
No-one can compete with McLaren when
he is ranting like a highly-strung washer-
woman about his favourite subject:
himself.
*James Delingpole – 'Sunday Telegraph'
(1989)*

'House of the Blue Danube' (1989) – You
must have been to one of those awful
small village pubs, all fake pewter, *Daily
Mail* readers and ploughman's lunches . . .

That's what it sounds like, honestly.
David Stubbs – 'Melody Maker'

Meatloaf
After the first album, Meat just lost it
completely. Grunt! Grunt! Grunt! Grunt!
I had to listen to that for nine months.
That pig can't sing a f***ing note!
Jim Steinman (1989)

Megadeath
Fancies itself rotten, but it is so much
bedroom rebellion on a short lead.
'Melody Maker' (1992)

Freddie Mercury [Queen]
'The Great Pretender' (1992) – Dead but
still crap.   *Jim Arundel – 'Melody Maker'*

'The Freddie Mercury Album' (1992) – Mr
Teeth's solo hits 'The Great Pretender'
(early rock'n'roll as glazed ham), 'Love
Kills' (electro-disco as melodrama) and
'Barcelona'(opera as bollocks). You want
the album for a Christmas present like
you want a gift-wrapped box of veruccas.
Let's face it, he was overrated and he
wasn't that funny.
David Bennun – 'Melody Maker'

Most posthumous eulogising of Freddie
respectfully touched on what a 'great
entertainer' he was. Well, true in part, but
then so is Bruce Forsyth.
Dave Morrison – 'Select' (1992)

**Freddie Mercury and Montserrat
Caballé**
'The Golden Boy' (1988) – Time Rice has
got his hand up Mercury's aria, which
might account for the awful noises he's
making.
Edwin Pouncey – 'New Musical Express'

Jim Morrison [The Doors]
Do we need a two-and-half hour movie
about The Doors? I don't think so. I'll
sum it up for you. I'M DRUNK-I'M
NOBODY-I'M DRUNK-I'M FA-
MOUS-I'M DEAD. 'Big Fat Dead Guy
in a Bathtub', there's your title.
Denis Leary

Morrissey

As soon as Morrissey started making shit records, which were basically sad pastiches, he became one of the crappiest people who ever lived.

Brett Anderson (1993)

He sometimes brings out records with the greatest titles in the world, which somewhere along the line he neglects to write songs for. *Elvis Costello (1989)*

A bleary, parochial fool . . . the Peregrine Worsthorne of pop.

'Melody Maker' (1992)

The boring bard of bathos.

'Time Out' (1992)

'Jack the Ripper' – Another of those fodder tuneless murder tracks he's made so unworthily famous.

Will Woodward – 'Time Out'

Gary Numan

A man who was even crap at turning sideways . . . The Steve Davis of Pop . . . his gun-metal hair shines, like a cunningly arranged android cow-pat.

Mick Mercer – 'Melody Maker'

If he'd been given a rifle for his birthday present instead of a synthesizer, Hungerford would have happened a whole lot earlier. *Simon Price (1989)*

Yoko Ono

We live in a country where John Lennon gets six bullets in the chest. Yoko Ono's standing right next to him, not a f***ing bullet. Will you explain that to me, God?

Denis Leary

Ozzie Osbourne

While you can't hold Ozzie responsible for the deaths of suicidal idiots, you can appreciate their motivation. I'd like to ensure I have never have to hear him again, as well.

Mick Mercer – 'Melody Maker'

'Miracle Man' (1988) – The run-off groove on *Led Zeppelin II* sounds better than this offal.

Edwin Pouncey – 'New Musical Express'

Tom Petty

'Free Fallin'' (1989) – Oh God, I've just played a record written and produced by Jeff Lynne. No wonder it's shite!

Ian McCann – 'New Musical Express'

'Free Fallin'' (1989) – Co-written with ex-ELO man Jeff Lynne, which means one could scarcely take it less seriously if it had been co-written with Jeffrey Archer.

David Stubbs – 'Melody Maker'

Pink Floyd

'The Wall' – This fourth-form philosophising meander across the fretboards of the consciousness, attempting to be Orwell, ending up being awful.

'Melody Maker'

'The Wall' – The last brick in Pink Floyd's own towering edifice. The rock musician's equivalent of the tired executive's toy, a gleaming, frivolous gadget that serves to occupy midspace. It's misplaced boredom with graphics by Gerald Scarfe.

'New Musical Express' (1979)

The Pogues

The Pogues, without the mouldering Shawn McGowan, seem like an alarmingly meaningless proposition. Like Morecambe and Wise without Morecambe. Or Wise. *'Melody Maker' (1992)*

Poison

'Nothing But a Good Time' (1989) – Banal bacchanalia, musically reminiscent of Chicory Tip.

David Stubbs – 'Melody Maker'

Police

If Punk gave voice to the aimlessness of the first pessimistic post-war generation, then the Police were prime parasites of the new negativity. *Dave Hill*

Elvis Presley

Unspeakable, untalented and a vulgar young entertainer. *Bing Crosby (1956)*

If Elvis had eaten green vegetables, he'd still be alive today.   *Ian Dury*

I'm not putting Elvis down, but he was a shitass, a yellow belly and I hated him, the f***er.   *Jerry Lee Lewis*

Presley did not become a worthless shit: he always was one. *Charles Shaar Murray – 'New Musical Express'*

Quireboys
'Brother Louie' (1993) – A hard rock cross between Rod Stewart and Phil Collins. Bleaagh!   *Laura Lee Davies – 'Time Out'*

Railway Children
New Musical Express had this bunch in their centre spread a couple of weeks ago, which suggests they don't know something we do.

David Stubbs – 'Melody Maker' (1988)

Lou Reed
He looked, as ever, as cheerful as a tombstone.

Spencer Bright – 'Daily Mail' (1992)

Cliff Richard
Appearing on 'Oh Boy!' – His violent hip-swinging was revolting – hardly the kind of performance any parent could wish their children to see. If we are expected to believe that Cliff was acting naturally, then consideration for medical treatment may be advisable.   *'The Alley Cat' – 'New Musical Express' (1958)*

This man forgot how to sound or look natural thirty years ago.

Dave Jennings – 'Melody Maker' (1989)

There is something uniquely nauseating about his combination of inexhaustible commercial ambition, vacuous piety, and suggestive squirming and cavorting when he actually performs.

A. N. Wilson – 'Sunday Telegraph' (1990)

Keith Richards [Rolling Stones]
Though he is only 50 next year, he looks ready for a free bus pass.

Tony Parsons – 'Sunday Telegraph' (1992)

'Talk Is Cheap' (1988) – Talk is cheap, and this album is almost as worthless.

Terry Staunton – 'New Musical Express'

Rolling Stones
They are called the ugliest group in Britain. They are not looked on very kindly by most parents, or by adults in general. They are even used to the type of article that asks big brother if he would let his sister go out with one of them.

'Daily Mirror' (1964)

'Mixed Emotions' (1988) – It's just turgid cack. Any pub band could have done it.

Graham Poppie

I promise you they'll never be back on my show. I was shocked when I saw them.

Ed Sullivan (1964)

David Lee Roth
He comes on like a cross between a toreador and Miss World. Shortly after he opens his mouth, any critical response leaps into the fox-hole and tries to come to terms with describing the indescribable.*Paul Mathur – 'Melody Maker' (1988)*

Kevin Rowland
'Young Man' (1988) – The sound of early senility stealthily creeping in. Bugger off grandad.

Edwin Pouncey – 'New Musical Express'

Roxette
'Queen of Rain' – Take heed: neo-lusty words and loud crashing drums do not an epic make.

Ross Fortune – 'Time Out' (1992)

Scatterbrain
'Scamboogery' – Unless they wish to be the King Kurt of the current metal-funk wave, they'll have to grow up and smell the 90s.   *Ted Kessler – 'Rage'*

The Screaming Trees
I've scraped stuff out from underneath my fingernails that's got more panache than this motley, lumbering, mumbling bunch of hairy gray dollopfuls of f*** all!

Mr Agreeable – 'Melody Maker' (1993)

Sharon Shannon

Her tunes should please the three people who thought that The Waterboys never really got folksy enough.

Andrew Collis – 'Select'

Sheep on Drugs

'Track X' (1992) – Their songs are second-rate Carter USM copies, a concept so grim who'd have thought it possible? *Mark Morris – 'Select' (1992)*

Gene Simmons [Kiss]

He looks like a goat that's OD'd on testosterone. *'Melody Maker'*

Carly Simon

'You're So Vain' – If a horse could sing in a monotone, the horse would sound like Carly Simon, only a horse wouldn't rhyme yacht, apricot and gavotte.

Robert Christgau

Simple Minds

'Glittering Prize: Video' (1992) – Yes, at last the truth can be told. All along Simple Minds were really Genesis . . . with syrup. For people who think that Hey-We'll-Do-The-Video-Right-Here-At-This-Gig promos are still a smooth idea.

Andrew Collis – 'Select'

Skid Row

They aren't the worst metal band in existence – stand up Warrant – but that's not for lack of trying.

'Melody Maker' (1992)

Robert Smith [The Cure]

Wipe off the lipstick, put him in a suit, and you might make a proper performer of Robert Smith.

Bruce Dessau – 'Time Out' (1992)

Bruce Springsteen

He plays four-and-a-half hour sets. That's torture. Does he hate his audience? *John Lydon (1989)*

'Human Touch' (1992) – Pub-rock on a NASA budget. *'Melody Maker'*

'Lucky Town' (1992) – People like Bruce Springsteen are slowly boring music to death. *'Melody Maker'*

He's the Walt Disney of street poets – as useful a social commentator as Donald Duck. *Chris Rea*

'Human Touch and Lucky Town' (1992) – The 24 songs here make up such a mixed bag that you can't help wondering why the Boss didn't get off the production line and take an interest in what was happening over in quality control.

Robert Sandall – 'Sunday Times'

Dave Stewart [Eurythmics]

He must go down as one of the all-time biggest jokers in pop history – from his beard to his part in foisting the appalling Curve on an unsuspecting world . . . There should be a public health warning against the man.

Mark Morris – 'Select' (1992)

Rod Stewart

A sort of wiggly-bottomed Mike Baldwin. *Craig Brown – 'Sunday Times' (1993)*

'Tom Traubert's Blues' (1992) – Rod sings Tom Waits. Yeah, and I've been commissioned to make a new recording of Richard Strauss's *Four Last Songs* by Heinrich Goebbels.

Nick Coleman – 'Time Out'

Sting

'Russians' (1985) – Buy this and hear the most fatuous, mock-innocent 'concerned' pop song since 'I'd Like to Teach the World to Sing'. *Dave Hill*

'They Dance Alone' – I'm not surprised they dance alone, Sting, me old mucker, what with you coming on like Jess Yates in their ears.

Paul Mathur – 'Melody Maker'

He sings like he wants to be a hungry African. *David Stubbs – 'Melody Maker'*

Submarine

'Dinosaurs' (1992) – Submarine make a pleasant grown-up shoegazing sound that

has you gently floating off to sleep after a couple of minutes. *Mark Morris – 'Select'*

Tin Machine
'*Maggie's Farm*' *(1989)* – This is a load of old tosh . . . Just what you'd imagine the Rolling Stones would be doing if they were still alive.
Everett True – 'Melody Maker'

Pete Townshend [The Who]
For the last 23 years he's been a constant embarrassment. There's nothing worse than a pub-rocker with pretentions.
Jonah Wilde – 'Melody Maker' (1989)

Tina Turner
La Trina Turner – these days she's as tasty and hygenic as a mouthful of Domestos.   '*Melody Maker*' *(1988)*

U2
We could end up as awful as U2.
Barney [New Order] (1989)

'*Zoo TV*' *(1992)* – What have zoos and U2 got in common, apart from the fact that enlightened people would like to abolish them and they're both full of shite?   *Mr Agreeable – 'Melody Maker'*

'*Zoo TV*' *(1992)* – With its CNN out-takes and William Burroughs' cut-ups, *Zoo TV* began to look about as revolutionary as the out-takes from the Genesis video 'Jesus, He Knows Me.'
Jim Shelley – 'Guardian'

'*Zoo TV*' *(1992)* – With *Zoo TV*, U2 have managed to do something no one thought possible – eradicate the memory of their *Rattle and Hum* image and replace it with one that is even more ridiculous. U2 are still preaching, still self-regarding, self-righteous, self-promoting. Any irony they did discover has been, typically, bludgeoned to death.   *Jim Shelley – Ibid*

Do you know who the most boring group in the world is? F***ing U2! Give me Barry Manilow anytime.
Jim Steinman (1989)

'*Desire*' *(1988)* – Fellows have asked me for 10p on street corners for more substantial musical fare.
David Stubbs – 'Melody Maker'

'*Rattle and Hum*' *(1988)* – I hate U2. *Rattle and Hum* – a work of monstrous ego, suggesting all rock led to them. They're usurping our heritage, they're stealing my past and I hate it.
Steve Sutherland – 'Melody Maker'

Ugly Kid Joe
'*America's Least Wanted*' *(1992)* – UKJ prove it's possible to be old enough to vote and still think it's funny to eat with your mouth open, while their aspirations to Guns N'Roses rock noise make the Beastie Boys attempt at 'attitood rap' look like a triumph of mature social comment. This is average heavy rock with burping jokes to make up for lack of musical imagination.
Laura Lee Davies – 'Time Out'

Ultravox
They combined the hot-blooded passion of Kraftwerk with the elegance and restraint of Queen.
Simon Reynolds – 'Melody Maker' (1993)

Suzanne Vega
I could put on my Suzanne Vega tape and bore myself to death.
Sean Hughes (1990)

Nan Vernon
'*No More Lullabies*' – I'd rather be stuck in a lift with Garth Brooks than listen to these pathetically overwrought amateur dramatics again.
Ross Fortune – 'Time Out' (1992)

Gene Vincent
'*Be Bop-A-Lula*' – A junior idiot chant . . . strictly from the booby hatch.
'New Musical Express' (1956)

Whitesnake
They only imagine they make a big noise, and David Coverdale still believes he sounds like William Bell, which he does not. *Ian McCann – 'New Musical Express'*

Roger Waters
'Amused to Death' (1992) – Humourless to the point of absurdity.   *'Rolling Stone'*

The Who
'Tommy' – This still-born, over-anxious stretch of bilge. We needed rock opera like we needed rock morris dancing.
'Melody Maker'

REGGAE & CALYPSO

Zeke Manyika
Listening to his calypso nonsense is like being forced to go to the Notting Hill Carnival with all those poor people demonstrating their happiness and love of life. *Chris Roberts* – *'Melody Maker' (1989)*

Shabba Ranks
'Rough and Ready Volume One' (1992) – Volume One? What earthly need could there be for a second volume of this stuff?
'Melody Maker'

'X-Tra Naked' (1992) – His monotonous bark of a voice, sounds impressive at first but palls, like a party bore . . . For the most part this is just bedroom boasting with a beat.
Robert Sandall – *'Sunday Times'*

Snow
'Informer' (1993) – The Vanilla Ice of the reggae world . . . We can only pray he melts away.   *Ray Douglas* – *'Time Out'*

RHYTHM, BLUES & GOSPEL

Ghetto blacks 'speak jazz' (or blues or gospel) as their native tongue as Italians 'speak opera.'   *Frank Kofsky (1970)*

Rhythm and blues is not music, it's a disease.   *Mitch Miller*

A wave of vulgar, filthy and suggestive music has inundated the land. Nothing but ragtime prevails, and the cake-walk with its obscene posturings, its lewd

gestures . . . It is artistically and morally depressing, and should be suppressed by press and pulpit. *'Musical Courier' (1899)*

The mambo craze is passing and rhythm and blues will pass away too – the sooner the better as far as I am concerned.
Johnny Ray (1955)

PERFORMERS

The Silhouettes
'Get a Job' – This is one of the worst rock'n'roll records I have ever heard. This opens with a fair imitation of hens clucking, but is monotonous, meaningless, miserable, mumble jumble.
Keith Fordyce (1958)

The Yardbirds
They want to play the blues so badly and that's how they play it – badly!
Sonny Boy Williamson (1963)

Unknown gospel choir
On U2's 'I Still Haven't Found What I'm Looking For' (1988) – featuring, horror of horrors, a full blown gospel choir who are about as welcome as a flock of aunts at Christmas.
David Stubbs – *'Melody Maker'*

SOUL, DANCE & RAP

I love rap music. It's such a versatile art form. I mean every rap record sounds so different from the others.
Ade Edmondsen – *'Juke Box Jury' (1989)*

In the Top 40 half the songs are secret messages to the teen world to drop out, turn on and groove with the chemicals and light shows at discotheques.
Art Linkletter

Disco music is a kind of background music that is louder than anything in the foreground.   *Miles Kington*

With acid house they just sit with a synthesizer for half an hour and make squiddly-diddly noises.   *Robert [Loop]*

That rap stuff is noise pollution.
Kiefer Sutherland (1989)

PERFORMERS

808 State
Mule-drawn muzak.
Jonah Wilde – 'Melody Maker'

Adamski
He'd had his day almost the moment he
appeared.   *'Melody Maker' (1992)*

A House
Like an uncamp Smiths or Lloyd Cole,
without his redeeming pretensions.
Steve Reynolds

Tori Amos
'Crucify' (1992) – A stuck-up, affected,
mewing, tiresome tenth-rate Kate Bush
wannabe who pushes her body for
middle-aged, hormonally underactive,
white middle-class liberals to wank over.
'Melody Maker'

Rick Astley
'Ain't Too Proud to Beg' (1988) – The lad
is obviously not Eddie Kendricks; you
can practically hear him taking a run up
at the falsetto bits.
Stuart Maconie – 'New Musical Express'

He just can't do anything right can he, yet
he's a thoroughly good egg. So, let's
smash his head in.
Mick Mercer – 'Melody Maker'

'She Wants to Dance With Me' (1988) – It
bounces around with the wet enthusiasm
of a would-be husband promising his
fiancee that when they're married, he'll
always help with the dishes and take the
Ford Fiesta up to Safeway at the weekend
to do the shopping.
David Stubbs – 'Melody Maker'

Azizi
'Don't Say That It's Over' – That it's over.
Andy Cowan – 'Rage'

Bananarama
'More, More, More' (1993) – Less, less,
less, please.   *Ray Douglas – 'Time Out'*

The Beautiful South
'Old Red Eyes is Back' (1992) – More
horrid than shit on your pillow.
'Melody Maker'

The snivelling pits of pop music.
Chris Roberts – 'Melody Maker'

Andy Bell [Erasure]
The man whose soul is lodged
uncomfortably in his larynx, like a
fishbone.   *David Stubbs – 'Melody Maker'*

Boy George
Doesn't Boy George remind you of Su
Pollard?   *John Lydon (1989)*

I won't be photographed with that over-
made-up tart.
Princess Margaret [attrib] (1984)

Bros
'I Quit' (1988) – This rush-hour at
Oxford Street of a single, which the world
needs like an anal boil.
David Stubbs – 'Melody Maker'

Brother Beyond
A band at the very cutting edge of flower
arranging. *Mick Mercer – 'Melody Maker'*

James Brown
On his prison sentence – Papa's got plenty
of brand new mailbags to sew.
Len Brown – 'New Musical Express' (1989)

Belinda Carlisle
'Leave a Light On' (1989) – It's kind of like
watching a chicken try to fly, you wish it
would stop, or turn into a swan, or even
just stop trying so hard.
The Stud Brothers – 'Melody Maker'

Charles and Eddie
'NYC (Can You Believe the City?)' (1993)
– Not as good as the weakest track on a
George Michael album. Get the picture?
Laura Lee Davies – 'Time Out'

Neneh Cherry
Appearing on Channel 4's 'The Word' –
Neneh looked even less credible than the
show's presenters.   *'Select' (1992)*

Gary Clark

His sickly croon makes you feel like you're being force fed caramel.

Simon Reynolds – 'Melody Maker' (1993)

Simon Climie

'Soul Inspiration' (1993) – As emotionless as a catatonic Tibetan toad-owl. *Soul Inspiration* will no doubt sell to the kind of people who hang suits up in the back of Cavaliers. But this is no recommendation, even if you own a suit and a Cavalier.

The Stud Brothers – 'Melody Maker'

Climie Fisher

The name makes you feel nauseous, the feel of it in your mouth, the connotations, clammy fishy, Yukyukyukyukyukyuk.

Steve Reynolds – 'Melody Maker' (1989)

They proved that, to the punters, nothingness was better than nothing.

Chris Roberts – 'Melody Maker'

'Fire on the Ocean' (1989) – Yet another blue-eyed plodder which possesses all the grace of a menstruating sow.

Jonah Wilde – 'Melody Maker'

Natalie Cole

'Starting Over' (1989) – If you want to avoid dire rubbish like this, just look on any records for the names Michael Masser and Narada Michael Walden. If you see either name or both names, run like you'd hade an offer of sex with Cyril Parkinson.

Ian McCann – 'New Musical Express'

Deacon Blue

'Love and Regret' (1989) – This is what Geoffrey Howe plays on his Walkman when he's standing in the dole queue.

The Stud Brothers – 'Melody Maker'

Listening to DB attempting to lighten up is about as pleasurable as watching your loved ones grow old.

John Tague – 'New Musical Express' (1988)

Chris De Burgh

The ugliest man alive. The Valium of

The Menopusal Generation.

Barry Egan – 'New Musical Express' (1988)

Sandy Dennis

'Falling' (1993) – Teeny-boppy disco music for restless schoolgirls.

Ray Douglas – 'Time Out'

Depeche Mode

Perhaps they should try telling some jokes on their records, it might cheer them up a bit. *Laura Lee Davies – 'Time Out' (1993)*

Jason Donovan

You're not one of those rock stars who smash up hotel rooms, are you? You just leave the hot water tap running a bit longer than necessary.

Clive Anderson – 'Clive Anderson Talks Back' (1992)

On his apearance on 'Good Morning Britain' – A fearsomely hetereosexual Jason Donovan sang 'As Time Goes By', doing more damage to *Casablanca* in the process than the Nazis ever achieved. He wore fake glasses, attempting to look like Arthur Miller but looking more like Windy Miller.

Victor Lewis-Smith – 'Evening Standard' (1992)

East 17

'Walthamstow' (1992) – All the irritant qualities you'd expect from an LP produced by a bunch of spotty urchins only recently graduated from loafing in East End amusement arcades. Even taking into account previous models (Bros, New Kids, Take That) East 17 are the least stimulating arrivals for some time. Bargain-bin, Fisher-Price breakbeats team up with a whole series of baby-talk endearments and still-born musings on what a nasty world we live in.

Rupert Howe – 'Select'

'Deep' (1993) – 'I want to do it till my belly rumbles' mumbles the lead nerd. I guess that passes for romance in Walthamstow.

Dave Jennings – 'Melody Maker'

'*Walthamstow*' – It's so generalised that it's an abstraction masquerading as a rallying cry . . . E17 deal solely in desires that can never be acted upon, the easiest kind to sell. *Walthamstow* is an instruction manual for non-starters.

Jon Selzer – '*Melody Maker*' *(1993)*

Carmen Electra

'*Fantasia Erotica*' – The karaoke Madonna impersonation of your dreams.
Nick Coleman – '*Time Out*' *(1993)*

Electronic

'*Disappointed*' *(1992)* – You will be.
'*Melody Maker*'

En Vogue

Comparing En Vogue to the greats of soul is like comparing the Monkees to the Beatles. *David Sinclair* – '*The Times*' *(1992) [Davy Jones preferred a Monkees-Beatles comparison of 'Star Trek' to 'General Hospital']*

Enya

She makes All About Eve sound like Public Enemy.
Stuart Maconie – '*New Musical Express*'

A foul, cold-hearted technician whose music is so sterile that were it possible to bottle it, you could use it to clean lavatories.   '*Melody Maker*' *(1992)*

Erasure

Music to take back slightly shop-soiled shirts to Next for a refund to.
David Stubbs – '*Melody Maker*' *(1989)*

Gloria Estefan

She sings like she's got Babycham coursing through her veins rather than blood.
Simon Reynolds – '*Melody Maker*' *(1989)*

Eurythmics

If music be the food of love, why do the Eurythmics insist on serving up spam and chips all the time?   *Pauline [Pluto] (1989)*

'*Revival*' *(1989)* – Ignore the title . . . this simply repeats their tired prog-rock formula.   *Robert Yates* – '*Melody Maker*'

Fairground Attraction

'*Perfect*' – Surely Shakin' Stevens never made a worse record than 'Perfect'?
Chris Roberts – '*Melody Maker*'

Bryan Ferry

'*Let's Stick Together*' – This sounds as though it was remixed by Bryan's drunken chauffeur, who happened to be hanging out in the studio one night.
Jonah Wilde

Five Thirty

'*Super Nova*' – The aural equivalent to finding slugs in your salad sandwich.
Andy Cowan – '*Rage*'

Julia Fordham

'*Woman of the Eighties*' – Yuppie Soul! Words can't go far enough to say how abhorrent this muck is. Burn her at the stake! Aretha for the eighties, designed by a committee.
Ian Gittins – '*Melody Maker*'

Aretha Franklin

'*Check This Out*' *(1989)* – Unfortunately, Aretha's *Check This Out* reminds me of our local Brixton bobby who rather clumsily insists on shouting 'Yo!' whenever a kid passes by.
Robert Yates – '*Melody Maker*'

Sophie B. Hawkins

'*Damn, I Wish I Was Your Lover*' *(1992)* – She should get out more.   '*Melody Maker*'

Nick Heyward

'*You're My World*' *(1988)* – He wants to be Bros, which may be financially sound, but is as spiritually dignified as biting your toenails in Pizzaland.
Paul Mathur – '*Melody Maker*'

Hithouse

Add a big capital 'S' to the beginning of their name and you'll get the idea.
Edwin Pouncey – '*New Musical Express*'

The Housemartins
The Shit-House Martins. Alas the wind
has blown them away like whitened dog
turds.   *'Melody Maker'*

Whitney Houston
'I'm Every Woman' (1993) – I'll tell you
one woman who you certainly f***ing
aren't. And that's f***ing Chaka Khan.
Leave soul songs to the actual human
beings they were written for in the
f***ing first place. Whitney, you walking,
smooching, cooing, f***ing MTV
android from designer jean hell!
            Mr Agreeable – 'Melody Maker'

Mick Hucknall
He looks like Charlie Drake and he's a
midget.   *Carol Decker [T'Pau] (1988)*

We talk of the death of soul, and all he
wants to do is sing for his supper.
            Ian Gittins – 'Melody Maker'

The Jacksons
'2300 Jackson Street' (1989) – Listening to
it feels not unlike being drowned in sweet
sherry.   *Dave Jennings – 'Melody Maker'*

Jermaine Jackson
He has the mental acumen and agility of a
hedgehog. If Michael is a pair of pristine
white socks, Jermaine is the old grubby
nylon pair with the big toes sticking out.
            Ian Gittens – 'Melody Maker' (1989)

Michael Jackson
'*The Michael Jackson Interview' with
Oprah Winfrey (1993)* – With his womanly
voice, stark white skin and Medusa hair,
his gash of red lipstick, heavy eyeliner,
almost non-existent nose and lopsided
face, Jackson was making this appearance
in order to scotch all rumours that he is
not quite normal.
            Craig Brown – 'Sunday Times'

The boy's got more plastic on him than a
Co-op bag.   *'Melody Maker' (1992)*

Wembley Stadium Concert (1992) – He
hasn't just lost the plot, he's lost the whole
f***ing library!   *'Melody Maker'*

'Bad' (1989) – Michael Jackson's album
was only called *Bad* because there wasn't
enough room on the sleeve for 'Pathetic'.
                    Prince

Since his hair caught fire during a Pepsi
commercial, he now takes no chances,
maintaining a permanent wringing look,
as if he showers under a tea-pot and then
puts it through a strainer – like he's just
stepped out of Ceylon (or Darjeeling).
    Mark Steyn – 'Mail on Sunday' (1993)

He now looks like a Barbie doll that has
been whittled at by a malicious brother.
    Thomas Sutcliffe – 'Independent' (1993)

Jive Bunny
Read my lips, f*** off and die, vacuous
sheep-felchers.
            Everett True – 'Melody Maker'

Grace Jones
Today the Ice Queen is a soggy
(micro)chip, about as risque as a *double-
entendre.*   *Paul Lester (1989)*

Junior
'Renewal' (1992) – Poor old Junior. He's
outgrown his name, whilst the public
have outgrown his music.
            Adam Mattera – 'City Limits'

Mark King [Level 42]
King is the most boring bass player I've
ever heard in my life. He plays lead guitar
on a bass. It's shit. I hate him, bastard!
        Porkbeast [Crazy Heads] (1988)

Kris Kross
A gnat's cock away from paedophilia.
            'Melody Maker' (1992)

I blame the parents. *'Melody Maker' (1992)*

The Lilac Time
A group who sound like they've spent
their lives spotting trains.
            Chris Roberts – 'Melody Maker'

Lovetrain
In the Scottish B & Q league of pop,
where Wet, Wet, Wet are Rangers,

Lovetrain are suspiciously
Stenhousemuir.
Stuart Maconie – 'New Musical Express'
(1988)

Madonna

It amazes me that lesbians have adopted
Madonna as an icon. Madonna wouldn't
go down on you if her life depended on it.
Sandra Bernhard (1992)

Q. What's the difference between
Madonna and a Rottweiler?
A. Lipstick. *'Bitch' (1993)*

'Erotica' – On the best of days, Madonna
has an average voice. Wearing her heart
on her g-string, she has raided the
cupboard for ideas, only to discover that
far more talented artists have beaten her
to the cookie jar.
Mike Cowton – 'Daily Express' (1992)

I acted vulgar, Madonna IS vulgar.
Marlene Dietrich

Wembley Stadium Concert (1990) – The
show was like watching a Space Shuttle
launch: the wonders of science but, hello,
hello, is anyone in there?
Simon Garfield – 'Independent on Sunday'

'Like a Virgin' (1985) – Like hell.
Dave Hill (1986)

That ugly, shapeless, toe-sucking slut
Madonna . . . the difference between
Marilyn Monroe and Madonna is the
same difference as exists between
Champagne and cat's piss.
John Junor – 'Mail on Sunday' (1992)

Madonna is sleazy. She's an exercise in
utter cynicism and has practically no
talent. *Irma Kurtz (1992)*

'Erotica' (1992) – What is this, a tribute to
Benny Hill, or something? *'Melody Maker'*

'Truth and Dare' (1991) – What a tramp .
. . depraved shameless hussy . . . If there
was ever an emotional cripple it is
Madonna. *'New York Post'*

She's absolutely crap and the fact that the
only people who buy her records are 13-
20-year-olds proves that scientifically.
You never hear a man say 'I listen to
Madonna'. *Jerry Sadowitz (1989)*

Marky Mark

'You Gotta Believe' (1992) – It all unravels
on 'Super Cool Mack Daddy' when he
pleads 'I'm the baddest white boy in
Boston' – which is like boasting you're
top dog in Tunbridge Wells. You gotta
believe? You wanna bet?
Rupert Howe – 'Select'

George Michael

'Too Funky' (1992) – George has always
managed to keep a hairy finger on the
pulse of the moneyed wally.
'Melody Maker'

He's a wimp in disguise. He should go
home and shave. *Keith Richards (1988)*

Kylie Minogue

Kylie – her name means boomerang (but
she hasn't yet). *Andrew Burroughs (1990)*

I'm writing Kylie Minogue's biography.
It's called 'Superstar: Jesus Christ!'
Barry Cryer

Like one of those nine-year-olds from
Dagenham done up in her mother's
lipstick, to appear on a talent show.
Jonathan Margolis – 'Mail on Sunday'
(1992)

Her name sounds like a disease plants get
. . . Has there been a less charismatic pop
singer? *Chris Roberts – 'Melody Maker'*

New Kids on the Block.

New Kids Off The Production Line.
Andrew Burroughs (1990)

Stevie Nicks

She sounds like Carol Decker's granny.
Robert Yates – 'Melody Maker' (1989)

Sinead O'Connor

A cow that can't sing.
Danny Baker – 'Have I Got News for You'
BBC TV (1992)

Sinead O'Connor has taken 'looking like a bloke' so far that she actually resembles Alexei Sayle.   *Barbara Ellen –*
'New Musical Express' (1988)

'Don't Cry for Me Argentina' (1992) – The Ross Perot of pop. It's ugly.
'Melody Maker'

Sinead, thin voice and no hair, looks beautiful and sounds awful.
'Time Out' (1992)

The sweet-voiced spamhead – talk about one track short of a compilation album.
'Time Out' (1992)

Robert Palmer
'Ridin' High' at the Albert Hall (1992) – This is the night Palmer committed professional suicide.   *Anon*

Languid to the point of coma.
Ian Gittins – 'Melody Maker'

'It Could Happen to You' (1989) – The wine-and-wassailing Palmer, the tubby Sheffield bacchus . . . aims for the late-night sophistication of an intimate cabaret in Berlin, but hits the level of a social club in Bradford.
Robert Yates – 'Melody Maker' (1989)

Marti Pellow [Wet, Wet, Wet]
The ponderous Pellow . . . His voice made gutteral sounds that presumably passed for emotion.
Spencer Bright – 'Daily Mail' (1992)

Ce Ce Peniston
'Inside That I Cried' (1992) – Slick pap for sofa-bound soul boys.
Laura Lee Davies – 'Time Out'

Pet Shop Boys
Music for malls and motorways.
Simon Frith – 'Observer' (1990)

Prince
'Purple Rain' (1984) – Ultimately as spineless as it sounds.   *Dave Hill (1986)*

He's sort of a cross between Liberace and Johnny Mathis.
'Motion Picture Guide' (1984)

'Morning Papers' (1993) – Sounds like Michael Jackson singing 'We Are the World' with one arm lifting a Slushy Pup, the other balancing a Parisian cookbook . . . Not a recommendation.
Everett True – 'Melody Maker'

Ruins
'Burning Stone' (1992) – They make a humungous racket, but so does your baby sister, and she's sweeter. They hit the odd uncluttered groove, but then there's a strong case for denying these guys access to their instruments.
Andrew Perry – 'Select'

Sade
The best thing about Sade is that at her worst she's never actually bad, just very dull.   *Ross Fortune – 'Time Out' (1992)*

An over-rated crock of crap, who has seen one too many Soho nightclubs.
Jane Solanas (1988)

Sandy B
'Feel Like Singin'' (1993) – Don't you just love words that aren't properly ended? Like groovin', lovin', and clubbin'. Predictab.   *Laura Lee Davies – 'Time Out'*

Shakespear's Sister
'Break My Heart' (1988) – Typical hoofer for the Hippodrome hordes. She should be bard.
Edwin Pouncey – 'New Musical Express'

The Shamen
'Phorever People' – Phorever? Only the sort of people who still wear 'Smiley Smile' acid-house tee-shirts and say things like 'Jack Your Body' still cultivate the irritating, f***ing clubland habit of spelling their 'f's' as 'ph's'! Get out of the late eighties, you useless ph***wits!
Mr Agreeable – 'Melody Maker' (1993)

Jimmy Somerville
'Run for Love' – Will Mr. Potato Head cut a new record? Does anybody really care? This dates back to Bronski Beat days and

then, as now, bores the pants off me.
Andy Cowan – 'Rage'

He isn't very attractive. He looks not quite finished – as if there's still a lot of work to be done on him.
Richard Fairbrass [Right Said Fred] (1992)

Sonia
She dances like a spaz and sounds like that Debbie Gibson . . . She just prances about like one of those precious little shits in kilts that for some unfathomable reason cause a sensation at the *Royal Command Performance*.
Stud Brothers – 'Melody Maker'

Spandau Ballet
'Diamond' – Putting the Spands on a double album is like buying a garage for a bicycle. *'Melody Maker'*

Dusty Springfield
'In Private' (1989) – What Have We Done To Deserve This?
Chris Roberts – 'Melody Maker'

Stock, Aitken and Waterman
Stock, Take One and Water It Down.
Chris Roberts – 'Melody Maker'

Stock and Waterman
The combination gives new meaning to mediocrity.
Ray Douglas – 'Time Out' (1993)

Take That
'Do What U Like' – A puke-inducing slice of shite. Projectile vomiting is infinitely preferable. *Andy Cowan. – 'Rage'*

'It Only Takes a Minute' (1992) – An astonishing and actually quite nauseating case of the young being used to exploit the younger. *'Melody Maker'*

Neil Tennant [Pet Shop Boys]
He emits the contrivances without the crucial element of joy, without the punchline.
Chris Roberts – 'Melody Maker' (1988)

The Thieves
'Through the Door' (1992) – Limpid, trite and lifeless, in all the best senses of the words. *Ross Fortune – 'Time Out'*

Thule
'321 Normal 2' (1992) – Thule would probably have been fashionable in 1983 and are, inevitably, challengingly rubbish.
Adam Higginbotham – 'Select' (1992)

Ruby Turner
'Motown Song Book' (1988) – The presence of the Temptations, Four Tops, Jimmy Ruffin and Junior Walker on some tracks does little to improve matters; it's a bit like trying to put TCP on a gunshot wound.
Terry Staunton – 'New Musical Express'

Luther Vandross
'Never Too Much: Remix' (1989) – For some reason I can't shake off this mental image of Gary Davies slow-dancing in a tacky disco. This would be the soundtrack. *Ian Gittins – 'Melody Maker'*

Vanilla Ice (real name: Robert Van Winkle)
Rap Van Winkle.
'New Musical Express' (1991)

Village People
'Macho Man' – Lyrics so camp they have to be held down by tent pegs.
'New Musical Express' (1979)

Jane Weidlin
'Inside A Dream' – . . . festering sub-Bananarama baby's stools.
Mick Mercer – 'Melody Maker'

Jackie Wilson
'Reet Petite' – I thought the strange collection of noises, ranging from gargling to an outboard motor, was obviously Stan Freberg indulging in one of his satires.
Derek Johnson (1957)

OTHER

Karaoke
'Karaoke' comes from the Japanese 'kara'

('empty') and 'oke' (supposedly from 'okesutura' – the Japanese version of 'orchestra' – now thought to mean 'headed'). *'Classic CD' (1993)*

MEDIA

The media is the main enemy of democracy and socialism in Britain.
Tony Benn – 'Diary'

The fallacy of the press is still rampant in this decaying and foolish world.
Noël Coward – 'Pomp and Circumstance'

The press can be best compared to haemorrhoids. *Gareth Davies*

In my experience a newspaper is not a well-ordered bureaucracy.
Sir Gordon Downey (1990)

I love the media. They should all be working from Dachau. *Jerry Lewis (1992)*

On the whole I would not say that our Press is obscene. I would say that it trembles on the brink of obscenity.
Lord Longford (1963)

The Press should take a lesson from the under-tens – it might learn something.
John McEnroe (1984)

THE PRESS

From the American newspapers, you'd think America was populated by naked women and cinema stars.
Nancy Astor (1957)

America is a country of inventors, and the greatest of inventors are the newspaper men. *Alexander G. Bell (1917)*

It is an ordeal reading the British papers every day. *Jacques Delors (1992)*

That ephemeral sheet of paper, the newspaper, is the natural enemy of the book, as the whore is of the decent woman. *Edmond and Jules De Goncourt – 'Journal' (1858)*

Once a newspaper touches a story, the facts are lost forever, even to the protagonists.
Norman Mailer – 'Esquire' (1960)

The British newspapers are edited by Kitty Kelley. They are only interested in character assassination.
Rudolf Nureyev (1991)

The newspaper and magazine business is an intellectual brothel from which there is no escape. *Leo Tolstoy*

Most of the current literary and arts magazines are written by the self-indulgent or pretentious.
Rupert Vandervell – 'The Auteur' (1992)
[*'Time Out' remarked on this comment –* Spot the Kettle.]

NEWSPAPERS & MAGAZINES

British 'quality' newspapers
The *Sun* is far less casually corrupt, if less of an insult to journalism, than those piss-elegant broadsheets whose review and literary sections amount to nothing more than an extension of the PR industry.
Julie Burchill – 'New Statesman' (1990)

Church Times
I am increasingly convinced that the *Church Times* is now edited by the devil in person. *Bishop Gore*

Counterfeit
If you continue to publish slanderous pieces about me, I shall feel compelled to cancel my subscription.
Groucho Marx – 'Letter'

Country Living

Like the Moonies, this glossy magazine leads perfectly sane middle-class people to behave in staggering ways . . . One of the most distressing features of *Country Living* is the regular appearance of Paul Heiney dressed like an escaped extra from *Far from the Madding Crowd*.

Stephen Pile – 'Punch' (1990)

Daily Express

The paper written by the undead for the undead. *John Sweeney – 'Observer' (1990)*

Daily Star

It will be all tits, bums, QPR and roll your own fags. *Derek Jameson*

Fleet Street, London

A certain squalid knot of alleys where the town's bad blood once slept corruptly.

Robert Browning

What a squalid and irresponsible little profession it is at the moment. Nothing prepares you for how bad Fleet Street really is until it craps on you from a great height. *Ken Livingstone*

London Evening Standard

Good evening, sir. I'm from the *Evening Standard*. *Journalist*
The Standard! What a dreadful paper, I certainly shan't talk to you.

Prince Edward (1992)

News of the World

'Wankers' Weekly', a.k.a. 'News of the Screws'. *'Private Eye'*

Private Eye

An infected organ. *Robert Maxwell (1986)*

Boring, very establishment, full of in-jokes for the in-crowd.*Simon Regan (1992)*

Punch

The essence of humour is surprise; that is why you laugh when you see a joke in *Punch*. *A. P. Herbert*

Q Magazine

Can anyone read *Q* without an instant greying of hair? *Everett True (1989)*

Regina Leader (Canada)

'The MisLeader'. *Anon (1923)*

Sounds

Those seventies' retards.
Steve Sutherland – 'Melody Maker '(1988)

The Spectator

The Young Fogey Weekly.
Peregrine Worsthorne – 'Sunday Telegraph' (1989)

The Sun

Murdoch has found a gap in the market – the oldest gap in the world. *Anon*

It is a dreadful paper, which panders to what it believes to be working-class prejudices; worse than that, it patronises its readers by assuming that its views must be theirs.

Julian Critchley – 'Daily Telegraph' (1990)

'There's more Fun in *The Sun*' – that's your catchphrase. Unfortunately, like everything else in *The Sun* this is not true.
E. J. Thribb – 'Private Eye' (1989)

Murdoch's *Sun* has only one voice: loud, frantic and insistent. It has the class of a polyester shirt, and the soul of a Colombian hit-man.

'Washington Post' (1989)

Sunday Telegraph

Don't believe everything you read in the papers: especially in the *Sunday Telegraph. Bill Dare [Spitting Image] (1992)*

Sunday Times

'The Sunset Times'. *'Private Eye'*

Time Out

All *Time Out* journalists want to write for the *Evening Standard*.

Lindsay Anderson (1992)

I don't care to hear about *Time Out. Time Out*'s a f***ing asshole magazine.
Robert de Niro – 'Guardian' (1993)

The Times

The Turnabout. *Nickname*

On Irish home rule – The Times is
speechless and takes three columns to
express its speechlessness.
                    Sir Winston Churchill (1908)

Toronto Globe
A literary despotism which struck without
mercy.   *Goldwin Smith (1883)*

EDITING & PUBLISHING

If there is anything tougher than a sports
editor, I should not like to meet it.
                    Earl of Arran (1962)

Perhaps, an editor might divide his paper
into four chapters; heading the first,
Truths; the second, Probabilities; the
third, Possibilities, and fourth, Lies.
                    Thomas Jefferson

The modern editor of a paper does not
want facts. The editor wants novelty. He
would prefer a novelty that is not a fact to
a fact that is not a novelty.
                    William Randolph Hearst

EDITORS & PUBLISHERS

Anon Editor of *The Los Angeles Times*
I can but wonder what will become of the
editor of the *Los Angeles Times* when the
breath leaves his feculent body and death
stops the rattling of his abortive brain. He
cannot be buried in the sea lest he poisons
the fishes. He cannot be suspended in
mid-air, like Mahomet's coffin, lest the
circling worlds, in their endeavour to
avoid contamination, crash together,
wreck the universe and bring about the
return of chaos and Old Night. The
damn scoundrel is a white elephant on the
hands of the Deity, and I have some
curiosity to know what He will do with
him.   *W. C. Brann*

Bruce Anderson (*Sunday Telegraph*)
Hagiographer-in-chief to the Tory party.
                    Simon Heffer – 'The Spectator' (1992)

Harold Brooks-Baker (Editor of *Burke's Peerage*)
He knows as much about the Queen as an

Ayrshire cow knows about the Exchange
Rate Mechanism . . . He is a rent-a-royal-
quote buffoon.
                    Peter McKay – 'Evening Standard' (1991)

William F. Buckley Jr. (Editor of *New Republic*)
It's great to be with Bill Buckley because
you don't have to think. He takes a
position and you automatically take the
opposite and you know you're right.
                    J. K. Galbraith

Chris Davis (Assistant Editor of the *Sun*)
Mr Davis may not be the most engaging
of characters (waking up to hear him on
the *Today* programme was rather like
finding a Colorado beetle in one's early-
morning tea).
                    'The Weasel' – 'Independent' (1993)

Cecil Harmsworth King (Chairman of *Mirror Newspapers*)
He was an outsized man both in
physique, ambition and self-esteem.
                    Denis Healey

Frank Harris (Editor of *Vanity Fair* and *Evening News*)
Can there ever have been, since St Paul,
such a pompous, conceited, opinionated,
patronising ass? Patronising Ruskin,
Carlyle, Whitman, Wilde and the Prince
of Wales; patronising the Parthenon or
the whole continent of North America;
patronising the arts, patronising
philosophy, patronising God. Prose
stodgy and repetitious; moralising at once
trite and windy; and as for the celebrated
sex, orgasms going off as a noisily and
monotonously as a twenty-one gun salute
– to Frank Harris, of course. *Simon Raven*

Hugh Hefner (*Playboy* magazine)
His philosophy would not impress anyone
with as much knowledge of the subject as
can be gained by catching sight of a copy
of a popular philosophical digest in a
book-case on the other side of a fairly
large room.   *Anon*

ITV's 'The World of Hugh Hefner' (1974) –
Mocking Hugh Hefner is easy to do, and

in my mind, should be made easier.
Clive James – 'Observer'

Ian Hislop (Editor of *Private Eye*)
He looks rather like King Edward – the
potato not the monarch.   *Anon*

I don't think people like midgets,
especially pushy midgets. I think he is a
deeply unpleasant man.
Nigel Dempster (1986)

**Kelvin MacKenzie (Editor of
The Sun)**
Kelvin MacFilth.   *'Private Eye'*

**H. L. Mencken (Editor of *The
Smart Set*)**
The world's greatest alphabetical
montebank, perpetually suffering from
logomachitis, or acute inflammation of
the stylus. If all he writes is true, he is a
very sick man.   *'Chicago Step-ladder'*

If he and the pusillanimous curs who are
backing him are right, Judas Iscariot
should be sainted, and an American
shrine should be erected to the memory
of Benedict Arnold.   *L. L. Hayden*

Mr Mencken's prose sounds like large
stones being thrown into a dump-cart.
Robert Littell

Mr Mencken did not degenerate from an
ape, but an ass. And in the process of
'revolution' the tail was eliminated, the
ears became shorter, and the hind parts
smaller; but the ability to bray was
increased, intensified, amplified, and
otherwise assified about one million
times.   *J. B. Tedder*

**Rupert Murdoch (Publisher of *The
Sun* and *The Times*)**
The man's charm is lethal. One minute
he's swimming along with a smile, then
snap! There's blood in the water. You're
head's gone.   *John Barry*

He believes that people crave rubbish and
that he has the right to grow rich
providing it.
Simon Hoggart – 'Observer' (1992)

The Dirty Digger.   *'Private Eye'*

No self-respecting dead fish would want
to be wrapped in a Murdoch newspaper,
let alone work for it.   *George Royko (1986)*

Rupert Murdoch has made a fortune
from selling excrement and, in the
process, has debauched our culture and
corrupted our youths, producing a
generation of lager louts, sex maniacs and
morons. *Francis Wheen – 'Literary Review'*

**John Middleton Murry (Founder
Editor of *The Adelphi*)**
His very frankness is a falsity. In fact it
seems falser than his insincerity.
Katherine Mansfield [Mrs Murry]

**Andrew Neill (Editor of the *Sunday
Times*)**
That Bordes boudoir boy, the oleaginous
editor of the *Sunday Times*.
John Junor – 'Mail on Sunday' (1990)

Andrew 'Brillo Pad' Neill.   *'Private Eye'*

**Harrison Gray Otis (Publisher of *Los
Angeles Times*)**
In the city of San Francisco we have
drunk to the very dregs of infamy; we
have had vile officials, we have had rotten
newspapers. But we have nothing so vile,
nothing so low, nothing so debased,
nothing so infamous in San Francisco as
Harrison Gray Otis. He sits there in senile
dementia, with gangrened heart and
rotting brain, grimacing at every reform,
chatting impotently at all things that are
decent, frothing, fuming, violently
gibbering, going down to his grave in
snarling infamy.   *Hiram Johnson*

**Eve Pollard (Editor of *Sunday
Mirror*)**
Eve Pollard a.k.a. 'La Stupenda', a.k.a.
'La Bollard' a.k.a 'Dame Edna Cleavage'
a.k.a. 'ET'.   *'Private Eye' (1988)*

**Harold Ross (Editor of *The New
Yorker*)**
At first view, oddly disappointing. Even
in dinner jacket he looked loosely
informal, like a carelessly carried
umbrella.   *James Thurber (1927)*

Ross, a man who knew nothing and had contempt for everything he didn't understand, which was practically everything.   *Alexander Woollcott*

JOURNALISM

Journalism could be described as turning one's enemies into money.
                    Craig Brown (1990)

Skin a hard-boiled journalist and you find a thwarted idealist.   *Russell Green*

Reporters are puppets. They simply respond to the pull of the most powerful strings.   *Lyndon B. Johnson*

The lowest depth to which people can sink before God is defined by the word 'journalist'. If I were a father and had a daughter who was seduced I should despair over her; I would hope for her salvation. But if I had a son who became a journalist and continued to be one for five years, I would give him up.
                    Soren Kierkegaard

Women journalists are harlots. Harlots of the day, not the night.   *James Pickles (1992)*

Journalists belong in the gutter because that is where the ruling classes throw their guilty secrets.   *Gerald Priestland (1988)*

American female hacks tend to psychoanalyse everything, including household pets.   *Taki – 'Spectator' (1992)*

Journalism is a low trade and a habit worse than heroin, a strange seedy world full of misfits and drunkards and failures. A group photo of the Top 10 journalists in America on any given day would be a monument to human ugliness.
                    Hunter S. Thompson (1988)

There is much to be said in favour of modern journalism. By giving us the opinions of the uneducated, it keeps us in touch with the ignorance of the community.
                    Oscar Wilde – 'Intentions' (1891)

The American President reigns for four years, and journalists govern for ever and ever.   *Oscar Wilde (1891)*

A journalist makes up his lies
And takes you by the throat.
W. B. Yeats – 'The Old Stone Cross' (1938)

JOURNALISTS

Anon American columnist
She's one great stampede from nose to navel.   *Noël Coward*

Julie Burchill
Julie Burchill is despicable for two reasons. The first is that she will not appear on television or in the public forum to account for what she's written, which means that two, she is a coward. And if she is a coward, then the moral authority behind most of her statements simply does not exist.
                    Jon Savage – 'Observer' (1993)

Philip Hodson
He thinks he's writing for the 'Journal of Psychology' . . . his column is going down like a cup of cold sick.   *Anon (1992)*

John Junor
He likes to think of himself as the columnist who articulates the opinions of the average reader. But, in fact, if he articulates anything at all, he is the bigoted, homophobic, barrack-room lawyer in the snuggery.
                    Logan Gourlay – 'Guardian'

Bernard Levin
It takes Bernard Levin five hundred words to get to the point.
                    Jeffrey Bernard – 'Spectator' (1992)

Paul Morley
For Paul Morley to attack media culture is like hearing Jeremy Beadle criticize game shows.
          Cosmo Landesman – 'Modern Review' (1993)

Tony Parsons
Tony has become the Hyacinth Bucket of journalism. Forever trying to distance himself from the Onslows of this world, but too trapped into a middle class lifestyle to realise that the majority of

working class people are still honest and decent.

Garry Bushell – 'Modern Review' (1992)

Nick Rufford and David Leppard
The Laurel and Hardy of investigative journalism.   *'Private Eye'*

Hannen Swaffer
Whenever I see his fingernails, I thank God I don't have to look at his feet.

Athene Seyler

Israel Zangwill
His face shining like Moses, his teeth like the Ten Commandments – all broken.

Sir Herbert Beerbohm Tree

TELEVISION

TV – a clever contradiction derived from the words Terrible Vaudeville. However, it is our latest medium – we call it a medium because nothing's well done. It has already revolutionised social grace by cutting down parlour conversation to two sentences: 'What's on television?' and 'Good night!'

Goodman Ace – Letter to Groucho Marx

Life doesn't imitate art. It imitates bad television.   *Woody Allen*

There's no way anybody's going to take you seriously if you're on a TV show.

Shaun Cassidy

I don't like television, it's for dedicated non-thinkers.   *Billy Connolly (1989)*

There are film buffs and opera buffs, but there is no such thing as a telly buff. Nor should there be, because only the retarded and TV critics should pay so much attention to such an ephemeral, transitory medium.

Victor Lewis-Smith – 'Evening Standard' (1992)

Everbody watches television. But no one really likes it.   *Mark C. Miller*

NETWORKS

British Broadcasting Corporation [BBC]
The BBC does itself untold harm by its excessive sensitivity. At the first breath of criticism the Corporation adopts a posture of a hedgehog at bay.

'Annan Committee Report' (1977)

Why should a little old lady from Barnsley pay £100 per year so that Michael Ignatieff can toss himself off on the *Late Show*?   *Richard Littlejohn*

British Sky Broadcasting [B Sky B]
On satellite TV, there is too much of everything: at Sky, pigging out is a way of life.   *Tony Parsons – 'Observer Magazine' (1992)*

Public Broadcasting Service [PBS] (USA)
P.B.S. = Paid for by Bored Spectators.

Anon

TV SHOWS

Soap operas are simply corn on the sob.

Anon

A lot of TV pop is like nouvelle cuisine. It looks great and tastes shite.

Malcolm Gerrie – 'Wired' (1988)

24-hour news is the ultimate in television repeats.   *'Mail on Sunday' (1992)*

2point4 Children (BBC TV)
An witless exercise involving a charmless couple called Bill and Ben, who will appeal only to lovers of alliteration.

Maureen Paton – 'Daily Express' (1992)

After Dark (Channel 4)
The drinking class's equivalent of therapy.

Garry Bushell – 'Modern Review' (1992)

A Bit of a Do (ITV)
A sort of very low-rent Alan Bennett.

Alkarim Jivani – 'Time Out' (1992)

A Word in Your Era (BBC TV)

A comedy show that has the effect of making you think you have forgotten how to laugh. A desperately arch panel game show, full of embarrassingly, unfunny jokes and compered, with all the zest of a man awaiting his own execution, by Rory McGrath.

Craig Brown – 'Sunday Times' (1992)

Americana (Channel 4)

I tuned in to only one show and learned that Americans ate a lot of junk food. Jonathan Ross might just as well have taken his cameras to Wigan and discovered there are fish and chip shops.

Jack Tinker – 'Daily Mail' (1993)

Beverly Hills 90210 (ITV)

Just one long advert for consumer durables with a cupful of caring poured over. *Elaine Paterson – 'Time Out' (1992)*

The Big Breakfast (C4)

Has reduced morning TV to the level of *Sesame Street* banality.

Garry Bushell – 'Modern Review' (1992)

Channel 4 has devised a special programme for all those who want to know what it's like to be pregnant. *The Big Breakfast* guarantees morning sickness ... It makes Saturday morning stuff for children look like *Mastermind* and Philip Schofield like David Dimbleby.

Jilly Parkin – 'Daily Express' (1992)

'End of the Year Show' (1992/3) – The end of *The Big Breakfast* would have been a much more attractive proposition, but hyper-active children and intellectually challenged adults need to celebrate like the rest of us.

Mark Sanderson – 'Sunday Times'

Blackeyes (BBC TV)

Reminiscent of Disney's Snow White doing an underwear ad.

'Daily Mail' (1989)

After four episodes of *Blackeyes*, I feel as if I had dined on a soggy fricassee of

chopped-up recipe books.

Noel Malcolm – 'Sunday Telegraph' (1989)

In *Blackeyes*, the pretentious and prurient are most unappealingly mixed ... *Blackeyes* reveals a morbid fascination with the nastier recesses of Denis Potter's mind.

Charles Spencer – 'Sunday Telegraph' (1989)

A load of old cobblers. *'The Sun' (1989)*

Boon (ITV)

The acting and dialogue suggested that RADA must now have an entire course module on playing brash, humourless business executives in the style of those total, total nerds in the Mercury commercial. (Remember, 'Like' is a word I will not tolerate in this office, 'like' is for wimps) ... Outstandingly awful stuff.

Jonathan Margolis – 'Mail on Sunday' (1992)

The Borgias (BBC TV)

Never drawing breath, *The Borgias* bores on like a bore at a party who, having bored everybody else into the wall, stands alone in the kitchen and bores himself.

Clive James – 'Observer' (1974)

The Camomile Lawn (Channel 4)

Television works wonders with Dickens, so why can't a novel about the late Thirties and early Forties be dramatised without becoming a cardboard 'cut-out'?

Jeanette Kupfermann – 'Daily Mail' (1992)

Children in Need (BBC TV, hosted by Terry Wogan)

Why, in order to help children, should we have to tolerate One Man and His Wig surrounded by a bunch of Egos in Need – the minor celebrities from the BBC's worst shows? It makes my flesh creep.

Victor Lewis-Smith – 'Mail on Sunday' (1992)

The Cleopatras

Getting the costumes right in *The Cleopatras* was like polishing the fish knives on the *Titanic*. *Julian Barnes*

Clive James Meets Ronald Reagan (1989) **(BBC TV)**
The two of them could well have been auditioning to be Santa Claus in the next Macey Christmas parade.
> *Sheridan Morley – 'The Times'*

Crime Limited **(BBC TV)**
There's something about this leering, lip-smacking show that gave me the creeps. It seemed to be shot in semi-darkness, on a set looking like a torture dungeon . . . If real life (and death) crime is to become entertainment, where will it end? With Jeremy Beadle presenting 'You've Been Mugged'?
> *Charles Catchpole – 'News of the World' (1992)*

Presenters Nick Ross and Sue Cook of *Crimewatch UK* are now asking for a separate series of ten weekly offences to be taken into consideration: *Crime Limited* on Tuesday nights.   *'Private Eye' (1992)*

Dame Edna's Neighbourhood Watch **(ITV)**
This probing show is more 'Down the Toilet Bowl' than 'Through the Keyhole'.
> *'Time Out' (1992)*

Darling Buds of May **(ITV)**
It is, of course, famous for nothing ever happening: Ma wobbles her chest and makes the odd whoopee cushion sound-effect: Pop goes 'Perfick!'. It's perfick family viewing: instead of sitting around doing nothing, we can watch some other family sitting around doing nothing.
> *Mark Steyn – 'Mail on Sunday' (1992)*

Another sunlit story written with a stick of rock dipped in syrup.   *'Time Out' (1992)*

Desmond's **(Channel 4)**
The less than side-splitting sitcom. Will you laugh uproariously? Will John Major be spotted in one of Norma's frocks?
> *Elaine Paterson – 'Time Out' (1992)*

Diana: Her True Story **(Sky TV)**
Royal performance: the TV soap that spreads the dirt.
> *W. F. Deedes – 'Daily Telegraph' (1993)*

The monarchy is portrayed as having all the charm, sensitivity and finesse of the *Bash Street Kids*.
> *Pam Francis – 'Today' (1993)*

Much of the dialogue is hilariously plonking scenario-writing . . . Other exchanges are simply tabloid editorials press-ganged into dialogue form.
> *Martyn Harris – 'Daily Telegraph' (1993)*

Every member of the Royal Family . . . is cruelly lampooned as heartless, vindictive, stuffy and poisonous. Some of the performances are obviously derived lock, stock and barrel from *Spitting Image*.
> *Peter Paterson – 'Daily Mail' (1993)*

Don't Tell Father **(BBC TV)**
Any programme which has 'Father' in the title is likely to be the mother of all stinkers. *Don't Tell Father* is well down to the standard of such comedy classics as *Father, Dear Father* and *Bless Me, Father*.
> *Charles Catchpole – 'News of the World' (1992)*

Out of that scrabble bag of clichés where 'The Time of Your Wife' cuddles up with 'How's Your Father?' and 'Where Did You Last See This Punchline?'
> *Allison Pearson – 'Independent on Sunday' (1992)*

Eldorado **(BBC TV)**
It looks like pornography without the sex.
> *Anon (1992)*

Looking more like a holiday commercial than the soap operas we are used to on British TV . . . Judging a new series by only its first episode is as tricky as gauging a restaurant by only reading its menu.   *Joe Joseph – 'The Times' (1992)*

If this is life in the land of Spanish sun, sea, sangria and sex, I'll put up with the drizzle and grizzle in Blighty a bit longer, thanks.
> *Hilary Kingston – 'Daily Mirror' (1992)*

Calling it 'the Golden Place' was asking for it. 'El Brasso' might have been better.
Hilary Kingston – 'Daily Mirror' (1992)

The first eight bars of the signature tune are enough to send most of us scuttling to the video shop.
Mark Steyn – 'Mail on Sunday' (1992)

Emmerdale (ITV)
Formerly *Emmerdale Farm* . . . the last time I tuned in, it was little more than Emmerdale allotment . . . *Emmerdale* was never more than a pop-up book of *The Archers*.
Victor Lewis-Smith – 'Evening Standard' (1993)

Every Second Counts (BBC TV)
It certainly does, whenever Paul Daniels is on the air . . . Each show last for 1800 seconds. It just seems an awful lot longer.
Charles Catchpole – 'News of the World' (1992)

Flamingo Road (BBC TV)
The worst stretch of imported American trash.   *Clive James – 'Observer' (1981)*

Food and Drink (BBC TV)
A *Blue Peter* for greedy pigs.
Craig Brown – 'Sunday Times' (1992)

Fresh Fields (ITV)
About as sexy as cleaning your ears with cotton buds.   *'Time Out'*

The Gladiators (ITV)
The novelty of watching people named after pet Rottweilers hit each other over the head with giant cotton buds was always going to wear off.
Charles Catchpole – 'News of the World' (1992)

Where presenters [John Fashanu and Ulrika Johnsson] read 'enthusiasm' off an autocue, and the commentator [John Sachs] sounds like a machine.
Margaret Forwood – 'Daily Express' (1992)

The Good Guys (ITV)
Pitched at a level marginally less than

Danger Mouse . . . it's terrifyingly inane . . . Compared with *The Good Guys*, even 'International Darts from Droitwich' seems an attractive proposition.
'Private Eye' (1992)

Good Morning Britain (TV-AM)
Radio 3 is a country gent reading the *Telegraph*, LWT a shell-suited youth with a six-pack, Channel 4 a baggy-jacketed design consultant. Using this technique (of brand personification) TV-am emerges as a mustachioed herbert from Crawley whose philosophy of life is drawn from the pages of the *Readers Digest* . . . The show is cheap and trashy. *Hello!* with moving pictures but without the celebrity cast.
Victor Lewis-Smith – 'Evening Standard' (1992)

Good Morning with Anne and Nick (BBC TV)
The show was the most vapid I have ever watched, a grisly mixture of fawning and fumbling, a cackhanded exercise in sponsored time-wasting.
Craig Brown – 'Sunday Times' (1992)

Head Over Heels (Carlton TV)
I'll never be head over heels with this rock'n'droll.
Margaret Forwood – 'Daily Express' (1993)

A Gaggia machine and a *Rebel Without a Cause* poster do not a seven-part drama make.
James Rampton – 'Independent on Sunday' (1993)

These may not be human actors at all. Watch any scene involving more than two people: like early episodes of *Stingray*, they only change the direction in which their heads are pointing between shots.
Mark Steyn – 'Mail on Sunday' (1993)

Hearts of Gold (BBC TV)
Appearing on this programme is the media equivalent of being awarded the British Empire Medal, for the Heart of Gold is a patronising and meaningless decoration given only to 'lowly' punters,

as a pretext for wallowing in cheap sentimentality at their expense . . . This is the furthest that Esther Rantzen has yet gone in taking Light Entertainment down the road of 'let's take the smoked windows out of the ambulance so we can enjoy the suffering'.
Victor Lewis-Smith – 'Evening Standard' (1992)

Hearts of Gold is all about physical courage, since you need an awful lot to watch it . . . This is not simply tabloidal TV, it is worse. This is the stuff that local rags are made of – mawkish, sentimental, ignoble junk. The sooner it is axed, the better.   *Victor Lewis-Smith – Ibid*

Home and Away (ITV)
Consider this, the people who watch this are the same people responsible for keeping Bryan Adams at No. 1 for two years.   *'Bitch' (1992)*

The House of Elliot (BBC TV)
Upstairs Downstairs without the knobs on.
Bruce Dessau – 'Time Out' (1992)

Inspector Morse (ITV)
A dull TV detective acclaimed as great intellect yet who takes two hours to solve crimes, compared to one hour for Miss Marple, Poirot, Bergerac, etc.
Mike Barfield – 'The Oldie' (1992)

Lovejoy (BBC TV)
The series is a pain in the commode, just as predictable as a metronome, and as deep as the shine on a fake Regency cabinet.
Peter Paterson – 'Daily Mail' (1993)

The Love Weekend (Channel 4)
A naked chat-show, in which Richard Jobson threatens to reveal all, is almost as horrifying as the thought of Margi Clarke, Su Pollard and Nina Myskow with their clothes ON.
Charles Catchpole – 'News of the World' (1993)

May to December (BBC TV)
Bad even by British sitcom's lamentable standard. Weaker than a cup of BR's Maxpax.   *Julian Astor – 'Time Out' (1993)*

Mission Impossible (BBC TV)
Glop from the schlock-hopper.
Clive James – 'Observer' (1974)

Murder She Wrote (US TV)
For whatever the critics of British-made television may say, I don't think that we make anything as shamelessly anodyne, cynical and mediocre as *Murder, She Wrote*. It's not a show anyone can be proud of.   *Marcus Berkmann – 'Daily Mail' (1992)*

Nature (BBC TV)
As with BBC's *Nature* series, you're left wondering why so many environmentally-friendly TV shows have to be pumped full of artificial additives.
Mark Steyn – 'Evening Standard' (1992)

Neighbours (BBC TV)
The show you can listen to while talking on the phone, while reading Bertrand Russell, while decoding the genetic information in a DNA molecule, all without missing a single nuance of the plot.   *Victor Lewis-Smith – 'Evening Standard' (1992)*

With furniture that looks like MFI rejects and walls that wobble whenever an actor picks up the phone. The designs may be cheap and shoddy, but not nearly as cheap and wooden as the acting and the dialogue; it soon becomes clear that the most moving thing on this show is the scenery.   *Victor Lewis-Smith – Ibid*

As the end credits rolled Reg Grundy Productions informed us that 'all events depicted in this photoplay are purely fictitious' and that 'any similarity to persons living or dead is purely coincidental'. Come on, Reg. Any similarity would not just be coincidence. It would be a miracle.
Victor Lewis-Smith – Ibid

News at Ten (ITN)
On the new format – B.L.T. : Bright, Light and Trite.   *Anon ITN staff (1992)*

On the new format – You begin to wonder whether they have all watched *Broadcast News* too often and started to believe in their own star quality.

Chris Dunkley – 'Mail on Sunday' (1992)

Noel's House Party (BBC TV)

There is a terrible programme called *Noel's House Party* in which all the jokes refer to other telly programmes; when Noel Edmonds opens the front door or cupboard of his 'house', more figures-as-seen-on-TV are discovered. This programme is the modern equivalent of hell, and the figures trapped in Noel's house – stray characters from *Neighbours* or *Last of the Summer Wine* mingled with sports stars or ex-politicians – are like the tormented souls in Dante.

A. N. Wilson – 'Sunday Telegraph' (1992)

Nurses (Channel 4)

Give me *Surgical Spirit* any day.

Charles Catchpole – 'News of the World' (1992)

On the Buses (ITV)

Rerun for ghastly '70s bus-based sitcom continues with all the grace of a late 2B . . . With a script that makes Attila the Hun look the paragon of political correctness, it's series like these that make you wonder whether nostalgia is a flimsy virtue.

'Time Out' (1992)

Oprah Winfrey Meets Michael Jackson (BBC 2)

The longest piece of spindoctoring in the history of modern broadcasting.

Thomas Sutcliffe – 'Independent' (1993)

Ps and Qs (BBC TV)

Naffer than *Bullseye*, dafter than *3-2-1*, with less charm than *Play Your Cards Right*, the whole thing stank.

Hilary Kingsley – 'Daily Mirror' (1992)

The designers covered every angle save one; they forgot to insert a free sick bag at the appropriate page in the *Radio Times*.

John Naughton – 'Observer' (1992)

Pallas II (Channel 4)

In which real footage is dubbed with a fake script. This is like all the losing entries in a caption competition being strung together, stretched over 25 minutes, and the joke running out after 30 seconds.

Allison Pearson – 'Independent on Sunday' (1992)

The Pallisers (BBC TV)

A bit of a dud . . . the acting takes place in the range from minor league to outright incompetent, and the direction only occasionally rises to the uninspired.

Clive James – 'Observer' (1974)

The Piglet Files (ITV)

Secret agent piglet, licensed to swill.

Garry Bushell – 'The Sun' (1992)

Points of View (BBC TV)

Anne Robinson's lopsided pout of self-congratulation.

Gilbert Adair – 'Sunday Times' (1993)

All monitored by Anne 'Autocue' Robinson. If this is meant to prove viewers' opinions matter, it is a pointless exercise.

Mark Sanderson – 'Sunday Times' (1992)

Prime Suspect 2 (ITV)

Not prime at all. Just suspect.

Charlie Catchpole – 'News of the World' (1992)

Not nearly so gripping as your average Ruth Rendell mystery . . . I was positively longing for the interval; and it surely takes a pretty boring programme to make you think some interest is to be derived from nice Trevor McDonald telling you about Sunday trading restrictions.

A. N. Wilson – 'Sunday Telegraph' (1992)

Primetime (BBC TV)

Its extraordinarily wild, computer-generated opening credits suggest *Def 2*, but your first glimpse of the frail studio audience suggests too deaf.

Victor Lewis-Smith – 'Evening Standard' (1992)

Private Schulz (BBC TV)

A supposedly comic series like *Private Schulz* would be an offence even if it were funny. In fact it is no funnier than a cold sore on the lip.

Clive James – 'Observer' (1981)

Roseanne (Channel 4)

I have chosen not to return to the show next season. Instead my wife and I have decided to share a vacation in the relative peace and quiet of Beirut.

Anon producer – 'Variety'

Sale of the Century (ITV)

They call Nicholas Parsons's show *Sale of the Century* because you feel a hundred years old when you watch it.

Bernard Manning

Screen One: Ghostwatch (BBC TV)

Listen! Is that the sound of things going bump in the night? Or is it just the tumbling viewing figures?

Elaine Paterson – 'Time Out' (1992)

Screen Two: The Law Lord (BBC TV)

This time-wasting piece of nonsense was an entirely unsuccessful marriage between a feebly unpromising farce, 'Carry On up the Woolsack', perhaps, and a political thriller concocted from a reading of the manifesto of the Conspiracy Tendency . . . a Hammer House-style production of 'A Teddy Bear Lawyer's Picnic'.

Peter Paterson – 'Daily Mail' (1992)

Sean's Show (C4)

Channel 4 insist on calling Sean Hughes' sitcom 'surreal'. I call it unreal.

Charles Catchpole – 'News of the World' (1992)

Side by Side (BBC TV)

The overworked BBC comedy computer spews out plot 217(b).

Charles Catchpole – 'News of the World' (1992)

This stuff is so depressing it gives you half a mind to have a go yourself. Make

that a quarter.

Allison Pearson – 'Independent on Sunday' (1992)

The Simpsons (Sky TV)

America needs to be more like *The Waltons* and less like *The Simpsons*.

George Bush

Spitting Image (ITV)

It isn't funny – never has been . . . It has all the subtlety of a nightclub bouncer's wedding speech.

Peter McKay – 'Evening Standard' (1992)

Strathblair (BBC TV)

'Strathbore' – looks as cold an unwelcoming as yesterday's porridge.

Charles Catchpole – 'News of The World' (1992)

Surprise Party (Carlton TV)

This Is Your Life (Not!)

Charlie Catchpole – 'Sky News' (1993)

Take Your Pick (ITV)

This has always been a legendary cheapskate show: I mean, who can distinguish between the star prizes and the booby prizes?

Mark Steyn – 'Mail on Sunday' (1992)

Telly Addicts (BBC TV)

I have always thought of *Telly Addicts* as an awful programme, but it turns out I am quite wrong: it is now in its eighth year, which makes it an awful old programme . . . And eight years of lavatory humour is almost more than I can bear.

Craig Brown – 'Sunday Times' (1992)

We all know the effects of prolonged in-breeding and both *Telly Addicts* and its host Noel Edmonds display the classic symptoms.

Victor Lewis-Smith – 'Evening Standard' (1992)

Terry and Julian (Channel 4)

Julian Clary's latest vehicle – that comedy Skoda . . . Twice as many viewers preferred repeats of *Rising Damp* to this relentless rising camp.

Garry Bushell – 'Modern Review' (1992)

This Is Your Life (ITV)

The show is antiseptic to a mawkish degree: 'This Is Your Ideal Life' . . . The campaign for euthanasia is steadily gaining ground and this is a programme that deserves to be put out of its misery.

Victor Lewis-Smith – 'Evening Standard' (1992)

A Time to Dance, written by Melvyn Bragg (BBC TV)

Undoubtedly the most accurate and moving portrait of a retired Cumbrian bank manager by a Hampstead television presenter since the war.

Wallace Arnold – 'Independent on Sunday' (1992)

This Cumbrian Cookie has written a raunchy love romp to set the whole nation's hearts a-bumpin' and a-thumpin'! What next? 'The South Bonk' Show? If we want the sexual fantasies of a dirty ol' man a-humpin' and a-thumpin' all over the Lake District, Melv, we'll give you a ring! Meanwhile, give us a break and clear off back to Cockermouth (geddit?) or wherever it is you are from?!

'Private Eye' (1992)

Wish You Were Here . . . ? (ITV)

It is so remorselessly cheerful that they would describe the cess pit at the bottom of my garden as charmingly unspoilt.

Craig Brown – 'Sunday Times' (1992)

The Word (Channel 4)

The Word is tabloid TV as an art form. Which means it's kitsch, it shocks, it's vulgar and it's banal.

Chrissie Iley – 'Sunday Times' (1993)

The Word is innovative, it's *The Tube* recycled and injected with a hefty dose of bad taste and ineptitude masquerading as dangerous television.

Elaine Paterson – 'Time Out' (1992)

TV tat for the young at heart and the soft in the head. *'Time Out' (1993)*

Your Best Shot (BBC TV)

If this is the BBC's best shot at prime time entertainment, God help us!

'Time Out' (1993)

PERSONALITIES

Newsreaders

Another lazy breed like actors. These are likewise too lazy to read through their material before delivering it and constantly misemphasise it, pause in the wrong place, etc.

Kingsley Amis – 'The Spectator' (1988)

Female Sky TV newscasters – Dollies who read the news as if they're reading a menu. *Peter Sissons (1990)*

Scott Bakula

'Quantum Leap' – Scott becomes a Chippendale! A nice change. He normally looks like a chipolata.

Garry Bushell – 'The Sun' (1992)

Jeff Banks (presenter of *The Clothes Show*)

Banks rummaged among the industry's princelings of haute couture like a tabloid sports reporter, a flushed Max Miller lookalike. *Anon*

Dani Behr (presenter of *The Word*)

Amanda de Cadenet was replaced by Dani Behr – the very name sounds like a cartoon – who is blander, blonder, smilier, hostessier and hollower.

Chrissie Iley – 'Sunday Times' (1993)

Christopher Biggins

Games-shows presented by Christopher Biggins, some people feel, should be suppressed for the good of the nation.

Marcus Berkmann – 'Daily Mail' (1992)

Melvyn Bragg

The André Previn of literature. *Anon*

Modest? He's as modest as Larry Adler!

Jonathan Miller

Melvyn Barg – this adenoidal 'as been sounds like the guy in the 'Tunes' ad on telly. *'Private Eye'*

Trevor Brooking (on *Match of the Day*)

England's most cultured ex-midfielder and now leading BBC television barbiturate . . . he still manages to make Nigel Mansell sound like Murray Walker on acid. And he looks like Virginia Wade.
'Zit' (1993)

Frank Bruno

'Do They Mean Us?' (1989) – Even a f***ing mongol could present a show better than he does.   *Jerry Sadowitz*

Ian Carmichael

'Strathblair' – Poor old Ian Carmichael, boy how he has become bloated over the years . . . He has literally doubled in size since I was last aware of seeing him, as Lord Peter Wimsey. He should ring up Nigel Lawson and ask him for some diet tips.   *A. N. Wilson – 'Sunday Telegraph' (1992)*

Judith Chalmers (*Wish You Were Here*)

Satsuma-skinned Judith Chalmers – a walking warning about spending too long in the sun.   *Charlie Catchpole – 'News of the World' (1992)*

Keith Chegwin

The cheeky alcoholic shocks the world with the revelation that he is a secret celebrity and a fully paid up member of Celebrities Anonymous.   *'Bitch' (1993)*

Terry Christian (presenter *The Word*)

One day someone will join two Terry Christians together and make one long plank.   *Rory Bremner (1993)*

Noel Edmonds

Television is going from bad to Edmonds.   *Rory Bremner (1993)*

He looks just the sort of person to chip in 'You can tell it's only ketchup' halfway through a horror movie.
Craig Brown – 'Sunday Times' (1992)

With his streaked hair, his nudge-nudge common touch, his self-assured smug manner and his schoolboy puns, he is the archetypal smooth local rep from a package holiday firm. *Victor Lewis-Smith – 'Evening Standard' (1992)*

I find Noel Edmonds insufferable and I reach for the zap-button every time the beard looms into view. This could be a bit unfair on the old facial cladding, which is providing a valuable public service by hiding half of Mr Edmonds. If those innocent whiskers could only appear in place of the man himself . . . my cup of happiness would runneth over.
Maureen Paton – 'Daily Express' (1992)

A telly personality whom I imagine to have no existence outside telly.
A. N. Wilson – 'Sunday Telegraph' (1992)

Michael Fish (BBC weather forecaster)

As dull as the day is wet and the weather he reports on. Fish is the Sheikh of Drab Chic.
Peter Freedman – 'Glad to Be Grey' (1985)

Bob Geldof –(*The Big Breakfast*)

The interview itself [with Chris Patten] was proof that Geldof, for all his fund-raising feats, is a loss to the road-sweeping profession, as well as actually looking like something swept up.
Jilly Parkin – 'Daily Express' (1992)

Muriel Gray

Sounding as though she had just spat out a pint of Angostura bitters.
James Delingpole – 'Sunday Telegraph' (1989)

A face which looks as though it has been through a pencil sharpener.
Noel Malcolm – 'Sunday Telegraph' (1989)

Jimmy Greaves (presenter *Good Morning Britain*)

A walrus in a woolly jumper affected his customary objectionable they-call-me-Joe-Blunt persona . . . spoke fluent bilge. In short, he was as illuminating as the average taxi driver, without the saving grace of getting you anywhere.

Victor Lewis-Smith – 'Evening Standard'
(1992)

Loyd Grossman –(presenter of *Through the Keyhole*)

Loyd's preposterous voice is a sound that makes peaceable folk want to put a brick through his teeth . . . Loyd is now up there in the ludricrousness grand prix with the greatest exponent of vocal idiocy Dick Van Dyke in Mary Poppins.

Jonathan Margolis – 'Mail on Sunday'
(1992)

Alan Hansen (on *Match of the Day*)

Thunderbirds puppet who's now made a career out of bleating on and on about Liverpool's injury problems on *Match of the Day*. Was never exactly Mr Controversial in his playing days – and same can be said of his TV career. His strong accent is a problem, but viewers should be able to understand him better when he finally manages to extricate his tongue from Bob Wilson's arse.

'Zit' (1993)

Alan Hansen and Gary Lineker (on *Match of the Day*)

Mr and Mrs Mogadon.   *'Zit' (1993)*

Clive James

In his quest to become the thinking man's Terry Wogan, there are few barrels that Mr James is unwilling to scrape.

John Naughton – 'Observer' (1989)

Dr. Hilary Jones (medical expert *Good Morning Britain*)

A mannequin who has stepped out of the window of C&A.

Victor Lewis-Smith – 'Evening Standard'
(1992)

Richard Keys (Sky sports presenter)

A presenter with a dinky Sky logo on his blazer presides over the grim revelry with a fixed, moronic grin. It is a vision of holiday camp hell.

Tony Parsons – 'Observer Magazine'
(1992)

Robert Kilroy-Silk

'Kilroy' (1990) – A terrible warning about what can happen to politicians who resign.

Mark Lawson – 'Independent on Sunday'

Belinda Lang

'2point4 Children' – Belinda Lang, as Bill, has all the guilt-racked look of the token harassed TV mother, who cannot decide whether to administer Bovril or strychnine to a son in a coma.

Maureen Paton – 'Daily Express' (1992)

Jan Leeming

She is the winner of the 'Award of the Death Watch Beetle' for being so gloomy.

Anon daily newspaper

Ian McShane

'Lovejoy' – There are even doubts about Ian McShane's staying power as a sex symbol. Isn't there a bit of a tum under the T-shirt? The result is that *Lovejoy*'s distinctive style is gradually disappearing, and soon we'll have just another identikit comedy-drama series, starring an ageing Ian Botham lookalike.

Marcus Berkmann – 'Daily Mail' (1992)

Richard Madeley (presenter of *This Morning*)

Tessa Sanderson had travelled to Manchester under the impression that she was appearing on *This Morning* so it appeared only natural that, when the [*This Is Your Life*] big red book was thrust in her face, she collapsed on the floor. The relief that she would not, after all, have to spend half an hour in the company of Richard Madeley was quite understandable.   *Victor Lewis-Smith –*
'Evening Standard' (1992)

Peter Marshall (ITV linkman)

'Miss World' (1980) – Who showed all the signs of having been passed through that famous BBC processing room where front-men go to be deprived of charisma.

Clive James – 'Observer'

Jonathan Meades

'Ps and Qs' – He looked as though he had

agreed to be on the show after a very big lunch.

Marcus Berkmann – 'Daily Mail' (1992)

Mike Morris (TV-am presenter)

One of the few people who could re-enact the squashy nose Dime Bar commercial without recourse to a pane of glass. Some people are born with presence, adding oxygen to the room simply by walking into it. Mr Morris, by contrast, is a human vac-u-vin, sucking the atmosphere out of the studio with a single movement of his mouth.   *Victor Lewis-Smith – 'Evening Standard' (1992)*

Des O'Connor

'Des O'Connor Tonight' (1992) – Perhaps his boyish blandness is what persuades the occasional megastar to appear on his show – as an interviewer, he has all the bite of a baby armadillo.

Mark Sanderson – 'Sunday Times'

The man with the nylon hair.

'Time Out' (1992)

Nick Owen

On the launch of 'Good Morning with Anne and Nick' (1992) – Nick's wooden face bravely concealed the fact he has been unemployed since being voted the sixth most boring man in Britain.

Peter Dunn – 'Independent on Sunday'

Living proof of Oscar Wilde's dictum that, 'Only dull men are bright at breakfast', TV-am presenter, Owen has been hailed as high priest and prophet of the Cult of Ordinariness.

Peter Freedman – 'Glad to Be Grey' (1985)

Maggie Philbin (*Primetime* presenter)

Some interviewers shine, but only Maggie dulls, bowling hopeless underarm deliveries that don't even reach the wicket.   *Victor Lewis-Smith – 'Evening Standard' (1992)*

Dennis Potter

Den Plodder – the whingeing playwright.

'Private Eye' (1989)

Esther Rantzen

Scientists are working on the theory that Rantzenitis is a mutant strain of Monkhouse syndrome, a terrible affliction that often struck Bob during *The Golden Shot* when he was describing the disability of someone he didn't know and broke down on camera.

Victor Lewis-Smith – 'Evening Standard' (1992)

Esther Rantzen's teeth (formerly the property of Arkle the race horse).

Victor Lewis-Smith – 'Mail on Sunday' (1993)

To me there is something rather creepy about a television personality setting herself up as a national child-abuse guru.

Peter McKay – 'Evening Standard' (1991)

Jonathan Ross

The sinking man's David Letterman.

Garry Bushell – 'Modern Review' (1992)

Now there's a useless plank of wood. He should be in real estate. *John Lydon (1989)*

'Americana: Dumb' (1992) – Not that I'm saying Jonathan Ross is dumb. It's just that he isn't clever enough to front a programme which sets itself above its subjects.

Martin Plimmer – 'Evening Standard'

A man who talked like a joke policeman.

Martin Plimmer – Ibid

He's a f***ing plastic piece of yuppie talentless shit and proof that Channel 4 are lazy bastards who won't step outside their own offices to look for talent. He was shit at being a post boy as well.

Jerry Sadowitz (1989)

'Saturday Zoo' (1993) – I sat in mounting bewilderment last weekend trying to discover any sign of recognisable human intellect at work on his behalf in the aptly-named *Saturday Zoo* . . . the entertainment equivalent of the *Emperor's New Clothes*.   *Jack Tinker – 'Daily Mail'*

Philip Schofield

Definitely looks like the boy-next-door, which is unfortunate because where we live the boy next door is in fact a screaming queen who breeds hamsters.

'Zit' (1993)

Jack Scott (BBC weatherman)

'Under the Weather' (1981) – No longer confined to his fleeting half-minute, Jack has now been given the bore's equivalent of a heavy goods vehicle licence. It is children's television, except that children wouldn't watch it. *Clive James – 'Observer'*

Mike Smith

Mike Smith – living proof of the need for ejector seats in helicopters.

Victor Lewis-Smith – 'Evening Standard' (1992)

Barbara Walters

She is said to sleep standing up so the silicone won't move.

Taki – 'Spectator' (1992)

James Whale

A talentless Aquarian smug git.

'Bitch' (1993)

Alan Whicker

Not for nothing are Whicker videos now sold in chemist shops. They are the best cure for insomnia since Mogadon, and can be obtained without a prescription.

John Naughton – 'Observer' (1992)

Francis Wilson (weather forecaster)

Listen to him, and it's like sitting on wet seaweed at Land's End at the end of February. *Jean Rook*

Terry Wogan

What is the correct ethical decision to make about a living cadaver that has demonstrated no brain activity for years, yet whose body lingers on in a state of persistent vegetative stasis? Pull the plug? Keep him switched on in the futile hope of a miraculous mental recovery? In the end my conscience could stand it no

longer, so I did the humane thing and switched Wogan off.

Victor Lewis-Smith – 'Evening Standard' (1992)

Think how much better Wogan would be if instead of rolling his eyes and beaming so complacently at his audience, Mr Wogan actually listened to what his interviewee was saying.

Noel Malcolm – 'Sunday Telegraph' (1989)

Victoria Wood

'Mens Sana in Thingummy Doodah' (1989) – Most of her humour here was as predictable as – well, as a studio audience guffaw. *Noel Malcolm – 'Sunday Telegraph'*

TV EXECUTIVES

John Birt (Director-General of BBC TV)

Birtism: which could roughly be translated as a Stalinist determination that audiences should be instructed, not entertained.

Peter McKay – 'Evening Standard' (1992)

Liz Forgan (Director of Programmes for Channel 4)

She is not fit to be in charge of any programmes which have any bearing on matters industrial or political. She might do well on gardening programmes, although the flowers featured would be mostly red, a few yellow and none blue.

Lord Wyatt (1992)

Sir Marmaduke Hussey (Chairman of BBC TV)

Sir Marmalade Gusset. *'Private Eye'*

Jeremy Isaacs (Chairman of Channel 4)

In November 1982 Jeremy Isaacs launched Channel 4 with a mission to refresh the parts other telly couldn't reach . . . Like the Maastricht Treaty and John Major's Citizen's Charter, it was an idea of precious little vision and even less appeal.

Garry Bushell – 'Modern Review' (1992)

**Waldemar Januszczak
(Commissioning Editor for
Channel 4)**
A superannuated art critic raised to loftier
things.
Brian Sewell – 'Evening Standard' (1992)

Gerry Robinson (Granada TV)
Dear Gerry Robinson, F★★★ off out of it
you ignorant upstart caterer.
John Cleese – Fax (1992)

**Ted Turner (President of TBS and
CNN networks)**
The Mouth of the South. *'Private Eye'*

RADIO

The airwaves are packed with atrocious
sounds that wouldn't sell to a starving
man if made of Christmas cake.
Jonathan King – 'Music Week' (1992)

Radio is death in the afternoon . . . and
into the night. *Arthur Miller*

Sir Arthur Bliss (Master of the Queen's
Music) once described the BBC's pop
programme as 'aural hashish', but it's not
that good.
Richard Neville – 'Playpower' (1970)

RADIO STATIONS

Capital Radio
A station where you are shouted at, over a
Stock, Aitken and Waterman backing
track . . . Yapital Radio.
Peter Young – 'Jazz FM' (1992)

BBC Radio One
At 65, Alan Freeman is to retire from
'Pick of the Pops'. He will be replaced by
'The Man' Ezeke, 49, whose media track-
record amounts to an appearance on the
long defunct BBC TV programme
Nationwide. Affectionate devotees of
Radio One will be assured that its
tradition of spectacularly failing to be
young and hip is to be stoutly maintained.
'Evening Standard' (1992)

**One Hundred Best Tunes (BBC
Radio 2)**
That musical morgue.
*James Delingpole – 'Sunday Telegraph'
(1989)*

DISC JOCKEYS

Radio One DJs
The prospect of Dan Quayle running the
world if George Bush drops dead is like
having a Radio One DJ running the
world. *John Peel (1988)*

Bruno Brooks
Bruno Brooks is to Alan Freeman what
we are to Napoleon.
Chris Roberts – 'Melody Maker' (1988)

Alan Freeman
Freeman announces each record as if it
were the greatest song he'd ever heard.
*James Delingpole – 'Sunday Telegraph'
(1989)*

Brian Hayes
I rarely listen to Radio 2, in case I happen
to hear that smug, pompous, little twerp
Brian Hayes.
*Charles Catchpole – 'News of the World'
(1992)*

Liz Kershaw
Is there anything that can be done to rid
the airwaves of the terrible Liz Kershaw?
Corinne (1988)

Brian Redhead
Mr Redhead looks like every Morris
dancer you have ever seen.
Stephen Pile – 'Punch' (1990)

Kate Smith
Are you going to tell me how to make an
entrance? You fat tub of lard.
Tallulah Bankhead

Wally Whyton
Radio 2 needs longer news bulletins like
Scud FM needs Wally Whyton.
Russell Twisk – 'Observer' (1992)

POLITICS

Every government carries a health
warning.   *Anon*

The trouble with some of the big guns in
politics is that they are of small calibre
and are big bores.   *Anon*

Political animal: Rat, toad, snake, ass,
worm, louse, etc.
          Mike Barfield – 'The Oldie' (1992)

Conferences at the top level are always
courteous. Name-calling is left to the
foreign ministers.
              W. Averell Harriman (1955)

I don't think modesty is the outstanding
characteristic of contemporary politics.
                  Edward Heath (1988)

A dilemma is a politician trying to save
both of his faces at once.   *John A. Lincoln*

In political discussion, heat is in inverse
proportion to knowledge.   *J. G. Minchin*

A man should always be drunk when he
talks of politics – it's the only way in
which to make them important.
              *Sean O'Casey – 'The Shadow of a
                                    Gunman'*

In politics people give you what they
think you deserve, and deny you what
you think you want. *Cecil Parkinson (1990)*

Politicians – a number of anxious dwarfs
trying to grill a whale.
          J. B. Priestley – 'Outcries and Asides'

Politicians are people who, when they see
the light at the end of the tunnel, order
more tunnel.
          Sir John Quinton – 'Money' (1989)

It is a pity, as my husband says, that more
politicians are not bastards by birth
instead of vocation.
              Katherine Whitehorn (1964)

The wrong sort of people are always in
power because they would not be in
power if they were not the wrong sort of
people.   *Jon Wynne-Tyson –
                  'Times Literary Supplement'*

POLITICAL DOCTRINES

Communism
The corruption of the dream of justice.
                  Adlai Stevenson (1951)

Fascism
Fascism is capitalism plus murder.
                          Upton Sinclair

Socialism
A socialist is a person who is so disgusted
by the way the power is controlled by a
few huge corporations that he proposes to
place it in the hands of one giant
corporation.   *Miles Kington*

He had one peculiar weakness; he had
faced death in many forms but he had
never faced a dentist. The thought of
dentists gave him just the same sick
horror as the thought of Socialism.
                  H. G. Wells – 'Bealby'

UNITED KINGDOM

PARTY SYSTEMS

Conservative
Past Tory manifestos may have had some
chance of winning the Booker prize for
fiction. But as a guide to what they
actually did in power they were a lot less
reliable than even *Old Moore's Almanack*.
                      Bryan Gould (1992)

Our partners in Europe don't know
whether to laugh or cry. The generalship
shown by the Government over
Maastricht makes Fred Karno look like
the Duke of Wellington.
                      Denis Healey (1993)

Citizen's charter – Mr Major has issued a citizen's charter. It is as worthless as the piece of paper Neville Chamberlain brought back from Munich.
Paul Johnson – *'Sunday Times' (1992)*

There are now more zig-zags in Government policy than on a ski slope.
'Mail on Sunday' (1992)

1992 manifesto – Like Stockhausen, the Conservative manifesto contained too many notes and not enough tunes.
'Sunday Telegraph' (1992)

It is not quite accurate to say this is a do-nothing government; the problem is that when it does something, it invariably makes it worse. The scale of the Government's incompetence is breathtaking.   *'Sunday Times' (1992)*

Labour
'New Hope for Britain' (1983) – The longest suicide note in history.
Gerald Kaufman

The CBI are as anxious for a Labour government as I would be for my daughter to go to an all-night party at the Kennedys'.   *David Mellor (1991)*

Liberal
If God had been a Liberal, there wouldn't have been ten commandments, there would have been ten suggestions.
Malcolm Bradbury and Christopher Bigsby – *'After Dinner Game'*

I never use words like Republicans or Democrats. It's liberals and Americans.
James Watt – *'Philadelphia Inquirer' (1982)*

Liberal Democrats
They are the political Kiss of Death.
Paul Johnson – *'Daily Mail' (1992)*

Three party politics is now back with us in the form of the traditional two majors, neither of whom people particularly like, and a useful bucket to spit into as a third option.   *Austin Mitchell (1990)*

They are not so much a party, more like a disease.   *David Owen*

'Loony Left'
Maggot extremists.   *Neil Kinnock*

The Crazed Hattonistas.   *'Private Eye'*

The Loony Left are always hovering in the wing. They have a loony defence policy and a loony economic policy and, in the main, when they appear on television, they look pretty loony themselves.   *William Whitelaw*

Social Democrats
I saw David Owen on television the other week. He was heckling a small number of bystanders in Torquay. And then I realised they weren't bystanders – they were his party.   *Kenneth Baker*

None of the Liberal-Democratic Alliance's leader's are household names – not even in their own homes.
David Mellor

GOVERNMENT DEPARTMENTS & POSTS

Lord Privy Seal
It has been said that this Minister is neither a Lord, nor a privy, nor a seal.
S. D. Bailey

Ministerial departments
The ten empty bottles of hypocritical and intellectually fraudulent Ministries misbehaving everywhere from schools to parks.
Melvyn Bragg – *'Literary Review' (1992)*

Royal commission
A Royal commission is a brood hen sitting on a china egg. *Michael Foot (1964)*

The Treasury
The ministers on the Treasury Bench remind me of a marine landscape on the coast of South America. You behold a range of exhausted volcanoes.
Benjamin Disraeli

The Treasury could not, with any marked success, run a fish and chip shop.
Lord Harold Wilson (1984)

POLITICIANS

It was as dark as the inside of a Cabinet Minister.
Joyce Cary – 'The Horse's Mouth'

In France there are politicians of merit who began life as professors. But in England politicians seem to have been politicians from birth, with Personal Advancement as their fairy godmother.
Stanley Casson

Ulster M.P.s – Rickety old knights in rusty armour riding into Parliament on ancient steeds who only appear when there is a debate on Ulster.   *Edwina Currie (1990)*

American politicians will do anything for money; English politicians take the money and won't do anything.
Stephen Leacock

Politicians – Six hundred beefy men (but mostly gas and suet).   *Ezra Pound*

As ugly a devil as you would wish to see outside the House of Commons.
P. G. Wodehouse – 'Money for Nothing' (1928)

He's got about as much intelligence as a Cabinet minister.
P. G. Wodehouse – 'Much Obliged, Jeeves' (1971)

Jeffrey Archer
Jeffrey Archersickofhim.
'Private Eye' (1988)

Lord Archer of Victoria Station.
'Private Eye'

Paddy Ashdown
His boyish charm has begun to petrify into an empty adolescent grin. At his press conferences, you expect the first question to be, 'Is there anybody in?'
Keith Waterhouse – 'Daily Mail' (1992)

Herbert Asquith and Arthur Balfour
The difference between Balfour and Asquith is that Balfour is wicked and moral, Asquith is good and immoral.
Sir Winston Churchill

Stanley Baldwin
Not even a public figure. A man of no experience. And of the utmost insignificance.   *Lord Curzon*

Stanley Baldwin always hits the nail on the head, but it doesn't go in any further.
G. M. Young

Margaret Beckett
Not even her best friends would describe her as a glamour puss, whose face would be likely to turn on many voters. Except perhaps those who are members of the British Horse Society.
John Junor – 'Mail on Sunday' (1992)

Tony Benn
It remains a mystery why having decided to adopt a revolutionary sobriquet, he did not go for broke and call himself 'El Tornado' or 'Tony Terror'.
Clive James – 'Observer' (1981)

Ernest Bevin
He objects to ideas only when other people have them.   *A.J.P. Taylor*

David Blunkett
Blunkett is one of the most eloquent exponents of old-fashioned, unreconstituted bossy-boots, Stafford Cripps-style Stalinism.
A. N. Wilson – 'Evening Standard' (1993)

Sir Robert Boothby
He could make the most ridiculous statements sound as if they'd been inscribed on tablets brought down from the mountain.   *Edgar Lustgarten*

Peter Brooke
He is about as sensitive as a barbed-wire salesman.
Peter McKay – 'Evening Standard' (1992)

James Callaghan
Just an old Tory warmonger.
Tony Benn – 'Diary'

Edward Carson
The starry hero of all the politest young ladies of Belfast, has not done anything to promote the well-being of Ireland, never has done anything, and never will.
St. John Ervine

Austen Chamberlain
A noodle, a walking compendium of vulgar, insular prejudice.   *G. B. Shaw*

Neville Chamberlain
A retail mind in a wholesale business.
David Lloyd George

Chamberlain (who has the mind and manners of a clothes-brush) aims only at assuring temporary peace at the price of ultimate defeat.   *Harold Nicolson*

Earl of Chatham
William Pitt was a noble statesman; the Earl of Chatham was a noble ruin.
Woodrow Wilson

Randolph Churchill
A chain drinker.   *Anon*

Dear Randolph, utterly unspoiled by failure.   *Noël Coward*

At social gatherings he was liable to engage in heated and noisy arguments which could ruin a dinner party, and make him the dread of hostesses on both sides of the Atlantic. The tendency was exacerbated by the always generous and occasionally excessive, alcoholic intake.
Obituary – 'The Times' (1968)

After he had a benign lump removed – A typical triumph of modern science to find the only part of Randolph that was not malignant and remove it.   *Evelyn Waugh*

Sir Winston Churchill
He has spoilt himself by reading about Napoleon.   *David Lloyd George*

A flat-footed bastard of a drunken old Jew.   *GSI Propaganda Radio (1941)*

If you think I'm gaga, you should see Winston.   *W. Somerset Maugham*

Alan Clark
A sod-you-all aristocrat. Clark is about as politically incorrect as you can be.
Jilly Parkin – 'Daily Express' (1992)

Terence Clark
He was the nearest thing to Neanderthal man on the Tory benches.   *Denis Healey*

Julian Critchley
The trouble with people who try very hard not to be boring is that they often end up boring, but in a different way.
Julie Burchill – 'Sunday Times'

Edwina Currie
That poisonous lady with the poisonous tongue.
John Junor – 'Mail on Sunday' (1990)

A junior minister with an uncontrollable tongue and an insatiable desire to self advertisement.   *Robin Maxwell-Hyslop*

Hugh Dalton
Apart from his loud voice, he had little to commend him.   *Harold Wilson*

Terry Dicks
He is to the arts what James 'Bonecrusher' Smith is to lepidoptery.   *Tony Banks*

Anthony Eden
His speeches consist entirely of clichés – clichés old and new – everything from 'God is love' to 'Please adjust your dress before leaving'.   *Winston Churchill*

Michael Foot
A sort of walking obituary for the Labour Party.   *Anon (1983)*

On succeeding James Callaghan as Labour leader – The Labour Party was led by Dixon of Dock Green. Now it is being led by Worzel Gummidge.   *Kenneth Baker*

The ghost of an old left-winger coming back and desecrating his own grave.
Tony Benn – 'Diary'

The human duffel bag.
Peter Freedman – 'Glad to Be Grey' (1985)

William Gladstone

Posterity will do justice to that unprincipled maniac . . . with his extraordinary mixture of envy, vindictiveness, hypocrisy and superstition; and with his one commanding characteristic – whether Prime Minister or Leader of Opposition, whether preaching, praying, speechifying or scribbling – never a gentleman!
Benjamin Disraeli

It was said that Mr Gladstone could persuade most people of most things, and himself of anything.   *William R. Inge*

He is really half crazy, half silly, a man who listens to no one and won't hear any contradictions or discussion.
Queen Victoria

Harry Greenaway

The Ealing Comedy.   *Anon*

John Gummer

John Selwyn Gummer, an agriculture minister who makes sheep look charismatic.
Mark Lawson – 'The Independent' (1992)

He has to be a cabbage because he's not a patch on the rest of the cabinet.
'The Sun' (1992)

Roy Hattersley

That great bloated unsmiling accuser.
Philip Larkin – 'Letter'

Derek Hatton

If you really want to insult someone nowadays, try calling them an 'Eighties person'. Eighties person equals flashy and

trashy, someone who mistakes style for substance, thinks power-dressing and a portable phone is all that is necessary for success. Derek Hatton . . . is a quintessential eighties person.
Geraldine Bell – 'Independent on Sunday' (1992)

Edward Heath

There is an element of stony rigidity in his make-up which tends to petrify his whole personality in a crisis. *Denis Healey*

Margaret Thatcher and Ted Heath both have a great vision. The difference is that Margaret Thatcher has a vision that Britain will one day be great again, and Ted Heath has a vision that Ted Heath one day will be great again.   *Robert Jones*

Michael Heseltine

He looked like a tall, blond marionette on a jerky string.
Paul Callan – 'Daily Express' (1992)

The President of the Board of Trade is exposed as an unprincipled hypocrite.
'News of the World' (1992)

The President of the Board of Makes-You-Weep.
William Scammell – 'Elegy at Closedown' (1992)

Ropey Tarzan.   *'The Sun' (1990)*

Sir Samuel Hoare

No more coals to Newcastle, no more Hoares to Paris.   *King George V*

Geoffrey Howe

Sir Geoffrey Howedullcanyouget – perhaps the dullest figure of his generation, and the dullest foreign secretary of any generation . . . As a public figure he has all the dash and panache of the Hush Puppies which are his favourite footwear.
Peter Freedman – 'Glad to Be Grey' (1985)

After a speech in the House of Commons – I think we've all enjoyed another lugubrious concatenation of meaningless

clichés from the foreign secretary.
Denis Healey

It may not in the long run pay dividends to have as a foreign secretary someone, who, far from arousing animosity in the hearts of foreigners, only makes them want instead to put a protective arm in his and guide him across a busy road?
John Junor

David Icke
The Young Turquoise.
Mark Steyn – 'Evening Standard' (1991)

Gerald Kaufman
He had a bald head, wore tinted glasses and looked remarkably like Kermit the Frog. In this election the 'Shadow' Foreign Minister has become the Lord Lucan of the campaign trail . . . For the dismal truth, in this electronic age, is that the fourth most important politician in Labour's front line is deemed to have the kind of looks that are likely to make people throw things at their TV screens. The word unappealing is used whenever he is described. In short, he is a turn-off.
Gordon Greig – 'Daily Mail' (1992)

Robert Kilroy-Silk
He looks like a refugee from his sunlamp.
John Major

Neil Kinnock
On his interview technique – Boastful, wordy and weak . . . like processed cheese coming out of a mincing machine.
Tony Benn – 'Diary'

My eyes glaze over every time Kinnock appears on TV, he's so deadly boring.
Shirley Conran (1992)

He has the consistency of the chameleon and the wisdom of the weathercock.
Michael Howard

On his sudden change in policy –
Sometimes he's described as a windbag. I prefer to think of him as a windsock.
Charles Kennedy (1990)

Nice chap. Thick as a plank.
Richard Littlejohn

When it comes to the crunch, the Trade Unions will put their arms around Mr Kinnock's and say 'Neil!'. And he will, he will.
John Major (1990)

I think that Neil Kinnock is not a bad chap. But he's rather a bit of a bore and you wouldn't want to spend too much time with him.
John Major (1992)

Kinnochio.
'Private Eye' (1988)

He has never had a job. I tell you, if he applied to me for work, I wouldn't hire him.
Sir Gordon White (1990)

David Knox
The wetter-than-thou Tory.
'Private Eye'

Norman Lamont
He is an onion because he reduces the country to tears. That's shallot, Norman.
'The Sun' (1992)

There was never a gloomier Chancellor of the Exchequer – if ever a minister's face fitted it is Norman Lamont's glum look.
John Williams – 'Evening Standard' (1992)

Nigel Lawson
He looks like an Armenian might whilst on holiday in Florida.
Anon

He is to economic forecasting what Eddie the Eagle is to ski-jumping.
Neil Kinnock (1989)

You snivelling little git!
Brian Sedgemore MP (1985)

David Lloyd George
He spoke for a hundred and seventeen minutes – in which period he was detected only once in use of an argument.
Arnold Bennett

Oh, if I could piss the way he speaks.
Georges Clemenceau

177

He would have a better rating in British mythology if he had shared the same fate as Abraham Lincoln.   *John Grigg (1963)*

He was the wizzard of England and the blizzard of Wales.   *Jack Jones*

Ramsay MacDonald
During his last Commons speech – Sit down, man. You're a bloody tragedy.
James Maxton

Harold Macmillan
I would have said that Mr Macmillan had a tiny, tiny flavour of mothballs about him.   *Malcolm Muggeridge – 'Ancient and Modern' (1981)*

John Major
Why does it take two days for a Polaroid of John Major to appear?
Barry Cryer (1992)

John Major is like King Midas in reverse. Everything he touches turns to dross.
Frank Dobson (1992)

It's quite a change to have a Prime Minister who hasn't any political ideas at all.   *Michael Foot (1988)*

He delivers all his statements as though auditioning for the speaking clock.
Stephen Glover – 'Evening Standard' (1992)

He is looking like a weak leader, a Prime Minister who dithers. *Bryan Gould (1992)*

John Major is becoming the thieving magpie of British politics.
Bryan Gould (1992)

If you are looking for a man of principle, strike John Major off your list.
Roy Hattersley (1992)

The Monarch of Muddle Through.
Simon Jenkins – 'The Times' (1992)

This man is a consummate failure. He will always fail our country.
Neil Kinnock (1992)

Major is a very wishy-washy personality. And what we do with his puppet reflects that.   *Roger Law [Spitting Image] (1992)*

Grey John sounds more and more like a Dalek every day.   *Richard Littlejohn*

Only Alice was missing last week from John Major's Blunderland.
'The People' (1992)

John Major is to leadership what Cyril Smith is to hang-gliding.
John Prescott (1992)

U-turn-ip!   *'The Sun' (1992)*

John Major – the ignominious failure.
'Sunday Mirror' (1992)

His definition of honour is more like what the rest of us call saving one's face.
'Sunday Telegraph' (1992)

He needs to tear up the script and start again, casting himself as the Franklin Roosevelt of the decade. At present he is destined to be the Ramsay MacDonald.
'Sunday Times' (1992)

When he first became Prime Minister I found his gormlessness rather endearing: now it sets my teeth on edge.
'The Weasel' – 'Independent' (1993)

Tony Marlow
He is of the goose-stepping tendency.
Dennis Skinner

Colin Moynihan
On scrapping football I.D. cards – I would like to thank Colin Moynihan and those who are higher than him. Most of us are.
Brian Clough (1990)

The Anti-Christ made manifest in the form of a Sports Minister; whose role is that of the implacably hostile pip-squeak ally of the playground bully.
Andy Lyons – 'Melody Maker' (1988)

Albert Murray
A mere flatulent lightweight.
Sir Gerald Nabarro

David Owen
Four fairies attended the birth of David
Owen. Number One said, 'You'll be
good-looking.' Number Two said, 'You'll
be clever.' Number Three said, 'You'll be
very ambitious.' And Number Four said,
'You'll be all these things and you'll also
be a shit.' *Denis Healey*

He possesses an ego fat on arrogance and
drunk on ambition. *Neil Kinnock*

You are a small rump making bombastic
claims.
David Steel (1988)

Cecil Parkinson
Being called a political bungler by Cecil
Parkinson is rather like being called ugly
by Ross Perot.
'The Weasel' – 'Independent on Sunday' (1992)

John Profumo
A great party is not to be brought down
because of a squalid affair between a
woman of easy virtue and a proved liar.
Lord Hailsham (1963)
[See Lord Hailsham p.180]

Francis Pym
Mrs Mona-Lot. *Anon*

Norman St John Stevas
Why should anyone look up to a man like
that? What's he done for anyone but
himself? I bet his real name is Norman
Stephens. *Richard Littlejohn*

Dennis Skinner
He needs a verbal strait-jacket.
John Major

John Smith
A prissy, pompous little bantam-cock of a
man. *John Junor – 'Mail on Sunday' (1992)*

Norman Tebbit
A jumped-up engine driver.
Richard Littlejohn

Margaret Thatcher
Her impeccable accent is like some
devilish Roedean water torture.
Anon (1965)

Mrs Thatcher may be a woman, but she
isn't a sister. *Anon feminist (1979)*

Thatcherites: People who say you can't
make omelettes without breaking eggs but
imagine that the mere breaking of the
eggs will produce omelettes.
Julian Critchley – 'Some of Us' (1992)

She ate journalists for breakfast and,
feeling peckish, bit off some reporters'
heads at a press conference.
Trevor Fishlock

She is the Castro of the Western world –
an embarrassment to her friends – all she
lacks is a beard. *Denis Healey*

I often compare Margaret Thatcher with
Florence Nightingale. She stalks through
the wards of our hospitals as a lady with a
lamp – unfortunately, it is a blowlamp.
Denis Healey

Thatcherism: it will be in the history
books. It may be a footnote at the bottom.
Edward Heath (1992)

This woman is headstrong, obstinate and
dangerously self-opinionated.
ICI personnel report

When I hear the Prime Minister feeling
sorry for the rest of the world, I
understand why she has taken to calling
herself 'we' – it is less lonely. *Neil Kinnock*

Ugly as sin. If indeed it be a woman. I
think she's just a bad, bad brain with an
unused fanny. *John Lydon (1989)*

The trouble isn't having a woman as
Prime Minister. It's having that woman as
Prime Minister. *David Steel (1979)*

George Villiers
Stiff in his opinions, always in the wrong;
Was everything by starts, and nothing
long;

But in the course of one revolving moon,
Was chymyst, fiddler, statesman, and
buffoon.   *John Dryden*

The Lord of useless thousands.
                    Alexander Pope

William Waldegrave
Q. What is the difference between a
Government bond and William
Waldegrave?
A. Willie will never mature.
                    House of Commons joke

If William Waldegrave believes that the
spirit of Nye Bevan supports his changes
to the NHS, then there is a wheel missing
from his ouija board.   *Robin Cook (1992)*

Harold Wilson
Q. How can you tell when he's lying?
A. His lips are moving.
                    'That Was The Week That Was'

He's a rugby linesman who think he's a
three-quarter.   *Charles De Gaulle (1968)*

He has no sense of direction, and rarely
looked more than a few months ahead.
His short-term opportunism allied with a
capacity for self-delusion which made
Walter Mitty appear unimaginative often
plunged the government into chaos.
Worse still, when things went wrong he
imagined everyone was conspiring against
him.   *Denis Healey*

His very presence in Labour's leadership
pollutes the atmosphere of politics.
Anthony Howard – 'New Statesman' (1972)

The dismal-voiced, dough-faced and
discredited twister.
    Andrew Marr – 'The Independent' (1992)

He's going round the country stirring up
apathy.   *William Whitelaw*

David Winnick
I can never quite understand why he
walks that way. He either has a very bad
tailor or he has filled his pants.
                    Norman Tebbitt

HOUSE OF LORDS

The cure for admiring the House of
Lords is to go and look at it.
                    Walter Bagehot

Whose only function these days is to
stand in the way of something more
sensible.
    Martyn Harris – 'Spectator' (1992)

If Mrs Thatcher wants a hereditary title
as countess, she should have it. It sticks in
the throat that her son Mark might one
day sit in the Lords as a belted earl. But
what is one more twit among so many?
                    'The Sun' (1992)

LORDS AND LADIES

Lord Alexander of Hillsborough
Has the striking distinction of being the
only member of the House of Lords who
looks more like a frog than Lord
Beaverbrook.
    Bernard Levin – 'The Spectator' (1957)

Lord Carrington
Duplicitous bastard. European friends –
just plain cowardly. British, lying through
their teeth.   *Alexander Haig (1982)*

Lady Falkender [Marcia Williams]
Lady Fork-Bender.   *'Private Eye' (1975)*

Lord Hailsham
*On Lord Hailsham's comments on the
Profumo scandal* – From Lord Hailsham
we have had a virtuoso performance in
the art of kicking a fallen friend in the
guts . . . When self-indulgence has
reduced a man to the shape of Lord
Hailsham, sexual continence requires no
more than a sense of the ridiculous.
                    Reginald Paget (1963)

Lord Howe
The Welsh, to judge from the likes of
Lord Howe of Aberavon, have no sense
of humour at all.
    Simon Heffer – 'The Spectator' (1992)

Lord Longford
The only thing I really mind about going

to prison is the thought of Lord Longford coming to visit me.   *Richard Ingrams*

Lord Teviot
Could there be a worse advert for hereditary peers?
Gary Bushell – 'The Sun' (1992)

A perfect specimen of that cultivated idiocy which is the armour of the upper classes. *Martyn Harris – 'Spectator' (1992)*

Lord Ted Willis
The real sickening set-up is YOU, an out and out Communist, accepting a peerage! What an hypocrite! It is people like you who make this world the rotten place it is today.   *Anon letter*

Lord Wyatt
On his call for press reforms – It would be kindest to dismiss this nonsense as the rambling of an old man for whom senility is an overdue bedfellow. *'The Sun' (1992)*

TRADE UNIONS

Unions run by workers are like alcholic homes run by alcoholics, a sure recipe for tyranny.   *Roy Kerridge –*
'The Lone Conformist' (1984)

Unionism seldom, if ever, uses such power as it has to ensure better work; almost always it devotes a large part of that power to safeguard bad work.
H. L. Mencken

A trade unionist is a man who hates his job and is terrified someone may take it from him.   *Richard Needham –*
'A Friend in Needham' (1969)

The recent TUC conference was like listening to an old 78 record – scratchy, distorted, indistinct, running down and repeating itself.
Denys Randolph – 'Daily Telegraph' (1979)

Norman Gallagher (Builders' Labourers' Federation)
He has been a union official since he was 18, which is the best advertisement for limited tenure of trade union officials I have ever seen.
Meredith Burgmann (1982)

Lord Hill (Leader of the Boilermakers' Union)
It obviously hurt him to wear the dinner-jacket of respectability instead of the boiler-suit of revolt.
Cassandra – 'Daily Express'

'Autobiography' (1974) – Like the slag-heap calling a polar bear black.
Bernard Levin – 'Observer'

Arthur Scargill (Chairman of the National Union of Mine-workers)
You wouldn't run a darts club the way he runs the union.
Anon NUM executive (1990)

If the kamikaze pilots were to form their own union, Arthur Scargill would be an ideal choice for leader. *Jimmy Reid (1988)*

Norman Willis (Leader of the TUC)
First I get Maxwell, then I've got the second sumo wrestler on my back.
Arthur Scargill (1990)

UNITED STATES OF AMERICA

Trying to get the Presidency to work these days is like trying to sew buttons on a custard pie.   *James D. Barber*

The office of Presidency is such a bastardised thing – half royalty, half democracy – that nobody knows whether to genuflect or spit.   *Jimmy Breslin*

Remember, everybody, let sleeping dogs lie, but somebody wake up the President.
Bill Cosby

The outcome of 25 years of Republican rule (Jimmy Carter was a mere blip in 1976) is that Americans have learnt to hate themselves, like children of repressive, conformist families.
Cynthia Heimel – 'Independent on Sunday'
(1992)

This year, like every year, two teams will face each other in the Super Bowl. One team will win and know what it's like to be a champion. The other team will lose

and know what it's like to be a
Republican. *Jay Leno (1993)*

Scrubbing floors and emptying bedpans
has as much dignity as the Presidency.
Richard Nixon

Wisdom is essential in a President, the
appearance of wisdom will do in a
candidate. *Eric Sevareid*

All the President is is a glorified public
relations man who spends his time
flattering, kissing and kicking people to
get them to do what they are supposed to
do anyway. *Harry S. Truman*

POLITICAL FIGURES

John Q. Adams
It is said he is a disgusting man to do
business with. Coarse and dirty and
clownish in his address and stiff and
abstracted in his opinions, which are
drawn from books exclusively.
William H. Harrison

Spiro Agnew
Agnew reminds me of the kind of guy
who would make a crank call to the
Russians on the hotline. *Dick Gregory*

A medicine man whose remedies would
put an end to the patient as well as the
problem. *Tom Wicker*

William J. Bryan
A mouthing, slobbering demagogue
whose patriotism is all jawbone.
Thomas Dixon (1896)

We put him to school and he wound up
stealing the schoolbooks.
Ignatius Donnelly

George Bush
George Bush has alway been wet, now
he's washed up. *Bumper sticker (1992)*

I found out where George Bush is today.
He's visiting his economists. He's at
Disneyland right now.
Lloyd Bentsen (1988)

He is moaning like a pig stuck under a
gate. *Bill Clinton (1992)*

George Bush is a fake, a fool and a wimp.
Jules Feiffer – 'New York Village Voice'
(1988)

A weaseling pragmatist devoid of
principle. *William Safire (1992)*

On losing the Presedential election – George
Bush's mistake was to run a big-band
campaign in a rock'n'roll country.
Ralph Whitehead (1992)

The unpleasant sound Bush is emitting,
as he traipses from one conservative
gathering to another, is a thin, tinny, 'arf'
– the sound of a lapdog. *George Will*

George Bush and Dan Quayle
Putting Bush and Quayle in charge of the
economy is like making General Sherman
the fire marshal of Atlanta.
Bill Clinton (1992)

George Bush, Bill Clinton and Ross Perot
A wimp, a wonk and a wacko. *Anon (1992)*

Jimmy Carter
When Carter gave a fireside chat, the fire
went out. *Anon*

He couldn't even hold his own attention.
Anon

I would not want Jimmy Carter and his
men put in charge of snake control in
Ireland. *Eugene McCarthy*

A hayseed with a toothy grin.
P. J. O'Rourke

Bill Clinton
On Clinton becoming President – It's a
great day for Arkansas. We're on the map
at last. Better still, Bill Clinton's not our
governor anymore.
Anon Arkansas businesswoman (1992)

Bill Clinton is a dope-smoking, draft-dodging liar, whose wife never knows where he is.
Anti-Clinton rally placard (1992)

The failed governor of a small state.
Jim Baker (1992)

A stumblebum, spud-faced Little League Lothario.
Julie Burchill – 'Mail on Sunday' (1993)

On his views on the Gulf War – I bit the bullet, and he bit his nails.
George Bush (1992)

A two-faced pumpkin from Arkansas.
George Bush (1992)

Being attacked on character by Governor Clinton is like being called ugly by a frog.
George Bush (1992)

Governor Clinton talks about change, change, change. Well, that's all you're going to have in your pockets if he's elected.   *George Bush (1992)*

Hilary's husband elected.
'Die Tageszeitung' (1992)

Comparing Clinton, his wife and running mate to characters from 'The Wizard of Oz' – Al Gore is looking for a brain, Hilary is looking for a heart. I hope the national media is not listening, but people tell me that Clinton is looking for Dorothy.
Bob Dorman (1992)

Even I would take offence at being called a liar by a governor of Arkansas, whose career as an evader of truths is hardly less distinguished than Emmett Smith's [Dallas Cowboys] as an eluder of open field tackles.   *Murray Kempton – 'New York Review of Books' (1992)*

We, in the Republican Party, have never said to the press that Clinton's a philandering, pot-smoking draft-dodger.
Mary Matalin (1992)

It's a crime that George Bush should be defeated by a sleaze bag.
Sally McKenzie (1992)

On becoming Governor of Arkansas – I hear you have been elected King of some place with two men and a dog.   *Douglas Millin*

This fellow they've nominated claims he's the new Thomas Jefferson. Well, let me tell you something: I knew Thomas Jefferson. He was a friend of mine. And Governor, you're no Thomas Jefferson.
Ronald Reagan (1992)

Clinton plays golf . . . he wore jogging shoes, and his shirt was hanging out over painter's pants. Golf needs Clinton like it needs a case of ringworm.
Rick Reilly – 'Sports Illustrated' (1992)

Bill Clinton and Al Gore
My dog Millie knows more about foreign affairs than these two bozos.
George Bush (1992)

Governor Taxes and Mr Ozone.
George Bush (1992)

Hilary Clinton (wife of Bill Clinton)
That smiling barracuda.
'US National Review' (1993)

Michael Dukakis
He's the stealth candidate. His campaign jets from place to place, but no issues show up on the radar screen. *George Bush*

Pinchgut Mickey.   *P. J. O'Rourke – 'Parliament of Harlots' (1991)*

John F. Dulles
He stirred whisky with a thick forefinger, his socks drooped, his suits were green-hued, his ties were indifferent, and his breath was chronically bad. Hunched forward as he talked, he droned on in a flat voice.
Walter Isaacson and Evan Thomas

Dwight D. Eisenhower
I doubt very much if a man whose main literary interests were in works by Mr Zane Grey, admirable as they may be, is particularly well equipped to be chief executive of this country.   *Dean Acheson*

General Eisenhower employs the three-monkeys standard of campaign morality:

see no evil – if it's Republican; hear no evil – unless it's Democratic; and speak no evil – unless Senator Taft says it's all right.   *Adlai Stevenson*

Why, this fellow don't know any more about politics than a pig knows about Sunday.   *Harry S. Truman*

Gerald Ford
He could even f*** up a two-car funeral.
                                          Anon

John Wesley Gaines
John Wesley Gaines!
John Wesley Gaines!
Thou monumental mass of brains!
Come in, John Wesley for it rains.   *Anon*

John Glenn
Senator Glenn couldn't electrify a fish tank if he threw a toaster in it. *Dave Berry*

Al Gore
Q. How do you tell Al Gore from the secret service agents?
A. He's the stiff one!
                          Campaign joke (1988)

John Hancock
A man without head and without heart – the mere shadow of a man – and yet Governor of old Massachusetts.
                                    John Adams

Warren Gamaliel Harding
When Warren Gamaliel Harding was the twenty-ninth President of these States in 1920, he made an inaugural address that was described as 'the most illiterate statement ever made by the responsible head of a civilised government.'
                                      A. J. Hanna

W. Averell Harriman
He's thin, boys. He's thin as piss on a hot rock.   *William E. Jenner*

Barbara Honegger
A low-level munchkin. *Tom DeCair (1983)*

Thomas Jefferson
The moral character of Jefferson was repulsive. Continually puling about liberty, equality and the degrading curse of slavery, he brought his own children to the hammer, and made money of their debaucheries.   *Thomas Hamilton*

Lyndon B. Johnson
Hey, hey, LBJ,
How many kids did you kill today?
                                Vietnam protest

When Johnson wanted to persuade you of something you really felt as if a St Bernard had licked your face for an hour.
                              Benjamin C. Bradlee

One of the few politicians with whom I found it uncomfortable to be in the same room. Johnson exuded a brutal lust for power which I found most disagreeable.
                                      Denis Healey

How does one tell the President of the United States to stop picking his nose and lifting his leg to fart in front of the TV camera and using 'chicken shit' in every other sentence?   *Stuart Rosenberg*

Henry Kissinger
Henry's idea of sex is to slow down to thirty miles an hour when he drops you off at the door.   *Barbara Howar*

Ed Koch
Ed Koch is like Richard Nixon. He is forever rearranging his Enemies List in his mind. Mr Koch is a practitioner of political sadomasochism: inflicting pain gives him pleasure.   *Jack Newfield*

Fiorello La Guardia
Anyone who extends to him the right hand of friendship is in danger of losing a couple of fingers.   *Alva Johnston*

Abraham Lincoln
He was responsible for the state of the West today. He was a manic depressive, paranoid schizophrenic.
                              Thurston Moore (1989)

I say here, in my place in the Senate of the United States, that I never did see or converse with so weak and imbecile a man as Abraham Lincoln . . . .If I wanted to paint a tyrant, if I wanted to paint a despot, a man perfectly regardless of every constitutional right of the people, whose sworn servant, not ruler, he is, I would paint the hideous form of Abraham Lincoln.

Willard Saulsbury (1863)

On his 'Gettysburg Address' – Anything more dull and commonplace it wouldn't be easy to reproduce.   *'The Times' (1863)*

An enemy of the human race, and deserves the execration of all mankind.

Robert Toombs

John Lindsay
You are nothing but a juvenile, a lightweight and a pipsqueak. You have to grow up.   *Michael J. Quill*

Bruce Lindsey
This colourless, odourless, almost invisible person – who looks like John Major in a button-down shirt.

Jeremy Campbell – 'Evening Standard' (1992)

Edward Livingstone
He is a man of splendid abilities, but utterly corrupt. Like rotten mackerel by moonlight, he shines and stinks.

John Randloph

Henry Luce
Mr Luce is like a man that owns a shoe store and buys all the shoes to fit himself. Then he expects other people to buy them.   *Earl Long*

Joseph McCarthy
A sadistic bum from Wisconsin.

Hank Greenspun

The policeman and the trashman may call me Alice. You cannot.

Alice Roosevelt Longworth

A pathological character assassin.

Harry S. Truman

George C. Marshall
An errand boy, a front man, a stooge, or a conspirator for this administration's crazy assortment of collectivist cut-throat crackpots and Communist fellow-travelling appeasers.   *William E. Jenner*

Robert Martinez
Governor Martinez exudes the warm personal charm of a millipede. *Dave Berry*

Walter F. Mondale
He has all the charisma of a speed bump.

Will Durst

He has all the charisma of a magnum of chloroform.

Peter Freedman – 'Glad to Be Grey' (1985)

During a Presidential TV debate – I am not going to exploit for political purposes my opponent's youth and inexperience.

Ronald Reagan (1984)

Richard Nixon
Nixon's motto was: If two wrongs don't make a right, try three.   *Norman Cousins*

You have to scrape diligently at Mr Nixon's skin to find a value traditional or otherwise.   *Howard Fast*

If he had an affair while in office, I misjudged him. I thought he was just doing that to the rest of the country.

John Gavin

All that stands between the US and a dictatorship.   *L.L. Levinson*

The election of 1972 simply goes to prove that America is a land where the lowest common man can become President. And he did.   *Kirkpatrick Sale*

Nixon without his sanctimony is a man half-dressed.   *Wilfred Sheed*

When Nixon is alone in a room, is there anybody there?   *Gloria Steinem*

Nixon is a no-good lying bastard. He can lie out of both sides of his mouth at the same time, and even if he caught himself telling the truth, he'd lie just to keep his hand in.   *Harry S. Truman*

He not only doesn't give a damn about the people; he doesn't know how to tell the truth. I don't think the son-of-a-bitch knows the difference between telling the truth and lying.   *Harry S. Truman*

H. Ross Perot

A.A. Milne's Piglet come to life.
                              'Bitch' (1993)

Perot is the sort of man of whom it is said, 'In your head, you know he's right; in your guts, you know he's nuts'.
    Chris Buckland – 'Daily Express' (1992)

Chattering like a chimp high on PG Tips.
    Allison Pearson – 'Independent on Sunday'
                              (1992)

Being called a political bungler by Cecil Parkinson is rather like being called ugly by Ross Perot.
The Weasel – 'Independent on Sunday' (1992)

Dan Quayle

After he misspelt 'potatoe' – DUMPE QUAYL!   *Banner (1992)*

Senator, you are no Jack Kennedy!
                    Lloyd Bentsen (1988)

He represents white bread with no nutritional value what so ever.
                              Jarboe (1989)

The prospect of Dan Quayle running the world if George Bush drops dead – is like having a Radio One DJ running the world.   *John Peel (1988)*

The choice of an utter nincompoop as Vice President is absolute insurance against impeachment to end with J. Danforth Quayle.   *Michael M. Thomas*

Nancy Reagan

A senescent bimbo with a lust for home furnishings.   *Barbara Erhenreich*

Ronald Reagan

The most widely beloved American since E.T.   *Roy Blount Jr.*

I listen to Reagan and I want to throw up.
                    Henry Fonda (1981)

He doesn't dye his hair – he's just prematurely orange.   *Gerald Ford*

One hesitates even to speculate about the polyester levels of his outfits. The dyed hair is an outrage, as is the rouge on the cheeks. (Will the President soon proceed to eyeshadow and liner?)   *Paul Fussell*

Naming a national forest after Ronald Reagan is like naming a day-care centre after W. C. Fields.   *Bob Hattoy*

He is the first man in twenty years to make the Presidency a part-time job, a means of filling up a few of the otherwise blank days of retirement.   *Simon Hoggart*

When you meet the President, you ask yourself, 'How did it occur to anybody that he should be governor, much less President?'   *Henry Kissinger*

The consummate electronic candidate of our time.   *Max Lerner*

You've got to be careful quoting Ronald Reagan, because when you quote him accurately it's called mud-slinging.
                    Walter F. Mondale

The battle for the mind of Ronald Reagan was like trench warfare in World War I: never have so many fought so hard for such barren terrain.   *Peggy Noonan*

President Ray-Gun.   *Arthur Scargill*

He has achieved a political breakthrough – the Teflon-coated Presidency. He sees to it that nothing sticks to him.
                    Patricia Schroeder

I know for a fact that Mr Reagan is not clear about the difference between the Medici and Gucci. He knows that Nancy wears one.   *Gore Vidal*

He does not dye his hair – he bleaches his face. *Gore Vidal*

Thomas B. Reed
He does what he likes, without consulting the administration, which he detests, or his followers, whom he despises.
Cecil Spring-Rice

Walter Reuther
You are like a nightingale. It closes its eyes when it sings and sees nothing and hears nobody but itself. *Nikita Khrushchev*

James W. Riley
The unctuous, overcheerful, word-mouthing, flabby-faced citizen who condescendingly tells Providence, in flowery and well-rounded periods, where to get off. *Hewlett Howland*

Franklin D. Roosevelt
Roosevelt wasn't a bump on a pickle compared to what I'd have been in the White House. *Huey Long*

One-third sap, two-thirds Eleanor.
Alice Roosevelt Longworth

He had every quality that morons esteem in their heroes. He was the first American to penetrate to the real depths of vulgar stupidity. *H. L. Mencken*

Theodore Roosevelt
A dangerous and ominous jingo.
Henry James

The mere monstrous embodiment of unprecedented resounding noise.
Henry James

Theodore Roosevelt was an old maid with testosterone poisoning. *Patricia O'Toole*

His idea of getting hold of the right end of the stick is to snatch it from the hands of somebody who is using it effectively, and to hit him over the head with it.
G. B. Shaw

Harold Stassen
A political nymphomaniac. *Relman Morin*

Eugene Talmadge
His chain-gang excellency. *Harold Ickes*

Harry S. Truman
The president would lick any Jewish arse that promised him a hundred votes.
Ernest Bevin

Henry Wallace
Henry's the sort of guy that keeps you guessing as to whether he's going to deliver a sermon or wet the bed. *Anon*

George Washington
Treacherous in private friendship and a hypocrite in public life, the world will be puzzled to decide whether you are an apostate or an imposter, whether you abandoned your good principles or whether you ever had any.
Thomas Paine – Letter (1796)

James G. Watt
The Secretary of the Interior has gone bonkers. It's time the white-coat people took him away. *Gaylord Nelson*

Daniel Webster
The most meanly and foolishly treacherous man I ever heard of.
James R. Lowell

EUROPEAN COMMUNITY

The European Community is run in a thoroughly un-British way.
Lord Bethell (1990)

The constitution and administrative structure of the Community is a buck passer's and paper pusher's dream.
Sir John Hopkins – 'Daily Telegraph'
(1989)

Jacques Delors
He is like a slimy dead sheep stuffed down the back of a sofa. *'Private Eye'*

REST OF THE WORLD

AUSTRALIA

Malcolm Fraser (Prime Minister)

He is the cutlery man of Australia. He was born with a silver spoon in his mouth, speaks with a forked tongue and knifes his colleagues in the back.

Bob Hawke (1975)

Bob Hawke

An ego without purpose.

Gough Whitlam (1992)

Paul Keating

He has made references to individuals as scumbugs, scum, suckers, thugs, dimwits, swill, a pigsty, fools and incompetents, perfumed gigolos and stupid foul-mouthed grubs. He is the most offensive Prime Minister in Australia's history.

Robert Hill (1992)

CANADA

Robert Baldwin

The man of one idea.   *Anon (1840)*

Harold C. Banks

He is the stuff of the Capones and the Hoffas, of whom the dictators throughout history, from the earliest times to the totalitarians, Hitler and Stalin, are prototypes. He is a bully, cruel, dishonest, greedy, power-hungry, contemptuous of the law.

Canadian Royal Commission on disruption of shipping on the Great Lakes (1963)

Richard B. Bennett

A tough guy who wants to be kissed.

Bob Edwards

Edward Blake

Ed Blake was a failure in politics. He was the most tragic figure that has yet appeared in our Canadian public life.

Frank H. Underhill

John G. Diefenbaker

The besetting disease of Canadian public life for almost a decade had been Diefenbakerism: the belief that promises were policies, that rhetoric was action and that the electorate believe in Santa Claus.

Ramsay Cook – 'The Maple Leaf Forever' (1971)

It is scarcely an exaggeration to say that fewer tears were shed over the fall of Canadian Prime Minister John Diefenbaker than over the upset of any major Commonwealth political figure since Oliver Cromwell.

Robert Estabrook – 'Washington Post' (1963)

A platitudinous bore.   *John F. Kennedy*

Mitchell Hepburn

He is not fit to be premier of a pub.

George C. McCullagh (1937)

W. L. McKenzie King

McKenzie King was chiefly concerned to avoid committing himself to anything.

L. S. Amery (1953)

The paramount egotist of our time.

Bruce Hutchinson (1953)

Sir Wilfrid Laurier

He was never any good at figures, other than those of speech.

Paul Bilkey (1940)

Arthur Meighen

Meighen had the gift of being admired by those who agreed with him.

C. G. Power (1966)

J. R. Ramsay

He was a half-cut schoolmaster and a quarter-cut poet.   *Robertson Davies*

Henry W. Wood

He is an American wolf in the Canadian sheep-fold in the skin of a Missouri mule.

'Canadian Milling & Grain Journal' (1926)

FRANCE

Valéry Giscard d'Estaing
A bogus Count.   *Margaret Thatcher*

Charles de Gaulle
A head like a banana and hips like a
woman.   *Hugh Dalton*

General de Gaulle is again pictured in our
newspapers looking as usual like an
embattled codfish. I wish he could be
filleted, and put quietly away in a
refrigerator.   *Sylvia T. Warner*

GERMANY

Nazism
The foulest and most soul-destroying
tyranny that has ever darkened and
stained the pages of history.
        Winston Churchill (1940)

Adolf Hitler
He is formless, almost faceless, a man
whose countenance is a caricature, a man
whose framework seems cartilaginous
without bones. He is inconsequent and
voluble, ill-poised, insecure. He is the
very prototype of the Little Man.
        Dorothy Thompson

GUYANA

The form of government is a mild
despotism tempered by sugar.
        Anthony Trollope – 'The West Indies and
        the Spanish Main' (1859)

INDIA

A despotism of office-boxes tempered by
an occasional loss of keys.   *Lord Lytton*

IRELAND

Charles Haughey
I have a theory about Charles Haughey.
Give him enough rope and he'll hang
you.   *Leo Enright (1992)*

If I saw Mr Haughey buried at midnight
at a crossroads, with a stake driven

through his heart – politically speaking – I
should continue to wear a clove of garlic
round my neck, just in case.
        Conor Cruise O'Brien

ITALY

Political parties in Italy repeat themselves
like broken gramophone records.
        Professor Pedarotti – 'BBC Newsnight'
        (1980)

Benito Mussolini
Mussolini is the biggest bluff in Europe.
        Ernest Hemingway – 'Toronto Daily Star'
        (1923)

JAMAICA

Edward Seaga (Prime Minister)
An arrogant, stupid fool.
        Michael Manley (1985)

PHILIPPINES

Dewi Sukarno (First Lady)
On being slashed by a broken glass – She
says I called her a whore. I probably
would have, but I didn't have time.
        Maria Victoria Osmena (1992)

POLAND

Lech Walesa (President)
He was an extraordinary leader of
workers. He is a terrible head of state.
        Gustav Herling (1992)

RHODESIA

Cecil Rhodes
I admire him, I frankly confess. When his
time comes I shall buy a piece of rope for
a keepsake.   *Mark Twain*

SERBIA

Dr Radovan Karadicz
A rambling, inconsistent, sentimental
bouffanted crook.
        John Naughton – 'Observer' (1992)

SOUTH AFRICA

In racial matters the Union today is a kind of shabby cross between Germany in 1933 and backwoods Tennessee in the 1880s.

John Gunther – 'Inside Africa' (1955)

SPAIN

Dolores Ibarruri (La Pasionaria)
One of the most despicable and self-seeking careerists of the communist movement. *Franz Borkenau*

LAW & ORDER

Lawyers and painters can soon turn white to black. *Danish proverb*

Woodpeckers and lawyers have long bills.
Dr. K. C. Allen

A lawyer starts by giving $500 worth of law for $5, and ends up giving $5 worth for $500. *Benjamin H. Brewster*

Lawyers Can Seriously Damage Your Health. *Michael Joseph (1984)*

LAWYERS & JUDGES

Jim Garrison (New Orleans District-Attorney)
I cannot think anything but evil about him. He was a menace and anyone who thinks otherwise is insane.

Pershing Gervais

Mr Justice Harman
He is absolutely the best example to give anyone to get rid of the judiciary. He is rude, offensive and intolerant.
Anon lawyer – 'Observer Magazine' (1992)

Judge James Pickles
He has had his fifteen minutes of fame, which is more than he deserves. Let us now put him back in his box.
Lynn Barber – 'Independent on Sunday' (1992)

Lord Justice Taylor
A bit of a bruiser with a strain of arrogance. *James Pickles*

The Law Society
The Law Society officers should be committed for contempt, but they are imprisoned by sin already . . . they are a wicked organisation which has no reverence for other people.

Roy Oddy (1991)
[Mr Oddy, a solicitor, was struck off for these comments and others he made about certain members of the Society e.g. A bent little git and a useless pillock who had influenced judges with about as much integrity as a cow pat.]

POLICE

The Metropolitan Police Force is abbreviated to the 'Met' to give more members a chance of spelling it.
Mike Barfield – 'The Oldie' (1992)

A vague uneasiness: the police. It's like when you suddenly understand you have to undress in front of the doctor.
Ugo Betti – 'The Inquiry' (1944)

Detectives are only policemen with smaller feet.
Whitfield Crook – 'Stage Fright'

How I hate the French police! And what rottenness there must be in a social system which needs or tolerates such lawkeepers.
Eric Muspratt – 'Wild Oats' (1932)

EDUCATION

The aim of education is to induce the largest amount of neurosis that the individual can bear without cracking.
W. H. Auden

Hell hath no fury like a wallflower with a sociology degree.   *Julie Burchill (1986)*

The difference between education and intelligence is intelligence will make you a good living.   *Charles Kettering*

Education is the inculcation of the incomprehensible into the indifferent by the incompetent.   *John M. Keynes*

What is the point of the English upper-class girl's education, or rather, lack of education, if not to prepare her for a life tolerating the boringness of the English upper-class man?
Charles Moore – 'The Spectator' (1992)

Education is the method whereby one acquires a higher grade of prejudices.
Laurence J. Peter

Education is what survives when what has been learnt has been forgotten.
B. F. Skinner

EDUCATORS

The most formidable headmaster I ever knew was a headmistress. She had X-ray pince-nez and that undivided bust popularized by Queen Mary. I think she was God in drag.
Nancy Banks-Smith – 'Guardian' (1977)

Academic and aristocratic people live in such an uncommon atmosphere that common sense can rarely reach them.
Samuel Butler – 'Notebooks'

The schoolteacher is certainly underpaid as a child-minder, but ludicrously over-paid as an educator.   *John Osborne*

I am inclined to think that one's education has been in vain if one fails to learn that most schoolmasters are idiots.
Hesketh Pearson

God forgive me for having thought it possible that a schoolmaster could be out and out a rational being.   *Sir Walter Scott*

Everybody who is incapable of learning has taken to teaching.   *Oscar Wilde*

Headmasters of private schools are divided into two classes: the workers and the runners-up-to-London.
P. G. Wodehouse – 'The Little Nugget' (1913)

SEATS OF LEARNING

They teach you anything in university today. You can major in mud-pies.
Orson Welles

Boarding schools
For all the smooth talk of modern headmasters, most English boarding schools were still hotbeds of racism and social prejudice . . . when the inevitable happens, and the majority of these places go bust, we should all heave a sigh of relief.
A. N. Wilson – 'Evening Standard' (1992)

British universities
British universities are becoming more like trains in India, where one cannot actually see the train because of the number of people who are hanging on to the outside of it.   *Lord Quinton (1993)*

Business schools
Business schools dampen entrepreneurship.
Anita Roddick – 'Daily Telegraph' (1987)

English public schools
Anyone who has been to an English public school and served in the British Army is quite at home in a third world prison.   *Roger Cooper (1991)*

Harrow School, Middlesex
I hated it. I hated everyone there for arrogantly assuming that they had a right to their wealth and position without having to work for it.
        John Bentley – 'Daily Mirror' (1972)

Harvard, Massachusetts
Q. Why do they have to nail all the windows at Harvard shut?
A. To keep the fairies from flying out.
                College joke (c. 1950)

Ivy League colleges
I am not impressed by the Ivy League establishments. Of course they graduate the best – it's all they'll take, leaving to others the problem of educating the country. They will give you an education the way banks will give you money – provided you can prove to their satisfaction that you don't need it.
    Peter De Vries – 'The Vale of Laughter'

Trinity College, Cambridge
Trinity is like a dead body in a high state of putrefaction. The only interest of it is the worms that come out of it.
        Lytton Strachey – Letter (1903)

Winchester College
C'est magnifique, mais ce n'est pas la gare.   *Anon*
[*The College's entrance is dominated by a large clock*]

'The Robbins Report on Higher Education' which advocated that higher education should address the problem of untapped talent
Tapped untalent.   *Kingsley Amis*

RELIGION

Prayers are to men as dolls are to children. They are not without use and comfort, but it is not easy to take them seriously.
        Samuel Butler – 'Notebooks' (1912)

It is no accident that the symbol of a bishop is a crook, and the sign of an archbishop is a double-cross.
                Dom Dix (1977)

The most tedious of discourses are on the subject of the Supreme Being.
    Ralph W. Emerson – 'Journals' (1836)

Church leaders can no more pontificate on economics than the Pope could correct Galileo on physics.
        John Gummer – 'The Times' (1984)

Good God, how much reverence can you have for a Supreme being who finds it necessary to include such phenomena as phlegm and tooth-decay in His Divine system of Creation?
                Joseph Heller – 'Catch 22'

Operationally, God is beginning to resemble not a ruler but the last fading smile of a cosmic Cheshire cat.
        Julian Huxley – 'Religion Without Revelation'

My only phobia is I'm afraid one day of getting a religious conversion. That would be a fate worse than death. Becoming a born-again something or other.   *Dave Faulkner (1989)*

The identification of a church and a state is about as farcical as a vegetarian joining the Butcher's Union.

Malcolm Muggeridge – 'Ancient and Modern' (1981)

I have noticed again and again since I have been in the Church that lay interest in ecclesiastic matters is a prelude to insanity.

Evelyn Waugh – 'Decline and Fall'

Religions are such stuff as dreams are made of.

H. G. Wells – 'The Happy Turning' (1946)

WORLD RELIGIONS

CHRISTIANITY

Those who talk of the Bible as a 'monument of English prose' are merely admiring it as a monument over the grave of Christianity.   *T. S. Eliot (1935)*

The whole religious complexion of the modern world is due to the absence from Jerusalem of a lunatic asylum.

Havelock Ellis

The two greatest curses of civilization were Christianity and journalism.

Frank Harris

[*To which Arthur, Lord Balfour replied:* Christianity naturally, but why journalism?]

Better sleep with a sober cannibal than a drunken Christian.

Herman Melville – 'Moby Dick'

Nothing is more depressing and more illogical than aggressive Christianity.

Gerald Vann – 'The Heart of Man'

Mormonism

I don't call them Mormons – I call them Nazi Amish.   *Roseanne Barr (1989)*

The Mormons are a nice crowd, with one drawback: you have to wear a blue suit

and a permanent grin and tell everybody about this wonderful book of yours.

Alan Coren – 'Sunday Express' (1992)

Roman Catholicism

After ripping up a picture of the Pope on 'Saturday Night Live' – Fight the real enemy. There's only ever been one liar and it's the Holy Roman Empire.

Sinead O'Connor (1992)

ISLAM

Islam is the enemy of the tree, as it is the enemy of all patient and continuous effort.   *Hilaire Belloc – 'Places' (1942)*

MEN OF GOD

Bishop of Durham

It wouldn't be spring, would it, without the voice of the occasional cuckoo.

Margaret Thatcher (1985)

The Bishop of Durham is a dangerous joker who by some error has been allowed to creep into the Congregation of Bishops.   *Nicholas Winterton – 'Poles Apart' [BBC TV] (1984)*

Monsignor José Maria Escriva (Founder of Opus Dei)

He had a vile character.   *Miguel Fisac*

Jesus Christ

No one ever made more trouble than 'gentle Jesus sweet and mild'.

James M. Gillis – 'This Our Day'

A Jesus-freak: the dreariest conversationalist of them all.

Kenneth Hurren – 'Mail on Sunday' (1993)

We always like our pop-stars to be like Greek gods: bigger, better and uglier than us. We hate the bores: Jesus Christ and the Dutch.   *Malcolm McLaren (1989)*

Jesus Christ is derivative. You might even call him a third-rate Socrates.

Dieter Meier (1989)

A parish demagogue. *Percy Bysshe Shelley*

Martin Luther
Luther was the foulest of monsters.
Pope Gregory XV

Cardinal John Henry Newman
How odious Newman was! Chock-full of egotism, self-importance, self-pity, self-concern, the most tedious aspects of femininity – a real stinker.
Rupert Hart-Davis

Pope Pius XII
You get the impression this was another dirty wop, an organ grinder. *W. H. Auden*

Rev Al Sharpton
I've got three words for Al Sharpton:
Martin Luther King. *Denis Leary*

John Wyclif
The devil's instrument, church's enemy, people's confusion, heretics idol, hypocrite's mirror, schism's brother, hatred's sewer, lies' forger, flatteries' sink; who at his death despaired like Cain, and, stricken by the horror of God, breathed forth his wicked soul to the dark mansion of the black devil.
Sir Thomas Walsingham

MILITARY

As busy as a Swiss admiral. *Anon*

If it's natural to kill, why do men have to go into training for it?
Joan Baez – 'Daybreak'

Any man who liked marching had been given his brain for nothing: just the spinal column would have done. *Albert Einstein*

New weapons would seem to be regarded merely as an additional tap through which the bath of blood can be filled all the sooner. *B. H. Liddell-Hart (1925)*

With mercenaries your greatest danger is from their cowardice. *Niccolò Machiavelli*

An army without culture is a dull-witted army, and a dull-witted army cannot defeat the enemy. *Mao Tse-tung (1944)*

Soldiers ought more to fear their general than their enemy. *Michel de Montaigne*

The Army Selection Board told me I had the voice of a gentleman and the spelling of a clown. What spelling had to do with winning wars is beyond me.
Oliver Reed (1971)

There are three kinds of intelligence – the intelligence of man, the intelligence of animals, and the intelligence of the military. In that order. *Gottfried Reinhardt*

I am tired and sick of war. Its glory is all moonshine. War is hell.
General William Sherman (1879)

The professional military mind is by necessity an inferior and unimaginative mind; no man of high intellectual quality would willingly imprison his gifts in such a calling. *H. G. Wells*

We want to get rid of the militarist not simply because he hurts and kills, but because he is an intolerable thick-voiced blockhead who stands hectoring and blustering in our way of achievement.
H. G. Wells – 'The Outline of History' (1920)

MILITARY LEADERS

Napoleon Bonaparte

If utter selfishness, if the reckless sacrifice of humanity to your own interest and passions be vileness, history has no viler name.

Goldwin Scott – 'Three English Statesmen'
(1807)

Che Guevara

Guevera was a powerful theoretician but no soldier.

Shelford Bidwell – 'Modern Warfare'
(1973)

Paul von Hindenburg

The wooden Titan. *A. J. P. Taylor (1963)*

Adolf Hitler

Hitler's achievements as Supreme Commander in the Second World War were inferior to his achievements as an ordinary soldier in the First.

J. Strawson – 'Hitler As a Military Leader'
(1971)

Saddam Hussein

As far as Saddam Hussein being a great military strategist, he is neither a strategist, nor is he schooled in operational arts. He's not a tactician. He's not a general. He's not a soldier. Other than that, he's a great military man.

General H. Norman Schwarzkopf (1991)

Duke of Wellington

I should pronounce him to be a man of little genius, without generosity, and without greatness of soul.

Napoleon Bonaparte – Letter (1817)

WARS & BATTLES

Battle of Crete (1941)

Like German Opera, too long and too loud. *Evelyn Waugh*

Boer War

This war will not add an ounce of glory to the English flag. *Henry Bourassa (1900)*

Falklands War

The Falklands Conflict was a quarrel between two bald men over a comb.
Jorge Luis Borges (1983)

Korean War

The wrong war, at the wrong place, at the wrong time, and with the wrong enemy.
General Omar Bradley (1951)

Vietnam War

It's worse than immoral, it's a mistake.
Dean Acheson

Clean out my cell
And take out my tail
On the trail
For the jail
Without bail
Because it's better in jail
Watchin' television fed
Than in Vietnam somewhere dead.
Muhammad Ali (1966)

Vietnam was as much about a laboratory experiment as a war. *John Pilger (1978)*

All the noises of this war have an unaccountably Texan ring.
Nicholas Tomalin – 'Sunday Times' (1966)

OTHER

British Expeditionary Force

A contemptible little army.
Kaiser Wilhelm II (1914)

British military leaders

Ludendorff: The English soldiers fight like lions.
Colonel Max Hoffman: True. But don't we know that they are lions led by donkeys.
(1915)

Egyptian cavalry

As soldiers they lack both vices and virtues. *Sir Winston Churchill (1899)*

Mexican army

I don't fight Mexicans with cartridges, I fight them with rocks and keep the cartridges to fight the white soldiers.
Chief Geronimo

Nuclear weapons

The atom bomb is here to stay. But are we?   *Anon*

Let not the atom bomb be the final sequel
In which all men are cremated equal.
                                        Kaye Phelps

It is not enough to ban nuclear weapons, for nuclear weapons can always be manufactured. The thing you have to ban is war.   *Bertrand Russell*

The arms race is based on an optimistic view of technology and a pessimistic view of man.   *I. F. Stone –*
                        'New York Review of Books' (1969)

The tremendous menace of this day and age is not the stockpile of nuclear weapons which human ingenuity has devised, but the grim fact that the men in charge of them are as mediocre as those who invented them are brilliant.
                                Peter Ustinov (1968)

Pacifists

On Vietnam War protestors – Their signs said, 'Make love not war!' It didn't seem to me as if they were capable of either.
                                Ronald Reagan

The Pentagon

The Pentagon has five sides on every issue.   *Anon Russian*

A Pentagon committee is a group of the unwilling, picked from the unfit, to do the unnecessary.   *David Brinkley*

Royal Air Force

The RAF do not have traditions, they have habits.   *Anon Petty Officer –*
                        Letter to 'The Times' (1977)

V2 rocket

It was very successful, but it fell on the wrong planet.   *Wernher von Braun*

ROYALTY

I have nothing but contempt for the aristocracy.
    Robert Maxwell – 'Daily Express' (1974)

We're all anti-royalist and anti-patriarch, 'cos it's 1989. Time to get real. When the ravens leave the Tower, England shall fall they say. We want to be there shooting the ravens.   *Ian Brown (1989)*

There are no credentials. They do not even need a medical certificate. They need not be sound either in body or mind. They only require a certificate of birth – just to prove that they are first of a litter. You would not choose a spaniel on these principles.
                        David Lloyd George (1909)

The British people prefer their royalty stupid, selfish and greedy. The more

ridiculous and philistine they are, the easier it is to identify with them.
    Paul Foot – 'Sunday Correspondent' (1990)

The monarchy, as presently constituted, is, like St George's Hall at Windsor, a nineteenth-century imitation of ancient splendour which creates the illusion of real antiquity.
            Roy Hattersley – 'Observer' (1992)

Strange, but in England they think soccer is football. Of course, in England they think princes and princesses live happily ever after.   *Jay Leno (1993)*

The British Royal Family are a tax-evading bunch of adulterers.
                            Richard Littlejohn

Your Royal Family, I've never seen such ugly people.   *Mojo Nixon (1989)*

My objection to the Royal symbol is that it is dead, it is the gold filling in a mouthful of decay.
            John Osborne – 'Declaration' (1957)

Kings and such like are just as funny as politicians.   *Theodore Roosevelt*

I would not be a queen for all the world.
        William Shakespeare – 'Henry VIII'

The idea of Prince Charles conversing with vegetables is not quite so amusing when you remember that he's had plenty of practice chatting to members of his own family.
        Jaci Stephens – 'Sunday Times' (1993)

I certainly do not want to marry a member of the British aristocracy, because I am not a necrophiliac.
            Taki – 'Spectator' (1980)

Authority forgets a dying king.
    Alfred, Lord Tennyson – 'Idylls of the King'

Unlike the male codfish which, suddenly finding itself the parent of three million five hundred thousand little codfish, cheerfully resolves to love them all, the British aristocracy is apt to look with a somewhat jaundiced eye on its younger sons.   *P.G. Wodehouse*

These comfortably padded lunatic asylums which are known, euphemistically, as the stately homes of England.
    Virginia Woolf – 'The Common Reader'

ROYAL PERSONAGES

Princess Alexandra

'Good but Dull' royalty. *Viviane Ventura – 'A Guide to Social Climbing'*

Queen Caroline of Ansbach (wife of King George II)

Her conduct present, no censure affords

She sins not with courtiers, but sleeps with Lords.   *Anon*

Charles, Prince of Wales

Prince Charles loves nostalgia – pitched roofs, pastiche, detail, Victorian architecture. The institution of monarchy is preposterous in a technological society – you can't wear a crown in midtown Manhattan. But if the gentry are in the Palladian houses, the stoical artisans in the pebble-dash house tugging their forelocks – if you recreate the past, then the institution of monarchy and class privilege is tenable.   *J. G. Ballard*

All the speeches on the rainforests and the buildings pale when you're two-timing the most popular woman in England.
            Anthony Holden (1992)

Diana, Princess of Wales

Di Hard – the pop princess.
        Julie Burchill – 'Modern Review' (1992)

King Edward VII

A corpulent voluptuary.   *Rudyard Kipling*

A descendant of a Hanoverian imposter . . . He is an inveterate romancer whose crimson inventions suggested that he had been brought into the world by a union of Victor Hugo and Ouida.
                G. B. Shaw (1906)

King Edward VIII

The most damning epitaph you can compose about Edward is one that all comfortable people should cower from deserving: he was at his best only when the going was good.
            Alistair Cooke – 'Six Men'

Reviewing Philip Ziegler's 'Edward VIII' (1990) – This book confirms Edward VIII as the nastiest human being in 20th century British history – with the possible exception of his wife.
        Paul Foot – 'Sunday Correspondent'

He had hidden shallows.   *Clive James*

Prince Edward

Eddie the Beagle. *'Bitch' (1993)*

It's a mystery why Prince Charles needs to talk to flowers . . . when he has Edward.

Jilly Parkin – 'Daily Express' (1992)

Mr Major told a shocked House that it was 'a matter of some sadness for the Prince that he was unable to announce his formal separation from anyone.' 'However,' the Prime Minister went on, 'should the Prince ever marry, I can assure the House that he will immediately separate from his partner, whomsoever he or she may be.' *'Private Eye' (1992)*

Queen Elizabeth I

As just and merciful as Nero, and as good a Christian as Mahomet.

John Wesley – 'Journal' (1768)

Queen Elizabeth II

An undeniably dull fish. Her dress sense – the epitome of Drab Chic . . . Her annual Christmas broadcast to the Commonwealth is a dull highlight of any year, which only watching *The Great Escape* for the twelfth time afterwards can match.

Peter Freedman – 'Glad to Be Grey' (1985)

Sarah Ferguson, Duchess of York

On her weight problem – The Duchess of Pork. *Anon*

Frederick, Prince of Wales (son of King George II)

Here lies Fred,
Who was alive and is dead:
Had it been his father,
I had much rather;
Had it been his brother,
Still better than another;
Had it been his sister,
No one would have missed her;
Had it been the whole generation,
Still better for the nation;
But since 'tis only Fred,
Who was alive and is dead –
There's no more to be said. *Anon*

King George II

You may strut, dapper George, but will all be in vain.
We know 'tis Queen Caroline, not you, that reign. *Anon*

King George III

A better farmer ne'er brushed dew from lawn
A worse king never left a realm undone.
Lord Byron – 'The Vision of Judgement'

On his nine sons – They are the damnedest millstones about the neck of any government that can be imagined.
Duke of Wellington

King George IV

A noble, nasty course he ran,
Superbly filthy and fastidious;
He was the world's 'first gentleman,'
And made the appellation hideous.
Winthrop M. Praed

King George V

Lousy but loyal. *Jubilee banner (1935)*

If he ever sets foot in Chicago, I'll punch him in the snoot. *William H. Thompson*

King Hussein of Jordan

On Queen Noor's visit to London after the Gulf War – I think she's come to London to get a pair of pliers to get the splinters out of her husband's backside, he's sat on the fence so long. I think the little wretch should stay out of this country and keep his family with him. *Terry Dicks (1991)*

Valerie Messalina (wife of Emperor Claudius)

Unfaithful bitch! Messalina, Medusa! Gorgon! *Claudius*

Princess Michael of Kent

On his idea of the worst possible Christmas present – Dinner with Princess Michael of Kent. *Viscount Linley (attrib)*

Princess Pushy.   *'Private Eye'*

Queen Mother
I have heard that everyone in the East
End regards the Queen Mother as their
best friend. This is sheer fantasy. It is
rather like regarding Father Christmas as
your best friend.   *A. N. Wilson*

Louis Mountbatten of Burma
Dickie, you're so crooked that if you
swallowed a nail you'd shit it corkscrew.
Gerald Templer

Marina Mowatt (née Ogilvy)
She previously posed for one of the
tabloids in a rubber *Avengers* outfit. *You*
magazine described her as a Boy George
lookalike, but this is unfair. Boy George is
pretty.   *Lynn Barber –*
'Independent on Sunday' (1990)

William IV
He was not a man of talent or of much
refinement.   *'The Times' – Obituary (1837)*

COMMERCE

The aim of commerce is not to sell what
is best for people or even what they really
need, but simply to sell: its final standard
is successful sale.   *Sir Richard Livingstone*

Operating in America is like swimming in
a shark pool.   *Gerald Ronson (1992)*

CAPITALISM

The inherent vice of capitalism is the
unequal sharing of blessings.
Sir Winston Churchill (1945)

Capitalists are no more capable of self-
sacrifice than a man is capable of lifting
himself up by the boot-straps. *V. I. Lenin*

Show me a capitalist, I'll show you a
bloodsucker.   *Malcolm X (1965)*

Man is born perfect. It is the capitalist
system which corrupts him.
Arthur Scargill (1981)

BUSINESSMEN & WOMEN

John Cleese
I find it rather easy to portray a

businessman. Being bland, rather cruel
and incompetent comes naturally to me.
'Newsweek' (1987)

**Richard Branson (Chairman of
Virgin)**
A reptilian little shit.   *'Private Eye' (1981)*

**Sir Michael Edwardes (Chairman of
British Leyland)**
Looks like a victim of forceps delivery.
Auberon Waugh – 'Private Eye'

Milton Friedman (economic adviser)
Any country that can stand Milton
Friedman as an adviser has nothing to
fear from a few million Arabs.
John M. Galbraith (1979)

John Paul Getty (US industrialist)
Paul Getty, who had always been vastly,
immeasurably wealthy, and yet went
about looking like a man who cannot
remember whether he remembered to
turn the gas off before leaving home.
Bernard Levin

Sir James Goldsmith
Goldenballs.   *'Private Eye'*

Ralph Halpern (Chairman of the Burton Group)

You make Al Capone look like a petty shoplifter.   *Cynthia Israel (1982)*

Leona Helmsley (New York hotelier)

The Queen of Mean.   *Anon*

Sir Freddie Laker (Chairman of Laker Airlines)

On his knighthood – Pity the sword didn't slip and hack that son of a bitch's jugular.
                    Anon U.S. airline executive (1982)

If I gave Laker three tickets on Concorde every time he gets married. I should go broke the way he did.   *Lord King (1985)*

Robin Leigh-Pemberton (Governor of the Bank of England)

This appalling dead-beat.
                    Brian Sedgemore (1985)

Robert Maxwell

Cap'n Bob, the Bouncing Czech.
                    'Private Eye'

A talk on 'The Art of Letter Writing' is being given by Elisabeth Maxwell, described in the programme as 'widow of the celebrated publisher'. How about an apology?
          The Vulture – 'Modern Review' (1992)

An emperor of excess, a grand vizier of gluttony – in short, a greedy pig.
     Francis Whelan – 'Literary Review' (1993)

Sir Ian McGregor (Chairman of the National Coal Board)

When the Queen invests him, she should bring the sword down with a horizontal movement across the shoulders, perhaps with a little flick of the wrist.
          Peter Heathfield [N.U.M.] (1986)

Michael Milken ('The King of Junk Bonds')

The ultimate insight of Michael Milken, was that there is no limit to greed, no shackles on avarice, no end to cupidity, and that there is a seemingly endless supply of crooks and suckers.
                    Maxwell Newton

Tony O'Reilly (Chief Executive of Heinz)

He makes blarney and hot air a fine substitute for real cash.
                    Conrad Black (1992)

'Tiny' Rowland (Chairman of Lonrho)

The unacceptable face of capitalism.
                    Edward Heath

Of course, being called the acceptable face of capitalism would be equally insulting.   *Tiny Rowland (1985)*

He is, of course, a pirate, the kind of man who would walk into a revolving door behind you and emerge, the other side, in front.
          Stewart Stevens – 'Daily Mail' (1973)

Alan Sugar (Chairman of Amstrad)

His computers take twice the gestation period of an elephant to load up . . . He has the looks and charm of a warthog long since ostracised by polite warthog society on the grounds of looks and lack of charm.   *'Media Guardian' (1993)*

Donald Trump

The Prince of Swine.   *Michael M. Thomas*

COMPANIES

Exxon

The corporation? Hype! They fund the arts, they give out grants for programmes for public TV about dancing, and then they turn around and show what their real interest is: disaster.   *Jarboe (1989)*

General Motors

I come from an environment where, if you see a snake, you kill it. At General Motors, if you see a snake, the first thing you do is hire a consultant on snakes. Then, you spend a year talking about snakes.   *H. Ross Perot (1988)*

Habitat

Shabitat.   *Anon*

Ratners [jewellers]
People say, 'How can you sell this for so little?' I tell them, 'Because it is total crap!'   *Gerald Ratner (1991)*

The House That Crap Built.
'The Sun' (1991)

Spud-U-Like
I think we should definitely fire-bomb Spud-U-Like. Not for any reason apart from its the worst name I've heard in my life.   *Dave Stewart (1989)*

THE CITY OF LONDON

He's called a broker because after you deal with him you are.   *Anon*

Most City analysts remind me of the old bookies' runners.   *George Davies (1989)*

The Stock Market is a hotbed of cold feet.   *Financial Times (1981)*

I abhor the city. I think they're whores, all of them.
Harvey Goldsmith – 'The Times' (1988)

I would not take too much notice of teenage scribblers in the City who jump up and down in an effort to get press attention.   *Nigel Lawson (1988)*
[*Morgan Grenfell analyst Steve Bell replied* The Chancellor's description of us as 'teenage scribblers' is about as accurate as his forecast of the current account deficit – 100% wrong]

The City is like an orgy where no one stops to have a bath.
Charlie Richardson (1988)

There should be professional exams for these City analysts. Most of the time they talk through their backsides.
Alan Sugar (1990)

ACCOUNTING

Accounting is a malicious extension of the banking conspiracy.   *Henry Ford*

Accountants are the witch doctors of the modern world.   *Mr Justice Harman – 'Miles v Clarke' (1953)*

An accountant is a man who puts his head in the past and backs his ass into the future.   *Ross Johnson*

ACTUARIES

An actuary is someone who moved out of accountancy because he couldn't stand the excitement.   *Anon*

Actuaries are to market research what brain surgeons are to foot massage.
George Pitcher

Actuaries have the reputation of being about as interesting as the footnotes on a pension plan.   *George Pitcher (1988)*

AUDITORS

Auditors are the troops who watch a battle from the safety of a hillside and when the battle is over, come down to count the dead and bayonet the wounded.
Anon

Who says auditors are human?
Arthur Hailey – 'The Money Changers' (1975)

CONSULTANTS

I don't like to hire consultants. They're like castrated bulls – all they can do is advise. *Victor Kiam – 'Going for It' (1986)*

Consultants are people who borrow your watch to tell you the time and then walk off with it.   *Robert Townsend (1970)*

ECONOMICS

You can make even a parrot into a learned political economist – all he must learn are the two words 'Supply' and 'Demand'.   *Anon*

An economist is a man who knows one hundred ways of making love but doesn't know any women. *Art Buchwald*

Economists are like Bangkok taxi-drivers; put two of them together and you will have four opinions, any of which will take you careering in the wrong direction at great expense. *Mike Carlton (1986)*

Economists are the Respectable Professors of the Dismal Science. *Thomas Carlyle*

Economists are people who think the poor need them to tell them that they are poor. *André Drucker*

Old economists never die, they simply change their assumptions. *Sir Geoffrey Howe (1989)*

Most of the modern economics as taught is a form of brain damage. *Ernst F. Schumacher – 'The Reader' (1977)*

Give me a one-handed economist! All my economists say, 'On the one hand . . . on the other hand'. *Harry S. Truman*

SCIENCE

Science is but an exchange of ignorance for that which is another kind of ignorance. *Lord Byron*

The two big tricks of the twentieth century are: technology instead of grace, and information instead of virtue. *Ulysée Comtois*

Verily, it is easier for a camel to pass through the eye of a needle than for a scientific man to pass through a door. *Sir Arthur Eddington*

Science has 'explained' nothing; the more we know about, the more fantastic the world becomes and the profounder the surrounding darkness. *Aldous Huxley – 'Views of Holland'*

How many learned men are working at the forge of science – laborious, ardent, tireless Cyclopses, but one-eyed! *Joseph Joubert – 'Pensées' (1842)*

We have genuflected before the god of science only to find that it has given us the atomic bomb, producing fears and anxieties that science can never mitigate. *Martin Luther King – 'Strength Through Love'*

Our scientific power has outrun our spiritual power. We have guided missiles and misguided men. *Martin Luther King – Ibid*

Science is what one Jew copies from another. *Dr Karl Lueger*

Science has taught us to kill before philosophy has taught us to think. *Lester S. Sinclair (1945)*

SCIENTISTS

Francis Crick
Already for thirty-five years he had not stopped talking and almost nothing of fundamental value had emerged. *James Dewey Watson – 'The Double Helix'*

Charles Darwin

'The Origin of the Species' – The question
is this: Is man an ape or an angel? I, my
Lord, am on the side of the angels.
Bejamin Disraeli

'Origin of the Species' – A brutal
philosophy – to wit, there is no God, and
the ape is our Adam.   *Cardinal Manning*

Albert Einstein

I'd have given ten conversations with
Einstein for a first meeting with a pretty
chorus girl.   *Albert Camus*

As a rational scientist, Einstein is a fair
violinist. Einstein is already dead and
buried alongside Andersen, Grimm and
the Mad Hatter.   *George F. Gilette (1929)*

Louis Pasteur

It is absurd to think that germs causing
fermentation and putrefaction come from
the air; the atmosphere would have to be
as thick as pea soup for that.
Dr. Nicolas Joly

ASTRONOMY

An observatory is where astronomers
conjecture away the guesses of their
predecessors.   *Ambrose Bierce*

*On visiting Mount Wilson Observatory, in
California, and being told 'One of the
principal functions of all this sophisticated
paraphernalia is to find out the shape of the
Universe'* – Oh, my husband does that on
the back of an old envelope. *Mrs. Einstein*

MATHEMATICS

It is easier to square the circle than to get
round a mathematician.
*Augustus de Morgan – 'A Budget of
Paradoxes' (1872)*

Mathematics may be defined as the
subject in which we never know what we
are talking about, not whether what we
are saying is true.   *Bertrand Russell*

MEDICINE

B.U.P.A. is a company that docks your
pay to pay your doc.   *Anon*

The first operation carried out in the
private sector is a biopsy of your wallet.
Anon

In America, a revolutionary technique is
being developed of asking the patient how
he feels on the new treatment, etc., and
paying attention to what he says.
Kingsley Amis – 'The Spectator' (1985)

A plastic surgeon is one who has credit
card facilities.
Mike Barfield – 'The Oldie' (1992)

First physicians try to get on, then they
get honour, then they get honest.
Humphrey Rolleston

Preachers say, 'Do as I say, not as I do'.
But if the physician had the same disease
upon him that I have, and he should bid
me do one thing, and himself do quite
another, could I believe him?
John Selden – 'Table Talk'

MEDICAL PRACTICES

Alternative medicine

That medieval fairground of
technophobia and make-it-at-home
philosophy.
*Thomas Sutcliffe – 'The Independent'
(1993)*

Dentistry

A dentist is a prestidigitator who, putting
metal in your mouth, pulls coins out of
your pocket.   *Ambrose Bierce*

PHILOSOPHY

The difference between gossip and
philosophy lies only in one's way of
taking a fact.   *Oliver Wendell Holmes Jr.
– 'Youth's Companion' (1896)*

Philosophers have always been happier in felling the orchards of their predecessors than in planting new ones. *Lambert Jeffries*

Inertia rides and riddles me;
The which is called Philosophy.
Dorothy Parker – 'Enough Rope' (1926)

Friedrich Nietzsche

He belongs, body and soul, to the flock of mangy sheep.
Max Nordau – 'Degeneration'

Thomas Paine

Like Judas he will be remembered by posterity; men will learn to express all that is base, malignant, treacherous, unnatural and blasphemous by the single monosyllable – Paine. *William Cobbett*

A mouse nibbling at the wing of an archangel. *Robert Hall*

Bertrand Russell

One of the most fabulously stupid men of our age. *Brian Appleyard*

A desiccated, divorced and decadent advocate of sexual promiscuity.
'The Tablet'

PSYCHIATRY

Forget about smacking children, when are adults going to start hitting child psychologists?
Julie Burchill – 'Mail on Sunday' (1992)

Psychiatry's chief contribution to philosophy is the discovery that the toilet is the seat of the soul.
Alexander Chase – 'Perspectives' (1966)

Psychiatrists have a financial interest in being wrong; the more children they can disturb, the larger their adult clientele.
Geoffrey Robinson

Carl Jung

Jung's latter-day philosophy, with its esoteric archtripe, fitted wonderfully with the Nazi endeavour to befuddle people's minds, make them mistrust the evidence of their own senses, and obey an elite with pure blood and impure motives.
Frederic Wertham

PSYCHOLOGY

I refuse to endure months of expensive humiliation only to be told that at the age of four I was in love with my rocking-horse. *Noël Coward*

James Baldwin

A hustler who comes on like Job.
Ishmael Reed

Havelock Ellis

He had the air of a false prophet, like Santa Claus at Selfridges. *Graham Greene*

Mr Ellis has a tendency to dwell on excrement. *'London Mercury'*

Sigmund Freud

I always loathed the Viennese quack. I used to stalk him down dark alleys of thought, and now we shall never forget the sight of old, flustered Freud, seeking to unlock his door with the point of his umbrella. *Vladimir Nabokov*

THE TECHNOLOGICAL AGE

If the human race wants to go to hell in a basket, technology can help it get there by jet. It won't change the desire or the direction, but it can greatly speed the passage.   *Charles M. Allen (1967)*

An inventor is a person who makes an ingenious arrangement of wheels, levers and springs, and believes it civilization.
                    Ambrose Bierce

If civilization has risen from the Stone Age, it can rise again from the Wastepaper Age.
    Jacques Barzun – 'The House of Intellect' (1959)

The Atomic Age is here to stay – but are we?   *Bennett Cerf*

Take the so-called standard of living. What do most people mean by 'living'? They don't mean living. They mean the latest and closest plural approximation to the singular prenatal passivity which science, in its finite but unbounded wisdom, has succeeded in selling their wives.   *e. e. cummings (1954)*

The danger of the past was that men became slaves. The danger of the future is that men may become robots.
    Erich Fromm – 'The Sane Society' (1955)

Don't get smart alecksy
With the galaxy
Leave the atom alone.   *E. Y. Harburg*

If there is a technological advance without social advance, there is, almost automatically, an increase in human misery.
    Michael Harrington – 'The Other America' (1962)

It is said that one machine can do the work of fifty ordinary men. No machine, however, can do the work of one extraordinary man.   *Tehyi Hsieh (1948)*

Technological progress has merely provided us with more efficient means of going backwards.   *Aldous Huxley*

The trouble with our age is that it is all signpost and no destination.
    Louis Kronenberger – 'The Spirit of the Age' (1954)

Electronic calculators can solve problems which the man who made them cannot solve; but no government-subsidized commission of engineers and physicists could create a worm.   *Joseph W. Krutch – 'The Twelve Seasons' (1949)*

Progress has its drawbacks; you can't warm your feet on a microwave.
                    Doug Larson

You cannot endow even the best machine with initiative; the jolliest steam-roller will not plant flowers.
    Walter Lippman – 'Routineer and Inventor' (1914)

Everywhere in this world the industrial regime tends to make the unorganized or unorganizable individual, the pauper, into the victim of a kind of human sacrifice offered to the gods of civilization.
    Jacques Maritain – 'Reflections on America' (1958)

By his very success in inventing labour-saving devices, modern man has manufactured an abyss of boredom that only the privileged classes in earlier civilizations have ever fathomed.
    Lewis Mumford – 'The Conduct of Life' (1951)

We have created an industrial order geared to automation, where feeble-mindedness, native or acquired, is necessary for docile productivity in the factory; and where a pervasive neurosis is the final gift of the meaningless life that issues forth at the other end.

Lewis Mumford – Ibid

One has to look out for engineers – they begin with sewing machines and end up with the atomic bomb.

Marcel Pagnol (1949)

We cannot get grace from gadgets. In the bakelite house of the future, the dishes may not break, but the heart can. Even a man with ten shower baths may find life flat, stale and unprofitable.

J. B. Priestley (1956)

The technology of mass production is intently violent, ecologically damaging, self-defeating in terms of non-renewable resources and stultifying for the human person. *E. F. Schumacher – 'Small Is Beautiful' (1973)*

Sir, I have tested your machine [an early gramophone]. It adds a new terror to life and makes death a long-felt want.
Sir Herbert Beerbohm Tree

No test tube can breed love and affection. No frozen packet of semen ever read a story to a sleepy child. *Shirley Williams*

If automation keeps up, man will atrophy all his limbs but the push-button finger.
Frank Lloyd Wright – 'New York Times' (1955)

TECHNOLOGICAL ADVANCES

Computers

Computer software cannot replace greyware. *Anon*

To err is human, but to really foul up requires a computer.
Philip Howard – 'The Times' (1987)

Computers are useless, they only give you answers. *Pablo Picasso*

Telephones

Public telephones in Europe are like our pin-ball machines. They are primarily a form of entertainment and a test of skill rather than a means of communication.
Henry Beard (1981)

That plastic Buddha jars out of Karate screech
Before the soft words with their spores
The cosmetic breath of the gravestone
Death invented the phone it looks like the altar of death.
Ted Hughes – 'Do Not Pick Up the Telephone'

Typewriters

The typewriter, 1/2ike all mac&ines, has amind of it sown. *A. P. Herbert*

I have tried noiseless machines, but they put me off; it is like typing on a steak and kidney pudding. *J. B. Priestley*

TRAVEL

AIR TRAVEL

Airline travel is hours of boredom
interrupted by moments of stark terror.
Al Boliska

There's nothing like an airport for
bringing you down to earth.
Richard Gordon

In the space age, man will be able to go
around the world in two hours – one hour
for flying and one hour to get to the
airport.   *Neil McElroy – 'Look' (1958)*

Ten years ago the moon was an
inspiration to poets and an opportunity
for lovers. Ten years from now it will be
just another airport.
Emmanuel G. Mesthene

The rings of Saturn are composed
entirely of lost airline luggage.
Mark Russell (1990)

AIRLINES & AIRPLANES

Alitalia
Always Late In Take-off, Always Late In
Arrival.   *Acronym*

Concorde
An aircraft which is used by wealthy
people on their expense accounts, whose
fares are subsidized by much poorer
taxpayers.   *Denis Healey*

I was delighted to hear that Concorde was
going to land at Dulles airport,
Washington – a unique spectacle of a
white elephant on another white elephant.
*Malcolm Muggeridge – 'Ancient and
Modern' (1981)*

MOTOR TRAVEL

New roads: new ruts.   *G. K. Chesterton*

The automobile has not merely taken
over the street, it has dissolved the living
tissue of the city. Its appetite for space is
absolutely insatiable; moving and parked,
it devours urban land, leaving the
buildings as mere islands of habitable
space in a sea of dangerous and ugly
traffic.
James M. Fitch – 'New York Times' (1960)

A conservation area is a place where you
can't build a garage but you can build a
motorway.   *James Gladstone*

As the horse-power in modern
automobiles steadily rises, the congestion
of traffic steadily lowers the average speed
of your car. This is known as Progress.
Sydney J. Harris – 'Strictly Personal'

The trouble is that too often there is forty
horsepower under the bonnet and one
asspower at the wheel.
John McNaughton (1933)

People on horses look better than they
are. People in cars look worse than they
are.
Marya Mannes – 'More in Anger' (1958)

What's the average man's life but a
succession of automobiles? When he dies
we should carve on his tombstone simply
the makes and years.
*Richard Needham – 'A Friend in Needham'
(1969)*

MOTOR CARS

Ford Motor Company
Dick Turpin wore a mask to rob the
poor, but Ford spared the nicety.
Anon striking Ford worker (1972)

Ford Cortina
We chose the name because it represents
something really cheap 'n' nasty.
Jeremy Valentine [The Cortinas pop group]

RAIL TRAVEL

I hate trains. I hate travelling down parallel lines, a rigid frieze of scenery stuck on smeary windows. As Ratners was to jewellery, British Rail is to trains. It is crap. *Reggie Nadelson – 'Evening Standard' (1992)*

RAILWAYS

British Rail
On the Tories' Citizen's Charter: Proving about as efficacious as a pomander was against the bubonic plague.
Victor Lewis-Smith – 'Mail on Sunday' (1992)

On staff: Porters are trained at the Pol Pot school of charm, while guards are either frustrated broadcasters, ceaselessly blaring out incomprehensible messages, or Trappist monks who have taken a holy vow forbidding any communication whatsoever.
Victor Lewis-Smith – 'Mail on Sunday' (1992)

On privatisation: Transport Secretary John MacGregor thinks he is building a new Jerusalem. Some of us think it will be more like Beirut. *Robert Adley (1993)*

Long Island Railway, New York
A nightmare on wheels . . . at rush hour it makes you wish you'd been mugged before you got on.
Reggie Nadelson – 'Evening Standard' (1992)

Waterloo-City Line
The Drain. *Anon*

THE WORLD

NATIONS

Heaven is an English policeman, a French cook, a German engineer, an Italian lover and everything organised by the Swiss. Hell is an English cook, a French engineer, a German policeman, a Swiss lover and everything organised by an Italian. *John Elliott (1986)*

The Italian seems wise, and is wise.
The Spaniard seems wise, and is a fool.
The Frenchman seems a fool, and is wise.
The Englishman seems a fool, and is a fool. *Thomas Scott (1623)*

Australia
Australia may be the only country in the world in which the word 'academic' is regularly used as a term of abuse.
Dame Leonie Kramer (1986)

British Isles
The British disease is considering others more responsible than ourselves.
Sir Geoffrey Howe (1986)

England
In settling an island, the first building erected by a Spaniard, would be a church; by a Frenchman, a fort; by a Dutchman, a whorehouse, and by an Englishman, an ale-house. *Proverb*

We're no longer a nation of shopkeepers, we're a nation of cowboys.
Kirsty MacColl (1989)

Book title – The English: Are They Human? *G. J. Reiner (1931)*

France
The French are either sadly optimistic or jolly pessimistic. *Ilya Ehrenburg*

Britain has football hooligans, Germany has neo-Nazis, France has farmers.
'The Times' (1992)

Germany
The human as opposed to the German
mind.   *William James*

The East German manages to combine a
teutonic capacity for bureaucracy with a
Russian capacity for infinite delay.
Goronwy Rees – 'Diary' (1964)

The great virtues of the German people
have created more evils than idleness ever
did vices.   *Paul Valéry*

Greece
Few things can be less tempting or
dangerous than a Greek woman of the
age of thirty.   *John Carne – Letter (1830)*

Holland
The Dutch fall into two quite distinct
physical types: the small, corpulent, red-
faced Edams, and the thinner, paler,
larger Goudas.   *Alan Coren*

Compared with Greece and Italy,
Holland is but a platter-faced, cold-gin-
and-water-country, after all, and a heavy,
barge-built, web-footed race are its
inhabitants.
Sir F. B. Head – 'Bubbles' (1834)

We always like our pop-stars to be like
Greek gods: bigger, better and uglier than
us. We hate the bores: Jesus Christ and
the Dutch. Especially the Dutch.
Malcolm McLaren (1989)

Ireland
Other people have a nationality. The Irish
and the Jews have a psychosis.
Brendan Behan – 'Richard's Cork Leg'

Japan
The Japanese have almost as big a
reputation for cruelty as young children.
*Dennis Bloodworth – 'Chinese Looking-
glass' (1967)*

I don't greatly admire Japanese women;
they have no figures to speak of, and look

as if a bee had stung them in the eye.
*Crosbie Garstin – 'The Dragon and the
Lotus' (1928)*

Korea
The Koreans have been called 'The Irish
of the East', but this is an insult to the
Irish.
James Kirkup – 'Streets of Asia' (1969)

Norway
F*** off, Norway!   *Paul Gascoigne (1992)*

Russia
The Russians seemed to me a nation of
sheep – angry sheep, but nevertheless
sheep, and in sheep's clothing.
James Kirkup – 'One Man's Russia' (1968)

Scotland
It is possible that all Scots are illegitimate.
Scotsmen being so mean and Scotswomen
being so generous.   *Anon*

Serbia
The Serbian countrymen came over as a
gang of brutal yokels with a cultural life
only marginally richer than that of
Neanderthal man.
John Naughton – 'Observer' (1992)

Sweden
Swedes are fake Norwegians.
Greg D'Alessio

Turkey
They are good people, but perfectly
useless.   *Horatio, Lord Nelson (1795)*

Will they ever be civilised? I think not.
Such a fine country ought to be in better
hands.   *John Webster – 'Notes' (1891)*

USA
The South: The beaten, ignorant, Bible-
ridden white South.   *Sherwood Anderson*

We're pigs! Americans are pigs! I really
hate America. We've turned into such
selfish bastards. If Adolf Hitler came back

and said, 'I will reduce taxes', he'd win by a landslide.   *Peter Buck (1988)*

Violence is as American as cherry pie.
                                    Stokely Carmichael

America is fundamentally the land of the overrated child.

   *Count Hermann Keyserling – 'Americans
                          Set Free' (1929)*

Americans have plenty of everything – and the best of nothing.
       John Keats – 'You Might As Well Live'

The American character looks always as if it just had a rather bad haircut.
                                    Mary McCarthy

The Americans don't really understand what's going on in Bosnia. To them it's the unspellables killing the unpronouncables.
            P. J. O'Rourke – 'The Sun' (1992)

A tasteless, efficient equalitarian society created by the European poor.
   William Toye – 'A Book of Canada' (1962)

Every time Europe looks across the Atlantic to see the American eagle, it observes only the rear end of an ostrich.
                           H. G. Wells (1907)

Wales

The older the Welshman, the more madman.   *Proverb*

Each section of the British Isles has its own way of laughing, except Wales which doesn't.

       Stephen Leacock – 'Humour' (1935)

They are treacherous to each other as well as to foreigners, covet freedom, neglect peace, are warlike and skilful in arms, and are eager for revenge.
                           Walter Map (1180)

The Welsh are a primitive tribe who speak an unintelligible language, practise

savage rites and customs and are untrustworthy and hostile to strangers.
                           Goronwy Rees (1972)

PLACES

Abroad

Never go abroad. It's a dreadful place.
                           Earl of Cardigan

Abroad is awful. I know because I've been there!   *King George V*

Addis Ababa, Ethiopia

Addis Ababa looks as if it had been dropped piecemeal from an aeroplane carrying rubbish.
       John Gunther – 'Inside Africa' (1955)

Albania

It's the sort of place you get into as late as possible, bring your own grub, go to bed, get up, go for a walk, play the game and get out.   *Jack Charlton (1993)*

Barnes, England

A London suburb which, aiming desperately at the genteel, achieves only a sordid melancholy.
       *W. Somerset Maugham – 'On a Chinese
                          Screen' (1922)*

Basra, Iran

The Persian Gulf is the arsehole of the world, and Basra is eighty miles up it.
                           Harry Hopkins (1941)

Beckenham, Kent, England

When you get to Beckenham, the country begins to assume a cockney-like appearance; all is artificial, and you no longer feel any interest.
       William Cobbett – 'Rural Rides' (1823)

Beirut, Lebanon

An artificial Babel.
   Henry Tanner – 'New York Times' (1976)

Birmingham, England

The longest chapter in Deuteronomy has

not curses enough for an Anti-
Bromingham.
John Dryden – 'To the Reader' (1681)

It's a disgusting town with villas and
slums and ready made clothes shops and
Chambers of Commerce.
Evelyn Waugh – 'Diary' (1925)

If you live in Birmingham, then being
awake is not necessarily a desirable state.
Tony Wilson (1988)

Blackpool, Lancashire, England
Blackpool is an ugly town, mean in its
vastness.
Arnold Bennett – 'Paris Nights' (1913)

Bogotá, Colombia
Bogotá seemed a cruel, towering place,
like an eagle's nest now inhabited by
vultures and their dying prey.
*Paul Theroux – 'The Old Patagonian
Express' (1979)*

Boulogne, France
The air of Boulogne encourages
putrefaction.
Tobias Smollett – 'Travels' (1766)

Bucharest, Romania
A town of one street, one church and one
idea.   *Romanian proverb*

Bulgaria
If this is Communism, they can keep it.
Arthur Scargill (1975)

Cairo, Egypt
I never saw a place I liked worse, nor
which afforded less pleasure or
instruction than Cairo; nor antiquities
which less answered their description.
James Bruce – 'Travels' (1790)

There is not perhaps upon earth a more
dirty metropolis.   *E. D. Clarke –
'Travels in Various Countries' (1817)*

Calais, France and Dover, England
What mean amorphous entrance portals
to great kingdoms! Mere grimy, untended
back-doors!
Arnold Bennett – 'Journal' (1897)

Calcutta, India
Calcutta is a definition of obscenity.
Geoffrey Moorhouse – 'Calcutta' (1971)

Calgary, Canada
It's going to look really great when it
finally gets uncrated.   *Anon*

California, USA
That advance post of civilisation, with its
flavourless cosmopolitanism, its charlatan
philosophers and religions, its lack of
anything old and well-tried, rooted in
tradition and character.
J. B. Priestley (1957)

I wouldn't like California even if the
weather was good.   *Jack Teagarden*

Cambodia
I have lived for 78 years without hearing
of bloody places like Cambodia.
Sir Winston Churchill (1953)

Cambridge, England
The least damaging place in England in
which not to be found funny.
Kingsley Amis – 'Encounter' (1964)

Canada
Canada is America's attic.
Robertson Davies

This two-cultured, multi-ghettoed, plural
community, this non-nation, nay-saying,
no-place of an un-Eden, this faceless,
unidentifiable blank on the map.
William Killbourn (1970)

Cape Hatteras, North Carolina
The Graveyard of the Atlantic. *Nickname*

Capri, Italy
A stewpot of semi-literary cats.
D. H. Lawrence – Letter (1920)

Charing Cross, London, England
All I can say is that standing at Charing
Cross and looking east, west, north and
south, I can see nothing, but dullness.
John Keats – Letter (1820)

Chelmsford, Essex, England
If any one were to ask me what in my

opinion was the dullest and most stupid spot on the face of the Earth, I should decidedly say Chelmsford.

Charles Dickens – Letter (1835)

Chicago, USA

Chicago's South side is like a vast, unorganized lunatic asylum. Nothing can flourish here but vice and disease.

Henry Miller – 'The Air-Conditioned Nightmare' (1945)

Copenhagen, Denmark

I see nothing here but ruins.

Mary Wollstencraft – Letter (1795)

Corsica

It is easier to deplore than describe the actual condition of Corsica.

Edward Gibbons – 'The Decline and Fall of the Roman Empire' (1788)

Costa del Sol, Spain

Costa del Crime.   *Nickname*

Danakil Desert, Ethiopia

The desert of Danakil is a part of the world that the Creator must have fashioned when He was in a bad mood.

Ladislas Farago (1936)

Delhi, India

Delhi is the capital of the losing streak. It is the metropolis of the crossed wire, the missed appointment, the puncture, the wrong number.

Jan Morris – 'Destinations' (1980)

A glorified Harrogate – not quite as 'refained' and about twenty times duller.

Julian Phillipson – Letter

Dessie, Ethiopia

The name, which means 'My Joy' in Amharic, seems peculiarly inappropriate.

Paul B. Henze (1977)

Eastbourne, England

Costa Geriatrica.   *Nickname*

East River, New York, USA

On being asked if she could repeat a 21-mile swim up the river she'd made in 1926 –

Sure, I'd float across the garbage.

Gertrude Ederle (1973)

Edinburgh, Scotland

This accursed, stinking, reeky mass of stones and lime and dung.

Thomas Carlyle – Letter (1821)

England

A little foggy island in the North-West corner of Europe. The witless mother of nations.   *Francis Adams (1893)*

I feel very sick with England. It is a dead dog that died of a love disease like syphilis.   *D. H. Lawrence – Letter (1921)*

Estoril, Portugal

An ugly little beach town.

Mary McCarthy – Letter (1955)

Exeter, Devon, England

Exeter is an ancient city, and has been so slow in adopting modern improvements that it has the unsavoury odour of Lisbon.

Robert Southey – Letter (1807)

Famagusta, Cyprus

The sound of it is so lovely, though when you visit it, you find it to be an undistinguished Cotswold village which has been whitewashed.   *Osbert Sitwell – 'The Four Continents' (1954)*

France

An expensive minefield between Dover and the Spanish border.

Roger Bray – 'Evening Standard' (1979)

Fujiyama, Japan

I once started to climb it, in company of about one million Japanese, but it was so unpleasantly like scrambling up a pile of coke that I gave up after five minutes.

James Kirkup – 'These Horned Islands' (1962)

The sacred rubbish dump. *James Kirkup – 'Japan Behind the Fan' (1970)*

Genoa, Italy

The untidiest port in the world.   *Robert Byron – 'First Russia Then Tibet' (1933)*

Glovelier, Switzerland
This is a place of no excellence whatever,
and if the thought did not seem extreme,
I should be for putting it to the sword and
burning it down.   *Hilaire Belloc (1902)*

Grantham, Lincolnshire
The most exciting thing to come out of
Grantham is the A1.   *Anon*

Centre of the dull world; where the dull
go when they die.
  Peter Freedman – 'Glad to Be Grey' (1985)

Guildford, Surrey
The Switzerland of England.   *Anon*

Harbin, China
Harbin is now called the Chicago of the
East. This is not a compliment to
Chicago.
  Maurice Baring – 'What I Saw in Russia'

Harwich, Essex, England
Harwich is not a merry town, towards
evening you might call it dull.
        *Jerome K. Jerome – 'Three Men on the
                        Bummell' (1900)*

Hoboken, New Jersey, USA
The Armpit of America.   *Anon*

Hyde Park, London
Hyde Park's not country. It's just an
underground car park with grass roof.
  *Alan Ayckbourn – 'Round and Round the
                              Garden'*

Japan
A land of disappointments.   *Anon*

Johannesburg, South Africa
If there is any place in the world where
love is dead, it is here.
        Mary Benson – Letter (1965)

Manchester under Fascism.
        Richard West (1965)

Kansas City, USA
It's not necessary to have relatives in
Kansas City to be unhappy.
        Groucho Marx – Letter (1951)

Keelung, Taiwan
A kind of low-life Venice of the Orient.
        James Kirkup – 'Streets of Asia' (1969)

Kingsgate, Kent, England
That half-crystallised nowhere of a place.
        D. H. Lawrence – Letter (1913)

Kingston, Canada
It may be said of Kingston that one half
of it appears to be burnt down, and the
other not to be built up.
  Charles Dickens – 'American Notes' (1842)

Lancashire, England
A dreary place and I have never passed
through it without wishing myself
anywhere but in that particular spot
wherein I then happened to be.
        *Nathaniel Hawthorne – 'Our Old Home'
                                      (1863)*

Las Vegas, USA
Glitter Gulch.   *Nickname*

A city both veneer and venereal,
dedicated to waste and excess, heartless
and without a heart.
        Trevor Fishwick (1980)

Leeds, England
Amongst all others the vilest of the vile.
        Barclay Fox

A little dingy town.
        Horace Walpole – Letter (1756)

Liverpool, England
I don't like Scouse humour, Derek
Hatton or the quaint local custom of
trampling Italian football fans to death.
        Julie Burchill – 'Modern Review' (1993)

No one goes to Liverpool for pleasure.
  *Graham Greene – 'Journey Without Maps'
                                      (1963)*

A most convenient and admirable point
to get away from.   *Nathaniel Hawthorne –
                          'Our Old Home' (1863)*

London, England
London is the most intensely reclusive

major city on the planet – an indoor, net-curtainish metropolis.

Douglas Kennedy – 'Literary Review'
(1992)

The worst place in the world for a good woman to grow better. *Sir John Vanbrugh*

Los Angeles, Spain
'The Angels' – where devils would not live could they help it.
Richard Ford – 'Travellers in Spain' (1855)

Los Angeles, USA
The city's layout is a tangle of circumferences which have lost contact with their centres.
Clive James – 'Postcard from L.A.' (1979)

It's all right, but it couldn't hold a candle to Blackpool. *Brian London*

A constellation of plastic.
Norman Mailer (1968)

When it's 100 degrees in New York, it's 72 in Los Angeles.
When it's 30 degrees in New York, it's still 72 in Los Angeles.
However, there are 6,000,000 intelligent people in New York and 72 in Los Angeles. *Neil Simon*

Lyons, France
It's a great nightmare – a bad conscience – a fit of indigestion – the recollection of having done a murder. An awful place.
Charles Dickens – 'Letter' (1844)

Macao, China
I found the Pearl of the Orient slightly less exciting than a rainy Sunday evening in Rochester.
S. J. Perelman – 'Westward Ha!' (1948)

Manchester, England
He chose to live in Manchester, a wholly incomprehensible choice for any free human being to make.
Mr Justice Melford Stevenson

Marbella, Spain
Bethnal Green in the sun. *Anon*

Margate, England.
Margate in February is like Nugget City after the gold-rush.
Lee Wilson – 'Evening News' (1979)

Massawa, Ethiopia
The less said about Massawa the better. It was one of those dark patches that are best forgotten. *Geoffrey Harmsworth (1935)*

Mississippi River, USA
An enormous ditch – running liquid mud six miles an hour. *Charles Dickens*

Monaco
Disneyland-sur-mer. *Anon*

Moscow
Los Angeles without sun or grass.
Lillian Hellman

Moscow, I saw at once, is Horrorsville.
James Kirkup – 'One Man's Russia' (1968)

Naples, Italy
Naples is the place that combines the vice of Paris, the misery of Dublin and the vulgarity of New York. *John Ruskin*

Nebraska, USA
My impression of Nebraska is twin steel rails running dead straight for ever and ever across a dead level plain of dead maize. *Crosbie Garstin (1928)*

Newcastle, England
To be out of hell, Newcastle certainly is the damnedest district of country anywhere to be found.
Henry Brougham – Letter (1813)

New England, USA
The most serious charge which can be brought against New England is not Puritanism, but February.
Joseph W. Krutch (1949)

Newfoundland, Canada
This poor bald rock. *Joseph Smallwood*

New York, USA
A city where wise guys peddle gold bricks to each other and Truth, crushed down to

earth, rises again as phoney as a glass eye.
Ben Hecht – 'Nothing Sacred'

New York looks as ever: stiff, machine-made, and against nature. It is so mechanical there is not the sense of death.
D. H. Lawrence – Letter (1924)

Purple-robed and pauper-clad
Raving, rotting, money-mad;
A squirming herd in Ammom's mesh,
A wilderness of human flesh
Crazed with avarice, lust and rum
New York, thy name's Delirium.
Byron R. Newton

New York isn't Mecca. It just smells like it. *Neil Simon – 'California Suite'*

Niagara Falls, Canada
The honeymoon bride's second disappointment. *Oscar Wilde*

North of England
Journeys North always felt like a descent into somewhere short-tempered nasty and barely British at all; not for nothing is the most sinister and depressing Underground line in London called the Northern Line . . . The South makes us think of heat and lust; the North of peat and dust.
Julie Burchill – 'Modern Review' (1993)

Nova Scotia, Canada
That dismal country that's nothing but an iceberg aground.
T. C. Haliburton – 'The Clockmaker' (1836)

Nova Scotia is very poor. Bangladesh on the St. Lawrence.
Simon Winchester – 'Daily Mail' (1979)

Ottawa, Canada
Ottawa doesn't know its art from a hole in the ground. *Anon (1968)*

Ouazazate, Morocco
'Diarrhoea City' – Oh, f***, yes, terrible place. You don't even have to eat anything for that. It's the dust from the camel shit. One of the worst places I've

ever been.
Michael Caine – 'Time Out' (1992)

Outer Mongolia
Outer Mongolia is such a terra incognita that Tibet is practically Coney Island by comparison.
James Gunther – 'Inside Asia' (1939)

Palm Beach, USA
Palm Beach looks like hell on wheels, Rolls-Royce of course.
Ronald Hastings – 'Daily Telegraph' (1977)

Paris, France
That monstrous growth on the Seine, the factory of greed and gaiety, of vice and art. *Thomas Craven*

Paris is a filthy hole. *Benjamin R. Haydon*

I've been to Paris, France and Paris, Paramount. Paris, Paramount is better.
Ernst Lubitsch

A week in Paris reduced me to the limpness and lack of appetite peculiar to a kid glove . . . It's my belief there's death in the kettle there.
Robert Louis Stevenson – Letter (1881)

Philadelphia, USA
A great, flat, over-baked brickfield.
Alexander Mackay (1849)

The City of Brotherly Love but more accurately called The City of Bleak November Afternoons.
S. J. Perelman – 'Westward, Ha!' (1948)

Piccadilly Circus, London, England
A distorted isochronal triangle, square to nothing of its surroundings . . . an impossible site in which to place any outcome of the human brain except possibly an underground lavatory.
Sir Alfred Gilbert [designer of the Eros Statue] (1890)

Quebec, Canada
Quebec is all steps and, at the bottom of the steps, poverty. *Norman Levine – 'Canada Made Me' (1958)*

215

Repulse Bay, Hong Kong
Repulsive Bay.   *Nickname*

Reykjavik, Iceland
About as exciting as Aberdeen on a
Sunday night.   *Anon*

Rhode Island, USA
Texas could wear Rhode Island as a
watch fob.   *Pat Neff*

Rome, Italy
The barbarians who broke up the Roman
Empire did not arrive a day too soon.
         Ralph W. Emerson – 'Conduct of Life'
                    (1860)

Rome reminds me of a man who lives by
exhibiting to travellers his grandmother's
corpse.   *James Joyce – Letter (1906)*

St. Louis, USA
A foul, stinking corpse, rising up from the
plain like an advertisement of Albrecht's
'Melancholia' . . . The houses seem to
have been decorated with rust, blood,
tears, sweat, bile, rheum, and elephant
dung.   *Henry Miller –*
    'The Air-conditioned Nightmare' (1945)

Samoa
Western Samoa – never confuse it with
American Samoa ruined by Yank sub-
culture.
    Ivor Herbert – 'Mail on Sunday' (1992)

San Francisco, USA
The poor man's paradise.   *Anon*

San Marino
I asked the Scottish Football Association
whether San Marino was a republic or a
principality, and they said it was a
technicality.
    Roddy Forsythe – BBC radio (1991)

Singapore
That modern apology for a romantic
eastern Port.   *Paul Scott (1968)*

South Kensington, London
Where sin stalks naked through the dark
alleys and only might is right.
    P. G. Wodehouse – 'Service with a Smile'
                    (1962)

Spain
A country that has sold its soul for
cement and petrol and can only be saved
by a series of earthquakes. Oh, for more
taste, less greed!   *Cyril Connolly –*
                    'The Evening Colonnade' (1973)

Suez, Egypt
The Paradise of thieves.   *Eliza Fry (1779)*

Swindon, England
The first rule of comedy: Never do
comedy in a town where they still point at
aeroplanes.   *Bobby Mills (1992)*

Switzerland
A country to be in for two hours, or two
and a half, if the weather is fine, and no
longer. *Ennui* comes in the third hour,
and suicide attacks you before night.
                    Lord Brougham

Switzerland has produced the numbered
bank account, Valium and Ovaltine.
    Peter Freedman – 'Glad to Be Grey' (1985)

I don't like Switzerland, it has produced
nothing but theologians and waiters.
                    Oscar Wilde

Tabas, Iran
The Persian for 'Get Lost!' is 'Go to
Tabas!'   *'The Economist' (1980)*

Tehran, Iran
Tehran, a boom town grafted onto a
village, is a place of no antiquity and little
interest, unless one has a particular
fascination for bad driving and a traffic
situation twenty times worse than New
York.   *Paul Theroux – 'The Great Railway*
                    Bazaar' (1975)

Telford, England
You live in a world of your own: Telford.
                    Sean Hughes (1990)

Tenerife, Canary Islands
Monstrous cement compounds by tourist
traps, rubbishy shops like sets for a
downmarket TV sitcom.
    Ivor Herbert – 'Mail on Sunday' (1992)

Toronto, Canada
A mournful Scottish version of America.
Percy Wyndham Lewis – Letter (1940)

Turkey
The sick old man of Europe.
Kaiser Wilhelm II

The sick old man of the east.
Tsar Nicholas II

Before World War I, Turkey was known
as 'the sick man of Europe' – now it is
almost terminal.   *Richard Nixon (1980)*

United States of America
In America you watch TV and think
that's totally unreal, then you step outside
and it's just the same.   *Joan Armatrading*

American cities are like badger holes
ringed with trash.
John Steinbeck – 'Travels with Charley'
(1962)

The land of the dull and the home of the
literal.   *Gore Vidal (1969)*

Venice, Italy
Abhorrent, green, slippery city.   ∙
D. H. Lawrence – 'Pomegranate' (1920)

Who wants a Renaissance Disneyland,
anyway, with entrance fees only the very
rich can afford?   *'Private Eye' (1978)*

Venice looked like a blocked sink.
'Sunday Times' (1979)

Victoria, Canada
Victoria is God's waiting room. It is the
only cemetery in the entire world with
street lighting.   *Anon*

Wales
There are still parts of Wales where the
only concession to gaiety is a striped
shroud.   *Gwyn Thomas – 'Punch' (1958)*

Widnes, Lancashire, England
They say that men become attached even
to Widnes.
A.J.P. Taylor – 'Observer' (1963)

Winnipeg, Canada
A sprawling, gap-toothed collection of
ghettos.   *James H. Gray (1970)*

Yakutsk
A more lifeless, depressing city does not
exist on the face of this planet. Even
Siberians call this 'the end of the world'.
Harry de Windt – 'From Paris to New
York' (1904)

Yorkshire, England
Yorkshire born, Yorkshire bred
Strong in t'arm, thick in t'ead.   *Saying*

I hold Yorkshire to be a mistake.
James Agate – 'Ego 9' (1946)

THE ANIMAL WORLD

ANIMALS

It's a fine day, let's go out and kill
something.   *Anon*

'orses and dorgs is some men's fancy.
They're wittles and drink to me.
Charles Dickens

Animals generally return the love you

lavish on them by a swift bite in passing.
Gerald Durrell

I do not like animals – of any sort. I don't
even like the idea of animals. Animals are
no friend of mine. They are not welcome
in my house . . . I like them just fine, in
the form of nice, crisp spare-ribs and
Bass Weejun penny-loafers.
Fran Lebowitz – 'Social Studies' (1981)

Beavers

The symbol of Canada is the beaver, that industrious rodent whose destiny it was to furnish hats that warmed better brains than his own. *Roy Daniels (1957)*

Canaries

The song of canaries
Never varies
And when they're molting
They're revolting.
Ogden Nash – 'The Canary' (1940)

Cats

God save all here, barring the cat.
Old Irish saying

A soft, indestructible automaton provided by nature to be kicked when things go wrong in the domestic circle.
Ambrose Bierce

The trouble with a kitten is THAT
Eventually it becomes a CAT.
Ogden Nash – 'The Kitten'

I am not a cat man, but a dog man, and all felines can tell this at a glance – a sharp, vindictive glance. *James Thurber*

The cat Percy, for all his sleek exterior, was mean and bitter. He had no music in his soul, and was fit for treasons, strategies and spoils. One could picture him stealing milk from a sick tabby.
P. G. Wodehouse – 'Cats Will Be Cats' (1933)

Dogs

It's the one species I wouldn't mind seeing vanish from the face of the earth. I wish they were like the White Rhino – six of them left in the Serengeti National Park and all males. *Alan Bennett*

Wanted: A dog that neither barks nor bites, eats broken glass and shits diamonds. *Goethe*

On James Thurber's cartoon dogs – Stop running those dogs on my page. I wouldn't have them peeing on my cheapest rug. *William Randolph Hearst*

For many of us, particularly myself, a dog is a set of sharp teeth mounted on four legs. *Robert Morley*

On W.C. Fields: Anybody who hates children and dogs can't be all bad.
Leo Rosten

Don't make the mistake of treating your dogs like a human or they'll treat you like dogs. *Martha Scott*

The indefatigable and unsavoury engine of pollution, the dog.
John Sparrow – Letter (1975)

I loathe people who keep dogs. They are cowards who haven't got the guts to bite people themselves.
August Strindberg – 'A Madman's Diary'

Any dog will tell you what these prize-ribbon dogs are like. Their heads are so swelled they have to go into their kennels backwards.
P. G. Wodehouse – 'The Mixer' (1917)

It was one of those hairy, nondescript dogs, and its gaze was cold, wary and suspicious, like that of a stockbroker who thinks someone is going to play the confidence trick on him.
P. G. Wodehouse – 'Blandings Castle' (1935)

It looked something like a pen-wiper and something like a piece of hearth rug. A second and keener inspection revealed it as a Pekinese puppy. *P. G. Wodehouse – 'Good-bye to All Cats' (1936)*

Dolphins

If dolphins are so intelligent, how come they ain't got Walkmans?
John Lydon (1989)

Donkeys

The Devil's walking parody
On all four-footed things.
G. K. Chesterton – 'The Donkey'

Gamecocks

If the gamecock was not meant for fighting, why was he created?
L. Fitz-Barnard

Gnu

The gnu's extraordinary movements . . .
could only be described as something like
an acute attack of St Vitus's Dance.

Gerald Durrell

Horses

I know two things about a horse
One of which is rather coarse.   *Anon*

Dangerous at both ends and uncomfortable in the middle.   *Ian Fleming*

I prefer a bike to a horse. The brakes are
more easily checked.   *Lambert Jeffries*

Insects

Two-legged creatures we are supposed to
love as we love ourselves. The four-
legged, also, can come to seem pretty
important. But six legs are too many from
the human standpoint.

*Joseph W. Krutch – 'The Twelve Seasons'
(1949)*

Pigeons

Pigeons are rats with wings.

'The Big Chill'

Those dull, unmysterious city
unemployables, dressed in their grey,
secondhand suits.

Anthony Carson – 'On to Timbuctoo'

Pigs

Of all the quadrupeds that we know, the
hog appears to be the foulest, the most
brutish, and the most apt to commit
waste wherever it goes. The defects of its
figure seems to influence its dispositions:
all its ways are gross, all its inclinations
are filthy, and all its sensations in a
furious lust, and so eager a gluttony, that
it devours indiscriminately whatever it
comes across.   *John Mills*

Rabbits

The rabbit has a charming face
Its private life is a disgrace.   *Anon*

ANIMAL PLACES

Circus

A place where horses, ponies and
elephants are permitted to see men,
women and children acting the fool.

Ambrose Bierce

Zoos

The zoo cannot but disappoint.

John Berger

Most of the zoos I have ever visited were
horrible, smelly places where I wouldn't
dream of keeping a dead cat.

Jacquie Durrell

The man who has to muck out the
monkeys is rarely if ever consulted when
the architects roll up in their limousines to
sketch out the new monkey-house.

David Taylor

SPORT

ATHLETICS

I don't think the discus will ever attract any interest until they let us start throwing them at one another.   *Al Oerter*

Sebastian Coe
L'Huomo Dull personified. Seb Coe in a C & A V-neck is like a square peg in a round hole.
Peter Freedman – 'Glad to Be Grey' (1985)

Carl Lewis
Mr Smarm – the interviewer's dream (though by all accounts, a bit of a madam in his dealings with other athletes).
Andy Lyons – 'Melody Maker' (1988)

AMERICAN FOOTBALL

I don't see the sense in football. I haven't since I became a vegetarian.
Dan Millman (1972)

Anon
There's this interior linesman who's big as a gorilla and strong as a gorilla. If he was smart as a gorilla he'd be fine.
Sam Bailey (1972)

He doesn't know the meaning of the word fear. Of course, there are lots of words he doesn't know the meaning of.
Sid Gilman (1963)

Commenting on accusations of drug taking – The way the [San Diego] Chargers played last year the drug must have been formaldehyde.   *Bill Curtis (1974)*

BASEBALL

Call me Un-American; call me Canadian or Swedish, I don't care. I hate baseball . . . I have lots of reasons to hate baseball. For one it's dull. Nothing happens. Watching baseball is like going to a lecture by a member of the Slow . . . Talkers . . . of . . . America. It's like turning on the TV . . . when the cable is out. It's like watching grass – no, Astro Turf – grow.
Jeff Jarvis – 'Entertainment Weekly' (1990)

Managing a baseball team is like trying to make chicken salad out of chicken shit.
Joe Kuhel

There is nothing remarkable about throwing or catching or hitting a ball. Jugglers in Yugoslavia do it better.
Jim Murray – 'Los Angeles Times' (1974)

(American) Football isn't some sport where you play 8,000 games and run out to second base and call time because you've got a hangnail. *Norm Van Brocklin*

Leo Durocher
Leo has the most fertile talents in the world for making a bad situation infinitely worse.   *Branch Rickey (1955)*

Tommy Heinrich
The most overrated underrated player in baseball.   *Larry Ritter*

Walter O'Malley
He's the only guy I know Dale Carnegie would hit in the mouth.   *Bill Veeck (1976)*

Ted Williams
If his noodle swells another inch he won't be able to get his hat on without a shoe horn.   *Jack Riley (1940)*

BASKETBALL

The game is too long, the season is too long and the players are too long.
Jack Dolph (1973)

Boston Celtics
The team is boring and lifeless. For over

twenty years the Celtics have stood for something. The only thing they stand for now is the anthem.

Bob Ryan – 'Boston Globe'

Los Angeles Clippers

Q. What do you call five black guys who can't play basketball?

A. The L.A. Clippers! *Arsenio Hall (1987)*

Earvin 'Magic' Johnson

A media freak-show.

Mark Lawson – 'The Independent' (1992)

BODY BUILDING

It does not befit a man to parade in front of the public flexing his muscles. Body-builders emerge from the basements. They don't walk. They carry their muscled torsos proudly – self-conceited, self-important, looking like roosters on a promenade. There are very many unbalanced persons among them and almost everyone seems to adore himself . . . Murderers and drunkards . . . men who take anabolic steroids and inject themselves with paraffin.

'Sovietsky Sport' (1978)

BOXING

Boxing is as cruel a blood sport as hunting; although the victims aren't dumb animals but poor blacks.

Michael Arditti – 'Evening Standard' (1993)

To hell with the Queen of Marksbury.

Pierre Bouchard (1973)

WBA, IBF and WBO – Alphabetical corporations which currently misrule professional boxing.

Patrick Collins – 'Mail on Sunday' (1992)

WBA Penta-Continental titles – This seems to be a part of world boxing's strategy to invent a prize for every boxer in the universe.

Andrew Shields – 'Time Out' (1993)

Muhammad Ali

He's phoney, using his blackness to get his way.

Joe Frazier (1971)

Nigel Benn

He is like washing-up liquid: built on hype and one day the bubble will burst.

Chris Eubank (1990)

Don Cockell

He is the biggest thing on canvas since 'The Wreck of the Hesperus'. *Anon (1955)*

Chango Cruz

After a loss – The bum was up and down so many times I thought he was an Otis elevator.

Harry Kabakoff (1977)

Chris Eubank

Eubank is as genuine as a three dollar bill.

Mickey Duff (1991)

Chris Eubank arrives in the a boxing ring posing and parading like a peacock, so risible that even his opponent and his opponent's corner men have to laugh . . . a preposterous pugilist.

Michael Herd – 'Evening Standard' (1992)

He tries to project himself as a deep-thinking and articulate gentleman, but fails miserably.

John Smith (1992)

Floyd Patterson

This old dumb pork chop eater don't have a chance. From eating pork he's got trillions of maggots and worms settling in his joints. He may even eat the slime of the sea.

Muhammad Ali (1965)

Billy Wells

He was all chin from the waist up.

Frank Moran

BOXING PROMOTERS & MANAGERS

A lot of boxing promoters couldn't match the cheeks of their backsides. *Mickey Duff*

Barry Hearn
He's still a legend in his own mind.
Mickey Duff

So many of his boxers end up in hospital, he should sell his limousine and buy an ambulance. *Mickey Duff*

Don King
Don King doesn't care about black or white. He just cares about green.
Larry Holmes

Frank Warren
The worst thing that's happened to boxing in this country. *Mickey Duff*

BULLFIGHTING

Antonio Fuentes (matador)
After me, there's nobody. And after nobody, there's Antonio Fuentes.
Raphael Guerra (1900)

CRICKET

The fixture list for the 1992 season could not indeed have been drawn up by a monkey with a typewriter. But that's only because monkeys are too clever to devise a programme which makes English cricketers play as much, rather than as well as possible . . . No self-respecting dog would dine on the unco-ordinated mess that English professional cricket has become.
Scyld Berry – 'Independent on Sunday'

The synthetic indignation of certain English cricketers over alleged Pakistani ball-tampering: the unedifying in pursuit of the unbeatable.
Patrick Collins – 'Mail on Sunday' (1992)

Sunday League cricket – multi-coloured pyjamas, two-tone umpires, and white balls with black seams. There is nothing like traditional English sport.
David Hunn – 'Sunday Times' (1992)

A cricketer – a creature very nearly as

stupid as a dog.
Bernard Levin – 'The Times' (1965)

Cricket? I thought it was an English food.
Alex Metreveli (1967)

Geoffrey Boycott
Now this next question has absolutely nothing to do with either music or sport . . . At which ground did Geoffrey Boycott hit his hundredth hundred?
'Classic FM' (1992)

Sunil Gavaskar
I feel personally quite disgusted and ashamed that I have played cricket with you. *Bishen Bedi (1990)*

Graham Gooch
On receiving the O.B.E. after losing the Ashes – It must stand for 'Overwhelmingly Beaten Englishman'
Ian Chadband (1991)

David Gower
A player of great innings but not a great player. *'Guardian'*

Devon Malcolm
Telling dear old Devon to bowl down the corridor of uncertainty is like asking bombers to demolish a city without hurting any civilians.
Peter Roebuck – 'Sunday Times' (1993)

Derek Pringle
Anything can happen in the 1992 World Cup. We know this because it already has. The world's best one-day team has lost three games. An off-spinner has opened the bowling. Derek Pringle has taken two diving catches. Pigs have seldom been seen travelling by land.
Tim de Lisle – 'Independent on Sunday'

Phil Tufnell
He's a great bowler and a complete dickhead. *Anon MCC player (1993)*

FOOTBALL

English First Division
The First Division – the new, hyperbolic

status for the erstwhile Second Division. This is a world of hard men and fluffed chances – park football writ large . . . The First Division is a greasy cheeseburger dressed up as an alfresco meat dish.
Tony Parsons – 'Observer Magazine' (1992)

English Second Division
Watching Channel 4's *Love Weekend* was all a bit much. You began to hanker for something love-free, like an Arnold Schwarzenegger film, or a Division 2 football match.
Marcus Berkmann – 'Daily Mail' (1993)

1989 England Team
The England soccer team are all bloody minor executives who can't kick the ball into the net.   *Mark E. Smith (1989)*

The Football Association
Everyone knows that a few clubs and some promotions men are now running the new Premier League. The organisation with the unfortunate initials seems to be doing, well, putting it politely, not much.
Norman Fox – 'Independent on Sunday' (1992)

Football hooligans
Get flame throwers out and burn the bastards. These people aren't human.
Bobby Robson (1976)

1978 Scottish World Cup Team
I feel ashamed for myself and Scotland, but I do not think some of the Scottish team have the brains to feel ashamed.
Martin Buchan (1978)

1990 World Cup Finals
They're going to bring this thing to the United States of America in 1994 and charge money for people to see it. Listen, if they were a Broadway show, it would have closed in one night.
Frank Deford – 'The National' (1990)

Wimbledon FC
I would rather watch Ice Hockey than see Wimbledon play. And I hate Ice Hockey.
John Bond (1991)

They have as much charm as a broken beer bottle.   *Tommy Docherty*

On their long-ball tactics – Football wasn't meant to be run by two linesmen and air traffic control.   *Tommy Docherty*

Anon Palace keeper (1989)
He's let in more than the West German government.   *Jimmy Greaves (1989)*

Roberto Baggio (Juventus)
A great footballer, but what an egregious haircut. It takes the damage Ian Botham inflicted on follicular sculpture a few frightening steps further. It's out beyond even the highlights zone . . . Would you walk down the street with someone with a semi-quiff, no sideburns and a pony-tail halfway up the back of his head?
Andrew Anthony – 'For Him Magazine' (1992)

George Best
The drunk we could all have become.
Michael Herd – 'Evening Standard'

Trevor Brooking (West Ham Utd FC)
Roy Race, the fictional Melchester Rovers heroic cardboard cut out still has more personality than Trevor Brooking.
'Zit' (1993)

Tommy Docherty
The human Scotweiler.   *Anon*

Who would have guessed that behind that arrogant Scots bastard image there lay an arrogant Scots bastard?
'When Saturday Comes'

Paul Gascoigne (Lazio)
Waddling around like a recently impregnated hippopotamus . . . Paul Gascoigne had become a bona fide wobble-bottom . . . But should football finally fail him, at least there's a whole range of alternative careers now on the horizon. Father Christmas . . . barrage balloon . . . spacehopper . . .
Marcus Berkmann – 'Independent on Sunday' (1993)

He asked me if I wanted to go on a midnight fishing trip, but I'd already seen his tiddler.

Madeleine Pallas – 'Daily Star' (1991)

Paul Gascoigne is a very well-known football player.   *Michael Silverleaf*

Rugby or Association?
Mr Justice Harman (1990)

Tony Hateley (Chelsea FC)

Tony had it all. The only thing he lacked was ability.   *Tommy Docherty*

Glenn Hoddle (Swindon Town FC)

Tame, cultured ball wizard who thought 'tackle' was something you put in your fishing bag.   *'Zit' (1993)*

Elton John (Chairman of Watford FC)

He decided to rename Watford, he wanted to call it Queen of the South.
Tommy Docherty

I hear he's made a bid for an Italian club – AC/DC Milan.   *Tommy Docherty*

Vinnie Jones (Wimbledon FC)

He must be a mosquito brain.
Sam Hammam (1992)

He is to fine and fair football what Count Dracula was to blood transfusions.
Michael Herd – 'Evening Standard' (1992)

A player who regards it as a matter of personal honour to intimidate the nation's finest, to castrate them with a shattering, late tackle early in the game, to rip their ears off and spit in the hole.
Jasper Rees – 'Independent on Sunday' (1992)

Vinnie (short for Vindictive).   *'Zit' (1993)*

Steve Kindon (Burnley FC)

They called him the 'Horse' because of his speed. It was also because he had the brain of a clothes horse and the control of a rocking horse.   *Paul Fletcher*

Gary Mabbutt (Spurs FC)

Dodgy defender who's often caught in two minds. Abbott and Costello's.
'Zit' (1993)

Jan Molby (Liverpool FC)

When the team trooped on, he looked like a fat man who had tagged on to the Liverpool line to live out every overweight's dream.   *Brough Scott – 'Independent on Sunday' (1992)*

Carlton Palmer (Sheffield Wednesday)

Carlton Palmer is the worst finisher since Devon Loch.   *Ron Atkinson (1991)*

Hugo Sanchez (Real Madrid)

He is a very dangerous man. He is as welcome as a piranha in a bidet.
Jesus Gil (1992)

Southend fans

At clubs like Newcastle the crowd is worth one and a half goals start to the home team but here it's probably minus six.   *Vic Jobson (1992)*

Ray Wilkins (QPR FC)

Dinner time at the Wilkins' home can take forever. Because true to form, if Ray's asked to pass the salt, it has to go sideways or backwards first.   *'Zit' (1993)*

GOLF

If I had my way the social status of professional golfers would be one notch below that of Nazi war criminals.
Andy Lyons – 'Melody Maker' (1988)

Golf is too slow a game for Canada. We would go sleep over it.
John B. McLenan (1891)

Nick Faldo

The only time he opens his mouth is to change feet.   *David Feherty (1992)*

Colin Montgomerie

He has a face like a warthog that has been stung by a wasp.   *David Feherty (1992)*

Greg Norman

The American players have a new name for the 'Great White Shark'. Greg Norman is referred to as the 'Carp'.
Guy Hodgson – 'Independent on Sunday' (1990)

ICE HOCKEY

The National Hockey League is so tightly organised that even the robber barons of old couldn't have devised a more monopolistic feudal system.
Nick Auf Der Maur – 'Last Post' (1971)

JOGGING

Joggers are basically neurotic, bony, smug types who could bore the paint off a DC-10. It is a scientifically proven fact that having to sit through a three-minute conversation between two joggers will cause your I.Q. to drop 13 points.
Rick Reilly – 'Sports Illustrated' (1992)

Exactly how intricate a sport is jogging? You were two years old. You ran after the cat. You pretty much had it mastered.
Rick Reilly – Ibid

MOTOR RACING

Auto racing is not an athletic sport.
Daniel R. McLeod (1961)

Some drivers grow the fruit. Others just come in and pick it. *Nigel Mansell (1992)*

The Indy 500 is not a sport for gentlemen. *Parnelli Jones (1965)*

Nigel Mansell

He is so brave, but such a moaner. He should have 'He Who Dares Whines' embroidered on his overalls.
Simon Barnes (1993)

Someone with about as much charisma as a damp spark plug.
Alan Hubbard – 'Observer' (1992)

Ayrton Senna

I feel no honour in racing against him, because he is not a man of honour.
Alain Prost (1989)

I thought he was one of the human race, but he is not. *Alain Prost (1990)*

SKIING

In St Moritz everyone who is anything goes around in plaster, which may be fashionable, but is damned uncomfortable. I value my legs as much as Marlene Dietrich values hers.
Noël Coward

SNOOKER

I swear my sons will never pick up a cue. Snooker can seriously damage your health. *Alex Higgins (1992)*

SURFING

A surfer is an American lemming.
Jacob Bronowski

TENNIS

A traditional fixture at Wimbledon is the way the [BBC TV] commentary box fills up with British players eliminated in the early rounds.
Clive James – 'Observer' (1981)

I may have exaggerated a bit when I said that 80 per cent of the top women tennis players are fat pigs. It's only 75 per cent.
Richard Krajicek (1992)

Bjorn Borg

Bjoring Borg . . . a Volvo among tennis stars.
Peter Freedman – 'Glad to Be Grey' (1985)

Chris Evert

Taut and tight-lipped mistress of the baseline, she is the all-American golden

girl become the champion of monotony.
Paul West

Ivan Lendl
He's never going to be a great player on
grass. The only time he comes to the net
is to shake your hand.
Goran Ivanisevic (1992)

John McEnroe
The Benson and Hedges Cup was won
by McEnroe . . . he was as charming as
always, which means that he was as
charming as a dead mouse in a loaf of
bread.   *Clive James – 'Observer' (1980)*

Ilie Nastase
When Nastase's winning he's
objectionable. When he's losing, he's
highly objectionable.   *Adrian Clark*

I feel like dog trainer who teach dog
manners and graces and just when you
think dog knows how should act with nice
qualities, dog make big puddle and all is
wasted.   *Ion Tiriac (1972)*

WATER SPORTS

Barefoot water skiing is no personal
ambition, particularly when the world
championships take place alongside an
Essex shopping centre car park.
David Hunn – 'Sunday Times' (1992)

SPORTS OFFICIALS

I wanted to have a career in sports when I
was young, but I had to give it up. I'm
only 6 feet tall, so I couldn't play
basketball. I'm only 190 pounds, so I
couldn't play football. And I have 20-20
vision, so I couldn't be a referee.
Jay Leno (1993)

Athletics judges
They're stupid. All you have to do to win
if it's close is throw up your arm just
before the finish and they think you're
first.   *Babe Didrickson*

Baseball umpires
Mama let me kill the umpire,
Let me hit him in the face.
19th-century American song

Basketball officials
You can say something to Popes, Kings
and Presidents, but you can't talk to
officials. In the next war they ought to
give everyone a whistle.
Abe Lemons (1977)

On females officiating in the NBA –
Incompetence should not be confined to
one sex.   *Bill Russell (1976)*

Boxing referees
Crippen got hung for less than some of
them referees have done.
Benny Jacobs (1960)

Cricket umpires
An umpire should be a man. They are for
the most part old women.
*'Quid' [Robert A. Fitzgerald] – 'Jerks in
from Square Leg' (1918)*

When a cricketer no longer had nerve,
eye or sinew left, then he was put out to
grass as an umpire.   *'Quid' – Ibid*

I have nightmares about having to
become an umpire.   *John Snow*

Harold 'Dickie' Bird – My only complaint
with 'Dickie' Bird is that he requires a
degree of certainty that is almost neurotic;
like the man who has to keep going to the
front door to make certain that he's
locked it.   *Mike Brearley*

Football referees
I feel I'm above referees.
Rodney Marsh (1971)

Tennis umpires
Natalie Cohen – I don't play if lady
umpires. I go to movies and have a few
beers.   *Ilie Nastase (1976)*

Edward James – I am not having points
taken off me by an incompetent old fool.
You're the pits of the world.
John McEnroe

SPORTS MEDIA

Sportswriters on TV have become as common as rats in a drain. Sportswriters should be read and not seen.
Norman Chad – 'Sports Illustrated' (1992)

Sportswriters have become the insurance salesmen of the 1990s. You don't ever want to get stuck in an elevator with one.
Norman Chad – Ibid

A colour commentator is a guy who's paid to talk while every one goes to the bathroom.   *Bill Curry (1968)*

On becoming a baseball columnist – I guess I'll have to gain 60 pounds, start smoking cigars, and wear clothes that don't match.
Gareth Iorg

A sports promoter is just a guy with two pieces of bread looking for a piece of cheese.   *Evel Knievel*

Match of the Day (BBC TV)
The BBC are just SO straight, SO respectable, they really can't do without the Housewives' Choice sort of people, people like Bobby Charlton and Trevor Brooking. They just will not rock the boat.   *'When Saturday Comes'*

Howard Cosell (US Sportscaster)
A voice that had all the resonance of a clogged Dristan bottle.   *'Encyclopaedia Britannica Year Book' (1973)*

Eamonn Dunphy
I think he is a bitter little man and I certainly do not want to talk to anyone who is ashamed to be an Irishman.
Jack Charlton (1990)

John Feinstein (US columnist)
You are a whore and a pimp.
Bobby Knight (1991)
[*Feinstein added:* I wish he'd just make up his mind, so I know how to dress]

Jimmy Hill (BBC soccer expert)
I don't think there's much doubt about who's the smuggest bastard among football's TV stars. Yes, it's that well-known wildlife slaughterer, Jimmy Hill . . . Take that chin away to the Natural History Museum, where it belongs.
'When Saturday Comes'

Christopher Martin-Jenkins (Radio 3 cricket commentator)
Born with a diamond-encrusted golden spoon thrust well down the throat.
Don Mosey – 'The Alderman's Tale' (1991)

Brian Moore (ITV soccer commentator)
Brian Moore is the only person who polishes his head before appearing on TV.   *'When Saturday Comes'*

Gary Newbon
If Gary Newbon were made of chocolate, he'd eat himself.   *Reg Gutteridge (1991)*

Bob Wilson (BBC sports presenter)
He just about sums Arsenal up – the verbal equivalent of a square ball across the back four. Watching him trying to make 'Football Focus' entertaining is like watching Doug Rougvie dribble – a painful experience.
'When Saturday Comes'

GAMES & PASTIMES

Barbie dolls
I hated Barbie dolls. I used to cut their hair off.   *Belinda Carlisle (1988)*

Cabbage Patch dolls
You didn't so much buy one as adopt it. Millions tried. Now, they just look like the rag dolls they are.
Hugh Pearman – 'Sunday Times' (1992)

Funfairs
A curious misnomer since they are neither fun nor fair . . . the rides (machines that Torquemada might have designed when he was in one of his moods) are 'supervised' by burly, tattooed maniacs hell-bent on pursuing underage girls: Neanderthals whose demeanour suggests that these travelling

folk are a closed community who have been inbreeding for centuries.
Victor Lewis-Smith – 'Mail on Sunday' (1992)

Pac-Man
It was a little all-to-devouring, just gobble, gobble, gobble. No social comment.
Ralph Nader

Sonic the Hedgehog
Super Mario the plumber must be the world's least likely hero, but at least he looks like a plumber: Sonic looks more like a skunk than a hedgehog.
Hugh Pearman – 'Sunday Times' (1992)

INTAKE

FOOD

Food, one assumes, provides nourishment; but Americans eat it fully aware that small amounts of poison have been added to improve its appearance and delay its putrefaction.
John Cage – 'Indeterminacy' (1961)

Food is a dangerous article. Too much food makes you fat, too little food makes you dead.
Mike Harding

Great eaters and great sleepers are incapable of doing anything that is great.
King Henry IV

FOODSTUFFS

Beans
There is no dignity in the bean. Corn, with no affectation of superiority, is, however, the child of song. It waves in all literature. But mix it with beans, and its high tone is gone. Succotash is vulgar.
Charles D. Warner (1871)

Bread
The white bread we eat is to corn bread what Hollywood will be to real American dramatic literature when it comes.
Sherwood Anderson

Those pock-marked wafers known as Scandinavian bread, which produce so cheerless an impression of Scandinavian home life.
Peter Fleming

Tell the cook of this restaurant with my compliments that these are the very worst sandwiches in the whole world, and that, when I ask for a watercress sandwich, I do not mean a loaf with a field in the middle of it.
Oscar Wilde

Cakes
Too many cooks, in baking rock cakes, get misled by the word 'rock'.
P. G. Wodehouse – 'Money in the Bank' (1946)

Dairy produce
Cottage cheese – there's no flavour in it. It's like kissing your sister.
Anon

In every restaurant, the hardness of the butter increases in direct proportion to the softness of the bread being served.
Harriet Markman (1991)

Desserts
My wife's banana split [from Pizza in the Park], laden with white cream and chocolate and with two wafers sticking out like wings from each end, looked like nothing so much as a squashed magpie.
Craig Brown – 'Sunday Times' (1992)

Fruit
A watermelon is a good fruit. You don't eat it, you don't drink it – you wash your face in it.
Enrico Caruso

Kiwi Fruit: What are these funny cucumbers?
Roy Kerridge

Haggis

To a sheep's stomach
containing permitted
amounts of oats, onions,
heart, lights, liver.
Dear god, I hope the sheep
is dead, for it's sake.

Miles Kington – 'The Times'

Health foods

Foods that are said to do one good
generally taste of sawdust and burnt
rubber.   *R. W. Howarth*

Meat

*On being asked by a waiter how his roast
woodcock had been –* Too much wood, too
little cock!   *Noël Coward*

A man of my spiritual intensities does not
eat corpses.   *G. B. Shaw*

Organic food and farming

Only bourgeois neurotics buy organic
food. If they want wacky food, we will
give it to them. But if all farming went
organic, the world would starve.

Chris Haskins (1989)

To the average British farmer, organic
farming is about as relevant as caviar and
a flight on Concorde.

Oliver Watson – 'Observer' (1989)

Sea food

In the past Naval cooking at sea involved
a choice between the lesser of two
weevils.   *Anon*

There is something sinister about
anchovy, something insect-like and
creepy, menacing, disturbing and fishily
unfishy (unofficially).

Craig Brown – 'Sunday Times' (1992)

To duplicate the taste of hammer-head
shark, boil old newspapers in Sloan's
liniment.   *Spike Milligan*

I hate that sushi crap. You have to drive a
Range Rover or BMW to eat it. Or wear
big chunky cardigans with green buttons
on.   *Marti Pellow (1988)*

TRAVELLER'S FARE

Airline food

Flying to New York – I've never really
cared for gutta-percha sandwiches and
purée of boot polish.   *Lord Mancroft*

The shiny stuff is tomatoes
The salad lies in a group
The curly stuff is potatoes
The stuff that moves is soup.

Steven Sondheim

British Rail food

Nobody expects the food at Government
Houses to be good, any more than one
expects the cooking on British Rail to be
good. It's just part of our tradition.

Noël Coward

A British Rail steward, sacked after being
accused of selling his own bacon
sandwiches, was 'unfairly dismissed'.
Quite so, British Rail must now stop
punishing stewards who sell eatable
sandwiches.   *'Evening Standard' (1991)*

Food (so disgusting that it is impossible
to tell where the paper plate ends and the
food begins) comes pinging out of the
sort of mephitic microwave ovens that
would get the Black Hole of Calcutta
Environmental Health Officers leaping
into action . . . I would prefer to stand in
line for seven hours outside Moscow's
GUM department store in pursuit of half
a cabbage than face a BR catering car
again. The old riddle has become my new
motto:
Q. If you have breakfast at King's Cross,
lunch in Peterborough and high tea in
Doncaster, where will you have dinner?
A. In hospital.   *Victor Lewis-Smith –
'Mail on Sunday' (1992)*

OTHER

Diets

Lizzie Webb's 'Total Health and Fitness' –
If you want to land up looking like a
badly-dressed Barbie doll this is the diet
book for you.

Alison Crenshaw – 'Bitch' (1992)

229

Your diet won't make you live longer, it will just seem that way. *Kerry Packer*

Gourmets
A gourmet who thinks of calories is like a tart who looks at her watch. *James Beard*

Microwaves
A microwave is an oven invented to prove that pub food could get worse.
Mike Barfield – 'The Oldie' (1992)

Nouvelle cuisine
With this so-called nouvelle cuisine there is nothing on your plate and plenty on your bill. *Paul Bocuse*

Cocktail parties
The cocktail party – as the name itself indicates – was originally invented by dogs. They are simply bottom sniffings raised to the rank of formal ceremonies.
Lawrence Durrell

Regional
The devil will not come into Cornwall for fear of being put into a pie.
Old Cornish saying

Once you get past breakfast, Italian food is not that bad.
Anon US soccer player (1990)

I begin to perceive that Americans regard food as something to sober up with.
James Agate – 'Ego 3' (1937)

Japan is so far away; and then you have to eat all that raw fish, tepid rice wine and live in cardboard houses. *W. H. Auden*

They cook worse in Undervelier, Switzerland, than any place I was ever in, with the possible exception of Omaha, Nebraska.
Hilaire Belloc – 'The Path to Rome' (1902)

The aftertaste of Middle Eastern food spoils the clean, pure flavour of gin.
Eddie Condon

Even a boiled egg tastes of mutton fat in England. *Norman Douglas (1915)*

Lunch kills half of Paris, supper the other half. *Charles de Secondat, Baron de Montesquieu – 'Variétés'*

The national dish of America is menus.
Robert Robinson (1977)

Vegetarian diet
A vegetarian diet may be best for those who would be beautiful but it does not seem to have done much for the elephant.
'Punch'

RESTAURANTS & HOTELS

Does anyone actually start the day with prunes, muesli, croissant and full English breakfast, except when they are visiting Hotel-land? As for the 'individual butter portions', the electron microscope which you would need to spread it is never supplied. *Victor Lewis-Smith – 'Mail on Sunday' (1992)*

Great restaurants are, of course, nothing but mouth-brothels.
Frederic Raphael (1977)

It is a very poor consolation to be told that a man who has given one a bad dinner, or poor wine, is irreproachable in private life. Even the cardinal virtues cannot atone for half-cold entrées.
Oscar Wilde – 'The Picture of Dorian Gray'

Anon restaurant in Bromley, Kent
Geographically, it is halfway between Elmer's End and Pratt's Bottom. Gastronomically, it is about the same.
Anon

Columbus, London
I ordered the Corn Masa Blinis with Salsa Verde and Sour Cream. With a dollop of sour cream perched on a generous helping of salsa verde, itself plopped upon the blinis, it looked as if someone had been sick over a passing plate. The taste, too, was not dissimilar.
Craig Brown – 'Sunday Times'

Jams, London
Jams in Albemarle Street, whose red pepper pancakes with a sweetcorn sauce, salmon caviar, creme fraiche and smoked salmon tasted like corn plasters with iodine.   *Craig Brown – 'Sunday Times'*

Le Gavroche, London
It's a silly place.   *Loyd Grossman*

The New Restaurant [Victoria & Albert Museum]
At the V&A's much vaunted Ace Caff the decoration is pupped by Habitat out of the Reject Shop and the food by Meals on Wheels out of School Dinners . . . The escalope of turkey was as large as a gardening glove and quite as chewy, catching the throat with lumps and leaving only a faint aftertaste of fowl . . . Poached cod Portugaise was a portion so meagre that a pensioner would starve on it . . . The baked potatoes looks as though they had been excreted by a buffalo.
    Brian Sewell – 'Evening Standard' (1992)

Phoenix Apollo, Stratford East
The satay . . . dessicated and served with a sauce that bears no relation to the genuine article: ointment plus grunge.
        Jonathan Meades – 'The Times'

COOKS & HOSTS

Anon
She did not so much cook food as assassinate food.   *Storm Jameson*

Ian Fleming
Whenever I ate with Ian at Goldeneye the food was so abominable that I used to cross myself before I took a mouthful. Stewed guavas and coconut cream – salt fish and ackee fruit. I used to say: 'Ian, it tastes like armpits!'   *Noël Coward*

Elaine Kauffman
'Elaine's' – The owner, Elaine, is notorious as a lady who sits spiking bills and glares with undiluted loathing at her clientele.   *Hugh Leonard*

Marco Pierre White
He's quite without equal in cooking. On the other hand, he's an arsehole, but he knows it.
        Anthony Worrall-Thompson (1992)

DRINKS

BEVERAGES

Coca-Cola
Coca-Cola can use its status as a main sponsor of the Olympic Games to proclaim, mystifyingly, that it is 'sharing the Olympic ideal.' What sport ideal, exactly, can a soft drink share?
        Richard Williams – 'Independent on Sunday' (1992)

Coffee
You can tell when you have crossed the frontier of Germany because of the badness of the coffee.   *King Edward VII*

In Europe, the most obstreperous nations are those addicted to coffee.   *Robert Lynd*

'Have you ever tasted such filthy coffee?' 'Never,' said Joe, though he had lived in French hotels.   *P. G. Wodehouse – 'Summer Moonshine' (1938)*

Perrier
On the 1990 mineral water scare – Those who live by the image die by the image. At this rate, in another month, we'll be back to burgers, fries and coke.
        Michael Kinsley

Soft drinks
No New Yorker has tasted a drink in his life, all refreshments being served cold enough immediately to paralyse the taste-buds.   *Richard Gordon*

Soft drink – it'll poison ye, poison ye, ruin a man's stomach.   *Dusty Rhodes*

Tea
If I had known there was no Latin word for tea, I would have left the vulgar stuff alone.   *Hilaire Belloc*

231

It's proper use is to amuse the idle, relax the studious, and dilute the full meals of those who cannot use exercise and will not use abstinence.   *Samuel Johnson*

ALCOHOL

He is a drunkard who takes more than three glasses, though he be not drunk.
        Epictetus (AD 110)

'Tis not the drinking that is to be blamed, but the excess.
        John Selden – 'Table Talk' (1689)

Drunkenness is simply voluntary insanity.
        Seneca (AD 63)

Alcohol increases a mild gloom while creating the illusion of numbing it.
        A. N. Wilson

Bailey's Irish Coffee
Baarf.   *Andrew Barr – 'Time Out' (1992)*

Ale, beer and lager
They who drink beer will think beer.
        Washington Irving – 'The Sketch-book' (1819)

Inflation is a man-made disaster – like Southern beer and nylon shirts.
        Roland Long (1990)

Corn Liquor
It smells like gangrene starting in a mildewed silo, it tastes like the wrath to come, and when you absorb a deep swig of it you have all the sensations of having swallowed a lighted kerosene lamp.
        Irving Cobb

Guinness
A couple of deathless bon mots from this page have found their way into the *Guinness Book of More Poisonous Quotes*. If they'd asked me what I thought of the black brew, they could have had three.
        Jilly Parkin – 'Daily Express' (1992)

Guinness Light – Ghastly!
        Mark Hely-Hutchinson (1986)

Sol Beer
Time for the sun to set on it.
        Andrew Barr – 'Time Out' (1992)

South African port
On its suitability for gout-sufferers – I prefer the gout.   *Lord Derby*

Travellers' Fare Lager
The only substance known to man which leaves the body in exactly the same state as it entered.
        Victor Lewis-Smith – 'Mail on Sunday' (1992)

Whisky
I wish to see beer become common instead of the whisky which kills one third of our citizens, and ruins their families.
        Thomas Jefferson – Letter (1815)

Wine
Some of the most dreadful mischiefs that afflict mankind proceed from wine: it is the cause of disease, quarrels, sedition, idleness, aversion to labour, and every species of domestic disorder.
        Francois de Salignac de la Mothe Fénelon (1699)

An infallible antidote to common sense and seriousness.
        Kin Hubbard – 'The Roycroft Dictionary' (1923)

Served in West End theatres – The stuff they sell as 'white wine' would strip distemper at 40 paces.
        Philip Norman – 'The Independent' (1993)

Le Piat D'Or wine – Les Francais abhorrent le Piat D'or.
        Andrew Barr – 'Time Out' (1992)

TOBACCO

Smoking is a dying art.   *Anon*

Smokers, male and female, inject and excuse idleness in their lives every time they light a cigarette.
        Colette – 'Earthly Paradise' (1966)

Tobacco surely was designed
To poison, and destroy mankind.
Philip Freneau – 'Tobacco'

Smoking is a custom loathsome to the
eye, harmful to the brain, dangerous to
the lungs, and in the black stinking fume
thereof, nearest resembling the horrible
Stygian smoke of the pit that is
bottomless.   *James I of England (1604)*

I have smoked 'carefully blended'
mixtures that tasted like a hayrick on fire.
J. B. Priestley

Nicotine is an awful curse,
It strains the heart and drains the purse.
K. T. Sarma

Finish smoking or it will finish you.
Lasse Viren (1977)

SOURCE INDEX

SOURCE INDEX

SUBJECT INDEX

SUBJECT INDEX

SUBJECT INDEX